CURRICULUM

D0076225

CRITICAL EDUCATION PRACTICE
VOLUME 12
GARLAND REFERENCE LIBRARY OF SOCIAL SCIENCE
VOLUME 1135

CRITICAL EDUCATION PRACTICE
SHIRLEY R. STEINBERG AND JOE L. KINCHELOE, *SERIES EDITORS*

CURRICULUM
TOWARD NEW IDENTITIES

EDITED BY
WILLIAM F. PINAR

GARLAND PUBLISHING, INC.
A MEMBER OF THE TAYLOR & FRANCIS GROUP
NEW YORK AND LONDON
1998

Library of Congress Cataloging-in-Publication Data

Curriculum : toward new identities / edited by William F. Pinar.
        p.   cm. — (Garland reference library of social science ; v. 1135.
Critical education practice ; v. 12)
    Includes bibliographical references (p.   ) and index.
    ISBN 0-8153-2550-9 (hardcover) (alk. paper)
    ISBN 0-8153-2522-3 (paperback)
    1. Education—United States—Curricula. 2. Curriculum change—United
States. 3. Critical pedagogy—United States.   I. Pinar, William.   II. Series:
Garland reference library of social science ; v. 1135.   III. Series: Garland
reference library of social science. Critical education practice ; vol. 12.
LB1570.C88377   1998
374'.006—dc21   97-37890
                                                                                CIP

Paperback cover design by Karin Badger and Robert VanKeirsbilck.

Printed on acid-free, 250-year-life paper
Manufactured in the United States of America

To Philip Jackson

Table of Contents

Introduction

William F. Pinar

It may seem odd for someone who—with William Reynolds, Patrick Slattery, and Peter Taubman—recently finished a study of the field to be suggesting that new configurations of scholarship are now appearing. It's not as odd as it may seem; in chapter 15 of *Understanding Curriculum* we tried to think about what might come next. While, I think, the picture of the field we present there remains accurate, it may be frayed at the edges. Just as in the geo-political world, boundaries are being contested, discourse borders crossed, new hybridities (or cyborgs, as Noel Gough might say—see his essay, in this volume) are appearing. While the basic borders and boundaries depicted in *Understanding Curriculum* remain intact, there are individuals—not all of whom are published here, of course—who are working on the edge and perhaps even outside "contemporary curriculum discourses."

This book was conceived in April 1994. Joe Kincheloe and Shirley Steinberg had organized a panel on identity for the 1994 American Educational Research Association meeting in New Orleans. I was still working on the final revisions of *Understanding Curriculum*; the last thing on my mind was editing a book pointing to "next steps." I remember Shirley walking into the courtyard of my French Quarter place directing me to simply "say yes... just say yes." I did. What I had agreed to was the editing of this volume. It was a while—I kept fiddling with *Understanding Curriculum* until December 1995—before I could turn my attention to this volume. Not until last summer did I write possible contributors about participating in the project.

Conceptions of the Field

Let me situate the idea for this collection historically. In his introduction to the *Handbook of Research on Curriculum,* Philip Jackson (1992) raised the question of identity implicitly when he studied the conceptions of curriculum work. In my estimation, this essay will become canonical. Jackson describes our profession over the course of the twentieth century. Never mind that the figures he identifies are all men, and all associated with the University of Chicago. No one disputes that these men are "giants" in the field. What the essay makes clear is the decisive shift in the profession over the past eight decades.

After reviewing the contributions of Bobbitt, Dewey, Tyler, and Schwab, Jackson focuses on what he regards as two major "identities" of curriculum specialists at the present time. The first is that of "consultant," which he links with the life history or narrative or autobiography movement (see Chapter 10, Pinar, Reynolds, Slattery, Taubman, 1995; Casey, 1995; Pinar, 1994). Jackson (1992) notes that a precedent exists for this version of curricularist in the United Kingdom, where historically, teachers have served as curriculum makers. Teacher groups and associations were very much involved with curriculum reform in the 1960s, in contrast to the American scene (see Chapter 3, Pinar, Reynolds, Slattery, Taubman, 1995). In the United Kingdom, university professors played roles much like those Joseph Schwab would recommend for American professors of curriculum. The contemporary North American expression of engagement with schools, for which the British example is an antecedent, is one that blurs the traditional distinction between curriculum development and in-service training or staff development. For illustrations of this group, Jackson cites the work of F. Michael Connelly and D. Jean Clandinin (1988), Freema Elbaz (1983), Robin Barrow (1984), and Antoinette Oberg (1987). Jackson (1992) says about this group:

> A sampling of books and articles written by adherents of a more practitioner-oriented point of view reveals plenty to write about after the goal of discovering general principles of curriculum has been abandoned.... The mixture of criticism and advice in Schwab's four essays is paradigmatic of this kind of writing (p. 33).

While noting the continuities among Bobbitt, Tyler, Schwab, and this contemporary interest in curricular practice, Jackson expresses a reservation regarding the work of those moving "closer to the practitioner" or curricularist-as-consultant:

> If the specialist brings no special knowledge or vision to the task of establishing the need for change, if he or she turns out to be only a facilitator of the change process without substantive involvement in the question of what needs changing and why, one then begins to wonder in what sense the label curriculum specialist is appropriate. Perhaps something like discussion leader or Schwab's term "deliberator," would be more suitable.... To give that [the visionary role of the generalist] up would indeed be to flee the field, though not quite in the way Schwab suggested (Jackson, 1992, p. 34).

The second path the contemporary field is traveling Jackson characterizes as "moving toward the academy: the curriculum specialist as generalist" (p. 34). Schwab (1983) imagined that the curriculum generalist would study American government and society, including the character of daily life in America. The curricularist-as-generalist might, for instance, study the intensity of competition in American life and ask how the schools might call its taken-for-grantedness into question. Racism and nationalism might legitimately preoccupy curriculum generalists (as in fact they do: see Chapters 5 & 6, Pinar, Reynolds, Slattery, Taubman, 1995). Developments in the academic disciplines, as well as in society, which might be important for consideration in the formulation of curriculum, would also be appropriate for curriculum generalists to study (Schwab, 1983). Who would constitute the audience of these generalists' essays? Schwab says that in addition to the colleagues of curriculum professors, former students and the public at large might take an interest. Jackson then observes:

> In the late 1960s and early 1970s there emerged a group of curriculum professors whose writing sounded as though they had taken Schwab's advice to heart, even though his fourth essay [from which the preceding quote was taken] was not to appear for at least a decade and Schwab himself was to be among those with whom the group as a whole was said to differ. Some members of this group spoke of what they were doing as reconceptualizing the task of the curriculum specialists, particularly with respect to the role of theory in curricular affairs (Jackson, 1992, p. 34).

Jackson describes this group—the Reconceptualists—as exhibiting three common features: 1) a dissatisfaction with the Tyler rationale, 2) the employment of eclectic traditions to explore curriculum, such as psychoanalytic theory, phenomenology, existentialism, and 3) a left-wing political bias "that drew on Marxist and neo-Marxist thought and concerned itself with issues of racial and ethnic inequalities, feminism, the peace movement, and so forth" (1992, p. 35). We examine the history of the Reconceptualization in detail in chapter 4 of *Understanding Curriculum*, and in chapters 5-14 outline just how these "eclectic" traditions and interests in race, gender, and politics became formulated and expressed in the American curriculum field during the last 15 years (Pinar, Reynolds, Slattery, Taubman, 1995).

In the aftermath of the Reconceptualization, the field has moved from a paradigmatic unity—the Tylerian rationale—to particularism—the various contemporary discourses. The situation today is particularistic and even balkanized. This proliferation of discourses can be traced to the vacuum created by the collapse of the Tyler rationale. In this vacuum scholars went to other fields as sources of new theory. This move away from the paradigm of curriculum development has been quite complete.

The current interest in becoming closer to practitioners may be an indication of just how far apart from practice (i.e., the procedural) the field has moved. Indeed, in the 1970s, when I first called for the field to distance itself from the school and from teachers, to my mind I was merely acknowledging what was the case—that education professors were distant from teachers. It was clear to me when I first started teaching (in 1972) at the University of Rochester that teachers were skeptical of education professors. The expert-client relationship typical of the traditional field had broken down. For many, undergraduate preservice teacher courses seemed intellectually lightweight at best, silly and arrogant at worse. True, a minority of graduate courses seemed tolerable to students, and a fewer number still seemed to be considered exciting. What was clear in the 1970s was that most teachers did not regard education professors as friends, and definitely not as experts. Suggesting that the field move away from the school as the institution was merely acknowledging what was the case.

Was there ever a "paradise lost" of teacher-professor relations, during the first decades of this century? If so, it probably expressed a client-expert relationship. John Dewey wanted "experts" consigned to an "advisory role," as democratic education would require. Further, Dewey insisted that expertise must be subordinated to "fully participatory, deliberative, democratic politics" (Westbrook, 1991, p. 188), recalling the emphasis upon "deliberation" the Schwabian wing of the contemporary field has emphasized. In Jackson's terms, the present-day curricularist-as-consultant would seem to satisfy Dewey's requirement, to a degree. Regardless of that, however, we curricularists are no longer the major stakeholders in school curriculum.

Acknowledging, then, that our influence upon the schools is reduced, what should we do? Where does our changed situation locate us, and how does this location affect our identities? Where we are, of course, is the university, a place of scholarship and teaching. Instead of wringing our hands over lost influence in the schools and rejection by teachers (and policymakers and parents and politicians), we might commit ourselves to understanding what curriculum is, has been, and might be. Of course, this does not mean fleeing from "practice," turning our backs on teachers, pretending to be like arts and sciences professors, as many educational foundations professors have pretended in the past. We curriculum theorists still offer friendship and colleague-ship to teachers. Of course, we continue to offer teachers our expertise, especially through the classes we teach and via consultancy relationships. We can offer politicians and policymakers that expertise, but we ought not be surprised and definitely not deflated when they decline to employ it. After all, their interests in the schools do not seem especially educational; they are instead political and economic.

In our insistence that we must fix the schools (which cannot be "fixed" in any case, given the present political and economic gridlock, and given that politicians will not let us try), an insistence that will only function to devalue our stock further, we risk missing the only way we might develop the sophisticated understanding which—should the school establishment and politicians ever attend to our advice—might indeed help in significant ways. Such understanding must be grounded in educational experience (not necessarily schooling), but it must not remain there. Like physics or art, curriculum as a field cannot progress unless some segment of the field explores phenomena and ideas that perhaps few will comprehend and appreciate, certainly not at first and perhaps never. Our field will not progress beyond a certain primitive point unless we support a sector of theory—such as the work printed here—that perhaps most in the field cannot fully understand initially. Imagine physics progressing if scholars in that discipline were limited to work which beginning students readily understood. Imagine art progressing unless forms of painting and dance were supported which, initially, very few could appreciate. In any field there must be a sector of advanced work; otherwise, a field cannot advance.

What I present in this collection is exactly "advanced work," work in advance of the mainstream of curriculum scholarship, work which points to future possibilities, including novel conceptions of what it means to be a curricularist and what it means to do curriculum work. The scholarship and theory collected here might well point to, someday, another "reconceptualization" of the field, drawing new boundaries and borders, occupying new terrains in innovative ways. For convenience we might use the concept of frontier, stripped, of course, of its colonial connotations.

What can we say about the frontier of the contemporary field? History is important (see Bill Doll's and Petra Munro's essays). So are gender (see Deborah Britzman's essay, as well as those by Wendy Atwell-Vasey, Suzanne de Castell and Mary Bryson, Annette Gough, and Petra Munro), race (see the essays by Shariba Rivers and Kofi Lomotey, and by Cameron McCarthy), and politics (Alan Block, Gaile Cannella, Suzanne de Castell and Mary Bryson, Joe Kincheloe, and the Peter McLaren interview). Ecology grows in importance (see Annette Gough's and Noel Gough's), as does autobiography (see Wendy Atwell-Vasey's essay, a well as those by Ivor Goodson, Noel Gough, Joe Kincheloe, Paula Salvio, and Dennis Sumara and Brent Davis). Post-modernism and poststructuralism remain powerful (see essays by Bill Doll, Ivor Goodson, Wen-Song Hwu, and Noel Gough). Curriculum-in-practice remains a topic, if in novel, theoretically rich ways (see Atwell-Vasey, Doll, Sumara and Davis, and Salvio). The field continues to move and shift. While it is premature to suggest a new map for the field, it is possible to point to new modes of scholarship, to possible trends (such as cultural studies). These may create new identities for us, including how we regard ourselves as scholars and teachers.

What does this collection tell us? As you see, we have taken the "linguistic turn," evidenced in our field by the continuing and perhaps increasing influence of poststructuralism and postmodernism. Not unrelated to this development is the appearance of "cultural studies." This interdisciplinary movement retains an interest in politics but is configured around postcolonialism, influenced by certain strands of feminist theory and in some ways by poststructuralism. As the effort to understand curriculum as political text continues to collapse (see Pinar,

Reynolds, Slattery, Taubman, 1995, pp. 293-314), more scholars can be expected to move to this terrain. The "self" remains crucial in several lines of scholarship, as the character of autobiographical and narrative theory continues to be debated, perhaps more contentiously than before. Pedagogy remains a central concern, now informed by theoretically rich traditions of feminist theory, psychoanalysis, autobiography, and political theory. Finally, there appears a new form of the effort to understand curriculum as homosexual text (see Pinar, Reynolds, Slattery, Taubman, 1995, p. 396 ff.), influenced by poststructuralism and feminist theory: queer theory. I am very pleased to reprint Deborah Britzman's important and pathbreaking essay, as well as Suzanne de Castell and Mary Bryson's exciting performative piece.

While the map of the field we drew in *Understanding Curriculum* remains accurate, clearly it will not last long—perhaps a decade. Then a new study of the field must be undertaken, one that reflects the new terrains being occupied, borders crossed, the new identities constructed, assumed, and contested. As a graduate student in the late 1960s I complained about the atheoretical character of the American curriculum field. Thirty-five years later the field has become theoretical, some would say with a vengeance. Now movement is rapid, profound, at times revolutionary, as we see in the essays that follow.

The Essays
The importance of historical and metatheoretical shifts for identity is clear in Ivor Goodson's essay, which opens the collection. He writes: "current changes in the economy and superstructure associated with postmodernity pose particular perils and promises for the world of education." One of the pioneers of autobiography in the field (see, for instance, Goodson, 1981), Goodson worries that current modes of "storying the self" reproduce the worst aspects of the marketplace. In making this provocative argument, he alleges that "much of the workplace knowledge currently being promoted is context specific and personal." This is a mistake. Instead, "we should be investigating and promoting more contextual and intertextual studies of the process of identity." Rather than pointing exclusively to our inner lives, as he is suggesting much contemporary autobiographical work does, the "use of personal stories and narratives in teacher education has to respond meaningfully to the new conditions of work and being in the postmodern world." In order to do so, perhaps autobiography, at least as it has been traditionally conceived, is not the most apt genre. Goodson

explains: "The self becomes a reflexive project, an ongoing narrative project. To capture this emergent process requires a modality close to social history, social geography, and social theory—modes which capture the self in time and space, a social cartography of the self." We must remember that, thanks partly to the omnipresence of the electronic media, the "experience of social life and self is more fluid." In order to avoid appropriation by the New Right, we need political grounding: "alongside narration, we need location and collaboration." He puts the matter plainly:

> Stories and narratives can form an unintended coalition with those forces which would divorce the teacher from knowledge of political and micropolitical perspective, from theory, from broader cognitive maps of influence and power.

Goodson's essay is a provocative challenge to those who promote narratives of personal experience which do not make explicit their grounding in the social and political world.

As the common wisdom has it, autobiography provides opportunities for self-exploration. In his remarkable essay, Wen-Song Hwu challenges the very notion of self. He begins by quoting Samuel Beckett: "What am I to do, what shall I do, what should I do, in my situation, how to proceed?" Of course, this is the question of professional identity in the field. What should I do next, in light of a reconceptualized but now balkanized field? How do I position myself vis-à-vis emerging discourses, vis-à-vis my own professional history, especially my graduate education, my teaching experience? What is the next step for me, intellectually, pedagogically, as a professional curricularist? Outside the institutional pressure to publish (anything, it seems, will do, as long as the journal is refereed), what work furthers my own education? These questions are complicated by Hwu's essay. He reminds us that "identity-formation is subject-positioned, context-situated, and discursively located." Our understandings of this process are very much situated in the West: "The Western notion of self is partly based on the limited subject of 'anthropological' thinking, which not only stigmatized and excluded the philosophical contemplation of the noumenal, it also exalted the autonomy of the individual subject." After Foucault, Hwu advises us:

> Not to look within to a true or authentic self, not to master one's time by holding it in one's thought, not to find a place for oneself within society or state, but to look out from oneself, to open

one's time to what has not yet been seen, to displace one's instituted, assigned identity at a time and place.

Quoting Deleuze, he continues: "What can I be, with what folds can I surround myself or how can I produce myself as a subject?" Not without humor, Hwu asks: "Does one or should one rule oneself as one rules a slave?" In other words, "my self-understanding...consists of constantly putting myself into question and a constant being-other." What is the Other? He answers by again quoting Deleuze: "Other = an expression of a possible world." The possible suggests:

> Transcendence...[which] gives to each person the power to start over, to begin anew and to transform the world.... The "trans" can be translated as over/across which has to do more with a relationship...rather than a separation...as that implied by "above" or "beyond."

What is the movement of transcendence? Hwu explains: "Breaking away from the traditional order constitutes an act of self-exile, a stage that allows the soul's own exploration, a journey, an open-ended one that defines, connects, and disconnects, that leads to possible transformation." It requires us "to think the unthinkable." In such a plane, what is pedagogy? What is its function? "[Pedagogy's]...function is to invent the conditions of invention."

The autobiographical method Paula Salvio employs illustrates, I think, Hwu's notion of pedagogy as creating the conditions of invention. Salvio uses the literacy portfolio in order to prepare teachers for "willful world traveling." She regards this portfolio as related in genre to Freire's "popular culture notebooks." She tells us that "to explore the history of our literacies is potentially to engage in an analysis of our cultural, social, and ethnic identities." As such, the literacy portfolio is "a collecting place." How does this work? Paula explains:

> Rather than imposing a linear, chronological story line to represent the meaning of our literacy practices, we build our stories by unpeeling the layers of meaning that are nestled in objects that are strewn about our attics, stored away in boxes or kept for us by members of our families.... We refer to these stories as social scenarios. Students play out their social scenarios through theatrical improvisation.

For Salvio it is clear that "the process of composing a series of social scenarios brings them face to face with dimensions of their cultural identities."

Such work, she continues, requires an "empathic engagement with the life of [those] communities we teach in. Before we can take up this project, however, we must first be able to study our own histories from an engaged rather than a disengaged stance." Such self-reflexive inquiry enables the teacher to avoid "creating a detached and static image of her cultural identity." Instead, "the literacy portfolio functions as...a deep desk drawer in which to store and interpret the myriad images, symbols, and artifacts that represent the complex and ever-changing elements of... cultural identity."

In fact, Salvio explains, the "narrative structure of the literacy portfolio is far more akin to the fluid, protean boundaries of culture and identity than it is to the more conventional, chronological story line." Cultural portfolios, she continues:

> offer no protagonists, no happy endings–rather, they are always subject to revision and re-interpretation. As teachers and teacher candidates pursue the emotional threads underlying the literacy practices they most identify with, as they seek out questions and theorize about the heritage of these practices, my hope is that they become more equipped as educators to teach their own students to articulate their place in history, as places of feeling, hope, and commitment.

Salvio's pedagogy is not only inventive and "critical," it is subtle and theoretically provocative as well.

So, too, is the pedagogy of Dennis Sumara and Brent Davis. They begin by observing that "private reading...is entangled in public meaning," a theoretical and pedagogical assumption they see grounded in a view of "literary anthropology...as a way of teaching." Such a view allows them to conceive of curriculum as "unskinning." What is unskinning? The term "all at once announces a process and its complement/opposite. We propose that identification and identity, the principal matters of curriculum, are also matters of unskinning—of simultaneously removing and imposing boundaries." Furthermore, "the need to inquire not just into the process of identification, but into the location of identity." Where are the locations of identity? They answer:

our personal identities are contained *inside* ourselves....[and]... they are imposed by the gazes of those who observe (identify) us,...they are located in the constellation of events and artifacts that we carry—that is,...they are somehow circumscribed in and by our relationships with others.

Therefore: "Unskinning...suggests both a removing (skinning) of recognizable markers—by stripping those boundaries that we use to identify—and a simultaneous re-marking of boundaries. An unskinning."

To illustrate the idea, Dennis and Brent describe a "curriculum commonplace...conducted by Dennis and classroom teacher Dolores van der Wey and her grade 5/6 students. This event was developed around Lois Lowry's novel *The Giver*." They explain:

It was within this newly mapped cultural space that we as university researchers, the teachers at this school, and the parents of school children came to a deeper understanding of the importance of curriculum events.... The boundaries between classroom teacher, parent, university researcher, reader were continually becoming unfixed, reconstituted, and reinterpreted.

Near the end of a meeting at the school, parents insisted that this book be read by their children. Why? Dennis and Brent think it was "not so much of the value of the text but, rather, because of the desire for their children to experience what they had just experienced—an event of unskinning."

In the new field, fiction is not only a subject in the school curriculum, it becomes a modality of scholarly inquiry and presentation. Perhaps no one has thought more carefully and innovatively about this possibility than Noel Gough. Noel begins by acknowledging that he wishes to "enlarge the provenance of fiction in curriculum inquiry." He declares: "Fact and fiction are much closer, both culturally and linguistically, than these narrative strategies imply." Fiction can be useful, he asserts, in suggesting possibilities, creating alternatives, especially moving toward novel ways of thinking and reasoning in curriculum theory. Some forms of fiction, he continues, "can function as a 'diffracting lens' for the narrator's eye and thus help to generate stories which move educational inquiry beyond reflection and reflexivity toward 'making a difference in the world.'" I think Gough does indeed persuade that fiction could be useful in curriculum inquiry. But this accomplishment isn't the endpoint of this intriguing essay. He reviews and criticizes major currents of autobiographical and narrative theory, including Barone, Clandinin, Connelly, Grumet, moi-même, worrying that all of us are too caught up in "a quest for truth." Fiction, including cyberpunk science fiction, can transport us toward "raising on-tologically-oriented questions." Such fiction "brings a sense of immediacy and urgency" to issues concerning subjectivity, what he terms "cyborg subjectivity." Acknowledging that we live in a world "ruled by fictions of every kind," we might well assume that the world is in fact a "complete fiction." He concludes this startling and important paper: "I prefer to situate myself in the world-as-fiction as a 'researcher-narrator' whose subjectivity is author of (that is, authorizes) his methodology."

Joe Kincheloe contributes significantly to autobiographical theory with his study of *currere* and hyperreality. It would be difficult to find as succinct a summary and as innovative a framing of *currere* as Joe has written. He points out that *currere* begins in politics as well as psychology: "grounded identity studies enable us to explain how the politics we located 'out there' in society are lived 'in here' in our minds, bodies, and everyday speech." Autobiography begins with the social constitution of subjectivity; consequently, "*currere* insisted on the exposé of white 'racialization.'" The subject is gendered as well as racial, and so *currere* has explored "masculinization, heterosexual male-male relations, and the tacit gender politics of social and curriculum theory." Usefully, Joe links *currere* with the notion of post-formal thinking, which he and Shirley Steinberg elaborated in their important *Harvard Educational Review* essay (Kincheloe & Steinberg, 1993). Joe concludes by noting that "exploring self-production" represents a form of "revolutionary pedagogy." He writes:

> Drawing upon their ability to produce integrated knowledge, students and teachers study both the forces that forge their identities and the ways such forces can be resisted. In such a con-text, students explore their place in the social hierarchy of their peer group, their romantic relationships, their vocational aspir-ations, their relationships with teachers, and their definitions of success. They become researchers, in other words, of their intrapersonal and interpersonal lives, in the process of gaining a post-formal meta-consciousness of who they are and how they constantly change in the hyperspace of the contemporary era.

Wendy Atwell-Vasey is interested, also, in power and status, especially as they position and identify women teachers, who live, she points out, at the intersections of history, society, and economics. But "woman" is not epiphenomenal. Wendy writes that, indeed, the "representation of maternal relations is crucial to our representation of reality." Relying on Kristeva, Atwell-Vasey asserts that it is "through reduplication of maternal structure, that is, identifying with the mother's body and what it does, that the infant assumes the ability to assimilate, repeat, and reproduce words, and becomes like the other: a subject." Furthermore, "language does not require giving up the mother's body, but being like it." Leading us on a path that takes us through—in addition to Kristeva—Winnicott, Freud, and especially Lacan, Wendy brings us to an extraordinary woman's place in a patriarchal field, a place of feminist, maternalist pedagogy. In this place, with this identity, "the model for a powerful teacher is one who accepts the child's ego and reflects his interests back to him, and who has strong interests and ties to the outside world that are visible to the child." What is required is a "more maternalistic system of teachers" who can help students "connect with power by helping them identify with their own power." Yes.

Teachers of young children have sometimes been sentimentalized as mothers, as if "caring" summed up teaching, or as if developmental theories constituted curriculum theory. No longer, if Gaile Cannella has anything to do with it. In an important paper, Cannella calls for a reconceptualized field of early childhood education. To do so requires first asking a series of fundamental questions:

> How has our historical and political context served to construct the values that have led the field? Do these beliefs lead to equity and social justice for all children? Are groups of children (and their families and communities) disenfranchised by the values that we have promoted in the field?

It is clear that Gaile believes the answer to each question is "yes." Next, she moves to the agenda for reconceptualizing the field:

> First, identify those 'images' in early childhood education that have created the field, problematizing them within our present day context. Second, I propose alternative images for the construction of a field whose goals would become social justice and the creation of revolutionary views in which children are seen as emancipatory agents in their own lives.

This is an revolutionary agenda indeed.

Among those taken-for-granted thematics of the field that Gaile contests are child-centeredness and developmentalism (including notions of "developmentally appropriate practice"). She observes, more generally, that "in the United States, we voice a rhetoric of concern for our children, but we have not accepted public responsibility for the well being of all of society's children and families." Finally, she sketches the broad outlines of a reconceptualized field:

> (1) the achievement of social justice and equal opportunity for younger members of society, (2) education as hearing and responding to the voices of younger human beings in their everyday lives, and (3) professionalism as the development of a critical disposition in the pursuit of social justice.

These themes and values will serve as the foundation for the new field. Gaile concludes: "Ideas can cause trouble. I contend we must cause trouble; our voices must be heard as advocates and activists for social justice and care, not only for the younger members of our society, but for everyone." Indeed.

Early childhood education is not the only field to be influenced by ideas associated with the reconceptualized field of curriculum. Traditional conceptualizations of science education are under siege, as we see in Annette Gough's powerful paper. Influenced especially by postcolonialism (a subject to which we return in Cameron McCarthy's essay), Gough works to go "beyond Eurocentrism in science education," a highly significant mission in itself. But her work sketches new territory for curriculum generalists as well. Like Hwu and other new theorists, Annette Gough situates her work in the "linguistic turn," terrains influenced by French poststructuralism. "I have," she qualifies, "taken an additional step, guided particularly by the work of Sandra Harding." That step involves going beyond Eurocentrism along a feminist path, outlining postcolonial critiques of Western science. She argues for a more democratic science and, in her final section, discusses both "the promises and problematics of these critiques for new directions in science education" and, I would add, in curriculum theory. Gough observes:

> Moving beyond Eurocentrism in science education will not be easy. Yet there are increasing challenges to the West imposing its values and standards on others, and these need to be both

acknowledged and taken into account in future developments in science education.... We need to be working toward less partial and less distorted accounts of nature and social relations in science education content and we need to be working toward pedagogies and research methodologies that are not in pursuit of "one true story." The principles I have proposed here, which are grounded in feminist and postcolonial critiques of science and science education and in feminist poststructuralism, are where I am starting on my work toward encouraging more democratic science content and science education practices.

She is, she tells us in the final sentence of the essay, "trying to stop being unconscious." An agenda for us all, this represents, as well as a significant shift in conception of curricularists' labor.

Being unconscious is in some respects comprised of what cannot be thought, at least consciously. Not a century ago homosexuality was "the love that dare not speak its name," or, more clinically, information the ego could not bear to hear, what it could bear to think. Deborah Britzman takes us into the realm of the "unthinkable," the gender unthinkable. Here gender is destabilized: "gay and lesbian demands for civil rights call into question the stability and fundamentalist grounds of categories like masculinity, femininity, sexuality, citizenship, nation, culture, literacy, consent, equality, and so forth." In queer theory there are "knowledge of bodies and bodies of knowledge," knowledges which pose a study of limits: "The study of limits is...a problem of where thought stops." What is identity? In queer theory "identity is examined as a discursive effect of the social and as constituted through identifications." In the reactionary straight world, the educational manifesto remains "back to the basics," whether understood in terms of skills or the Eurocentric canon. Queers behind enemy lines realize that "the problem of curriculum becomes one of proliferating identifications *not* closing them down." This is not a plea for tolerance as much as it is an assertion of a scheme for reading: "Reading for alterity begins with an acknowledgment of difference as the grounds of identity."

When identity is understood as in some way compensatory, as in relation to difference and otherness, we understand there is no "straight" man, no "heterosexual" woman in any definitive or self-identical sense: "So given these queer theories, identities and the self knowledge that render them intelligible and unintelligible suggest more about the social effects of the political than they do about essential selves." To think essentially is to misread the world, including oneself. To read the world, one must "stop reading straight."

Suzanne de Castell and Mary Bryson do not read straight. They don't write straight either: "This is a paper about location, identity, and signification. Its purpose is to try to move outside normal 'regimes' of academic/professional discourses...where Other things can be said." And other things they do say. They point out that in "heterosexist academic environments" our (i.e., queer) identities do not fit:

> The fact is, we (alongside other Others) are academics who can never really *be* Academics...we can never speak *as* Academics without in that very utterance, speaking against ourselves.... Thus to occupy the position of the "Professor," to "profess," is, inescapably to profess against ourselves, to speak our own illegitimacy, so long as we speak in the language, the tones, the cadences of the academy which has spawned us as impossible beings, as monstrous, aberrant eternal Outsiders who nevertheless dare to speak publicly about the *being* of being queer.

Where does this leave us? Well, for one thing, Suzanne and Mary, unlike our straight colleagues, are not in the business of creating knowledge. Rather, "where we want to begin as 'queer' educators, *inversely*, is with a very different interest, an interest in the *destruction* of knowledge, rather than its creation.... It is born...out of a frank amazement at the capacity of official discourse...entire universes of ignorance and deception." What can we hope for? "What we long for is a flood, a breaking through of forbidden knowledges, a tumultuous, uncontrollable release of what has been blocked, held back, dammed up for far too long." Business as usual won't do, for "participating in contemporary education...seems increasingly to involve a kind of 'lying game,'...to remain 'positive'...a kind of *studied* ignorance'...where full-grown 'men of good will' speak unashamedly of the 'wonderful world of education.'" What theory might be helpful?

> It is important to develop a theory of the epistemological significance of ignorance, and an understanding of the richness of its content. Ignorance represents a kind of knowing.... Systematic 'ignorances'...are not mere absences but active constructions of alterity, of otherness, of marginality, of deviance.

Where do de Castell and Bryson leave us? Their important, effectively performative paper has the effect of calling for revolution in our practice, requiring new identities: "New resources, then, in addition to new structures...these are the enticements to migrate to less well-chartered locations from which to articulate new identities for theory and praxis in education." Clearly Suzanne de Castell and Mary Bryson will be among the leaders of the new migration.

On another frontier of the contemporary field, not unrelated to queer theory, is a move toward "cultural studies." Who works here? In American curriculum studies, there are those who have worked to understand curriculum as political text, scholars such as Henry Giroux, Joe L. Kincheloe, and Peter McLaren. But cultural studies of curriculum are not just the political sector of scholarship renamed. It also has attracted scholars of race (such as Cameron McCarthy) of aesthetics and *Kinderculture* (such as Shirley Steinberg), as well as multi-sector scholars such as John Willinsky, whose recent work focuses on issues of postcolonialism. Cameron McCarthy writes about "The Uses of Culture: Canon Formation, Postcolonial Literature and the Multicultural Project." Cameron's most recent scholarship promises to play a role just as important in this emerging sector of scholarship as it did in the effort to understand curriculum as racial text (see McCarthy, 1990). "This essay," he tells us, "seeks to promote a rethinking of constructs such as culture, identity, and the relations between centers and peripheries."

"In literature and in popular culture," McCarthy explains, "the dynamism and contradictions of identity, community, and so forth are restored and foregrounded." He worries about "the tendency toward cultural exceptionalism and cultural purity that informs Eurocentric and ethnicity-based curriculum reform platforms now rampant in education." He introduces a mood, something perhaps like the global moods Heidegger postulated. For McCarthy, the mood is melancholic: "Melancholy is understood here, not as sadness and despondency but as a liberating skepticism toward cultural hierarchies and historical ruins. This hybridizing development is a central force in peripheries and metropolises alike." Just as multiculturalism must not be understood as an academic form of welfare for poor blacks, neither can postcolonial perspectives be confined to the Third World: "The founding of post-colonial literature is not simply to be located in the periphery, it must certainly be located in the metropole as well." Can its location in the metropole bring some self-reflexive awareness of "centeredness": "The cultural hybridity registered in the new postcolonial literature brings into view the subaltern gaze on the eye of power." McCarthy continues:

> [Theorists] often talk about identity and identity politics as though only minority groups...practice and benefit from the deployment of identity construction; and as if they are the only ones who experience the consequences of such identity construction: namely, group fragmentation, hybridity, entropy, and so forth.... Canon formation is itself a strategy of interpretation of historical crisis.... For example, the canonization of British literature occurred after World War I, in the 1920s and 1930s, at a time when Europe was in disarray and the British empire on the wane.... All of this, of course, would not prevent the empire from striking back as the migratory waves of postcolonial souls...descended on England....

What is McCarthy's advice in light of this understanding of canon formation and defense? "We need to get beyond the idea of teaching multiculturalism as corrective bits of knowledge." Sounding melancholic himself at the end, he wonders: "Maybe we are all exiles in a dehumanizing educational process.... It is these demons, these cyborgs, that now inhabit postcolonial literature in the periphery and in the center alike. In announcing their hybridity, they raise new possibilities of community, conflicted but bounded together for better or worse."

Of course, not only British literature is canonized. Curriculum history is as well. And curriculum history has emphasized narratives of men, white heterosexual men, silencing the voices and overlooking the contributions of women, African Americans, and other marginalized groups. In a pathbreaking paper Petra Munro, in a word, *engenders* curriculum history. In so doing she will "examine how the narrative structures of curriculum histories are implicated in the construction of gendered subjects." Why does curriculum history tend toward unitary narratives, stories of "struggle" in which the victors and the vanquished are always men? Perhaps, she suggests provocatively, history as master narrative may be driven by a castration fear. She writes: "I maintain that one sickness of contemporary theorizing is to continue to seek unitary theories despite our acknowledgment that knowledge is multiple, contradictory, and always in flux." By focusing on school history, for instance, the contributions of intellectuals and groups outside the school establishment are ignored: "Obscuring education in 'other' spheres outside of the public, erases women's, African

Americans', and other marginalized groups' forms of knowing and being as a source for theorizing curriculum." Typical curriculum histories, "predicated on this search [for origins], guarantees a unitary tale that can be traced." Isn't this oedipally and historically, "the work of the father?" It is clear, as she explains: "To conceive of history as the tracing of origins—Mann/Common School Movement; Hall/Child Study Movement; Dewey/ Progressivism; Tyler/Technical Rationalism—of establishing lineages, is to secure the exclusion, the invisibility of women." Referring perhaps to Kliebard's well-known scholarship, Munro describes the primary struggle of curriculum history as the tension between a "conventional narrative" (social efficiency) and a "liberation narrative" (social reconstruction). This story mirrors the oedipal father/son struggle which produces "a curricular master narrative bounded by the reproduction/resistance binary which situates control and individuation as central to the curricular plot."

What does this accomplish? With great insight she explains:

> This regulation of gender continues in current reform movements through the discursive formation of teacher identities as either "professionals" (reproduction) or as "intellectuals/activists/ cultural workers" (resistance). The father/son plot, remains the underlying structuring of the narrative.

Here is indeed an engendered conception of curriculum. It is long overdue. Petra Munro's project promises not only to reconceive the stories we tell about our past, but how in fact we see our present.

Bill Doll always seems to find the frontier of the field (see Doll, 1993). Here he is again, this time with a provocative piece of historical scholarship focused on control. He announces his intention, telling us that he will

> look briefly at the role this sense of (industrial) control has played in the curriculum, at a deeper sense of control as methodization, at John Dewey's attempt to find a sense of control neither externally imposed nor internally developed, and will conclude with a new view of control—one which does not represent imposition nor self-development but rather emerges from the dynamic interaction that constitutes all life.

Such historical scholarship is necessary, as "when the legitimacy of these rules and patterns (of control) is shrouded in mist; then indeed control becomes a ghost." Furthermore, he points out that: "All legitimacy, indeed all learning and knowledge, occur within temporally bounded networks. The control that lurks as the ghost in the curriculum will never be truly illuminated or exorcised until we wrestle with this fundamental fact."

Bill expresses his appreciation for David Hamilton's important scholarship (1989, 1990,1992, nd). Hamilton has

> done us all an immense service in resurrecting the educational origins of the word curriculum and its relation to the concept of "methodization," a movement which began in the latter sixteenth century and certainly received much attention in the seventeenth before it became a natural (and indeed "man-made") part of Western intellectual thought.

Understood as method, the concept of curriculum was/is quite Protestant: "John Calvin was a man of method...he advocated that each person read the Bible individually." That is not to say there is no apprenticeship: "Rather Luther, and those like him, studied with masters for as long as either party wished or until the master felt the student was ready to stand before the faculty for his disputation." Bill summarizes: "The rise of Protestantism with its individualism, commercialism, with its formation of a middle class, and scientism with its new methodology brought a new sense to education, a sense interested in and committed to simplicity and method." Curriculum appears as an educational word in 1576. Method becomes abstracted from context, and made universal two hundred years later: "This same sense of a universal methodology—still extant to a great degree in our curriculum 'methods courses'—surfaced in Descartes' method for 'rightly conducting reason for seeking truth.'"

It was, Bill continues, "Comenius...[who] played a direct role in moving education from a sense of study to a sense of teaching and learning, or from pedagogics to didactics." And "to this day, in the north European and Scandinavian counties (see for instance, Gundem, 1992, my note), curriculum and didactic are seen as one, curriculum and instruction." Bringing us to the twentieth century, Doll cites Dewey: "Only by wrestling with the conditions of the problem, at first hand, seeking and finding one's own way out, does one think." Moving through Dewey to chaos theory, Bill synthesizes method and curriculum: "Presently, though, I am excited...to try organizing my classes in a manner that allows for, indeed depends on, 'stability and flexibility.'"

Motion and space are themes in Alan Block's provocative essay as well, if in different ways. Here, Alan contests traditional notions of curriculum as journey and/or destination and calls into question concepts of identity as having arrived. He writes:

> I believe education ought to be an experience of dislocation in which the sense of lostness is given impetus and validation, and in which in that sense of lostness identity can be achieved.... Curriculum, in this view, is, in the words of the popular iconic hymn, "Amazing Grace," an engagement with the experience of lostness that the opportunity of being found may occur.

At present, Block argues,

> curriculum...represents the uninterrupted stream of writing which connects the center with the periphery, which serves as the pebbles by which the path is marked that the teachers and students might always find their way home, even though the father has long since absented himself from that path, ensconced himself at home and abandoned education for the thrill of exercising control by allowing the teacher and student to assume it.

Perhaps the state has replaced the nineteenth-century father and head of household. In our time, "education has become the functioning of the panopticon." He says that "we are defined—we define ourselves—by that position" that is, the "well-traveled, well-lit, and heavily marked path which is the curriculum." In such a time, what is education? Block answers that

> education is, or at least ought to be, not a discipline, not a matter of being found or finding self along a set path, nor of moving progressively along a path defined by others and by which we can define ourselves by our place along it; education might be understood as the opportunity of getting lost.

He quotes Thoreau, who told us that: "not till we are completely lost or turned around...do we appreciate the vastness and strangeness of nature." This view is in sharp contrast to the institutional organization of curriculum: "Curriculum...is organized around the rationality of order, of linearity, and of diachrony."

Block too is critical of current concepts of self and subject. He writes: "I return here to the orthodox Marxist belief that the notion of the subject is an entirely bourgeois concept.... I would prefer to replace the notion of subjectivity with the idea of identity." He explains:

> Unlike the notion of the subject, or the individual, or the more recent postmodern conjugation, subject-position, the notion of identity accounts for the effects of both ideological interpellation and resistance without accepting the powerless individual wholly subdued by the strategic position of the dominant powers.

To illustrate, Block goes to "the affichiste artists of the 1940s and 1950s [who] conjured up the look of daily life and the streets by using mass-produced ephemera in altered ways." What is instructive about these artists? "This yet–noncanonical art...offers us a model of curriculum as it produces knowledge in the active consumption of the everyday materials the world makes available. It is an art which is at once personal and social." And in the affichiste artists we see curriculum production which gets lost to be found, and in so doing supports novel, innovative, and politically-engaged identities as scholars and teachers.

Identity as social, even communal, born in the panopticon-world European Americans devised but do not self-reflexively understand: these are ideas not exactly new to students of the African American experience in the West. From "dual consciousness" to pan-African efforts to escape the debilitating gaze of the European and European American, understanding curriculum as racial text exhibits a broad thematic terrain populated with powerful concepts, such as identity. We see this power pedagogically in efforts to educate African American children. Shariba Rivers and Kofi Lomotey note that this effort has been "a long and tedious one," beginning "long before current discussions on multiculturalism and pluralism...long before the 'ethnic studies' movement of the 1960s." From slavery to segregation, black children have suffered the racism white people communicated in American public schools. Efforts to protect black children from the racism of white children and white teachers have taken many forms, including the development of independent black schools (or IBIs), which have existed since the 1700s. For contemporary IBIs, Rivers and Lomotey explain, "cultural knowledge is important," paralleling, we might note, the shift to cultural studies in the field. The curriculum at IBIs is multifaceted, relying on the Nguzo Saba (Kiswahili for "The

Seven Principles of Blackness") as the value system. Rivers and Lomotey list these:

> The seven principles are Umoja (Unity), Kujichagulia (Self-determination), Ujima (Collective work and responsibility), Ujamaa (Cooperative economics), Nia (Purpose), Kuumba (Creativity) and Imani (Faith).... The Nguzo Saba provide the moral foundation upon which the IBI stands.

Rivers and Lomotey point out that "familyhood is also a very important aspect of IBIs. Teachers are enjoined to treat their students as if they were their own children. Students, in turn, are encouraged to love and respect their teachers as they love and respect their parents." Not surprisingly, IBIs have been "more successful than their public school counterparts," not only in reference to standardized test scores, but in terms of attitude, self-esteem, and fostering relationships between school personnel, students, and families as well.

Does an Afrocentric curriculum function like the Eurocentric one? Rivers and Lomotey quote Joyce King: "In contrast to Eurocentric thought, this worldview does not rationalize or justify a universal or normative cultural model of being and way of knowing the world." Put another way, Rivers and Lomotey assert: "An African-centered curriculum does not exclude or negate other peoples and their histories/contributions." It is clear that "the public school system would do well by taking these schools as a model to restructure its curriculum to be more inclusive, truthful, and representative of its student body." European Americans might well support public efforts to endow and otherwise protect these independent black schools, which Shariba Rivers and Kofi Lomotey so succinctly describe.

This collection of essays on the edge concludes with an interview with a scholar who has thought on the edge for some time: Peter McLaren. For the *Journal of Mediterranean Education,* Carmel Borg, Peter Mayo, and Ronald Sultana interviewed Peter on the subjects of "revolution and reality." McLaren illustrates avant-garde thinking in the political sector, inspired and provoked as he is by postmodernism, postcolonialism, and feminism. McLaren tells the interviewers that "We cannot avoid as educators...standing before the concrete other who is in need of our help." In order to so do, we must "contest the anarcho-fascist politics of the splayed postmodern will.... My goal as a citizen and educator and cultural theorist is to make the world less exploitative, less cruel, less inhumane than if I had never been here."

Critical pedagogy survives in a sea of apathy: "How can we live with so little outrage against the evil of global capitalism?" Perhaps it is not apathy or some form of social indifference, perhaps it is more precisely understood as amnesia: "My work has tried to fathom how the process of motivated amnesia works on a national scale, through local circuits of subject formation tied together by national myths, so that people refuse to confront their complicity in relations of domination and exploitation."

Necessary, among other things, are new forms of subjectivity: "Lionnet's concept of *mestissage,* which refers to a type of creolization of subjectivity, a combination of the dominant language with outlaw languages of subaltern groups." Further, "we need to build our arch of social dreaming in the liminal, subjective mode of being." But this is not a reconfiguration of subjectivity alone: "We need to move towards a communicative democracy. Interest-based democracy is involved with one's own individual interests and preferences which are usually expressed in a vote. It doesn't really put pressure on engaging in a dialogue with other collectives in debate and discussion." Of course, political education cannot proceed without economics:

> Speaking about my own work on post-colonial education, I would say that for me the crucial issue is what Negri refers to as the imperialist process of capital, the ways capital can circulate on a global basis, and the opening up not only of ways of exploitation but also ways of contesting such exploitation.

And such exploitation is racial: "White people tend to believe they have transcended the 'lowliness' of ethnicity." Nor is class forgotten: "Class antagonisms thrive, although their forms and contexts differ." What can the scholar do?

> The role of the intellectual is important and I applaud much of what Gramsci has said about the role of the "organic intellectual" and Foucault has said about the "specific intellectual." I am also concerned with what I call the "border intellectual."

McLaren concludes with a self-reflective note: "My work is like an urban hallucination."

Prologue

Privileged (and disadvantaged) by his position at the University of Chicago, Philip Jackson provides an integrated historical narrative, one which allows us not only to link the contemporary field with the traditional one, but one which also asks us to think about our work, our identities as curricularists. True, he created a master narrative, a de-gendered, unracialized terrain in which great (white) men (most of whom either worked or studied at the University of Chicago), through the force of their apparently solitary thinking, pushed the curriculum field forward. Despite the limitations of this genre, Jackson's accomplishment is great.

In addition to linking past and present and compelling us to reflect on our professional roles, Jackson's essay allows us to turn our gaze to the "next step." What is on the frontier of American curriculum studies? One theme is certainly identity, and in this collection we have seen the idea explored from a variety of provocative and innovative points of view. There is, it is clear, no unitary concept of curriculum specialist, just as there is no unitary concept of "self" in the West. We are a complex, even self-fragmented field, but one very much in motion, exhibiting chaos and stability. To traditional scholars we might seem a lost generation, but as Alan Block has noted, it has been necessary to get lost in order to find new territory. Unlike our genocidal European American predecessors, we who are thinking on the frontier of the contemporary field of curriculum might join with those we find, support biospheric communities (however metaphoric the concept is for scholars and theoreticians), and together find passages to the new world.

Thanks to the *Journal of Education* (University of Malta) for permission to reprint the McLaren interview and to *Educational Theory* for permission to reprint Deborah Britzman's essay. Thanks to Joe Kincheloe and Shirley Steinberg for the idea of the collection and to Marie Ellen Larcada for her editorial expertise.

References

Barrow, Robin (1984). *Giving teaching back to teachers: A critical introduction to curriculum theory.* Totowa, NJ: Barnes & Noble.

Casey, Kathleen (1995). The new narrative research in education. In Michael W. Apple (Ed.). *Review of Research in Education* (211-253). Washington, DC: AERA.

Connelly, F. Michael & Clandinin, Jean (1988). *Teachers as curriculum planners: Narratives of experience.* New York: Teachers College Press.

Doll, Jr., William E. (1993). *A post-modern view of curriculum.* New York: Teachers College Press.

Elbaz, Freema. (1983). *Teacher thinking: A study of practical knowledge.* London, England: Croom Helm.

Goodson, Ivor. (1981). Life history and the study of schooling, *Interchange*, 11 (4).

Gundem, Bjorg (1992). Notes on the development of Nordic didactics. *Journal of Curriculum Studies* 24 (1), 61-70.

Hamilton, David. (1989). *Towards a theory of schooling.* London: Falmer.

Hamilton, David. (1990). *Curriculum history.* Geelong, Victoria: Deakin University Press.

Hamilton, David. (1992). Comenius and the new world order. *Comenius*, 46, 157-171.

Hamilton, David. (n.p.). Notes from nowhere. Liverpool, UK: University of Liverpool, School of Education, unpublished manuscript.

Jackson, Philip. (1992). Conceptions of curriculum and curriculum specialists. In P. Jackson (Ed.), *Handbook of research on curriculum* (3-40). New York: Macmillan.

Kincheloe, Joe & Steinberg, Shirley. (1993). A tentative description of post-formal thinking: The critical confrontation with cognitive theory. *Harvard Educational Review*, 63 (3), 296-320.

McCarthy, Cameron. (1990). *Race and curriculum.* London, England: Falmer.

Oberg, Antoinette (1987). Using construct theory as a basis for research into teacher professional development. *Journal of Curriculum Studies*, 19 (1), 55-65.

Pinar, William F. (1994). *Autobiography, politics, sexuality.* New York: Peter Lang.

Pinar, William F., Reynolds, William F., Slattery, Patrick, Taubman, Peter M. (1995). *Understanding curriculum.* New York: Peter Lang.

Schwab, Joseph (1983, Fall). The practical 4: Something for curriculum professors to do. *Curriculum Inquiry*, 13, 239-266.

Westbrook, Robert (1991) *John Dewey and American philosophy.* Ithaca, NY: Cornell University Press.

CURRICULUM

Chapter One

Storying the Self: Life Politics and the Study of the Teacher's Life and Work

Ivor F. Goodson

Preparing for Postmodernity: The Peril and Promise

The current changes in the economy and superstructure associated with postmodernity pose particular perils and promises for the world of education.

As Wolfe has argued, it is quite conceivable that it will not just be public social services which are dismantled in the new epoch but also aspects of the superstructure (Wolfe, 1989). In particular, some of the median associations such as universities and schools might be diminished and decoupled in significant ways. This means that institutional sites may no longer be the only, or major, significant sites of definition and contestation, and it also means that methodological genres which mainly focus on institutional analysis and institutional theorizing may be similarly diminished.

Associated with this restructuring of institutional life is an associated change in forms of knowledge, particularly the forms of workplace knowledge which will be promoted. Significantly, much of the workplace knowledge currently being promoted is context-specific and personal (Goodson, 1993, pp. 1-3). Putting these two things together means that different sites for definition and delineation will emerge in the postmodernist period. Firstly, there will be the continuing struggle for the theoretical and critical mission inside surviving but conceivably diminished institutional sites and existing social arenas.

Secondly, and probably progressively more important for the future, will be the site of everyday life and identity. It is here that perhaps the most interesting project, what Giddens calls "the reflexive project of the self," will be contested in the next epoch. Life politics, the politics of identity construction and ongoing identity maintenance, will become a major and growing site of ideological and intellectual contestation. In this regard, new modes of phenomenological work, with their focus on lived experience, may prove to be prophetic. The agenda standing before us is one in which identity and lived experience can themselves be used as the sites wherein and whereby we interrogate the social world theoretically and critically. If that sounds too grandiose (which it does), what it really means is that we should be investigating and promoting more contextual and intertextual studies of the process of identity, definition, and construction, especially the life history genre.

Here the important distinction is between life story and life history. The life story is the initial selected account that people give of their lives: the life history is the triangulated account, one point of the tripod being the life story and the other two points being other people's testimony, documentary testimony, and the transcripts and archives that appertain to the life in question.

Storying the Self

The use of personal stories and narratives in teacher education has to respond meaningfully to the new conditions of work and being in the postmodern world. As a number of social scientists have recently argued, this means we should reformulate our conceptions of identity and self-hood. The global forces which are undermining traditional forms of life and work are likewise transforming notions of identity and self. Identity is no longer an ascribed status or place in an established order; rather, identity is an ongoing project, most commonly an ongoing narrative project.

In the new order, we "story the self" as a means of making sense of new conditions of working and being. *The self becomes a reflexive project, an ongoing narrative project.* To capture this emergent process requires a modality close to social history, social geography, and social theory—modes which capture the self in time and space, a social cartography of the self.

The huge interpenetration of local and personal milieux with major global forces of information dissemination and economic redefinition is leading to a range of responses. One response undoubtedly is a new focus on the "reflexive project of the self"—this leads to a form of centering best expressed in a recent comment by a teacher in a recent interview: "what is home now—home is where I am." This response clearly links with a long tradition of romantic individualism in Western history. In this form the life story is seen as the individual construction of the autonomous self.

However, in such individualistic construction, the role of the collective subject is obscured. Tribal and collective identities continue to appeal. In fact one paradoxical response of growing global homogeneity is the stress on "the politics of minute difference." In this way countries fragment in pursuit of local tribal identity—the Balkan situation is perhaps an extreme example but the phenomenon can be viewed worldwide. This is not, as is sometimes claimed, an identity project harking back to old warrior tribes in Europe and Africa. It can, for instance, be as clearly evidenced in Canada, not only as French identity pushes Quebec towards independence but as western identity is pushing Western Canada towards the embrace of increasingly "regional" politics. In times of rapid global change we stress the "sense of place," of local identity, that we know.

Sigmund Freud argued that the smaller the difference between two people, the larger it was bound to loom in their imagination. He called this effect the "narcissism of minor difference" (see Ignatieff, May 13, 1993, p. 3). Life story work can, in fact, do much to *exacerbate* the "narcissism of minor difference" especially given the focus on the individual, the personal, the specific, the selective, and the idiosyncratic. The life history might restore aspects of the political, the collective, the general, the contextual, and the social.

For Giddens, the reflexive project of the self

> consists in the sustaining of coherent, yet continuously revised, biographical narratives, takes place in the context of multiple choice as filtered through abstract systems. In modern social life, the notion of lifestyle takes on a particular significance. The more tradition loses its hold, and the more daily life is reconstituted in terms of the dialectical interplay of the local and the global, the more individuals are forced to negotiate lifestyle choices among a diversity of options (Giddens, 1991, p. 5).

He spells out some of the implications of the emerging social order for life-cycles.

> Self-identity for us [in the late modern age] forms a *trajectory* across different institutional settings of modernity over the *durée*

of what used to be called the "life cycle," a term which applies
more accurately to non-modern contexts than the modern ones.
Each of us not only "has," but *lives* a biography reflexively
organized in terms of flows of social and psychological
information about possible ways of life. Modernity is a
post-traditional order, in which the question, "How shall I live?"
has to be answered in day-to-day decisions about how to behave,
what to wear and what to eat—and many other things—as well as
interpreted within the temporal unfolding of self-identity
(Giddens, 1991, p. 14).

The idea of the "life cycle"... makes very little sense once the
connections between the individual life and the interchange of the
generations have been broken... Generational differences are
essentially a mode of time-reckoning in pre-modern societies....
In traditional contexts, the life cycle carries strong connotations
of renewal, since each generation in some substantial part
rediscovers and relives modes of life of its forerunners. Renewal
loses most of its meaning in the settings of high modernity where
practices are repeated only in so far as they are reflexively
justifiable (Giddens, 1991, p. 146).

Above all, Giddens is arguing that the "situational geography" (p. 84)
(what we called earlier the social cartography) of modern social life and
modern social selves has been drastically repositioned by the electronic
media to the extent that the experience of social life and self is more
fluid, uncertain, and complicated than in previous epochs. In the global
marketplace, we are allowed to choose between a series of
decontextualized self-identities, rather like in the manner of the
commodified market place generally. Hence, the local and traditional
elements of self are less constitutive. This leads to the self as an
ongoing reflexive and narrative project, for as Giddens writes "at each
moment, or at least at regular intervals, the individual is asked to
conduct a self interrogation in terms of what is happening" (p. 76).

In Giddens' work, it is as if he is trying to re-assert the place of
individual self-storying at a time where the self is being ever more
commodified, saturated and legitimated. Storying the self then becomes
an ongoing process of self-building and self-negotiation; in this sense it
is possible to see the self as an ongoing project of storying and
narrative. This conceptionalization of self-building is not unlike the
conclusions arrived at by Leinberger and Tucker in their book *The New
Individualists* (1991). Here they are concerned with the offspring cohort

from the "organization men" of William Whyte's study in 1950. They argue that the whole epistemological basis of individual life has shifted because of the economic and social changes of the last decade. This economic and social change plays itself out in what they call a different "self ethic."

> As the organization offspring came of age in the sixties and seventies, they were exhorted to find themselves or create themselves. They undertook the task with fervor, as self-expression, self-fulfillment, self-assertion, self-actualization, self-understanding, self-acceptance, and any number of other *self* compounds found their way into everyday language and life. Eventually, all these experiences solidified into what can only be called the self ethic, which has ruled the lives of the organization offspring as thoroughly as the social ethic ruled the lives of their parents. Many people mistakenly regarded this development as narcissism, egoism, or pure selfishness. But the self ethic, like the social ethic it displaced, was based on a genuine moral imperative—the *duty* to express the authentic self (Leinberger and Tucker, 1991, pp. 11-12, Leinberger and Tucker's emphasis).

Leinberger and Tucker push the argument about self to the point where they argue that the (supposedly) authentic self is being replaced with by "an artificial self." In pursuing the ideal of the authentic self, the offspring produced the most radical version of the American individual in history, totally psychologized and isolated, who has difficulty "communicating" and "making commitments," never mind achieving community. But by clinging to the artist ideal, the organization offspring try to escape the authentic self and simultaneously to maintain it as the ultimate value. It is a delicate balancing act to which many of them have been brought by the search for self-fulfillment, but it is a position that they are finding increasingly hard to maintain.

> As our story will show, there are signs that the search for self-fulfillment is drawing to a close and with it, the era of the authentic self and its accompanying self ethic. The ideal of the authentic self is everywhere in retreat. It has been undermined from within; it has been attacked from all sides; and, in many ways, it simply has been rendered obsolete by history (Leinberger and Tucker, 1991, pp. 15).

In their study, they provide an important and exhaustive list of reasons for the end of the era of the authentic self. The list itself provides some glimpses of their implicit conception of authenticity and is worth reviewing in full:

- Self-fulfillment has proved to be unfulfilling, since the exclusive focus on the self has left many people feeling anxious and alone.

- The inevitable economic problems experienced by large generations, coupled with the long-term souring of the American economy, have introduced many members of the generation, even the most privileged among them, to limits in all areas of life, including limits on the self.

- Alternative and more inclusive conceptions of the self, especially those introduced into organizations by the influx of women, now challenge almost daily the more traditionally male conception of unfettered self-sufficiency.

- The macroeconomic issues of takeovers, buyouts, and restruc-turings that have dominated organizations for the past five years have left little room for psychological concerns in the workplace.

- The rise of a genuinely competitive global marketplace link-ed by instantaneous communications has accelerated the dif-fusive processes of modernity, further destabilizing the self.

- The centuries-old philosophical bedrock on which all our conceptions of individualism have rested, including the highly psychologized individualism embodied in the authentic self, is being swept away.

- Similarly, the most important developments in contemporary art *and popular entertainment* are subverting the conception of the artist on which the integrity of personalities who use the artist ideal to solve problems of identity depends.

- The rise of postmetropolitan suburbs, which are neither center nor periphery, and the emergence of organizational networks, which replace older hierarchical structures, have thrust the new generation into concrete ways of life to which

the authentic self is increasingly extrinsic (Leinberger and
Tucker, 1991, pp. 15- 16, their emphasis).

They argue then that the authentic self is being replaced by what they
call "the artificial person." While this would seem to polarize
authenticity and artifice too greatly, it is an interesting distinction to
pursue and the authors make clear the ambiguities that are present: Out
of this slow and agonizing death of the authentic self, there is arising a
new social character–the artificial person. This new social character is
already discernible among a vanguard of the organization offspring and
is now emerging among the remainder; it is likely to spread eventually
throughout the middle class and, as often happens, attract the lower
class and surround the upper.

It cannot be emphasized enough that the designation *artificial*
person does not mean these people are becoming phony or
insincere. Rather, it refers to a changing conception of what
constitutes an individual and indeed *makes* someone individual. In
the recent past, the organization offspring believed that
individuality consists of a pristine, transcendent, authentic self
residing below or beyond all the particular accidents of history,
culture, language, and society and all the other "artificial" systems
of collective life. But for all the reasons we have cited and many
more besides, that proposition and the way of life it has entailed
have become untenable. More and more the organization offspring
are coming to see that the attributes they previously dismissed as
merely artificial are what make people individuals—artificial, to
be sure, but nonetheless persons, characterized by their particular
mix of these ever-shifting combinations of social artificiality of
every variety. Starting from this fundamental, and often
unconscious, shift of perspective, they are evolving an
individualism that is "artificial" but particular, as opposed to one
that is authentic but empty. It is an individualism predicated not
on the *self,* but the *person:* while self connotes a phenomenon
that is inner, nonphysical, and isolated, *person* suggests an entity
that is external, physically present, and already connected to the
world. In effect, it is the realization that *authentic self is* more of
an oxymoron than is *artificial person* (Leinberger and Tucker,
1991, pp. 16-17, their emphasis).

The process of self-definition, or as Leinberger and Tucker would
have it, person building, is increasingly recognized as an emergent

process, an ongoing narrative project. In this emergent process, stories and narrative change and metamorphose over time. The life story changes and so does its meaning for both the person and the listener. The story or narrative then provides a contemporary snapshot of an ongoing process—every picture tells a story but as the picture changes, so do the stories. To establish a broader picture we need to locate the stories and collaborate in the discussion and understanding of stories and narratives. A life, it is assumed, is cut of whole cloth, and its many pieces, with careful scrutiny, can be fitted into proper place. But this writing of a life...is constantly being created as it is written. Hence the meanings of the pieces change as new patterns are found (Denzin, 1989, p. 20).

> [T]he beginning coincides with the end and the end with the beginning which is the end—for autobiography (like fiction) is an act of ceaseless renewal: the story is never "told" finally, exhaustively, completely (Elbaz, 1987, p. 13).

Narratives or life stories are a vital source for our studies of the social world in general and teaching in particular. But they are singular, selective, and specific (both in time and context). In these senses unless they are complemented by other sources they are of limited value in understanding the patterns of social relations and interactions which comprise the social world. Indeed a primary reliance on narratives or life stories is likely to limit our capacity to understand social context and relationships as well as social and political purposes. Sole reliance on narrative becomes a convenient form of political quietism—we can continue telling our stories (whether as life "stories" or research "stories") and our searchlight never shines on the social and political construction of lives and life circumstances. No wonder the narrative and life story have been so successfully sponsored at the height of New Right triumphalism in the west. As we witness the claim that we are at "the end of history" it's perhaps unsurprising that life stories are being divorced from any sense of history, any sense of the politically and socially constructed nature of the "circumstances" in which lives are lived and meanings made. Truly men and women make their "own history" but also more than ever "not in circumstances of their own choosing." We need to capture "agency" but also "structure": Life stories but also life histories.

In this sense the distinction between life stories/narratives and life histories becomes central. The life story comprises the person's account of her/his life (most often delivered orally) at a particular point in time. The life history supplements the life story with data drawn from other people's accounts, official records and transcripts, and a range of historical documentation.

The data, then, is distinctive but so too are the aspirations of life story and life history. In the first case the intention is to understand the person's view and account of his/her life, the story he/she tells about his/her life. As W.I. Thomas said, "if men define situations as real, they are real in their consequences." In the life history, the intention is to understand the patterns of social relations, interactions, and constructions in which lives are embedded. The life history pushes the question of whether private issues are also public matters. The life story individualizes and personalizes; the life history contextualizes and politicizes.

In moving from life stories towards life histories we move from singular narration to include other documentary sources and oral testimonies. It is important to view the self as an emergent and changing "project" not a stable and fixed entity. Over time our view of our self changes and so, therefore, do the stories we tell about ourselves. In this sense, it is useful to view self-definition as an ongoing narrative project.

As the self is an ongoing narrative project, we should think more of multiple selves located in time and space. To link with this ongoing narrative project, we have to *locate* as well as narrate since the latter is a snapshot, a contemporary pinpoint. To locate our ongoing narrative requires sources which develop our social history and social geography of circumstances and in many instances collaboration with others to provide contextual and intertextual commentary. Alongside *narration,* therefore, we need *location* and *collaboration.*

The reasons for location and collaboration arise from two particular features of life stories. First, the life story reflects partial and selective consciousness of subjective story building and self building; secondly, it is a contemporary pinpoint, a snapshot at a particular time. Collaboration and location allow us to get a finer sense of the emergent process of self-building and storytelling and allow us to provide a social context of the time and space in which the story is located.

Studying The Teacher's Life and Work

So a teacher as reader may say: "I am a teacher who tells stories that ignore social context. So what! I can see that's a theoretical problem for an educational scholar like you. Why should I worry—They're still good stories."

The reason to worry is that stories do social and political work as they are told. A story is never just a story—it is a statement of belief, of morality, it speaks about values. Stories carry loud messages both in what they say and what they don't say. They may accept political and social priorities without comment, or they may challenge those priorities.

Why would teachers' stories, particularly those directed to the personal and practical aspects of their work, be such a problem. Educational scholarship notwithstanding, why would such teachers' stories be a problem for teachers generally? How can giving someone a voice, so long silenced, be anything but a good thing?

Let us briefly review some of the changes currently going on in the teacher's life and work. Then let us see how stories of the personal and practical knowledge of teachers respond to such change. How, in short, do personal and practical teachers' stories respond to the forces that construct their work?

Martin Lawn (1990) has written powerfully about teachers' biographies and of how teachers' work has been rapidly restructured in England and Wales. The teacher, he argues, has moved from a moral responsibility particularly with regard to curricular matters, to a narrow technical competence. Teaching, in short, has had its area of moral and professional judgment severely reduced. He summarizes recent changes in this way:

> In the biographies of many teachers is an experience of, and an expectation of, curriculum responsibility not as part of a job description, a task, but as part of the moral craft of teaching, the real duty. The post-war tradition of gradual involvement in curriculum responsibility at primary and second level was the result of the wartime breakdown of education, the welfare aspects of schooling and the post-war reconstruction in which teachers played a pivotal, democratic role. The role of teaching expanded as the teachers expanded the role. In its ideological form within this period, professional autonomy was created as an idea. As the post-war consensus finally collapsed and corporatism was demolished by Thatcherism, teaching was again to be reduced, shorn of its involvement in policy and managed more tightly. Teaching is to be reduced to "skills," attending planning

meetings, supervising others, preparing courses and reviewing the curriculum. It is to be "managed" to be more "effective." In effect the intention is to depoliticize teaching and to turn the teacher into an educational worker. Curriculum responsibility now means supervising competencies. (p. 389)

Likewise Susan Robertson (1993) has analyzed teachers' work in the context of post-Fordist economies. She argues that again the teachers' professionalism has been drastically reconstructed and replaced by a wholly "new professionalism."

The new professionalism framework is one where the teacher as worker is integrated into a system where there is (i) no room to negotiate, (ii) reduced room for autonomy, and (iii) the commodity value of flexible specialism defines the very nature of the task. In essence, teachers have been severed from those processes which would involve them in deliberations about the future shape of their work. And while many teachers are aware that change is taking place and talk of the "good old days," few are aware of the potential profundity of that change even when it is happening in their midst. Clearly educators have been eclipsed by a core of interests from the corporate sector and selected interests co-opted in the corporate settlement (Mimeo).

Teachers' personal and practical stories typically relate stories about their work and practice. So stories in the new domain described by Lawn (1990) and Robertson (1993) will be primarily stories about work where moral and professional judgment plays less and less of a part. Given their starting point such stories will speak about that which has been constructed. By focusing on the personal and practical such teachers' stories forgo the chance to speak of other ways, other people, other times and other forms of being a teacher. The focus on the personal and practical teachers' stories is then an abdication of the right to speak on matters of social and political construction. By speaking in this voice about personal and practical matters the teacher loses a voice in the moment of speaking, for the voice that has been encouraged and granted, in the realm of personal and practical stories, is the voice of technical competency, the voice of the isolated classroom practitioner. The voice of "ours not to reason why, ours but to do or die."

In studying the teachers' lives and work in a fuller social context the intention is to collaboratively develop insights into the social construction of teaching. In this way, as we noted earlier, teachers' stories of action can be reconnected with "theories of context." Hence, teaching stories rather than passively celebrating the continual reconstruction of teaching will move to develop understandings of social and political construction. It is the move from commentary on what is to cognition of what *might be.*

Studying the teachers' lives and work as social construction provides a valuable lens for viewing the new moves to restructure and reform schooling. Butt et al. (1992) have talked about the "crisis of reform" when so much of the restructuring and reformist initiatives depend on prescriptions imported into the classroom but developed as political imperatives elsewhere. These patterns of intervention develop from a particular view of the teacher, a view which teachers' stories often work to confirm. All their lives teachers have to confront the negative stereotypes–"teacher as robot, devil, angel, nervous Nellie"– foisted upon them by the American culture. Descriptions of teaching as a "flat occupation with no career structure, low pay, pay increments unrelated to merit" have been paralleled with portrayals of teaching as "one great plateau" where "it appears that the annual cycle of the school year lulls teachers into a repetitious professional cycle of their own."

> Within the educational community, the image of teachers as semiprofessionals who lack control and autonomy over their own work and as persons who do not contribute to the creation of knowledge has permeated and congealed the whole educational enterprise. Researchers have torn the teacher out of the context of classroom, plagued her with various insidious effects (Hawthorne, novelty, Rosenthal, halo), parceled out into discrete skills the unity of intention and action present in teaching practices. (p. 55)

In some ways the crisis of reform is a crisis of prescriptive optimism—a belief that what is politically pronounced and backed with armories of accountability tests will actually happen.

I have recently examined the importance and salience of the belief in curriculum as prescription (CAP):

> CAP supports the mystique that expertise and control reside within central governments, educational bureaucracies or the university community. Providing nobody exposes this mystique, the two worlds of "prescriptive rhetoric" and "schooling as practice" can co-exist. Both sides benefit from such peaceful co-existence. The

promising as a focus for research and reflection. As teachers' work intensifies, as more and more centralized edicts and demands impinge on the teacher's world, the space for reflection and research is progressively squeezed. It is a strange time, then, to evacuate traditional theory and pursue personal and practical knowledge.

A promising movement might then throw the "baby out with the bathwater." At a time of rapid restructuring, the timing of these moves seem profoundly unfortunate. To promote stories and narratives without analysis of structures and systems shows how the best of intentions can unwittingly complement the moves to uncouple the teacher from the wider picture. Stories and narratives can form an unintended coalition with those forces which would divorce the teacher from knowledge of political and micropolitical perspective, from theory, from broader cognitive maps of influence and power. It would be an unfortunate fate for a movement that at times embraces the goal of emancipating the teacher to be implicated in the displacement of theoretical and critical analysis.

References

Butt, R., Raymond, D., McCue, G. and Yamagishi, L. (1992). Collaborative autobiography and the teacher's voice. In I.F. Goodson (Ed.) *Studying teachers' lives.* (pp. 51-98) London: Routledge.

Casey, K. (1992). Why do progressive women activists leave teaching? Theory, methodology and politics in life history research. In I.F. Goodson (Ed.), *Studying teachers' lives.* (pp. 187-208) London: Routledge.

Denzin, Norman, K. (1989). *Interpretive biography, Qualitative research methods series* 17, Newbury Park, London and New Delhi: Sage Publications.

Elbaz, Robert (1987). *The changing nature of the self: A critical study of the autobiographical discourse.* Iowa City: University of Iowa Press.

Giddens, A. (1991). *Modernity and self-identity: Self and society in the late modern* age. Cambridge: Polity Press (in association with Basil Blackwell).

Goodson, I.F. (1990). Studying curriculum: Towards a social constructionist perspective. *Journal of Curriculum Studies,* 22 (4), pp. 299-312.

Goodson, I.F. (1992). Studying teachers lives: An emergent field of inquiry. In I.F. Goodson (Ed.), *Studying teachers lives.* (pp. 1-17) London: Routledge.

Goodson, I.F. (1993). Forms of knowledge and teacher education. *Journal of Education for Teaching*, JET Papers No. 1.

Ignatieff, M. (May 13, 1993). The Balkan tragedy, *The New York Review of Books*, p. 3.

Lawn, M. (1990). From responsibility to competency: A new context for curriculum studies in England and Wales. *Journal of Curriculum Studies,* 22 (4), pp. 388-392.

Leinberger, Paul and Tucker, Bruce (1991). *The new individualists: The generation after the organization man,* New York: HarperCollins.

Robertson, S.L. (1993). Teachers' labor and post Fordism: An exploratory analysis. Mimeo.

Smith, L.M., Kleine, P., Prunty, J.J. and Dwyer, D.C. (1992). School improvement and educator personality: stages, types, traits or processes? In I.F. Goodson (Ed.), *Studying teachers' lives.* (pp. 153-166), London: Routledge.

Wolfe, A. (1989) *Whose keeper? Social science and moral obligation.* Berkeley: University of California Press.

Chapter Two

Curriculum, Transcendence, and Zen/Taoism: Critical Ontology of the Self

Wen-Song Hwu

> Being is the *transcends* pure and simple.
> (Heidegger, 1962, p. 62)

> The critical ontology of ourselves has to be considered not, certainly, as a theory, a doctrine, nor even a permanent body of knowledge that is accumulating; it has to be conceived as an attitude, an ethos, a philosophical life in which the critique of what we are is at one and the same time the historical analysis of the limits that are imposed on us and an experiment [épreuve] of their possible transcendence [de leur franchissement possible].
> (Foucault, 1987, p. 174)

Eastern philosophy has been either marginalized or mystified in curriculum discourses. Recent debates, "theory wars," on postmodernism/poststructuralism, critical theories, feminism, or new schools of thought, have shed new light on inquiry into non-Eurocentric approaches (Kellner, 1995). Zen and Taoism are provocative in such a confusion within the debate. This essay attempts to contrast post-structuralist thinking with Taoist and Zen perspectives.

Contemporary curriculum studies seem to reach the limit of the Foucauldian dimension of critique. By studying the notion of transcendence, the unconditional capacity to pass spontaneously beyond any and every specific limit that Kant called "freedom," and Nietzsche "will to power," it is to feel attuned to a mysterious spark within—transcendence in immanence, "to think differently." It is like "fording a river without wetting the feet" [*franchissement* can mean "crossing a river"] (Hwu, 1992). An additional pedagogical implication of critical ontology of self is that it illustrates how language constructs "self" and "other" and can marginalize and/or colonialize.

Introduction

> These few general remarks to begin with. What am I to do, what shall I do, what should I do, in my situation, how to proceed? By aporia pure and simple? Or by affirmations and negations invalidated as uttered, or sooner or later? Generally speaking. There must be other shifts. (Beckett, 1965, p. 290)

In recent decades, American education has been searching for diverse reasoning for practicing the right approaches. Curriculum scholars attempt to outline possible frameworks for studying curricular issues. Critical theorists reposition themselves as "critical intellectuals" who "must understand the historical specificity of the cultural practice of their own period with an eye to bringing their own practice and discourse in line with other oppositional forces in a society struggling against hegemonic manipulation" (Bové, 1986, p. 7). In other words, how to put theory into practice is the focus of teacher educators; bringing meaningful dialogues into public discourse and self-examination of curriculum discourse itself are pertinent.

Curriculum theorists now face the "century-old" problematic or paradoxical nature of the discrepancy between theory and practice, between immediacy and mediation. They recognize that "there are serious limits to our abilities to self-critique" (Lather, 1993, p. 674). These limits have been "contaminated" by the other, the marginalized—issues related to race, class, gender and the Other. As Jacques Derrida demonstrated in dealing with text and context, the "pure" level of descriptive or "constative" discourse is always already contaminated by the "impure" metaphorical level of performative rhetorical discourse, and context is "always, and always has been, at work *within* the place, and not only *around it*" (Derrida, 1988, pp. 95-102). The core is not always limited by the margins but traversed by them. Thus, the margins of curriculum discourses are found at work in curriculum itself, marginalizing various trends while "centering" others. For each case studied, we may resort to a variety of strategies, following the process of differentiation of the tradition itself and acknowledging that the truth of the phenomena studied can never be collected in a single intuition but has to be experienced through the constant oscillation of its alternative positions, at various stages along the process of its dissemination.

After theoretical debate throughout academic circles, curriculum scholars raise questions of self-identity and self-examination of reflective discourse. A sense of self-doubt or self-identity, thus, is generated by critical reflection. This sense of self-doubt is also caused by the discourse of the practitioner's everyday life and the dilemma of theory into practice. Nevertheless, the sense of "insecurity" is healthy and generative. The politics of identity is interrelated to the effect of difference and all contesting representation. From a deconstructionist perspective, the "double-bind" of identity is always already a struggle within the subject. The identity-formation is subject-positioned, context-situated, and discursively located. The subject-in-process, as Kristeva says, requires a new ethics operating as "the negativizing of narcissism within practice" (Kristeva, 1984, p. 233). Jean-Marc Ferry also remarks that "for the human subject, to be constituted is to be conscious of itself as an autonomous example of reflection and decision" (Ferry, 1994, p. 134). In this reflective process, we have to acknowledge the importance of seeing our discourses as contingent social practices.

Identity and Self

In a postmodern society, some argue that the self is saturated (Gergen, 1991). Others acclaim divided self, multiple selves, displaced self, and oneself as another self. I argue that there is no authentic self; however, it does not mean the self does not exist. Following Rorty's argument, when discussing and evaluating human behavior we need to speak less of the motivation for action and more of its occasions. Levinas (1993) also reminds that "to escape the 'there is' one must not be posed but deposed; to make an act of deposition, in the sense one speaks of deposed kings." This no-self, or *anatta* in Zen, is intimately involved with the heart of our misconceptions about ourselves. The Western notion of self is partly based on the limited subject of "anthropological" thinking, which not only stigmatized and excluded the philosophical contemplation of the noumenal, but also exalted the autonomy of the individual subject. In "The Anthropological Sleep," Michel Foucault foresees the space opened by the "disappearance of man" can evoke new philosophical language (Foucault, 1970). This new language is nothing negative, but rather, "the exact reversal of the movement which has sustained the wisdom of the west at least since the time of Socrates"

(Foucault, 1977, p. 43). It is this cessation of self that would make perfect wisdom possible and enable us to transgress the "dialectical man," the Western logic of contradictions and antagonism, as Foucault calls for "the disappearance of man" (Foucault, 1970). The self-conscious state of being is temporarily relinquished and dissolves into the act of creation.

The traditional recognition of the individual self in the West seems to be the center of society; relationships are considered by-products of interacting individuals. Curriculum and educational practices are built around improving the minds of single individuals. However, after our immersion in existentialism, phenomenology, and structuralism during the 1960s, the notion of self and "things in themselves" were called into question. Language and the structure or system that shape our understanding of ourselves and the world were modified. The truth about oneself has been viewed in the West as "a condition for redemption for one's sins" or as "an essential item in the condemnation of the guilty" (Foucault, 1993, p. 201).

In three volumes of *The History of Sexuality* (1980, 1986, 1988), Foucault outlines three strategies of self-constitution throughout the centuries: first, a critique of the self as rationalist by a strategy of reversal (madness—reason); second, a critique of the self as centered consciousness by a strategy of displacement (the locus of intelligibility shifted from subject to structure); third, a hermeneutics of the self using a strategy of historicism (the emphasis fell to the activity of self-constitution in discursive practices). One of Foucault's technologies of self might be said to be the art of seeing outside ourselves, or seeing the "absence" in our work. Not to look within to a true or authentic self, not to master one's time by holding it in one's thought, not to find a place for oneself within society or state, but to look out from oneself, to open one's time to what has not yet been seen, to displace one's instituted, assigned identity at a time and place. Deleuze explicates Foucault's triple root–knowledge, power, and self–of a problematization of thought:

> [W]hat can I know or see and articulate in such and such a condition for light and language? What can I do, what power can I claim and what resistance may I counter? What can I be, with what folds can I surround myself or how can I produce myself as a subject? (Deleuze, 1988, p. 114)

The "I" does not designate a universal but a set of particular positions occupied within a site one speaks, one sees, one lives. In other words, what can I do? what do I know? what am I? Foucault's work produces a redefinition of one's relations with oneself, the reflexivity of the self over the self; it is the development of a style of conduct that revolves around the question of the self. In other words, thinking from without. Does one or should one rule oneself as one rules a slave?

In Foucault's examinations of technologies of the self throughout history, he found that Christian technologies of the self or hermeneutics of the self imply the sacrifice of the self: no truth about the self without a sacrifice of the self. Today, one of the problems of Western culture has been to find the possibility of founding, not on the sacrifice of the self, but on a positive, on the theoretical and practical, emergence of the self. In addition, how could we save the hermeneutics of the self and get rid of the necessary sacrifice of the self which was linked to this hermeneutics since the beginning of Christianity? During the last two centuries, the problem has been:

> [W]hat could be the positive foundation for the technologies of the self that we have been developing during centuries and centuries? But the moment, maybe, is coming for us to ask, do we need, really, this hermeneutics of the self? Maybe the problem of the self is not to discover what it is in its positivity, maybe the problem is not to discover a positive self or the positive foundation of the self. Maybe our problem is now to discover that the self is nothing else than the historical correlation of the technology built in our history. Maybe the problem is to change those technologies (Foucault, 1993, p. 222-223).

For example, the construct of the teacher as expert tends to produce the image of the teacher as an autonomous and unitary individual who seems to have learned everything and consequently has nothing to learn. When knowledge is possession, when coupled with private property, its alterity, the relations between the said and unsaid and the relation between the self and the other cannot be acknowledged. It is easy to say what you mean and mean what you say and be understood perfectly as long as you belong to a social group or a community. It is only when one deals with outsiders that problems arise. My self is a matter of the continuity of my self-understanding, but this continuity consists of constantly putting myself into question and a constant being-other.

Self and Others

Popular common sense in America has always presumed individuals to be fully formed, autonomous beings who make their own way in the world, directed by the choices of an inner consciousness that is fully transparent to itself. Individual subjectivity is taken for granted "as an inherent characteristic of human beings, not in need of explication... [and] not open to any kind of social analysis" (Giddens, 1991, p. 120). On the other hand, Kenneth Gergen (1991) insists that one's identity is continuously emergent, re-created and re-constituted as one moves through the network of relationships with others. In present era, he remarks that "the self is redefined as no longer an essence in itself, but relational" (p. 156). In a sense, people do not acquire the languages needed for self-definition on their own. Rather, we are introduced to them through interaction with others who matter to us. The genesis of the human mind is in this sense not monological, not something each person accomplishes on his or her own, but dialogical. We need relationships to fulfill, but not to define, ourselves.

In current pedagogical settings, many educators are embracing dialogical principles and cooperative learning in their research and teaching. This dialogical orientation approach is centering on the relations between self and others, teacher and students, students and environment. Kanpol and McLaren's (1994) argument for understanding of "similarities within our differences" is a common reaction to the politics of difference that occurs in the postmodern debates. The major concern is of method-as-process rather than of result or product. A self-conscious dialogical pedagogy first of all recognizes and appreciates the difference between self and Other. The main understanding of self-Other relations, in the same underlying terms employed by Sartre and Barthes, has been that these relations are determined by the fact that one does not see oneself as one is seen by others, and this difference in perspective turns on the body. "The body is what others see but what the subject does not, the subject becomes dependent upon the Other in a way that ultimately makes the body the focus of a power struggle with far-reaching ramifications" (Jefferson, 1989, p. 153). The politics of body has been raised by numerous scholars, "bodymatters," "body teaching," "thinking through the body," or "embodied teaching"; the question remains: Is the body free and self-determining? Is it subject to the grip and grasp of the gaze of the Other?

Deleuze sees the problem in the Western philosophies is in sometimes reducing the Other to a particular object, and sometimes to another subject. The self is, for Deleuze, the development and the explication of what is possible, the process of its realization in the actual. The Other, as structure, is the expression of a possible world: it is the expressed, grasped as not yet existing outside of that which expresses it. In other words, "Other = an expression of a possible world" (Deleuze, 1990, p. 310). To refuse to name the Other, on whose body power is inscribed in figures of cruelty, subjectivation, and forced reterritorialization, is to silence the agent constantly mobilized in all deconstructive practices. Deleuze uses the notion of the "perverse" to demonstrate that the world of perversion is the world without the possible, in which the necessary has completely replaced the possible. Maxine Greene asks: "What is the existential meaning of a 'moral space' where the questions that arise do not inform and provoke action in a technicized and sterile world?" (Greene, 1991, p. 30). Too much stress on the "personal" over the public, Greene foresees, a new and dangerous mode of disengagement will promote a nihilist attitude toward social justice and human existence. However, this is not to say that emphasis on the public is more important than the personal or the personal has less value. Foucault's description of social practices (the public) has warned us that the goal of such practices is to reduce or marginalize behavior deemed deviant or eccentric (the personal).

It is the seeming tug-of-war between self and others, between autonomy and heteronomy, that opens many discussions of curriculum studies and initiates our more lucid notions of pedagogy and understanding of educational enterprise. The point is indeed aimed toward breaking one's boundary, dissolving one's self, and even integrating oneself with the Other, and ultimately the Self. This process of unlearning the learned is widely employed in the Zen teaching. The question of teaching the unteachable, for me, is still unanswered. In Levinas, we find that from one individual to another, there is already an established proximity that does not take its meaning from the spatial metaphor of the extension of a concept. We are taught to learn through abstraction via concepts, to concepts from one area organizing the totality of everything. One of the dialogical tasks is the engagement of contrasting theses. One needs to be self-conscious of his or her own ideological world view in order to practice one's "subject position" —although at times necessitated by the immediate situation, it works against and can inhibit the development of critical thinking on the parts of the other. The issue is not method or no method, but the unconscious or self-conscious. In this situational pedagogy, following

Zen teaching, uncertainty is a prerequisite for situational learning and students somehow need to be ready to be taught. The relationship between the self and others, the link of substantiality, is not subordinated to either subject; it "substantiates," it produces substance.

Transcendence in Immanence
The notion of transcendence has been religious in tone for centuries. The conception of transcendence has also been closely associated with transcendentalism, idealism, or mysticism. I would like to depict another aspect of the notion of transcendence. Transcendence, James Miller (1993) observes, is the starting point for all postwar French philosophers, and gives to each person the power to start over, to begin anew and to transform the world. The verb "transcend," deriving from the Latin *transcendere*, is to be understood as "to climb over" (*trans* = "over" and *scandere* = "to climb"). The "trans" can be translated as over/across which has to do more with a relationship, a contact with that which is being climbed, rather than a separation or a value-laden distance, such as that implied by "above" or "beyond" (Heidegger, 1982; Murphy, 1995, p. 98).

Levinas describes "a transcendence that is inseparable from the ethical circumstances of the responsibility for the other, in which the thought of the unequal is thought, which is no longer in the imperturbable correlation of the noesis and the noema, which is no longer the thought of the same. But, as non-transferable responsibility, it has received its uniqueness of self from the epiphany of the face in which a different requirement than that of the ontologies is taking on meaning" (Levinas, 1993, p. 94-95). Let me use Zen teaching as an example. The ultimate goal of Zen teaching is neither to transmit knowledge to learners, nor to help them construct their own knowledge. It strives to awaken in one's self-nature, the original "face," and to cultivate the wisdom to help others transcend their distorted perception and biased knowledge of the world. In other words, Zen teaching is a de/reconstructive process of self and others. It should, however, be recognized that Zen teaching is not anti-knowledge construction, but anti-knowledge construction with distorted beliefs and attitudes. It starts with the "dissolution" (or deconstruction) process of one's self in order to form one's self.

Levinas argues that "the human person, the 'I,' *hic et nunc*, bogged down in his or her problems or cares, is a means of sanctification. Here the human I is the reuniting of the profane and the sacred. It is not a substance but a relationship. Man is a bridge, as Nietzsche would have it, a passage, a going beyond" (1993, p. 7). He continues to remark, following Buber, "dialogue, through the *I and Thou*, is a dialogue that causes one to 'enter into dialogue,' so to speak" (p. 16). This dialogue, in Buber and Levinas' minds, is the "meeting," confrontation, or encounter before one enters the dialogue. It is a pure act, a transcendence without content, that cannot be told. The primal meeting is not part of dialogue; as soon as a dialogue takes place, the primal meeting leaves, as soon as something appears, dialogue reveals itself by hiding the meeting. This meeting is unknown to us, because what it "represents" cannot be represented. By saying this leads to mysticism, the relation or gap between the meeting and dialogue is dissolved, it leaves no trace.

The disparity between personal experience and social reality, between what we intend to mean and what we can mean, is as much a condition of speaking, reading, and thinking as it is a literary situation to be interpreted. There is no Archimedean point of view from which we can make absolute sense of the events and the moral issues at present; there are only limited and relative perspectives through which we can see and judge our understandings of the world and our actions. These "readings" offer us the opportunity to "re-describe" rather than "resolve" their formal and thematic irony. We simply understand the world or "texts" more as an occasion for compassion than as an immediate means of analysis and explanations. We need to "look within" ourselves to look beyond what we have already seen. Looking within is part of preparing ourselves for engaging in reflective and mindful practice.

The transcendental of relations is different from "conditions of possibility," argues Serres, although it's true that in Latin, *conditio* also means "the action of founding." One does not found a movement; a curtain of flames or "flame's dance" is not like a piece of solid architecture (Serres and Latour, 1995, p. 135). Serres argues for a new notion of relation which precedes substances or subjects that are encountered. Serres continues to argue this "because our scientific and technological powers make our transcendence flow continuously toward and in and for immanence. Here is the name of our new ethos: Natura sive homines-Nature, meaning human culture; human morality, meaning the objective laws of Nature" (Serres and Latour, 1995, p. 176). Therefore, the desire for transcendence turns into a radical immanence, and the sociological structure elaborated as an expedient tends to become "an end in itself" (Faure, 1991, p. 58). The phenomenal world in question is only nominally so, since it is seen (theoretically) from the point of view of awakening; its physical relativity turns into metaphysical truth.

In Zen philosophy or Taoism, the negation is used reflexively to delimit the discourse of the function of language, and it is a realization of this limitation which allows the break-through (transcendence) to an alternative mode of experience to occur. Yet the negation is not simply a statement concerning the impotence of language; it is posed as a problem–the reflexivity of the negation is also problematic. It is pointing to an area outside of its operation, and hints at something unsayable, which has nevertheless allowed language to speak of it. As Baudrillard observes that "hypersimilitude was equivalent to the murder of the original, and thus to a pure non-meaning" (Baudrillard, 1994, p. 108). Baudrillard's major concern is that of simulation and its relation to the real. Baudrillard does not believe in the real, he has totally removed the real from the order of things and replaced it with the idea of the simulacra. Baudrillard remarks that "present-day simulators attempt to make the real, all of the real, coincide with their models of simulation" (1994, p. 2). The difference between the real and the model, between one and the other, disappear all together. Baudrillard continues to remind us that "there is not only an implosion of the message in the medium, there is, in the same movement, the implosion of the medium itself in the real, the implosion of the medium and of the real in a sort of hyperreal nebula, in which even the definition and distinct action of the medium can no longer be determined" (1994, p. 82).

Experience and Language
The rapid change of self-presentation is one of the characteristics in a postmodern world. Through the changes of individuals, relations to others also undergo a dispersed constitution. We live on a threshold of cultural change, at a time when traditions are called into question and new alternatives are, or are yet to become, uncertain themselves. What we can do is to find creative and moving ways to re-describe ourselves and the world.

The anthropology of experience is sensitive to the socialization process via "social conditioning." For example, in terms of gender identity, Herdt (1981) argues that masculinity and femininity are embodied in individuals as a dimension of their experience. Social categories become the framework within which men and women behave in certain ways, but behavior is ultimately manifested by the individual. The search for a unitary identity remains an unspoken premise in the anthropology of experience. A different conception of self, as another, is tremendously empowering, since it also recognizes the Other as mutually another self in relation to self-constitution and calls for self-Other reorientation.

Our languages somehow replace our experiences. To some, the view of language is regarded as either an enclosed self-referential whole or as a reflection of the outside world, in favor of holding language to be a social practice (Sellars, 1963). The recognition is that there is no such thing as a "subject" before the accession of language. In educational practice, the learning/teaching processes are stripped of any tangible experience. These experiences are approached by phenomenology, but phenomenology has no sensation—everything via language only. Being lives in the house of language. "We need to recognize the existence of the other as a thing-in-itself" (Murphy, 1995, p. 22). Furthermore, humans are not only things-in-themselves and things-for-us but also things-for-others. In fact, we are the environment for one another. In terms of Zen teaching, in Zen master's mind, on the one hand, language is simply a medium, like a finger pointing to the moon, and we might use different fingers; on the other hand, we inevitably have to use more words to interpret or explain why we are limited by language itself. This paradoxical understanding is the gradual enlightenment of the teaching process of using words by forgetting them. As Derrida would say: the trace of traces.

Baudrillard warns us that "as long as the historical threat came at it from the real, power played at deterrence and simulation, disintegrating all the contradictions by dint of producing equivalent signs" (Baudillard, 1994, p. 22). Simulation, thus, can be considered as treating historical events being dissolved in the play of signs. This suspicion of the real is echoed in Foucault's thinking: Foucault never endorsed the possibility of a transparent, fully visible and meaningful reality. Foucault's major achievement is the conversion of phenomenology into epistemology, for seeing and speaking means knowledge, but we do not see what we speak about, nor do we speak about what we see; and when we see a pipe we shall always say "this is not a pipe," as though intentionality denied itself, and collapsed into itself. But knowledge is irreducibly double, since it involves speaking and seeing, language and light. In Zen we also find that the transcendental reality cannot be described by ordinary language and hence has to be stated in negative ways. So Zen negations, in this view, are really negations for affirmation and stand for something positive in the world.

De-marginalization

To marginalize is to exclude or to constitute the condition for the exclusion process. I am arguing that the excluded discourse not be moved or re-positioned into the central or dominant position. This re-positioning is initially similar to structuralist projects decentering the subject. However, the continuing process of decentering is intertwined with the search for subjective existence. The question, after decentering the subject and realizing the relationship, turns into "where did the subject go?" The notion of between or the boundary among various discourses is also called into question. "Between" is a mode of being: co-presence, *co-esse*" (Levinas, 1993, p. 23) or a speculative domain: a space of "neither representation nor knowledge nor ontology" (1993, p. xx). This space entails the critique of empiricism's attempt to naturalize consciousness, reducing it to an impersonal (or third-person) status. It is not by mere coincidence, nor by deviation, that rationalism and empiricism, observances of the percepts and transgression, coexist in practice, if not always in representation. This notion of between is connected with "serenity," as a middle-there, half-way from the self towards the Other. The so-called inner self or inner peace is a concern for others. In the Taoist mind, as we see the "Tai-chi" symbol, the involvement of Ying and Yang or *yu* (having) and *wu* (not-having)—a white dot in the black portion, a black dot in the white—represent poles of inclusion, indicating that the primary ontological concerns of Taoists are at once pluralistic and nonindividualistic.

In the fast moving technology of an information society, the postmodern consciousness of self-construction can be viewed as moving toward the possibility of changing perspectives. First, what has to happen is what Gadamer has called a "fusion of horizons." We must learn to move in a broader horizon, within which our newly developed and developing "vocabularies" of comparison can operate through the fusion of horizons. Consciousness is to achieve an understanding of what constitutes what we have taken for granted and "who we are today" that we couldn't possibly have had at the beginning. Second, we are in fact repressing the past, repeating it, and not surpassing it. Breaking away from the traditional order constitutes an act of self-exile, a stage that allows the soul's own exploration, a journey, an open-ended one that defines, connects, and disconnects, that leads to possible transformation. Third, the emerging dissolution of self and the proliferation of postmodern consciousness have created a discontinuous images of self. Discontinuous images in media have created a "rupture" in our consciousness and our sense of reality, this rupture moves us increasingly towards a sense of what Jean Baudrillard calls "hyperreality." As the boundaries give way, so does the assumption of self-identity.

It is not the proliferation of competing curriculum theories that dissolves curriculum itself but the subversive and hidden secret at its center—multiple interpretations. As Nel Noddings (1992) states: "if schooling is to have meaning for students, controversial issues must be discussed, and they must be discussed with full affect–that is, with attention to the responses of all those involved" (p. 129). Pinar et al. (1995) observes that "the field [curriculum] is very much a conversation, involving active participation (p. 867). Jerome Bruner also investigates the "transactional self" through reciprocity by arguing that "people act in accordance with their perceptions and their choices, and they reciprocate accordingly" (Bruner, 1986, p. 59). How much and in what forms the self develops will depend on the demands of the culture in which one lives–represented by particular others one encounters and by some notion of a "generalized other" that one forms (Mead, 1962). The aim of developing "self" is to challenge and problematize prevailing practices: for example, to cause those professionally engaged in education who no longer "know what to do" to rethink themselves. Critical teaching is directed toward a retrieval, amplification, and support of "localized," "marginalized," and minor forms of knowledge and a dislocation of commonly held conceptions about experiences, practices, and events (Hwu, 1993; 1994/1995).

The role of teacher is not to tell others what to do, not to issue edicts, nor to assist in the constitution of prophecies, promises, injunctions, and programs. The task of a teacher is not to affirm prevailing general politics of teaching but to question critically the self-evident, disturb the habitual, dissipate the familiar and accepted, making the strange familiar and the familiar strange (Greene, 1973; Hwu, 1993; 1994/1995). It is to open up the possibility of a new politics of teaching. Deleuze reminds us: "Nothing of what the great philosophers have written on the subjects grows obsolete, but this is why, thanks to them, we have other problems to discover, problems that save us from a 'return' that would only show our incapability to follow them" (Deleuze, 1991, p. 95).

Another ethics of teaching, as understood by Foucault, can be considered as "the elaboration of a form of relation to self that enables an individual to fashion him/herself into a subject of ethical conduct"

(Foucault, 1986, p. 251). The implication is not that codes or rules are unimportant but rather that the manner in which individuals are summoned to recognize themselves as ethical subjects offers analysis a richer and more complex field of study. In Foucault's mind, the question of "objects of discourse" is prior to the questions of methods of explanation and prediction. It is not simply an epistemological question, a question of what we can know, nor simply a political entanglement, a matter of what we can do. Rather, it is a study of "events in thought," to raise the issue of whether we need to restrict ourselves from, or our ways of finding the truth to, such objects, or whether we might discover yet other new ones (Foucault, 1986). It is to be free of the condition of other possibilities; it is to think otherwise, to think the unthinkable, as Deleuze would suggest. The classroom is therefore a place of invention rather than of reproduction. Michel Serres asserts that the aim of pedagogy in particular is to invent, and "to invent is not to produce, but to translate" (1983, p. xvii).

To have freedom we must "exercise" it, and to exercise it is to be able to question a kind of power, or refuse a kind of servitude, in the way we have been constituted. We need to think of freedom in terms of the historical process through which we come to "constitute" ourselves as subjects of the sort of activities through which we may be governed and may govern ourselves. We are not to issue a judgment of legitimating what is already known. Rorty suggests that "to create one's mind is to create one's own language, rather than to let the length of one's mind be set by the language other human beings have left behind" (Rorty, 1989, p. 27). The process of coming to know oneself, confronting one's contingency, is the same as the process of inventing a new language, as Zen masters utilize ordinary language in extraordinary ways.

Critical Ontology of Self

To study the self is "to forget the self" (Buksbazen, 1977). To forget the self is to "detach" from and to be enlightened by all things, by nature. This seems to be paradoxical in nature. It is a non-attachment, a possibility of many. It is similar to the way of Zen. The way of Zen is a way to an end, certainly—but there is no end. It is an end in and of itself. It is precisely such efforts to "free" oneself from oneself that makes one's work one's own; one finds who one has been by always getting away from oneself. For Heidegger, without an underlying unity, which represents the unified ultimate position in which the question concerning being itself forgets itself and loses itself, is what the technological era signifies, the era in which nihilism in fact brings about an endless return of the same. In *This Is Not a Pipe* (1983), Foucault pictures this process as an exercise of disengaging himself from himself in his "fragments of an autobiography," through "writing" that tries to alter his way of seeing things. Foucault emphasizes the power of sight to subvert the homogenizing drive towards the "same" implicit in naive linguistic versions of representation. The disciplinary power of the gaze and any search for essentializing immediacy are Foucault's primary concerns.

It was social values that determined the agon of self-mastery in Greece, and sociopolitical change that brings about an alteration in this cultivation of the self as it was experienced in the Roman Empire. In Foucault's case, the recognition of coalescence between the honor of the self and the honor of the city points to something powerful within the human condition: an ethics without morals. The honor of the city is one's relations to others; the honor of self is one's relation to oneself. The notion of struggle with the self has been of great importance, and essential to both personal and civic identity. The struggle consists of the attempt to free the self from the petrified connections forced on to the self by a repressing society. We also can comprehend through Zen and Taoism that the transmission of the supreme truth "without written signs and words" happens in deepest silence. Mute gestures take the place of words. This silence is rooted in our notion of transcendence. Zen philosophy offers us many examples of "body languages," but the wordlessness of such language is quite different from the sort of ineffable experience to which the mystics testify.

The search for an essentially good or conflict-free communal existence seems, Foucault observes, to have had disastrous consequences in the nineteenth century. Foucault's question was not about the presence or absence of community taken as goods in themselves, but about the kinds of community we may have with one another. It is a project of displacing the self rather than transforming the self. The modern principle that "the subject is not given" has eluded our freedom, and we cease to have an image of changing modes of living. For us the danger is not that we might fail to become what we are meant to be, but that we might only be what we can see ourselves to be. Rajchman reiterates Foucault's "aesthetics of existence" by saying that "one changes oneself as one comes to see what is dangerous in one's existence, and comes to see what is dangerous by changing oneself"

(Rajchman, 1991, p. 94). This means that through one's work one tries to say something as yet unsayable, or to see something as yet invisible, and so one opens out a space of a sort of rhythmic "disappearance" of oneself in and through one's work. This notion of self is always multiple; the self is constituted, constituting, and constitutive at the same time.

Some curriculum scholars have claimed that without the Other there is no self (Graham, 1991). Our sense of dislocation within current curriculum discourses lessens our sense of stability and social bonding. This sense of dislocation starts with the tension between tradition and disconnectedness. Foucault's point is not that "everything is bad, but that everything is dangerous, which is not the same as bad. If everything is dangerous, then we always have something to do" (Rabinow, 1984, p. 343). The practices of self are, Foucault insists, "not something that the individual invents by him/herself. They are patterns one finds in one's culture and which are proposed, suggested and imposed on one by one's culture, one's society and one's social group" (Foucault, 1986, p. 122). These processes of self-formation are not "natural" but are something done to the self, performed on the self. The self is not given or fixed but created by each individual. This eroding of the identifiable self is manifest in a wide range of practicing of self. The disappearance of the subject gives way to reflexive questioning, irony, and ultimately the playful probing of yet another reality. Our ways of understanding the self are thus displaced and move out of the confines of history and tradition into the preconditions of the possible as possible.

In this paradoxical or non-logical language, what Foucault calls "perverse," what has just been said is not contradicted but revoked and suspended. Foucault proposed a "slightly monstrous" language "where a division in two signals itself" (1977, p. 59). "Perversity" becomes purposeful pedagogy:

> The philosopher must be sufficiently perverse to play the game of truth and error badly; this perversity, which operates in paradoxes, allows him to escape the grasp of categories. But aside from this, he must be sufficiently "ill humored" to persist in his confrontation with stupidity, to remain motionless to the point of stupefaction in order to approach it successfully and mime it,... and to await, in the always unpredictable conclusion to this elaborate preparation, the stock of difference. Once paradoxes have upset the table of representation, catatonia operates within the theater of thought (1977, p. 190).

Foucault insists that "what must be produced is something that absolutely does not exist, about which we know nothing...the creation of something totally different, an innovation" (quoted in Miller, 1993, p. 336). This innovation refers to curriculum implications that are geared toward doing something quite different from what we have been doing. As we know, the teaching and learning process is a lifelong process, and it is a lifelong process "to become what one is." In other words, we teach and write to become what and who we are. Pedagogy lies at the heart of the transformation of our next generation; its function is to invent the conditions of invention.

This pedagogical intent is similar to the Zen master's teaching, leading from shock to transformation. We can see that "catatonia" is presented only as a transitional stage, a displacement, as a crisis; once thought is freed from its "catatonic chrysalis," it will rise, renewed and completely transformed (Foucault, 1977, p. 190). Even though we do not know exactly where to proceed from here, we do have some sense of where we are. Let me conclude with my translation of a Zen story.

> A monk once asked the Zen master, Chao-chou; "Master, I am still a novice. Show me the way of Zen!" The Zen master said, "Have you finished your breakfast?" "I have," replied the disciple. "Then go wash your dish!"

References

Barthes, R. (1975). *Roland Barthes by Roland Barthes* (R. Howard, Trans.). London: Macmillan.

Barthes, R. (1977). *Image, music, text* (S. Heath, Trans.). New York: Hill and Wang.

Baudrillard, J. (1994). *Simulacra and simulation* (S. F. Glaser, Trans.). Ann Arbor, MI: The University of Michigan Press. (Original work published 1981)

Beckett, S. (1965). *The unnamable: Three novels.* New York: Grove Press.

Bové, P. A. (1986). The ineluctability of difference: Scientific pluralism and the critical intelligence. In J. Arac (Ed), *Postmodernism and politics* (pp. 3-25). Minneapolis, MN: University of Minnesota Press.

Bruner, J. (1986). *Actual minds, possible worlds.* Cambridge, MA: Harvard University Press.

Buksbazen, J. D. (1977). *To forget the self.* Los Angeles, CA: Zen Center of Los Angeles, Inc.

Burke, S. (1992). *The death and return of the author.* Edinburgh, England: Edinburgh University Press.

Deleuze, G. (1988). *Foucault.* Minneapolis, MN: University of Minnesota Press.

Deleuze, G. (1990). *Logic of sense* (M. Lester with C. Stivale, Trans.). New York: Columbia University Press. (Original work published 1969)

Deleuze, G. (1991). A philosophical concept.... In E. Cadava, P. Connor & Jean-Luc Nancy (Eds.), *Who comes after the subject?* (pp. 94-95). New York: Routledge.

Derrida, J. (1972). Discussion. In R. Macksey & E. Donato (Eds.) *The structuralist controversy: The languages of criticism and the sciences of man* (pp. 265-272). Baltimore, MD: The Johns Hopkins University Press.

Derrida, J. (1988). *Limited Inc* (S. Weber, Trans.). Evanston, IL: Northwestern University Press.

Epstein, M. (1995). *Thoughts without a thinker.* New York: Basic Books.

Faure, B. (1991). *The rhetoric of immediacy.* Princeton, NJ: Princeton University Press.

Ferry, Jean-Marc (1994). Ancient, modern, and contemporary. In Mark Lilla (Ed.), *New French Thought: Political philosophy* (pp. 134-143). Princeton, NJ: Princeton University Press.

Foucault, M. (1970). *The order of things* (A. Sheridan, Trans.). London: Tavistock. (Original work published 1966)

Foucault, M. (1973). *The order of things: An archaeology of the human sciences.* New York: Vintage books. (Original work published 1966)

Foucault, M. (1977). *Language, counter-memory, practice* (D. F. Bouchard & S. Simon, Trans.). Ithaca, NY: Cornell University Press.

Foucault, M. (1980). *The history of sexuality, Vol 1: An introduction.* (R. Hurley, Trans.). New York: Vintage Books. (Original work published 1976)

Foucault, M. (1983). *This is not a pipe* (J. Harkness, Trans.). Berkeley, CA: University of California Press. (Original work published 1982)

Foucault, M. (1986). *The history of sexuality, Vol 2: The use of pleasure* (R. Hurley, Trans.). New York: Vintage Books. (Original work published 1984)

Foucault, M. (1987). What is enlightenment? In Paul Rabinow and William M. Sullivan (Eds.), *Interpretive social science: A second look* (pp. 157-174). Berkeley, CA: University of California Press.

Foucault, M. (1988). *The history of sexuality, Vol 3: The care of the self* (R. Hurley, Trans.). New York: Vintage Books. (Original work published 1984)

Foucault, M. (1993, May). About the beginnings of the hermeneutics of the self. *Political Theory*, 21(3), 198-227.

Gergen, K. J. (1991). *The saturated self: Dilemmas of identity in contemporary life*. New York: Basic Books.

Giddens, A. (1991). *Modernity and self-identity: Self and society in the late modern age*. Stanford, CA: Stanford University Press.

Graham, R. J. (1991). *Reading and writing the self: Autobiography in education and the curriculum*. New York: Teachers College Press.

Greene, Maxine. (1973). *Teacher as stranger*. Belmont, CA: Wadsworth.

Greene, Maxine. (1991, March). A tapestry of the self. *Educational Researcher*, 20(2), pp. 28-30.

Heidegger, M. (1962). *Being and time* (J. Macquarrie and E. Robinson, Trans.). New York: Harper & Row, Publishers. (Original work published 1927)

Heidegger, Martin. (1977). *Basic writings from being and time to the task of thinking*. New York: Harper & Row, Publishers.

Heidegger, Martin. (1982). *The basic problems of phenomenology* (A. Hofstadter, Trans.). Bloomington, IN: Indiana University Press. (Original work published 1975)

Herdt, G. H. (1981). *Guardians of the flute: Idioms of masculinity*. New York: McGraw-Hill.

Hwu, Wen-Song. (1992). Fording a river without wetting the feet: Displacing the self. Paper presented at Bergamo Conference, Dayton, OH.

Hwu, Wen-Song. (1993). *Toward understanding post-structuralism and curriculum*. Baton Rouge: Louisiana State University. Unpublished doctoral dissertation.

Hwu, Wen-Song. (1994/1995). Gilles Deleuze and the problematic of self. *Journal of Curriculum discourse and dialogue*, 2(1 & 2), 57-68.

Jefferson, A. (1989). Bodymatters: Self and Other in Bakhtin, Sartre and

Barthes. In K. Hirschkop and D. Shepherd (Eds.), *Bakhtin and cultural theory* (pp. 152-177). New York: Manchester University Press.

Kanpol, B. and McLaren, P. (Eds.). (1994). *Critical Multiculturalism: Uncommon voices in a common struggle*. Westport, CT: Bergin & Garvey.

Kellner, D. (1995). *Media culture: Cultural studies, identity and politics between the modern and the postmodern*. New York: Routledge.

Kristeva, J. (1984). *Revolution in poetic language* (M. Waller, Trans.). New York: Columbia University Press. (Original work published 1974)

Lather, P. (1993). Fertile obsession: Validity after poststructuralism. *The Sociological Quarterly*, 34(4), 673-693.

Levinas, E. (1993). *Outside the subject* (M. B. Smith, Trans.). Stanford, CA: Stanford University Press. (Original work published 1987)

Martin, L. H. and Gutman, H. and Hutton, P. H. (1988). *Technologies of the self: A seminar with Michel Foucault*. Amherst, MA: The University of Massachusetts Press.

Mead, G. H. (1962). *Mind, self and society* (C. W. Morris, Ed.). Chicago, IL: University of Chicago Press.

Miller, J. E. (1993). *The passion of Michel Foucault*. New York: Simon & Schuster.

Murphy, P. D. (1995). *Literature, nature, and other*. Albany, NY: State University of New York Press.

Noddings, N. (1992). *The challenge to care in schools*. New York: Teachers College Press.

Pinar, W. F., Reynolds, W. M., Slattery, P. and Taubman, P. M. (1995). *Understanding curriculum*. New York: Peter Lang.

Rabinow, P. (Ed.). (1984). *Foucault reader*. New York: Pantheon.

Rajchman, J. (1991). *Philosophical events: Essays of the '80s*. New York: Columbia University Press.

Rorty, R. (1989). *Contingency, irony and solidarity*. Cambridge, MA: Cambridge University Press.

Sellars, W. (1963). Empiricism and the philosophy of mind. In (Ed.), *Science, perception, and reality*. New York: Routledge and Kegan Paul.

Serres, M. (1983). *Hermes: Literature, science, philosophy*. Baltimore, MD: The Johns Hopkins University Press.

Serres, M. & Latour, B. (1995). *Conversations on science, culture, and time* (R. Lapidus, Trans.). Ann Arbor, MI: The University of Michigan University Press. (Original work published 1990).

Chapter Three

On Using the Literacy Portfolio to Prepare Teachers for "Willful World Traveling"

Paula M. Salvio

Introduction

My approach to using portfolios in teacher education is inspired by the Popular Culture Notebooks developed by Paulo Freire (Freire, 1992). Like Freire's popular culture notebooks, the literacy portfolios I describe are constructed from those language and literacy practices shaping the daily lives of teachers and teacher candidates.[1] These portfolios require that teachers and teacher candidates collect artifacts from their lives that represent their literacy practices in and out of school. Artifacts such as SRA cards and comic books are interpreted *as if* they were symbols. Because symbols refer to many domains of social experience and ethical evaluation, the reading of literacy artifacts as symbols transforms them into a powerful medium through which teachers and teacher candidates can critically focus on the social relationships that are established through reading and writing.[2] As teachers place these literacy practices in a historical, political and epistemic context they begin to understand that reading and writing are not neutral acts; rather, they are linked to cultural practices which make political, epistemic, and moral claims on our lives. Thus, to explore the history of our literacies is potentially to engage in an analysis of our cultural, social and ethnic identities.

We might think of the literacy portfolio as a collecting place,[3] an accordion file, or what Virginia Woolf has called "some deep old desk or capacious hold-all" that teacher candidates can use to select, document and interpret artifacts that represent the forms of communication and expression they value. In writing about the form she imagines her diary might take, Virginia Woolf describes "something loose knit and yet not slovenly, so elastic that it will embrace anything, solemn, slight or beautiful that comes into my mind."

> I should like it to resemble some deep old desk, or capacious hold-all, in which one flings a mass of odds and ends without looking them through. I should like to come back, after a year or two, and find that the collection had sorted itself and refined itself and coalesced, as such deposits so mysteriously do, into a mold, transparent enough to reflect the light of our life, and yet steady, tranquil compounds with the aloofness of a work of art (Woolf, 1978, p. 13).

The spacious images evoked by Woolf capture the fluid and protean qualities of the literacy portfolio. Rather than imposing a linear, chronological story line to represent the meaning of our literacy practices, we build our stories by unpeeling the layers of meaning that are nestled in objects that are strewn about our attics, stored away in boxes, or kept for us by members of our families. Each literacy artifact that is placed in the portfolio functions to build up the context of a teacher's reading history by provoking a story of literacy practices. We refer to these stories as social scenarios. Students play out their social scenarios through theatrical improvisation, autobiographical writing, and reflections which are subject to revision as old understandings and insights are shed.

As students interpret artifacts like *Teen Magazine*, personal diaries, and old letters, all of which represent their reading practices, they, in turn, read beneath the surface of their reading history. These subterranean readings enable them to re-visit and name the multiple relationships that have influenced how they read, what reading material they value, and which literacy practices may have conflicted with one another. By traveling back to an old classroom or the magazine section at the neighborhood newsstand, students begin to recognize the multiple and hybrid worlds that influence their reading practices, worlds that are wrought with contradictory social values, beliefs, and assumptions about who is worthy of learning and what forms of knowledge and understanding are valuable. The process of composing a series of social scenarios brings them face to face with dimensions of their cultural identities (Ferdman, 1990).

We draw on Bernardo Ferdman's use of the term cultural identity because it recognizes that literacy is not simply a social act but a "profound form of socialization" (Ferdman, 1990, p. 355) that is "continually re-defined and re-negotiated" (Ferdman, 1990, p. 353). His definition of a cultural identity also takes into account the *feelings and values* a person has toward the social groups to which s/he belongs. "A person's cultural identity," writes Ferdman,

> thus includes the individual's internalized view of the cultural features characterizing his or her group, together with the value and affect that the person attaches to those features. Thus, cultural identity involves those parts of the self–those behaviors, beliefs, values, and norms that a person considers to define himself or herself socially as a member of a particular ethnic group and the value placed on those features in relation to those of other groups. Changes in those features would imply a shift in the person's way of thinking about him/herself in a social context (Ferdman, 1990, p. 358).

He maintains that becoming literate requires that an individual understand how to interpret and use the symbolic media of a culture. According to Ferdman, literacy means more than engaging in transactions with print or writing. He extends his definition of literacy to include the ability to comprehend and manipulate cultural symbols and to do so in a culturally prescribed manner (Ferdman, 1990, p. 353).

The artifacts that teacher candidates collect in their literacy portfolio represent different symbolic media and offer them a way into the social worlds that shape their identities. Additionally, they function as "props" or cultural objects they can use to begin constructing the multiple social contexts in which they became and practice their literacies. Teacher candidates come to recognize the social scenarios and improvisational exercises they develop from these artifacts as useful for teaching their own students, many of whom face profoundly serious political and socio-economic struggles.

The political and socio-economic struggles of students who live in poverty or who have recently immigrated to this country pose serious challenges to educators, who with more and more frequency are female, in their early to mid-twenties, Anglo, and from a lower middle income to a middle income family (Cazden and Mehan, 1989). Their students, however, will most likely come from linguistic minority backgrounds and lower income families (Cazden and Mehan, 1989). These socio-economic and cultural differences often make teachers and their students more vulnerable to failure in the classroom, for their needs, characteristics, and ways of communicating differ broadly from one another (Birrell, 1993, quoted in Florio-Ruane, 1994, p. 54).

According to Kenneth Zeichner (1993), one of the most effective approaches to preparing teachers and teacher candidates to teach an increasingly diverse student population is to cultivate a *desire and ability* to continue learning about the communities in which they teach. This disposition toward inquiry requires particular skills as well as a particular orientation toward students that I want to call empathic.[4]

Empathic Inquiry
Although empathic identification has been under recent scrutiny in literature on multicultural education (Boler, 1994) Willinsky, 1990; Rosenberg, 1993) it has served as the cornerstone to important research in the areas of feminist research methodology (Lather, 1991; Gluck and Patai, 1991), philosophy, (Noddings, 1984), and feminist pedagogy (Grumet, 1988; Salvio, 1994). While I understand and appreciate the criticism that empathic identification is often conceived of as a cathartic experience that potentially allows educators to abdicate responsibility for social action (Boler, 1994), I also believe it serves complex communicative, moral, and cultural purposes, which influence how we view ourselves and our relationships with others (Salvio, 1994; Lutz, 1988).

Empathic identification, defined as the capacity for attending to how another person feels rather than merely imagining *ourselves* in his/her position, is a powerful index to the social attitudes of a given historical period. "The emotions," writes the playwright and director Bertolt Brecht, "are in no sense universally human and timeless. The emotions always have a quite definite class basis; the form they take at any time is historical, restricted and limited in specific ways" (Brecht, 1957, p. 145). Brecht maintained, as do anthropologists Catherine Lutz (1988), Michelle Rosaldo (1980), and Scheper-Hughes and Lock (1987), that social interests, values, and practices correspond to particular emotions. Emotion is, in this case, conceptualized as the means by which value is apprehended or perceived in the world (Lutz, 1988, p. 77). "Within the very language of emotion," writes Alison Jagger, "in our basic definitions and explanations of what it is to feel pride or embarrassment, resentment or contempt, cultural norms and expectations are embedded" (Jagger, 1989, p. 143).

Feminist philosopher Maria Lugones suggests that the process of empathic identification can be a source of creative action and strength for developing the desire and abilities necessary for traveling into the worlds of our students. Lugones warns, however, that before traveling to other worlds, we must begin to understand our own. Empathic identification, when practiced as a form of engaged thinking, can enable us to become more fully conscious of and to think critically about the social values that have shaped our literacy practices and the extent to which they are informed by racism and ethnocentrism. In writing about the role sympathetic and empathetic thinking can play in becoming a conscious critical practitioner of our culture, Lugones writes,

> I thought it realistic to reserve sympathetic and empathetic thinking for the rarity of deep friendship. But anyone who is not self-deceiving about racist ethnocentrism can begin to see us unbroken through *engaged thinking* that takes seriously her own participation in an ethnocentric culture in a racial state. Such thinking requires that she become and think as a self-conscious critical practitioner of her culture and a self-conscious critical member of the racial state. Furthermore, that thinking is possible because she is a participant in both (Lugones, 1990, p. 48, my emphasis).

Lugones suggests that if we are to become self-conscious critical practitioners of our culture and self-conscious critical members of the racial state, then we must first engage in empathic inquiry into our own histories and cultural practices. In the context of curriculum studies, this suggests that we develop reading practices that provoke each of us to more fully develop an awareness of our ethnicity as well as how we have been racialized within the culture and society we inhabit. Lugones states:

> One cannot think well about racism and ethnocentrism in one's culture and in oneself without an awareness of one's ethnicity, or one's being racialized as well as of the ties between the two.... Being unaware of one's own ethnicity and racialization commits the inquirer to adopt a disengaged stance, one from outside the racial state and the ethnocentric culture looking in. *But it is one's culture and one's society that one is looking at.* Such a disengaged inquirer is committed either to dishonest study or to ignoring deep meanings and connections to which she has access only as a self-conscious member of the racial state and as a sophisticated practitioner of the culture. (Lugones, 1990, p. 50).

If we intend to implicate ourselves in the process of self-conscious racialization, a goal I hold for both my students and myself, then we must first study our histories from an *engaged* rather than a *disengaged* stance. Lugones maintains that it is the disengaged stance that potentially abdicates educators from social action, for this position, like the seemingly value-neutral position of the positivist scientist, casts inquiry as a grand inquisition of the "other" that appears value free. The disengaged stance keeps educators at a distance, out of reach, out of touch, out of sight from the structures of feeling that inform our cultural, social, and ethnic identities (Williams, 1961). *Structure of feeling* is a term Raymond Williams uses to capture the characteristic approaches and tones in argument and communication of a given culture. These structures, although firm and definite, are also the least tangible and most delicate structures within a culture (Williams, 1961, p. 53) –consequently, they can be difficult to name. They can often, however, be felt, sensed, heard.

The disengaged form of inquiry Lugones is critical of presumes that "racialization and the having of a culture are what happens to others who are not her people and whom she can only know abstractly. One cannot disown one's culture. One can reconstruct it in struggle" (Lugones, 1990, p. 53).

For example, in an effort to construct a portrait of my own literacy history, I collect oral narratives from my great-aunts about the Italian American communities they grew up in, the family recipes that were not written, but literally handed down in their kitchens–venison, *zuppe inglese, torta pasqualina.* I include black and white photographs of my grandfather opening the season's new barrels of wine in his wine cellar in 1952 and old sheets of classical music that my mother has passed on to my sisters, my brother, and me. There are literacy practices here, there is talk, the making of food and wine, there is music, the staple of my mother's life, and, in my memory, there is the lively bantering and one up-manship with language akin to the uses of oral language Shirley Brice-Heath (1982) describes in her portrayal of the members of the Trackton community. There is the painful criticism I remember my paternal grandfather making of my mother's father for never having really become an "American," his Neapolitan accent thick as *sangue noce,* that rich, too-sweet jam my paternal grandfather would make each fall with honey, fresh figs, and almonds.

Yet, despite my paternal grandfather's commitment that his four children be well-educated, there was always a hidden suspicion of education, expressed in a saying I remember, *"Fesso chi fa il figlio meglio di lui"*–it's a stupid man who makes his son better than he is. American schools were not always regarded as the road to a better future by many of my relatives who immigrated from the Abbruzi; rather, they were more often seen as a threat to the family because they stressed a strict assimilation into American ways. In her discussion of the Italian American experience, Helen Barolini writes that "reading was ridiculed as too private, too unproductive, too exclusive an enjoyment–free time should be spent with the family group. Learning gave one ideas, made one different; all the family wanted was cohesion" (Barolini, 1987, p. 8). This was both true and not true in my parents' household. My parents were and encouraged us to be avid readers, but like them, we were also encouraged to bring what we read to the table, to discuss, to argue, and to make our thoughts about reading public.

The role orality has played in my own literacy and the emotional connections that this talk generates provides me with only one dimension of my literacy history and my life as an educator. As I travel back from New London, Connecticut, to collect artifacts and conduct family interviews, I begin to more fully comprehend the role that physical action and oral language play in the lives of my family and how I have integrated them into my own pedagogy through the use of theater, music, and autobiographical methods of inquiry.

What I have yet to construct, however, is the role my family's immigration to this country has played in the racial state. I read Daniella Gioseffi. From her, I learn that in certain southern states, Italians were segregated in schools and it was as unacceptable to intermarry with a "guinea, wop, or dago," as with a Jew or "Negro." In 1891, the murders and lynching of Italians continued from New Orleans as far west as Colorado and well on through the 1920s, or until the execution of Sacco and Vanzetti, who were sentenced by the bigoted Judge Thayer of Massachusetts, who dubbed the labor activists "dagos" (Gioseffi, 1992, p. 71).

As I read these accounts, I am first stunned and then deeply enraged, for I never studied these pages of my history. They were omitted, torn out from the history curriculum and replaced by the stereotypic, popular images of Italian Americans as gangsters, passive girlfriends, or wives of mobsters. Why have Italian Americans been so passive about the perpetuation of these images? Why haven't we taken a stronger stance in public to denounce these portrayals? I consider how these stereotypes create dense barriers to historical and social insights and envy the

Jewish Americans and African Americans who have worked publicly against such derogation.

Yet, the danger is that I equate the experience of Italian Americans with that of African Americans. This quick move to identification is what Susan David Bernstein has termed "promiscuous identification," a promotion of my circumstances as similar to others despite crucial differences in our history, class, ethnicity, and sexual orientation (Bernstein, 1992, p. 122). I must remind myself, as I work through my considerations, that my white ethnicity cannot be ignored. "To ignore white ethnicity," writes bell hooks, "is to redouble its hegemony by naturalizing it. Without specifically addressing white ethnicity, there can be no critical evaluation of the construction of the other" (hooks, 1990, p. 171).

As my students and I adopt an engaged form of inquiry into our histories, we work to locate the emotional threads that sustain the insidious logic of racism and ethnocentrism in our own pedagogies. This logic is formidable in its presence, in part because it is supported by emotional structures that are difficult to capture because they seem "natural"; hence, they limit, silence, or pathologize the emotions that threaten dominant perspectives. "[T]hey either prevent us from despising or encourage us to despise; they lend plausibility to the belief that greed and domination are inevitable human motivations; in sum, they blind us to the possibility of alternative ways of living" (Jagger, 1989, pp. 143-144).

The process of empathic inquiry that my students engage in is delicate and especially difficult to sustain in the context of institutional life and bureaucratic demands on time and space. As you will see, this process is subtle, slow, and oftentimes barely visible. I have chosen to draw on the case study I include here because Kathy Bellerose, a student with whom I have worked, has placed the insidious dangers of the passive attitude in relief for me. As Kathy re-visits the worlds she has inhabited, she begins to make portable the aspects of her world that are potentially instructive. Together, we explore the ways in which socio-economic class can pressure young girls to acquiesce to cultural codes that promote conformity and silence. Conformity and silence are recurring themes in my world as well. Although they mingle with themes of "taking a stand" and "speaking out," they echo louder; they are more shrill.

This passive attitude is what I will refer to as *emotional white-out.* Emotional white-out refers not to the erasure, but to the camouflaging of emotions that are incompatible with dominant perceptions and values. The word camouflage refers not only to altering our appearance, but to concealing ourselves from the enemy by making us appear to be part of the "natural" surroundings. "By forming our emotional constitution in particular ways," writes Alison Jagger, "our society helps to ensure its own perpetuation. The dominant values are implicit in responses taken to be precultural or acultural, our so-called gut responses" (Jagger, 1989, p. 143) Like liquid paper, emotional white-out may cover over our fear, outrage, or resentment, but it always leaves an unsightly mark.

By traveling into Kathy's world via her literacy portfolio, I have come to more fully recognize the inclination for young girls to "white out" their emotional life and hence become well schooled in adopting the passive attitude. This passivity, I believe, has serious political and epistemic implications for women who enter the teaching profession, for emotional white-out functions not only to numb a person's critical faculties but also to school students in avoiding actual rather than abstract commitments (Lugones, 1990, p. 53). Kathy's literacy portfolio exemplifies how emotional white-out is one of the most prevalent and dangerous emotional structures encouraged in schools for girls and thus is likely to become an integral part of many teachers' psyches. By employing particular methods of analysis for reading her portfolio, however, Kathy can take up forms of empathic inquiry into her literacy practices. These methods of empathic inquiry function to place the passive attitude in relief, thereby enabling Kathy to explore the actions she took to disrupt it.

Kathy's literacy portfolio does not represent a student recognizing the role she plays in the racial state, nor does it represent a student navigating the complex tension between literacy and white ethnicity. Rather, I have chosen to work with Kathy's portfolio because it represents an actual view of the subtle degrees of insight students who live in predominantly white communities develop as they become more fully aware of their own ethnicity, of their own racialization, and the ties between the two. These are small humble steps which can only be sustained over time and in educational communities which recognize the insidious dangers of emotional white-out. Although we, as educators, have a dangerous pre-disposition to white out our emotional lives, we also have the skills needed to recognize the social values embedded in our emotional lives. The project for teacher education is to begin uncovering these skills. This process might begin with what the contemporary Buddhist teacher Thich Nhat Hanh (1987) calls "being in touch with ourselves."

> In modern society, most of us don't want to be in touch with ourselves; we want to be in touch with other things like religion, sports, politics, a book–we want to invite something else to enter us, opening ourselves to the television and telling the television to come and colonize us. So first of all, "in touch," means in touch with oneself in order to find out the source of wisdom, understanding, and compassion in each of us (Thich Nhat Hanh, 1987, p. 85).

Empathic study into one's own literacy practices is preparation for an approach to teaching that is mindful of the realities in oneself and the worlds we are responsible to take social action in. This first stage of analysis is, I believe, a crucial step toward developing the desire and ability to learn about the communities in which we teach, and in so doing, to see through racism in our culture so as to loosen its grip on our pedagogical practices. The engaged orientation Zeichner evokes is akin to the disposition Lugones (1989) believes to be so necessary for educators and their students to travel into one anothers' worlds, an act she refers to as "world traveling and loving perception." She uses this phrase to describe the skills used by outsiders to the mainstream to move in and out of Anglo worlds. Lugones believes these skills need to be unearthed through empathic analysis if they are to be of educative value.

> I recognize that much of our traveling is done unwillfully to hostile white/Anglo "worlds." The hostility of these "worlds" and the compulsory nature of the "traveling" have obscured for us the enormous value of this aspect of our living and its connection to loving. Racism has a vested interest in obscuring and devaluing the complex skills involved in it. I recommend that we affirm this traveling across "worlds" as partly constitutive of cross-cultural and cross-racial loving. Thus I recommend to women of color in the U.S. that we learn to love each other by learning to travel to each other's "worlds" (Lugones, 1989, p. 276).

The failure of love Lugones speaks of, is, in part, a failure to identify with our students or with one another. This failure, which is prevalent in many classrooms, conditions us to render our students invisible, independent from us and finally, to feel no sense of self-loss for not knowing them (Lugones, 1989, p. 280).

"Those of us who are world travelers," writes Lugones, "inhabit more than one world at the same time as a matter of necessity and of survival. We have the distinct experience of being different in different worlds and of having the capacity to remember other worlds and ourselves in them" (Lugones, 1989, p. 235). There are worlds in which we feel at ease in and those in which we, like many of our students, feel vulnerable, angry, and defensive. Lugones is interested not only in those worlds in which we construct ourselves, but how we are constructed by those who stand outside our world.

Compulsory World Traveling

Compulsory world traveling is a performative act to the extent that we take on roles; however, it is not a form of acting, for it may not be willful or conscious. Perhaps most importantly, compulsory world traveling is done for purposes of survival and necessity and is devoid of joy or playfulness.

As compulsory world travelers, we venture into situations in which the standard behaviors required to feel a part of a group feel a bit snug, forced, or painful. This is a potentially good thing, for when we feel too easy among ourselves, argues Lugones, we are more inclined to *arrogantly perceive those unlike ourselves.* Arrogant perception is characterized by an absence of identification. It is the failure to identify with persons whom we perceive as unlike us. We think to ourselves, "I don't want them to rub off on me." "Being taught to perceive arrogantly," writes Lugones, "is part of being taught to be a woman of a certain class in both the U.S. and Argentina, it is part of being taught to be a white/Anglo woman in the U.S. and it is part of being taught to be a woman in both places: *to be both the agent and the object of arrogant perception"* (Lugones, 1989, p. 277, my emphasis). This way of seeing others is what Lugones believes to be the central property of racism–the internalization of the propriety of abuse without identification. I can abuse you because I feel no connection to you; I fail to see myself in your eyes.[5]

People who perceive arrogantly are often lazy and disrespectful to others unlike them and fail to appreciate any culture or cultural ways except their own (Lugones, 1990, p. 480). Feminist and activist Gloria Anzaldua believes that empathy can open the door to understanding and that the failure to empathize with another's experience is due, in part, to what she calls "selective reality," "the narrow spectrum of reality that human beings select or chose to perceive and/or what their culture 'selects' for them to 'see'" (Anzaldua, 1990, p. xxi). The failure to see those who stand outside our "field of vision" is a practice of disengagement Anzaldua recognizes as "a sanctioned ethnocentric racist strategy. An unmarked race is a sign of Racism unaware of itself..." (Anzaldua, 1990). "You do not see me because you do not see yourself and you do not see yourself because you declare yourself outside of culture. Whites not naming themselves while presume their universality" (Lugones, 1990). Thus, the failure to know one's own history potentially makes educators more vulnerable to racism and hence, I believe, more vulnerable to failure in the classroom. We cannot cultivate a desire and ability to learn about the community in which we teach if we are incapable of understanding the world in which we and our students live.

The literacy portfolio enables teacher candidates to mark their social, cultural and ethnic identities and the values and normative standards that constitute them. In the following sections of this chapter, I will describe an approach to using the literacy portfolio to cultivate a disposition for *empathic inquiry*. In the long run, I hope this approach to empathic inquiry can bring educators face to face with their own cultural, ethnic, and social identities. Such educative experiences, I believe, are contingent upon working to open up, to make broader, not only fields of vision but fields of emotion. The particular skills and disposition we need as educators to world travel and lovingly perceive our students are developed in relationship to Lugones' concept of empathic identification. This form of empathic identification has the following characteristics:

•   As we travel we consult something other than our own will and interests, fears and imagination (although we do not discount them).

•   We go into the worlds of others and attend to how we are constructed in this world; we attempt to witness our students' own sense of themselves in this world.

Because empathic identification is one important cornerstone of the theater, I introduce teachers and teacher-candidates to the forms of observation, reflection, interpretation, and artistic staging that are taken from the modern stage, specifically the rehearsal methods of Bertolt Brecht. Suspicious of forms of identification that enabled the audience to abdicate their obligation for social action, Brecht developed approaches to interpreting emotion that both engaged the audience in emotional response and distanced them from their emotions so they could reflect on the performance's social significance. His approach to reading scripts, the attention he gave to the social status of objects in space, whose hands these objects fell into, and the social interests of his characters provide a rich framework for teachers to study their own cultural identities. Moreover, these exercises provide opportunities for teachers to both engage in and reflect upon their educational histories as they stand in relation to one another, thus creating an enlarged story of literacy education.

Description of the Project

Setting and Participants
The setting for this work is in a course I teach each fall at the University of New Hampshire entitled "Foundations of Reading Instruction." I intentionally situate this research project in my own classrooms so that the pedagogical event can at the same time function as a process of research which continually involves teachers and teacher candidates in the construction and validation of the meaning I ascribe to the literacy portfolios (Lather, 1991). The students in this course are typically teachers and fifth-year interns in elementary and high school classrooms throughout southern New Hampshire. Many of the students are required to take this course to complete their masters degree in reading. Over the last two years, a total of fifty students have enrolled in this course, six of whom were men. The students are predominantly white women, and come from lower to middle income socio-economic backgrounds. The primary focus of this course is to explore a range of classic issues in progressive reading theory and instruction.

Beginning with the assumption that "the printed book is not merely a source of ideas and images, but a carrier of relationships" (Zemon-Davis, 1975, p. 192), we consider literacy as a social process. Toward this end, we begin by analyzing the social values of educators like Jean Jacques Rousseau (1762), Johann Heinrich Pestalozzi (1801), John Dewey (1963, 1956), and Sylvia Ashton-Warner (1963) and consider their influence on the teaching of reading in contemporary classrooms.

It is important to note that students use the readings in this course as theoretical lenses to interpret the significance of the artifacts they include in their literacy portfolio. The theoretical and literary material in this course functions as a diverse set of framing devices through which students can interpret and then re-interpret the meaning of their artifacts.

Excavating the Literacy Landscape: Collecting the Artifacts
I ask students on the first day of class to begin collecting five artifacts that represent their literacy practices (Christian-Smith, 1993; Luke, 1993). We include a wide-based set of literacy practices that include reading and writing in a variety of settings as well as expressive forms such as quilting and other fabric arts, drafting, and photography. Students have brought in journals from their childhood–comic books, bibles, recipes, musical lyrics, and personal correspondence. Students then use oral and written forms of expression to elaborate on the meaning of these artifacts with the intent of constructing a series of social scenarios that capture their cultural identities. These social scenarios are both descriptive and interpretive renderings which are worked on, discussed, performed, and formally presented in small and large groups throughout the term.

Rather than rendering a cultural identity that presents a seamless totality, we work to render complex portraits that capture the fluid, protean properties of identity and culture. We draw on, for example, the work of Bernardo Ferdman (1990), Perry Gilmore (1985), Audre Lorde (1982), Lisa Delpit (1992), Maria Lugones (1989) and Theresa Perry and James Fraser (1993) to locate and interpret behaviors, beliefs, values, and norms that we believe are important to sustaining our cultural, ethnic, and social identities while working toward an understanding of what it means to become educators who are *self-conscious critical practitioners of our cultures*. Teachers and teacher candidates are asked to consider the following issues as they begin to collect artifacts for their literacy portfolios:

- Which texts have played significant roles in your life?

- What particular social "group" do you associate this text with?

- Do you belong to a group that would not value or be interested in this text or the beliefs and values it holds?

- How was literacy taught? (many students bring in the actual primers they learned to read with, for example, the Dick and Jane series, SRA cards and lessons from DISTAR).

- Which of your literacy practices conflicted with one another? (Students often bring in collections of notes passed, like contraband, in the aisles and cafeteria—*sub rosa* literacy stashed in the barrels of pens, recovered from closets and under the bed).

We literally bring in and critically analyze objects from our world, consequently engaging the boundaries between home and school, neighborhood and classroom life.

I Thought I Was at Ease in My World

For many of the female teacher candidates I work with, compulsory world traveling is so imbued in their existence that it hardly seems like travel at all. Accommodating to other people's standards and being vulnerable to other people's constructions of them is a taken-for-granted part of daily life which is particularly evident in school. In reflecting on a series of artifacts in her literacy portfolio that capture her most memorable reading experiences, Kathy Bellerose recalls the importance of "fitting in," rather than excelling in her world.

> Growing up in a rural, white middle-class community, I was mostly formed by white, middle-class people, often conservative, mainly Christians who taught us non-controversial, textbook material. Rarely were projects wildly interesting, but always very basic.... The basic message I feel we received from the school was stay in the median range and "don't rock the boat." Creativity was allowed only within narrow confines. Ferdman asks the question of whether or not the learner "must change the nature of his or her self-concept in order to do what is asked." To answer this question for myself, I would say no. Mainly because I did not have a self-concept that was different from the school's. However, I did not find school at all stimulating and was rarely excited about what it had to offer me. But it was expected that I would passively go along with the curriculum whether I was excited or not. This was mandated from my family. My family was working class and just recently risen to white-collar status. My family was a mixture of French, English, Swedish, and Scottish. My mother's side of the family was Catholic. My father's side was Protestant. We attended

church, but were not devoutly religious. Education was not really
considered important. Fitting in was considered important,
though, so I knew excelling wasn't the goal, but passing was.

On the surface, it appears that Kathy did not have to alter her self-
concept to succeed in school. Like many of the students in her class,
she was white, middle-class and came from a Christian family. The
artifacts that Kathy includes in her literacy portfolio, her Smithsonian
Daily Calendar, a picture of the "travel quilt" she made for her daughter,
Amialya, *The Secret Garden,* by Frances Hodgson Burnett, a collection
of comic strips given to her by her high school boyfriend, *The Borning
Room,* by John Fleischman, and *Johnny Crow's Garden: A Picture
Book,* by Leslie Burnett, seem to testify to a sense of "being at ease in
her world." Being at ease in a world, according to Lugones(1989),
implies:

> I am a fluent speaker of the language; I know the moves; I am
> confident.
> I am normatively happy. I agree with the norms.
> I am humanly bonded.
> I share a history. (1989)

To say that Kathy is at ease in the world of school, is not only to
make a hasty evaluation, but it is to perhaps overlook the important
cultural structures which render Kathy more of a compulsory world
traveler than she first appears. While Kathy might know the moves of
her school culture, she does not appear to agree with them, "I did not
find school at all stimulating, rarely were projects wildly interesting,
but always very basic." Nor does she appear humanly bonded with those
in her community, "It was expected that I would passively go along
with the curriculum whether I was excited or not." Kathy may know the
moves for fitting in, but, these moves are not necessarily expressions
of her interests, desires, or pleasures, nor do they afford her confidence
in herself. As I read Kathy's narratives, I recognize the set of masks
worn by so many women, including myself, who struggle to get by
without breaching our relationships to the members of our community
and the values of our culture.

Writing about the many masks worn among Chicanas/*mexicanas,*
Anzaldua sees the manifestation of identity in the gestural life of the
body, particularly in the faces we make. "Face," writes Anzaldua,

is the surface of the body that is the most noticeably inscribed by social structures, marked with instructions on how to be *mujer, macho,* working class, Chicana. As mestizas–biologically and/or culturally mixed–we have different surfaces for each aspect of identity, each inscribed by a particular subculture. We are "written" all over, or should I say, carved and tattooed with the sharp needles of experience (Anzaldua, 1990, p. xv).

Kathy is not a *mestiza,* however, as a white Anglo American woman she wears masks that make her more acceptable to the image her working-class family and community have of her. In this piece of writing, it appears that Kathy wears the mask of *the girl fitting in* to engage in compulsory world travel in school. Fitting in requires a form of disengagement with school life which Kathy characterizes as passive, one of the very qualities that Lugones identifies as "the dulling of the ability to read critically and with maturity of judgment, those texts and situations in which race and ethnicity are salient" (Lugones, 1989, p. 53). The implications for adopting the passive attitude are serious, for it undermines the growth of engaged, critical judgment as well as the opportunities Kathy might have for articulating her specific interests and commitments.

While Kathy's written response to her portfolio artifacts brings her face to face with the mask of *the girl fitting in*, the pedagogical challenge remaining is to place this mask in relief so we can more fully explore the skills Kathy has learned in order to fit in and hence engage in compulsory world travel. How can a passive disposition be of value? By asking Kathy to travel back to the world she inhabited as a young girl, and interpret the normative standards that marked that world, I am asking her to develop an awareness of herself that, over time, I hope will enable her to be disloyal to any standard that schools girls in passivity, silence, and mediocrity. As I travel into the worlds Kathy has inhabited via her literacy portfolio, I become acutely aware of the insidious dangers in teaching students to be passive and how this attitude can become a seedbed for racism and ethnocentrism.

Lugones believes the skills we use for compulsory world travel, that is the recognition of and capacity to adopt particular faces (Anzaldua, 1990) and masks, gestures, and gaits for survival, actually have potential educative value because they are contingent upon the ability to interpret the pragmatic dimension of a social situation. This form of interpretation enables a world traveler to adopt the appropriate roles necessary for survival. In the context of Kathy's narrative, world traveling is done for purposes of survival and necessity, thus it is compulsory rather than willful.

Before Kathy can engage in willful world travel, she must identify the skills necessary for *adopting the passive attitude* as well as the skills she used to *transform* this attitude. Toward this end, Kathy re-interprets the artifacts that she has placed in her cultural literacy portfolio by adopting an attitude of inquiry into her own literacy practices that is at once empathic and critical. This attitude is what Brecht referred to as *verfremdung*, or the alienation effect. The alienation effect operates on the assumption that our emotional ties are the medium through which we most fully apprehend our social values. "This attitude," argued Brecht, "must be a socially critical one that points out alternative ways of taking action in the world" (Brecht, 1957). The a-effect helps students to look at the normative values and standards that have influenced their literacy practices as remarkable rather than "universally human." To identify the skills necessary for developing the passive attitude, Kathy breaks down the imperative to "fit in" into a set of gestures (or what Brecht would refer to as a set of social *gestes)* that make the passive attitude perceptible to an audience *as a social condition* rather than an idiosyncratic or individual dis-position.

For example, when asked to develop a social scenario by creating a social *geste* to represent the "passive attitude" she renders in her narratives, Kathy describes an image of a girl standing against a vast, white wall:

> As the action takes place in the center, I am standing on the periphery, silently watching. Not clutching the wall but leaning against it for support. Hoping to stay invisible, yet observing intently for any sign of recognition of my own experience; I want to connect with what is going on in the center.

This social *geste* signifies a cautious interest in fitting in with the social group located in the center. Rather than entering the center of action, Kathy remains on the periphery, where she can sustain a level of anonymity while looking for traces or signs of her own experiences. According to Kathy's social *geste,* a passive attitude is inculcated through silence and marginalization. Does this social *geste* portray Kathy's experience of schooling as one which delegitimized her interests and intentions? To what extent does this *geste* represent the ways in which texts, classroom relations, and teacher talk often silence female students? How can Kathy's experience of being silent on the margin prove to be a resource for willful world travel? What skills did she develop here?

Recall that Kathy writes about observing what transpires in the center as well as a desire to connect with the activity that unfolds there. Does the margin offer a social perspective that can serve to illuminate and transform classroom relations? In writing about the marginality she experienced as a child growing up in a small Kentucky town, bell hooks describes the margin as a place of resistance, a place that is much more than a site of deprivation.

> Living as we did–on the edge–we developed a particular way of seeing reality. We looked both from the outside in and from the inside out. We focused our attention on the center as well as on the margin. We understood both. This mode of seeing reminded us of the existence of a whole universe, a main body made up of both margin and center. Our survival depended on an ongoing public awareness of the separation between margin and center and an ongoing private acknowledgment that we were a necessary, vital part of that whole.
>
> This sense of wholeness, impressed upon our consciousness by the structure of our daily lives, provided us with an oppositional world-view–a mode of seeing unknown to most of our oppressors, that sustained us, aided us in our struggle to transcend poverty and despair, strengthened our sense of self and our solidarity (hooks, 1990, p. 149).

In this passage, hooks maintains that the margin can offer a larger world view; it can serve to broaden our perspectives by reminding us that the world is composed of a center with various locations at the margin and degrees of distance among them. The margin, according to hooks, can function as a site of resistance if one can develop an ongoing public awareness of the separation between margin and center and if those on the margin are seen as "a vital part of the whole." For hooks, the margin can provide us with different visions of the world. Part of the challenge is to understand what "central" resources can be put to use on the margin for creating just relationships in classrooms and what will perpetuate silence, alienation, and the marginalization of our students.

If we place *The Borning Room* in Kathy's hands, a book she values and one which she places in her literacy portfolio, is she more willing to move to the center and engage in dialogue? What language and forms of experience might this book give Kathy access to? In writing about why she includes this book in her portfolio, Kathy remembers her connection to other generations.

> I chose this book because it is about the importance of relationships in the fabric of our lives. In this book, Fleischman's main character discusses her connections to her mother and grandmother as she gives birth in the same borning room as both of them. "I had a strange sensation of shifting identities. Grandmother seemed to live where I lay, filling my form. Mama did the same. Other spirits swooped in and out of me. I felt slippery, changeable, shapeless as a river. I became an infant, leaving Mama's loins. And suddenly I realized that my own infant was leaving mine" (p. 96). Through his description of this transformation, Fleischman, through the printed word, has taught me something about myself. He...reminded me of connections I have had with people that I had forgotten.

With this book in her hand, might Kathy enter the "center" and engage in conversation about the myriad identities that fill her form as a young woman and have been carried to her through family allegiances and relations? What social values and norms are attached to being a daughter and a mother in this book? Do they underscore or contradict Kathy's values? Kathy, as a theatrical character, remains under her own observation as she hypothesizes about her actions and reads her *geste* against the writing of bell hooks (1990).

The function of traveling to worlds she has inhabited is an attempt to more fully understand the social contexts in which she became literate, and hopefully, to interrupt the practice of institutionalized passivity when she becomes a teacher herself. Perhaps what is most important is that when she does encounter young women who face society's demands to "stay in the median range," she will empathically recognize and work with them rather than turn away from or repudiate them.

In the following piece of writing, Kathy begins to explore how Audre Lorde describes a culture of womanhood that is separate from mainstream culture. She narrates this story by focusing on the sensual dimension of experience and using recursive rather than sequential narrative structures. The narrative structure Lorde employs, as well as the subject of her writing, subverts the traditional forms master narratives often take.

Zami: A Carriacou name for women who work together as friends and lovers (Lorde, p. 255)
In the first half of *Zami,* Audre Lorde begins to define her earlier world and...why she later calls herself Zami. She...explains how she sees herself now and how she got there. Also, Lorde attempts to build a relation to everywoman. She describes a culture of womanhood separate from the mainstream of society.... Kathy Carter's definition of stories (1993) could be a guide to what Lorde means when she calls *Zami* a biomythography.... It is not an autobiography in the sense of giving a chronological framework to her life. Reading *Zami* you do not find out the sequence of events in chronological order that have affected Lorde, instead you find a meshing of experiences, from different times during her life, that are brought together to describe distinctive experiences in her life. The experiences are often sensual in nature. Lorde takes a lot of time to describe events through what she remembers as sensual experiences. For example, her description of cooking with her mother's cooking bowl and pestle.

Carter (1993) describes the basic tenants of a story as

> a telling or recounting of a string of events that has at least three basic elements: (a.) a situation involving some predicament, conflict, or struggle; (b.) an animate protagonist who engages in the situation for a purpose; and (c.) a sequence with implied causality during which the predicament is resolved in some fashion.

Lorde's *Zami* does not stay within the narrow guidelines that Carter describes. She does recount a string of events, but not in a sequential order. There is no one predicament that must be resolved. She does describe herself in situations for a purpose, but there are many that are related and Lorde does not explicitly say—so far anyway—what purpose she may have when describing these situations. I look forward to finishing *Zami* to see whether Lorde further explores this personal definition of herself as Zami and what that means to her.

Kathy goes on to further explore the ways in which Lorde felt "white-out" was applied to her feelings toward being black within the gay community and being gay within the black community. As Kathy reads Lorde's account of her struggle she comes face to face with a woman who is asked to wear a mask to "fit in."

> Another struggle for Lorde is her feelings about being black within the gay community as well as being gay within the black community. Lorde says, "most black lesbians were closeted, correctly recognizing the black community's lack of interest in our position, as well as the many more immediate threats to our survival as black people in a racist society" (Lorde, p. 224). And as she describes the Bagatelle, a gay bar, she says, "...I, a black woman, saw no reflection in any of the faces there week after week..." (p. 220). The fact that she is unable to explain to any of her lesbian friends and lovers how much her color is a factor in how she is and has been defined within the many layers of her life, illustrates Bernardo Ferdman's point about what can be called the 'great equalizer" theory–that is creating standards in which we measure people by the same yardstick (Ferdman, p. 349). By actually ignoring cultural differences, everyone can receive the same set of values. Ferdman says that this is the manner in which current educational systems generally work with students. In Lorde's case, the gay community is too afraid of the issue of color to discuss it. Even close friends of Lorde's ignore it. When I first began reading Ferdman's article, I did not fully understand what he was trying to say. Later, as I jotted down notes while reading *Zami,* I began to understand the layered nature of his paper.

As Kathy juxtaposes her readings of *Zami* against the work of Ferdman, Carter, and her own writing, she begins to recognize the pain and loss people accrue through practices of normalization that white out our emotional lives. Throughout Kathy's readings of this material, she continually goes back to her own narratives and collection of artifacts to re-interpret the cultural norms, values, and beliefs that are represented in them and to study the social conditions in which she was most vulnerable to using white-out to camouflage her emotional life. Kathy's intentions are not to equate her life with Audre Lorde's. She is aware of the ways in which a quick move to identification with Lorde would gloss over important distinctions between them. Moreover, Kathy recognizes that engaged thinking about the life Audre Lorde renders in *Zami* will not cause the inequities and injustices that exist among socio-economic classes and ethnic groups to disappear. Engaged thinking is preparation for engaged social action.

The Art of Contradiction

As Kathy studies the social actions in her narratives, she must discover which social actions *contradict* the imperative to stay in the median range. Although Kathy is schooled in passivity on one level, she is also schooled in engagement by some of the older members of her community. Kathy finds that one of the important ways in which she experienced an engaged attitude was by reading literature. She discovers, through inquiry into her literacy practices, that she used literature to discover the emotional and social complexities within herself and through these discoveries to seek out others. Thus, reading became a way for Kathy to exercise her capacity for empathic engagement in worlds unlike her own.

In the following written narrative, Kathy renders the social landscape on which she read as a child. Her most vivid memory of reading is to use it, like her grandfather before her, to enter into the virtual worlds of others.

> Growing up I don't remember reading being an important activity in my household. My father occasionally read a murder mystery. My mother did not read at all, saying that she did not have the time for it. There were no books lined up on bookshelves encouraging us. Nor stacks of books or magazines for us to trip over or peek through. Nor do I have any memories of sleepily being read to. I believe my mother was too hurried with the responsibilities of four children, all one year apart....

> My only memories of a dedicated reader [are] of my grandfather who read books on World War II with unbelievable speed and interest. The borrowed library books were piled unsteadily near his red reading chair, where he sat forever absorbed in one more book. Although he died when I was seven or eight, I remember him always reading, light pitched over his book, eating a ham and cheese sandwich with mustard, and drinking coca cola from a thick glass bottle. I know the stories about him told to me by my uncle of what a vast vocabulary he had and of his insatiable appetite for reading. I know this was unusual for a man who worked as a janitor and a short-order cook in a diner.

With the exception of my grandfather, who never talked about his passionate interest to me, I do not remember anyone in my family being a voracious reader. Although this was the case, I don't remember a time after I was taught to read when I wasn't reading. I read mainly to escape and experience places and people that were not of my very small world.

Kathy elaborates on her collection of artifacts by using Judith Richard's piece, "Classroom Tapestry: A Practitioner's Perspective on Multicultural Education" (1993) as a theoretical lens through which to explore how place participates in the act of reading in part by holding particular social relationships. The places and relationships Kathy believes to have had an important impact on her interest in reading are subtle, quiet ones.

The actual places written about in my narratives generally do not reveal much about myself as a reader, with the one exception of the Hampstead library. It did have "mystery and airs" which caused me to feel an excitement about life and what opportunities it had to offer. Often I did have "gut deep feelings of excitement" which did make me feel "in time with that rhythm"...

The two most important points in my narrative that showed action were when I was handed my award for reading the most books in sixth grade and when I was placing books back on the shelves where I worked in the library. When I was handed my certificate, I felt the place of community because of the recognition of my achievement and the encouragement that I felt.

When I placed the library books back into their places on the shelf, I felt the pulse of the knowledge held within each book slip within my touch. The textures of the covers and the uneven pages created this sensation. The smell of old, well-read novels was the smell of history. All of my senses felt the pulse and the rhythm of that place. The action of putting the books on the shelf increased this feeling.

As Kathy empathically observes a taken-for-granted action in her narrative, like re-shelving the books at the Hampstead library, or receiving an award for reading, she begins to unearth the strong feelings she has for history. Set in the stacks of a quiet community library, Kathy is moved by the "pulse of the knowledge held within each book slip within my touch." Lodged in these feelings are distinct social values. Knowledge resides in books, knowledge is transmitted through books, and books come into our hands through distinct social relationships. The words of Zemon-Davis (1975) resonate throughout this piece: "The printed book is not merely a source of ideas and images, but a carrier of relationships" (p. 192).

The act of interpreting the meaning lodged in her portfolio artifacts enables Kathy to both unearth the passive attitude that was necessary for fitting in at school as well as recognize the particular ways in which the printed word, passed on to her by some of the older members of her community, carried relationships that functioned to transform this attitude. While Kathy begins to write about the library as a community in which she felt recognized, guided, and accepted, she does not yet fully elucidate the human relationships and social values that support the growing sense she had of herself as a reader. This move is important, for it is through the growing sense she held of herself as a reader that she resisted the larger community imperative to passively get along. She comes to recognize that her struggle was supported, in part, by specific people in her community who encouraged her growth. In future work, it is important that Kathy take a critical look at the social practices that are valued by this community. Who has access to these practices and who does not?

Kathy does come to recognize, however, that although the printed word can carry relationships, values, and norms that bring people into relationship with one another, the printed word can also fail to carry relationships, leaving people isolated or feeling utterly misunderstood. In the following reflection on a series of cartoons she included in her portfolio, Kathy writes the following:

> One item included in my literacy portfolio is a series of cartoons given to me by a boyfriend. Although I wanted to include them, they were so different from my other items.... I was not sure how they would fit in. What could they tell me about my own literacy? What could they tell me about my social and personal relationships?
>
> Throughout my three-year relationship with Paul, from time to time, he brought me a number of cartoons, mainly "Outland" by Berkely Breathed, "Calvin and Hobbs" by Bill Waterson and "Cathy" by Cathy Guisewite, about the roles of men and women and relationships between men and women....

Because I like it best when people use words to communicate, I encouraged him (sometimes threatened him) to communicate with me using words. But he couldn't or wouldn't do it. As a result, when he brought me a cartoon.... I often felt uncertain about his message. What was he trying to say to me...? Did he understand the implications of these cartoons? Although I have many theories concerning this message, I have never truly understood what it was he was trying to say, because it was never said directly. Our debate around male and female roles and about what a male/female relationship should be like continued, but was never resolved.... Literacy is a way to relate, to connect with someone. How can the "message" one person tries to convey to another become clear unless there is some sharing around the text. Two people bring their own ideas to a text. Without some negotiation of a middle ground or a discussion about the message, people can and do misconnect and this leads to a certain kind of isolation.

The cartoons represented unresolved issues on both social and personal levels. The external more social debate was the "appropriate" roles for both men and women.... On the more personal level was what each of us wanted in a relationship and how that played out within the confines of a relationship two people defined differently.

The printed word presents characters and information that can broaden our horizons and thus make us more accepting. In "Poets in the Kitchen," Paule Marshall describes the relationship between her mother and her mother's friends. She explains the importance of language and conversation to these women.

> They were women in whom the need for self-expression was strong, and since language was the only vehicle readily available to them they made of it an art form that–in keeping with the African tradition in which art and life are one–was an integral part of their lives (Marshall, p. 6).

Language, printed or spoken, can serve as a vehicle toward self-discovery and then connectedness.

By attending to herself *as if she is a character,* Kathy begins to critically inquire into her community's imperative to "stay in the median range and not rock the boat." The process of elaborating on the meaning her artifacts hold moves Kathy from a description of the artifacts to a reflective mode wherein she begins to elaborate on the emotional threads that run through the situations they are tied to by: (a.) making inferences about the social relationships that are established through reading, (b.) considering what skills and attitudes toward literacy are transmitted through interactions with the artifact, and (c.) hypothesizing about the normative/conflicting values present in these literacy practices.

In a final piece of writing where she analyzes her reading history, Kathy draws on Nel Noddings' (1991) concept of "interpersonal reasoning" to theorize about the ways in which reading might strengthen inner recognition of self, and, in turn, prepare readers to engage in Lugones' notion of "loving rather than arrogant perception." Lugones argues that by traveling to other people's worlds, whether it be by foot, through literature and art, or conversation, "we discover that there are *worlds* in which those who are the victims of arrogant perception are really subjects, lively beings, resistors, constructors of visions, even though in the mainstream construction they are animated only by the arrogant perceiver and are pliable, foldable, file-awayable, classifiable" (Lugones, 1990, p. 289).

The pedagogical challenge for Kathy is to extend the concepts of world traveling and interpersonal reasoning to her reading curriculum. By giving this theory life in her own classroom, the complexities of world traveling, and the pedagogical moves she will need to make to foster interpersonal reasoning among her students, will become more evident. Moreover, as I continue to work with Kathy, we will need to problematize the concepts of "interpersonal reasoning." How/in what way does this reasoning go against the grain of traditional reading pedagogy? What social conditions support this form of reasoning and under what social conditions might it become an emotional burden on the classroom community?

Some Concluding Thoughts

I have attempted to describe an empathic approach to interpreting the literacy portfolio that has been inspired by the rehearsal methods of Bertolt Brecht and the work of feminist philosopher Maria Lugones. This form of empathic inquiry is not romantic or sentimental. Rather, it suggests a form of engaged thinking that can enable us to detect instances of emotional white-out. We must remember that our emotional lives correspond to social interests, values, and social practices. Emotions are, in the words of Catherine Lutz, far more than genes and spleens. Emotions are the means by which value is apprehended or perceived in the world (Lutz, 1988, p. 77). The pedagogical function of Brecht's social *geste* is to indicate emotional life. It is something more than didactic–it complicates emotion by discerning the contradictory beliefs and values structuring it.

The prospect of cultivating the desire and the ability to learn about the communities in which we teach is contingent upon an empathic engagement with the life of those communities. Before we can take up this project, however, we must first be able to study our own histories from an engaged rather than a disengaged stance. Kathy Bellerose's portfolio depicts an approach to using empathic inquiry to unearth the social values, beliefs, and normative standards that mark her history as a reader. The rehearsal methods of Bertolt Brecht offer her methods to exercise engaged thinking; methods such as the social *geste* enable Kathy to work symbolically through the social values and attitudes that underlie her perceptions, assumptions, and beliefs about her literacy practices. Rather than creating a detached and static image of her cultural identity, the literacy portfolio functions as a "capacious hold-all," a deep desk drawer in which to store and interpret the myriad images, symbols, and artifacts that represent the complex and ever-changing elements of Kathy's cultural identity.

The narrative structure of the literacy portfolio is far more akin to the fluid, protean boundaries of culture and identity than it is to the more conventional, chronological story line. It resembles the recursive contradictory patterns of poetry and literature written by writers such as Christina Garcia, Paule Marshall, and Audre Lorde. Like their work, the cultural literacy portfolios are wrought with images upon images and readings upon readings. These portfolios offer no protagonists, no happy endings–rather, they are always subject to revision and re-interpretation. As teachers and teacher candidates pursue the emotional threads underlying the literacy practices they most identify with, as they seek out questions and theorize about the heritage of these practices, my hope is that they become more equipped as educators to teach their own students to articulate their place in history, as places of feeling, hope, and commitment.

I wish to thank Kathy Bellerose for the many hours of conversation we had about this paper as well as for raising important issues regarding the "passive attitude." For critical comments on earlier drafts of this paper I wish to thank Barbara Houston, Ann Diller, Madeleine Grumet, Dennis Sumara, and Diane Freedman.

Notes

1. For a description of Freire's popular culture notebooks, see *Education for critical consciousness*. Here, Freire describes the complex process of constructing and working with these notebooks in the Culture Circles he forms in Brazil. The Popular Culture Notebooks are literally hand-made from the social fabrics of the students' lives. Before the Culture Circle gets underway, coordinators (teachers) go out into the community and conduct what Freire refers to as "field vocabulary research," wherein the coordinator collects words, phrases, and activities that are typically used in the community. This material, chosen for its emotional weight, is later codified into visual representations. These "codifications" must correspond to the existential reality of the groups. Typical situations represented include men and women working on a potter's wheel, a group of men building a well and a picture of a *gaucho* from the south of Brazil. Through debate and detailed analysis of linguistic features, the members of the popular culture circle begin to discuss culture as the result of human labor and the creative acquisition of human experience. As the Culture Circle participants begin to read and write, they also come to understand that reading and writing are not neutral acts; rather, they are linked to cultural practices that make political, epistemic, and moral claims on our lives.

Ordinary acts like reading a romance novel, writing a letter to the editor of the local newspaper, or scanning the ingredients on a box of cereal are wrought with cultural values that position us in specific ways. What ingredients are you willing to tolerate in your cereal? Do you believe in the power of public opinion? What "tender traps" are adolescent girls lured to by reading the romance? (see Christian-Smith, 1993). The Popular Culture Notebooks document the very practices that are taken for granted, and consequently, are often most identified with.

Although I draw on Freire's use of these notebooks to create an analogous project for teacher candidates, I believe it is important to recognize the distinctions between the Brazilian population Freire works with and the populations I am working with in southern New Hampshire.

2. Here I refer to the definition of symbols used by Victor Turner in *The ritual process: Structure and anti-structure.* (1969) Chicago: Aldine Publishing Company. Turner maintains that symbols exhibit properties of *condensation, unification of disparate referents, and polarization of*

meaning. "A single symbol," writes Turner, "represents many things at the same time: it is multivocal, not univocal. Its referents are not all of the same logical order but are drawn from many domains of social experience and ethical evaluation. Finally, its referents tend to cluster around opposite semantic poles. At one pole the referents are to social and moral facts, at the other, to physiological facts" (p. 52). I ask my students to use Turner's framework to interpret artifacts like bibles, personal correspondences, SRA cards, and diaries.

3.   For a discussion about the use of the portfolio as a "collecting place," see Dennis Sumara's *Private readings in public: Schooling the literary imagination.* New York: Peter Lang.

4.   The term empathic is used to refer to a particular approach to inquiry that is concerned with the *structure of feeling* embedded in the contexts in which we read and write. For a discussion of elements that constitute the *structure of feeling,* see *The long revolution* by Raymond Williams.

5.   For a discussion of the ways in which submission and domination are rooted in western consciousness, see The bonds of love: Rational violence and erotic domination by Jessica Benjamin in *The future of difference* edited by Hester Eisenstein and Alice Jardine.

References
Anzaldua, Gloria. (1990). *Making face, making soul: Haciendo caras.* Aunt Lute Books: San Francisco.

Ashton-Warner, Sylvia. (1963). *Teacher.* New York: Simon and Schuster.

Barolini, Helen. (1987). *The dream book: An anthology of writings by Italian American women.* New York: Schocken Books.

Benjamin, Jessica. (1985). The bonds of love: Rational violence and erotic domination. In Hester Eisenstein and Alice Jardine (Eds.), *The future of difference.* Boston: G. K. Hall.

Bernstein, Susan. (1992). Confessing feminist theory: What's "I" got to do with it? *Hypatia, 7* (2), 120-147.

Boler, Megan (1994, March). Interrogating multiculturalism's gaze. Paper presented to the Philosophy of Education Society, Charlotte, North Carolina.

Brecht, Bertolt. (1957). *Brecht on theater: The development of an aesthetic.* John Willet (Ed. and Trans.). New York: Hill and Wang.

Brice-Heath, Shirley (1982). What no bedtime story means: Narrative skills at home and school. *Language in Society, 11*:1.

Britzman, Deborah (1991a). Decentering discourses in teacher education. Or, the unleashing of unpopular things. *Journal of Education, 173* (3), 60-80.

Britzman, Deborah. (1991b). *Practice makes practice: A critical study of learning to teach.* Albany: State University of New York Press.

Brooke, Leslie L. (1968). *Johnny crow's garden: A picture book.* New York: Frederick Warne.

Burnett, Frances Hodgson. (1962). *The secret garden.* Philadelphia: Lippincott.

Carter, Kathy. (1993). The place of story in the study of teaching and teacher education. *Educational Researcher,* Vol. 22, No. 1, Jan.-Feb., 5-12, 18.

Cazden, C.B. and Mehan, H. (1989). Principles from sociology and anthropology: Context, code and classroom. In M. Reynolds (Ed.), *Knowledge base for the beginning teacher* (pp. 47-57). Oxford: Pergamon.

Christian-Smith, Linda. (Ed.).(1993). *Texts of desire: Essays on fiction, femininity and schooling.* London: The Falmer Press.

Delpit, Lisa. (1992). The politics of teaching literate discourse. *Theory into Practice,* Vol. XXXI, No. 4, Autumn.

Dewey, John. (1938). *Experience and education.* New York: Macmillan.

Felman, Shoshanna.(1982). Psychoanalysis and education: Teaching terminable and interminable. *Yale French Studies, 63,* 21-44.

Ferdman, Bernardo. (1990). Literacy and cultural identity. *Harvard Educational Review,* Vol. 60, No. 2, May, 347-371.

Fleischman, Paul. (1991). *The borning room.* New York: HarperCollins.

Florio-Ruane, Susan. (1995). Conflict and consensus in teacher candidates' discussion of ethnic autobiography. *English Education,* Feb.

Florio-Ruane, S. (1994) The future teachers' autobiography club: Preparing educators to support literacy learning in culturally diverse classrooms. *English Education,* Feb.

Freire, Paulo. (1992). *Education for critical consciousness.* New York: The Continuum Press.

Gilmore, Perry. (1985). 'Gimme room': School resistance, attitude, and access to literacy. *Journal of Education,* Vol. 167, No. 1, 111-128.

Gioseffi, Daniela. (1992). Beyond stereotyping. *Ms. Magazine,*
    September/October, pp. 70-72.
Gluck, Sherna and Patai, Daphne. (1991). *Women's words: The
    feminist practice of oral history.* New York: Routledge.
Grumet, Madeleine. (1988). *Bitter milk: Women and teaching.*
    Amherst: The University of Massachusetts Press.
hooks, bell. (1990). *Yearning: Race, gender, and cultural politics.*
    Boston: South End Press.
Jagger, Alison. (1989). Love and knowledge: Emotion in feminist
    epistemology. In Ann Garry and Marilyn Pearsall (Eds.), *Women,
    knowledge and reality: Explorations in feminist philosophy* (pp.
    143-144). Boston: Unwin Hyman, Inc.
Lather, Patti. (1991). *Getting smart: Feminist research and pedagogy
    with/in the postmodern.* New York: Routledge.
Lorde, Audre. (1982). *Zami: A new spelling of my name.* Freedom,
    CA: The Crossing Press.
Lugones, Maria. (1989). Playfulness, 'world'-traveling, and loving
    perception. In Garry and Pearsall (Eds.), *Women, knowledge and
    reality: explorations in feminist philosophy* (pp. 275-290). Boston:
    Unwin Hyman.
Lugones, Maria. (1990). Hablando cara a cara/Speaking face to face: An
    exploration of ethnocentric racism. In Gloria Anzaldua (Ed.),
    *Making face, making soul: Haciendo caras: Creative and critical
    perspectives by feminists of color.* San Francisco: Aunt Lute
    Books.
Luke, Allan. (1993). Introduction to *Texts of desire: Essays on fiction,
    femininity and schooling.* London: The Falmer Press.
Lutz, Catherine. (1988). *Unnatural emotions: Everyday sentiments on a
    micronesian atoll and their challenge to western theory.* Chicago:
    University of Chicago Press.
Marshall, Paule.(1983). *Reena and other stories.* Old Westbury, New
    York: Feminist Press.
Noddings, Nel (1984). *Caring: A feminist approach to ethics and moral
    education.* Berkeley & Los Angeles: University of California Press.
Noddings, Nel.(1991). Stories in dialogue: Caring and interpersonal
    reasoning. In Carol Witherell and Nel Noddings (Eds.), *Stories
    lives tell: Narrative and dialogue in education.* New York: Teachers
    College Press.
Penley, Constance. (1986). Teaching in your sleep: Feminism and

psychoanalysis. In Cary Nelson (Ed.), *Theory in the classroom.* Urbana: University of Illinois Press.

Perry, Theresa and Fraser, James. (Eds.). (1993). *Freedom's plow: Teaching in the multicultural classroom.* New York: Routledge.

Pestalozzi, Johann (1801). *How Gertrude teaches her children.* (Ed. E. Cooke; trans. by L. Holland & F. Turner.) Syracuse, NY: C. W. Bardeen, Pub.

Richards, Judith J. (1993). Classroom tapestry: A practitioner's perspective on multicultural education. In Perry and Fraser (Eds.), *Freedom's plow: Teaching in the multicultural classroom.* New York: Routledge.

Rosaldo, Michelle. (1980). *Knowledge and passion: Ilongot notions of self and social life.* Cambridge: Cambridge University Press.

Rosenberg, Pearl. (1993). The presence of an absence. Paper Presented at the American Educational Research Association.

Rousseau, J-J (1762). *Emile: Or, concerning education.* (Trans. by Barbara Foxley.) New York: Everyman's Library Edition. (Also E.P. Dutton & Co, Inc. & L. M. Dent & Sons, Ltd.)

Salvio, Paula. (1994). What can a body know?: Re-figuring pedagogic intention in teacher education. *Journal of Teacher Education,* Vol. 45, No. 1.

Salvio, Paula. (1995). On the forbidden pleasures and hidden dangers of covert reading. *English Quarterly,* Vol. 27, No. 3, Spring, 8-15.

Scheper-Hughes, N. and Lock, M. (1987). The mindful body: A prolegomenon to future work in medical anthropology. *Medical Anthropology Quarterly, 1,* 1-36.

Sumara, Dennis. (1996). *Private readings in public: Schooling the literary imagination.* New York: Peter Lang.

Thich Nhat Hanh. (1987). *Being peace.* Berkeley, CA: Parallax Press.

Turner, Victor. (1969). *The ritual process: Structure and anti-structure.* Ithaca, New York: Aldine Publishing Company.

Williams, Raymond. (1961). *The long revolution.* New York: Columbia University Press.

Willinsky, John. (1990) *The new literacy: Redefining reading and writing in the schools.* New York: Routledge.

Witherall, Carol. (1991) The self in narrative: A journey into paradox. In Witherall and Noddings (Eds.), *Stories lives tell: Narrative and dialogue in education.* New York: Teachers College Press.

Woolf, Virginia. (1978). *The diary of Virginia Woolf, Vol. 2,* Anne Olivier Bell (Ed.). London: Hogarth Press.

Zeichner, Kenneth. (1993). *Educating teachers for cultural diversity.* East Lansing, MI: Michigan State University National Center for Research on Teacher Learning.

Zemon-Davis, N. (1975). *Society and culture in early modern France.* Cambridge: Harvard University Press.

An earlier draft of this paper was presented at the American Educational Research Association Conference in New Orleans, 1994.

Chapter Four

Unskinning Curriculum

Dennis J. Sumara and Brent Davis

> But here they were shedding skins. They could imitate nothing but what they were.[1]

In a focus group interview that followed the reading of a novel in a grade 5/6 classroom, twelve-year-old Heather was asked to comment on some of the group discussions that had occurred during the unit. She paused before beginning her response, and then announced that she was having trouble distinguishing among what she could remember of classroom interactions about the book, recollections of conversations she had had with her mother and brother on the same topic, and her memories of her own written responses to the text. "It's hard to tell them apart," she explained. "They're all about the same thing."

Heather's comment points to the complex relations among knowledge, experience, identity, curriculum, home, and school—phenomena that, within prevailing discourse about schooling, tend to be held apart by locating them within conveniently formulated and not-often-interrogated categories. However, although it is possible to *identify* individual readers, texts, students, teachers, and locations, the *experiences* of perceiving and of learning refuse the boundaries of such categories. When asked about what she remembered (that is, what was significant enough to have become re-symbolized and narrated), Heather had difficulty extricating home from classroom, conversations from written texts, the act of private reading from public meaning, and "herself" from "others." During the act of interpreting her learning, Heather necessarily narrated and interpreted an ever-evolving sense of individual and collective identity and, at the same time, narrated personal and collective knowledge.

In this chapter, we examine the culturally invented and reproduced boundaries that have been placed around and between knowledge, experience, identity, and curriculum. We endeavor to examine how private reading, as demonstrated by Heather, is entangled in public meaning—or, more broadly, how such categories as *teacher, learner, individual, collective, knowledge, perception, self,* and *other* are, within every curriculum happening, inextricable from one another.

In this task, we develop and use what we call a "literary anthropology"[2]—a hermeneutic practice that uses literary fictions as focal points for investigating beliefs and assumptions about reading, in particular, and education, in general. Our principal text here is Michael Ondaatje's 1992 Booker Prize novel, *The English Patient.* But our intent is not merely to present literary anthropology as a vehicle for our own theorizing. We also offer it as a *way of teaching,* a way of entering into pedagogical relations with others—a matter that is highlighted at the chapter's end through an elaboration of the teaching-and-research project that involved Heather and her classmates.[3]

Throughout the discussion, we focus on a notion that we have come to refer to as "unskinning"—a seemingly ambiguous term that, all at once announces a process and its complement/opposite. We propose that identification and identity, the principal matters of curriculum, are also matters of unskinning—of simultaneously removing and imposing boundaries. The trope "unskinning," then, functions in this article as a linguistic placeholder for a strange sort of postmodern hermeneutic understanding of curriculum.

Identification

> In the Pisa hospital she had seen the English patient for the first time. A man with no face. An ebony pool. All identification consumed in a fire.[4]

Common sense tells us that we distinguish one person from another by their appearances. We learn to identify—that is, to establish identities—by differentiating between male and female and among skin tones, heights, weights, and so on. But what happens when the culturally-sanctioned markers that we use to identify are removed? What happens when the *visual* is no longer privileged for purposes of identification?

In his novel, *The English Patient*, Michael Ondaatje presents four characters who, at the end of World War II, come together in a bombed-out and abandoned Italian villa. One of these characters is a pilot who has been badly burned in a plane crash—so severely, in fact, that his features have been obliterated; he is *unidentifiable*. During his time at the villa he is attended by the Canadian nurse Hana who, even though the war is over and the hospital abandoned, has insisted on remaining to care for him. The other characters are Caravaggio, an old friend of Hana's father who has come to the villa after hearing of Hana's presence, and Kip, a British soldier of East-Indian descent who is working in the area as a bomb defusing expert.

These four persons are faced with learning about one another—an activity that they quickly learn cannot be separated from learning about themselves. The strangeness of the setting and their respective circumstances thrust each into some crisis of identity. In some way, each character feels out of touch, inarticulate, beyond the bounds of remembered self. They enter into communal life at the villa unknown to one another, confronted with the strangeness of the others and of themselves. To overcome these feelings of estrangement, they each struggle with the need to re-negotiate and re-map the boundaries of their individual and collective selves amid these strange circumstances. Initially, several of the characters believe that they will create familiarity through the act of "reading" the other, of locating the trace of the hidden "personal" in the other. This, of course, follows conventional wisdom about learning about others. In time they find, however, that it is in shared action, shared responsibility, shared lives that knowledge of others—and of the sense of "self" that occurs with this knowledge of/with others—comes to feel familiar.

Among their joint projects, the most interesting is the identifying of the burned pilot as the "English patient." Although this identification is never verified by the pilot, and although there is little empirical evidence to suggest that he is, in fact, of English descent, he continues to be identified as such for much of the novel. This project of identification is focused around the English patient's commonplace book—a copy of Herodotus's *The Histories* that he has carried with him for the previous thirty years, and within which he has inscribed comments in the margins and pasted in drawings, maps, and clippings from newspapers and other books. For his companions in the villa, the book becomes a location where identifications are made, identities re-formed and re-written, and communal relations forged and sustained.

As we witness their efforts to identify, we come to realize that a sense of *personal* identity cannot be extricated from senses of communal/collective identity. They are, in fact, not two separate things. At the same time, because each person is always involved in many discursive systems, practices, and communities, the sense of personal and communal identity is always multiple. Our sense of who we are alters as our social relations and situations vary. Furthermore, our sense of identity always emerges from the fusing of previous, current, and anticipated experience. The memories we have of past selves can never really be fixed–as these become interrogated in relation to new experiences, they change.

In this formulation, we find that there is no clear boundary between the epistemological and the ontological: who we are is necessarily caught up in what we know; and, conversely, our knowing—that is, how we perceive and act toward the world—cannot be extricated from our senses of who we are. "Self" is not located within the body of the individual subject but, rather, is embodied in our (active) relations to and among persons and things. For the most part, these relations are seamless and invisible. It is usually only in moments of crisis that we become aware of the contested status of identity.

What is called into question with the notions of "shedding skins" and "unfolding of boundaries" are the modern beliefs in the autonomous self, the primacy of the individual, and the unitary and coherent subject. A sense of *self-identity* is not something that is "contained" within the boundaries of one's skin but, instead, occurs more ambiguously and tentatively amid the interstices of various interacting and overlapping phenomena. What is considered individual and what is considered communal cannot be caught within fixed, immutable categories, but *unfold* through the continual fusing of perceptions, understandings, and interpretations. Any conscious sense of self is always an interpretation of lived, remembered, and projected experiences.

Identification, then, is never a unidirectional process. The common phrase, "I can identify," for example, has a double meaning, used to announce *both* that I am able to relate to (that is, to insert my own sense of myself into what I am perceiving) *and* that I can recognize and name what I observe. "I can identify" is a phrase unique in the manner in which it simultaneously announces figure and ground while dissolving the membrane that separates them. It is thus we find that, as the other characters delve into the English patient's commonplace book in their efforts to identify him, their own identities are scrutinized, reformed, rewritten. It is as though when their gaze falls onto the English patient, whose body has been erased of all identifications, they can identify only themselves.

Within the villa, the remembering, narrating, interpreting, and shared reading serve to dissolve and to re-crystallize the boundaries of personal and collective identities. But such re-identification is not a process of discarding and replacing. When it is finally announced that the patient is not an English pilot, but a Hungarian spy, the novel's characters find it impossible to erase the "fiction" of Englishness. They have identified; they have become complicit in naming him and are unable to un-name. A skin was shed, but the new skin bears all the markings of its predecessor. The traces of past identifications remain. Histories are not lost, but, at the same time, they cannot be maintained as fixed entities.

This suggests the need to inquire not just into the process of identification, but into the location of identity. In *The English Patient,* we are presented with at least three possibilities on this matter: that our personal identities are contained *inside* ourselves, that they are imposed by the gazes of those who observe (identify) us, that they are located in the constellation of events and artifacts that we carry—that is, that they are somehow circumscribed in and by our relationships with others. These Ondaatje presents not as alternatives but as facets of the complex whole of personal and collective identity. Self and other, singular and plural, past and projected—all these exist in the relational fabric that constitutes our various and evolving senses of self.

Coming to know—that is, learning to identify—occurs amid our relationships with others and among the artifacts that are deposited about us in the form of a cultural world. In this way, the phenomena of who we are and what we know are inseparable, for both are matters of identification. Gadamer[5] develops this idea through the notion of "prejudice." Perception, he suggests, is not a matter of "taking in" information about an external world. Rather, every perception is an enactment of culturally-specific, historically-effected prejudices. "Prejudice" is thus divested of its overwhelmingly negative connotations, for such pre-judgment not only limits what we are able to perceive, it enables perception. Sight, hearing, touch, and our other senses are not givens, they are learned capacities, and, as such, they are inseparable from individual and collective identities. Knowing, being, perceiving, acting are all caught up in one another.

Learning, then, is not a simple process of accretion. While nothing is lost, displaced, or discarded, everything is transformed through learning. And it is here that we apply the trope of *unskinning*—a term introduced in the first few pages of *The English Patient*—to our thinking about curriculum. Like *identification,* unskinning announces a dual, bidirectional, and almost ambiguous sense. It suggests both a removing (skinning) of recognizable markers—by stripping those boundaries that we use to identify—and a simultaneous re-marking of boundaries. An unskinning.

Unskinning, for us, involves a deliberate attempt to render problematic the beginnings and endings of objects and events—an effort we feel is demanded in the conventional schooling culture of rigid organization, unambiguous demarcation, and clear definition. These artificial structures, supported by and contributing to the modernist conception of a coherent, unitary subject, are the very "objects" that we seek to unskin in our efforts to teach.

Marked Bodies

> We die containing a richness of lovers and tribes, tastes we have swallowed, bodies we have plunged into and swum up as if rivers of wisdom, characters we have climbed up as if in caves. I wish for all this to be marked on my body when I am dead.... We are communal histories, communal books. We are not owned or monogamous in our experience.[6]

As he reflected upon his life, the English patient began to understand that the human body is more than a physical-biological structure. It is also a location for relational marking: a communal and historical text. Each of us is, as Merleau-Ponty[7] put it, a network of relationships.

Merleau-Ponty recognized that human subjects are doubly-embodied: our bodies are simultaneously physical-biological structures and lived-phenomenological structures. Our bodies simultaneously separate us *from* as they place us in relationship *to* one another. Further, the body's shape is not a mere matter of physical unfolding or biological maturation. Ongoing daily experience—our continuous acting in the world—also plays a role. We are shaped by as we participate in the shaping of the contexts in which we live, physically and phenomenologically. The body, then, is not a mere locus of identity, nor a simple vehicle through which to exercise intention. It is, simultaneously, a material structure and a communal one. Whether it is a separate form or a component of a larger whole is more a matter of scale and prejudice than of factuality.

Such conceptions represent a profound challenge to what tends to be taken for granted with regard to cognition and knowledge. Generally framed as events and phenomena that exist in the invisible realm of the mental, thought and understanding have tended to be cast as "third things" that hang—suspended—in the gaps separating knowing agents and known objects. In modernist terms, knowledge is that *stuff* that links subject with what is regarded as not-subject, and cognition is that inner process through which knowledge is acquired/banked/constructed. Whether one adopts an objectivist or a subjectivist attitude toward "truth," it seems to be defined in the same way: as the extent of correspondence between a mutable thought and a stable reality. Both the nature of learning and the purpose of education are drawn out of such conceptions, with the goal of each being to creep ever closer to an optimal understanding of the universe that surrounds us.

The tactic of rendering the body a lived-phenomenological structure challenges such characterizations of cognition, shifting thought—like identity—outside of the individual and into the complex dynamic of (inter)activity. Knowing and (inter)acting are inseparable. When knowledge is pushed into the realm of action, "truthfulness" becomes more a matter of viability (following the proscriptive logic of maintaining *fit* with one's context) than validity (i.e., that modernist pursuit of a *fittest* match with a reality perceived to be separate and not directly accessible). In the former case, we situate ourselves as part of the universe, thereby leading us to the conclusion that the world changes with an event so mundane as a shifting thought. That thought is not merely in the universe, it is part of the universe.[8]

This (re)cognizing of the body as a unit of knowing-and-acting is also reflected in much of the discourse of cultural criticism. Working from a range of perspectives, theorists interested in this issue have announced the importance of attending to the embodied nature of our relations with one another, calling for a re-theorizing of the complex relations among race, class, gender, and sexuality. Their commentaries have been vital to prompting and supporting a rethinking of the modern educational project. However, and largely because the phenomenon of cognition has tended to be under-addressed, there has been a tendency to regard individuals as entirely socially-determined—thus committing an error that is complementary to that of those who focus exclusively on the thinking of individuals. The notion of individual autonomy, for example, varies in significance among critical and cognitive theorists, with extreme positions arguing what seem to be contrary points: autonomy as an elaborate fiction versus autonomy as the mainstay of thought and learning.

In our own work, we have attempted to side-step this binary by coupling the concept of "double-embodiment" with more recent theoretical offerings from such domains as the "new" biology[9] and the cross-disciplinary field of Complexity Theory.[10] Specifically, we have endeavored to develop and introduce an *enactivist* theory of cognition to discussions of and practices in the field of education.[11] In brief, enactivism is a theory of both individual and collective knowing/knowledge/action/identity. Embracing a tenet of hermeneutics—that the whole is enfolded in and unfolds from the part—enactivism endeavors to strike a "middle way" among the extreme positionings noted above. But this middle way is not a compromise between varied positions. It, in fact, calls for a different manner of thinking—and of thinking about thinking.

Founded more on the dynamic and ecological metaphors of neo-Darwinian theories of evolution than on the divisionary language of Descartes's *cogito,* enactivism casts such seemingly diverse phenomena as individual cognition, collective action, cultural knowledge, and species development as self-similar and inextricable processes. In so doing, the framework simultaneously embraces the insights of cognitive theorist and cultural critic—suggesting that these are not competing discourses, but ones that have perhaps not taken adequate account of each others' arguments. In terms of currently popular theories of cognition, for example, enactivism has much in common with radical constructivist accounts, but parts company with constructivism on its assumption that the individual cognizing agent is an adequate unit of analysis for understanding thought (not to mention the assumption that the individual is an appropriate unit of analysis for studying education). Similarly, enactivism incorporates much of what cultural and critical theorists have argued regarding social interaction and knowledge generation, but does not privilege metaphors of power and domination in its analysis of human collectivity. Rather, enactivism also embraces the figurative notions of ecologies, complexities, organisms/organizations, blurred edges. In a phrase, enactivism strives to *unskin* the phenomenon under study.

"Unskinning" is thus reflected in biologist and ecologist Gregory Bateson's[12] call to study neither organism nor environment, but the unity of the organism-in-its-environment. Following Geertz, Sumara[13] has announced a parallel notion in his formulation of the us/not-us relationship—by which the boundary that separates what we consider to be of ourselves and what we think of as not of ourselves is unstable, constantly negotiated, illusory. This does not mean that such boundaries are not useful or that they are deceiving—for they do seem necessary for language and thought (as we understand them). However, pragmatic utility should not be confused with some sort of essential truth. "Boundaries"—skins—are thus recast not in terms of unambiguous or clearly demarcated edges but, in Heidegger's[14] terms, as locations from which objects/phenomena/events unfold.

Returning to cognition, learning thus becomes a re-marking of boundaries, an unfolding, an enlarging the space of the possible—an unskinning that not only concerns matters of knowing and doing, but that is fully caught up in individual and collective identities. As Ondaatje announces (in the epigram to this section), histories of experience mark bodies, in the process dissolving the imposed borders between individual and collective, past and projected, fiction and fact.

Happenings

> She entered the story knowing she would emerge from it feeling she had been immersed in the lives of others, in plots that stretched back twenty years, her body full of sentences and moments....[15]

In reminding us of the Latin root of "curriculum"—that is, of *currere*, to run—Pinar[16] has helped to unsettle the once-pervasive (and, unfortunately, among school officials, still predominant) emphasis on the components of curriculum (e.g., texts, learning objectives, methods, teachers, students). With *currere*, Pinar has prompted us to be attentive to the complex, ever-evolving relations between individual and world and, as well, to the importance of autobiography, phenomenology, and hermeneutics for informing our thinking about curriculum. With the explicit acknowledgment that there can be no fixed or definable boundary between schooling and other lived experiences, we have been alerted to the need for detailed analysis and careful interpretation of the relations between events of curriculum and what tends to be regarded as the non-curricular. In this frame, the "path" of curriculum has been recast as a path laid while walking, rather than a prespecified route to be followed in pursuit of predetermined endpoints. Like Hana in *The English Patient*, as we participate in any event of curriculum, we become "immersed in the lives of others...[our bodies] full of sentences and moments."[17]

In focusing on the running of the course, *currere* brings with it a sensitivity to the contingencies of existence. Consistent with notions that have recently been developed in the fields of Chaos Dynamics[18] and Complexity Theory, *currere* embraces the unanticipated, the ambiguous, the complex, the strange, the queer, the incomprehensible. *Currere* compels us to focus on the moment—or, more accurately perhaps, on the weaving together of moments into lives.

We borrow Weinsheimer's notion of the "Hap" to highlight the importance of attending to the moment. An archaic term, and the root of such current words as happen, happy, mishap, hapless, and perhaps, "Hap" refers to an event, especially a fortuitous one. According to Weinsheimer, a Hap is something which

> makes its presence felt when one happens onto something, in the haphazard guess, the happenstance situation, in happiness and haplessness.... The Hap eludes the hegemony of method.[19]

The Hap, then, is what remains after method; it occurs beyond what we predict or strive to orchestrate; it exists beyond our willing and doing. The Hap exists in and consists of all the moment-to-moment events that await formulation, often slipping into the cracks (or, perhaps more appropriately, into the chasms) between the familiar and the expected—always reminding us of the fiction of having "control" over our learning, our curricula, our lives.

The Hap, then, is the warp and woof of daily existence. It is positioned against the scientistic ideal of an orderly, predictable universe—and, hence, it presents a challenge to the ideals of the modern classroom: those desires for clearly set goals, efficient instructional sequences, anticipated contingencies, unambiguously interpreted experiences. The Hap, in such settings, is to be avoided, suppressed, ignored—relegated to the uninterpreted space of "the remainder" in desperate efforts to create hapless curricula, for the Hap has the potential to unskin events of modern schooling.

The Hap thus announces a renewed relevance to the notion of *currere*. With *currere's* emphasis on movement (as opposed to the modern curriculum's focus on "progress"), the possibility emerges not just for the Hap to be noticed, but for it to become a location for interpretation—for identification, for marking. Attentiveness to the running of the course means being aware that there will be resistance, difficulty, ambiguity, surprise—and those elements are not just part of the course, they become the exceptional features that give it a recognizable form. Moreover, depending on the value they are ascribed through processes of hermeneutic interpretation, they might prompt fundamental reformulations of past, present, and projected experience.

We do not mean to suggest that our lives are determined by the course, nor that we ourselves determine the course. Rather, the point is that components of curriculum cannot be known in themselves. They must be unskinned, understood as co-evolving and mutually specifying—for it is not so much the parts (i.e., texts, persons, learning objectives, etc.) that make the curriculum, but the relations among them. Curriculum exists in our embodied relationships. In paying attention to what is *hap*pening during events of curriculum, we open the possibility of becoming more attuned to "the differences that make a difference"—as Gregory Bateson[20] puts it—helping us to more deeply understand the complexity[21] of any curricular form.

A Curriculum Commonplace

> She picks up the notebook that lies on the small table beside his bed. It is the book he brought with him through the fire—a copy of *The Histories* by Herodotus that he has added to, cutting and gluing pages from other books or writing down his own observations—so they are all cradled in the text of Herodotus.[22]

We have recently been involved in a research project that attempted to explore and to enact some of the principles of curriculum that are announced here. One facet of this research, which we call a "curriculum commonplace," was conducted by Dennis and classroom teacher Dolores van der Wey and her grade 5/6 students. This event was developed around Lois Lowry's novel *The Giver*.[23] Because Dolores and Dennis were interested in investigating the idea of readers "showing" their relations to the text in some material way (as the English patient did in his copy of Herodotus's *The Histories*), students were each given personal copies of the novel and asked to keep track of their thoughts and responses by actually inserting them into the text.

At the beginning of this curriculum event, the students were told about the English patient's copy of *The Histories* and were shown copies of Dennis's and Dolores's own favorite texts—ones filled with scribblings, Post-it notes, highlights, and scraps of paper. Students welcomed the thought of personalizing their books, and did so in a variety of ways. Some wrote in the margins or in the larger spaces at the ends of chapters, some used Post-its, some did both.

The activity proved to be extremely interesting during the first-class reading of the novel, allowing students to speak to initial and evolving opinions of the text. But it was not until the second reading[24] that the commonplace book activity proved to be most revealing. As students re-read the book, along with the comments made during their first readings, they developed much deeper understandings of the personal and collective interpretations that they were making. It was in this context that Heather commented on the inextricability of home, classroom, and herself. Her comment reflected only a small component of the larger discourse, part of which became evident during class conversations. The manner in which their readings were caught up in their home lives, their stages of biological maturation, other texts, other classes, other times became manifest during the second reading— through which it was clear to all that our lives *and* the text were different for having read and for having been read. The curriculum here came to be seen as a complex fabric of inter-relations. Because *The Giver* was read in relation to other texts, other experiences (remembered, invented, imagined) it was impossible for students to read and interpret the text (or themselves in relation to the text) without interpreting the world of significance that these interpretations announced. This "reading" activity, then, became a deeply hermeneutic activity where the *conditions* that provoked particular interpretations (and not others) were critically analyzed by the teacher and students.

We believe that the move from assigning meaning to a set of reader/text relations and toward exploring the conditions of inter-pretation became possible because of the material interventions students made in their novels. The act of actually writing inside of the book proved to be significantly different from "responding to" the text in some other, separated, manner. The juxtaposition of their own words with those of the author helped students to understand that reading is always a co-authoring. Further, it helped them to know that the act of reading is not experientially bounded by the opening and closing of the book nor by the ringing of bells; neither is it lodged in the deciphering of words and the extracting of meanings. Reading and deliberate interpretation—of the text, of beliefs, of lives—for these students, and for their teachers, became enmeshed in a complex fabric of relations.

It is important to note, however, that these "schooled" readings were unlike most that students and teachers experience—they did not exist in isolation from the families and communities to which students were attached. As part of the broader research project, we had earlier become involved with the teachers of this K-7 school, engaging in ongoing discussions of cognition and education. In one of our meetings, devoted to the topic of the role of literature in the classroom, we had focused on reactions to our reading of a book that had been selected purely on the recommendation of a bookseller: *The Giver*. This meeting proved to be the first in a chain of Hap-py events.

While all present acknowledged the novel to be a good one, there was also consensus among the teachers that the story would be un-suitable for the school's population. Because the novel depicts events of cultural genocide, the emergence of sexual desire, and the suppression of cultural memories, there was concern that some elements of the novel would offend community sensibilities. Not wanting to forego the opportunity of using the book as a classroom text on the basis of this suspicion—and curious as to the "personality" of the community—we suggested, and it was agreed, that parents should be invited to read the book and to respond at a later meeting. Most interesting to us was the way in which this "shared reading" and ensuing discussion among parents, teachers, and university researchers became, itself, an act of "unskinning" the usually thick hide that keeps these groups apart. The commonplace location of our shared interpretations sponsored an openness, a freedom to discuss our past experiences in relation to the "unfamiliarity and strangeness" of the world announced by the text. It was within this newly mapped cultural space that we as university re-searchers, the teachers at this school, and the parents of school children came to a deeper understanding of the importance of curriculum events that re-arrange the familiar so that it can be seen freshly. Rather than discussing the "appropriateness" of *the text* we became immersed in a conversation that explored the newly forming relations between and among the text and the readers who had gathered to continue the process of interpretation. These interpretations, of course, were never merely unidirectional or univocal (for example, What does this text mean?

What do you mean? Here's what I mean!) but, instead, became a complex reformulation of a set of cultural and social relations. The boundaries between classroom teacher, parent, university researcher, reader were continually becoming unfixed, reconstituted, and reinterpreted.

And so, it was not surprising that near the end of the meeting, parents *insisted* that this text be read by their children, not so much because of the value of the text but, rather, because of the desire for their children to experience what they had just experienced—an event of unskinning. Prior to beginning the unit in the grade 5/6 class, the curriculum event—that is, the interpretive process—had already begun. And, from the outset, it was one that transgressed the conventional boundaries that are so often used to separate school from community, student from teacher, reader from text, past from present, academic from personal. All of these were caught up in the *commonplaces* of the shared reading, the classroom collective, the community.

In brief, then, this project—which extended well beyond the details we have provided here (having also included, for example, a mathematics unit and community workshops, among other activities) —has further convinced us that in order for students and teachers to more deeply understand the complexity of the locations announced by curriculum events and our complicity in such events, curriculum must itself be understood as a deeply hermeneutic act. Identification, identity, happenstance, commonplaces all become facets of the interpretive process that involve the fluid and simultaneous naming of "us" and "not-us." They compel us to linger, to pause, to dwell on some matter—to re-read—rather than giving in to the temptation of "covering the curriculum" by glossing over fragmented concepts whose dynamic character and moral relevance have been obfuscated by *stating* them as *objectives*. What we are describing here is not another *prescription* for curriculum. Quite apart from that, it is a *proscription*—a movement toward thinking in terms of what is possible (based on what we know to be impossible) rather than focusing on what someone else has decreed must be.

We have pointed to several proscriptions in this writing, including: the impossibility of clear-cut distinctions between reader (interpreter) and text (interpreted); the impossibility of teaching (in the causal or control-of-learning sense of the term); the impossibility of inert knowledge; the impossibility of separating interpretations of who we are, what we know, and what we do. For us, these ideas have helped us to better understand that our identities as learners and teachers cannot be considered apart from one another. Developing commonplaces with students in schools means that we are engaged in unskinning—our selves, one another, communal relations, history. More particularly, as teachers we are continuously re-interpreting the manner in which we are situated in "the midst of things"—located as we are between individual and collective, past and future, actuality and possibility. It is here that we find and refine form, participating in the transformation of our culture even as (in our more unguarded moments) we attempt just to transmit.

And so, curriculum must unskin, recasting self-images, renaming, unfixing. It is not surprising, then, that an unskinning/unskinned curriculum feels risky, dangerous, forbidden—for within it we are able to imitate nothing but who we are [pretending to be (coming)].

> We had to keep moving. If you pause sand builds up as it would around anything stationary, and locks you in. You are lost forever.[25]

Notes

1. Michael Ondaatje, *The English patient* (Toronto: McClelland and Stewart, 1992), 117.

2. The phrase "literary anthropology" was originally used by Wolfgang Iser in *Prospecting: From reader response to literary anthropology* (Baltimore: The Johns Hopkins University Press, 1989). It has been adopted by Dennis Sumara, in *Private readings in public: Schooling the literary imagination* (New York: Peter Lang, 1996), and he has developed the notion for the dual purpose of informing teaching and framing research into those phenomena that involve shared reading.

3. We are limiting our focus in this paper to the English language arts classroom, but would like to note that we have also developed the notion of "mathematical anthropology." See Brent Davis, *Teaching mathematics: Toward a sound alternative* (New York: Garland Publishing, 1996).

4. Ondaatje, *The English patient*, 48.

5. Hans-Georg Gadamer, *Truth and method* (New York: Crossroad, 1990).

6.   Ondaatje, *The English patient*, 261.

7.   Maurice Merleau-Ponty, *Phenomenology of perception* (London: Routledge, 1962).

8.   We are borrowing here from Francisco Varela, Evan Thompson, and Eleanor Rosch's, *The embodied mind: Cognitive science and human experience* (Cambridge, MA: The MIT Press, 1991).

9.   For example, Gregory Bateson, *Mind in nature: A necessary unity* (New York: E.P. Dutton, 1979); Humberto Maturana and Francisco Varela, *The tree of knowledge: The biological roots of human understanding* (Boston: Shambhala, 1987); Varela et al., 1991.

10.   For example, M. Mitchell Waldrop, *Complexity: The emerging science at the edge of order and chaos* (New York: Simon and Schuster, 1992); Jack Cohen and Ian Stewart, *The collapse of chaos: Discovering simplicity in a complex world* (New York: Penguin, 1994).

11.   The word "enactivism" is drawn from the work of Bateson and Varela et al. See Davis, *Teaching mathematics*, and Sumara, *Private readings in public*.

12.   Bateson, *Mind in nature*.

13.   Clifford Geertz, *Work and lives: The anthropologist as author* (Stanford, CA: Stanford University Press, 1988). The notion is further developed in Sumara, *Private readings in public*.

14.   Martin Heidegger, *Basic writings* (San Francisco: HarperCollins, 1977).

15.   Ondaatje, *The English patient*, 12.

16.   William Pinar and Madeleine Grumet, *Toward a poor curriculum* (Dubuque, IA: Kendall/Hunt Publishing Company, 1976).

17.   Ibid.

18.   See, for e.g., James Gleick, *Chaos: Making a new science* (New

York: Penguin, 1987); William Doll, *A postmodern perspective on curriculum* (New York: Teachers College Press, 1993).

19. Joel Weinsheimer, *Gadamer's hermeneutics: A reading of "Truth and method"* (New Haven, CT: Yale University Press, 1985), 8.

20. Bateson, *Mind in nature.*

21. "Complexity" here means far more than merely *complicated.* Our use is drawn from the Complexity Theory–an emerging field of inquiry which examines the unexpected, unpredictable, self-organizing, and self-transcending behaviors that emerge as unities come together to form larger, more complex unities (such as cells forming organs, or organs forming bodies, or persons forming collectives).

22. Ondaatje, *The English patient,* 16.

23. Lois Lowry, *The giver* (New York: Dell, 1993).

24. Yes. The book was read twice by these 11- and 12-year-olds. And it was done without chapter questions, comprehension quizzes, or vocabulary word-catchers.

25. Ondaatje, *The English patient,* 137.

References
Bateson, Gregory. (1979). *Mind in nature: A necessary unity.* New York: E.P. Dutton.
Cohen, Jack and Stewart, Ian. (1994). *The collapse of chaos: Discovering simplicity in a complex world.* New York: Penguin.
Davis, Brent. (1996). *Teaching mathematics: Toward a sound alternative.* New York: Garland Publishing.
Doll, William. (1993). *A postmodern perspective on curriculum.* New York: Teachers College Press.
Gadamer, Hans-Georg. (1990). *Truth and method.* New York: Crossroad.
Geertz, Clifford. (1988). *Work and lives: The anthropologist as author.* Stanford, CA: Stanford University Press.
Gleick, James. (1987). *Chaos: Making a new science.* New York: Penguin.

Heidegger, Martin. (1977). *Basic writings.* San Francisco: HarperCollins.

Iser, Wolfgang. (1989). *Prospecting: From reader response to literary anthropology.* Baltimore: The Johns Hopkins University Press.

Lowry, Lois. (1993). *The giver.* New York: Dell.

Maturana, Humberto and Varela, Francisco. (1987). *The tree of knowledge: The biological roots of human understanding.* Boston: Shambhala.

Merleau-Ponty, Maurice. (1962). *Phenomenology of perception.* London: Routledge.

Ondaatje, Michael. (1992). *The English patient.* Toronto: McClelland and Stewart.

Pinar, William F. and Grumet, Madeleine. (1976). *Toward a poor curriculum.* Dubuque, IA: Kendall/Hunt Publishing Company.

Sumara, Dennis. (1996). *Private readings in public: Schooling the literary imagination.* New York: Peter Lang.

Varela, Francisco, Thompson, Evan, and Rosch, Eleanor. (1991). *The embodied mind: Cognitive science and human experience.* Cambridge, MA: The MIT Press.

Waldrop, M. Mitchell. (1992). *Complexity: The emerging science at the edge of order and chaos.* New York: Simon and Schuster.

Weinsheimer, Joel. (1985). *Gadamer's hermeneutics: A reading of "Truth and method".* New Haven, CT. Yale University Press.

Chapter Five

Reflections and Diffractions: Functions of Fiction in Curriculum Inquiry

Noel Gough

> Fiction in particular, narration in general, may be seen... as an active encounter with the environment by means of posing options and alternatives, and an enlargement of present reality by connecting it to the unverifiable past and the unpredictable future. A totally factual narrative, were there such a thing, would be passive: a mirror reflecting all without distortion.... [B]ut fiction does not reflect, nor is the narrator's eye that of a camera.... Fiction connects possibilities,...and by doing so it is useful to us (Le Guin, 1989, pp. 44-5).

> [F]or me, the most interesting optical metaphor is not reflection and its variants in doctrines of representation. Critical theory is not finally about reflexivity, except as a means to defuse the bombs of the established disorder and its self-invisible subjects and categories. My favorite optical metaphor is diffraction—the noninnocent, complexly erotic practice of making a difference in the world, rather than displacing the same elsewhere (Haraway, 1994, p. 63).

My purpose here is to enlarge the provenance of fiction in curriculum inquiry. I argue that fiction clearly is "useful to us" as a means of posing options and alternatives and for connecting "present reality" with past and/or future possibilities in curriculum inquiry and, indeed, that our purposes often may be better served by (re)presenting the texts we produce as deliberate fictions rather than as "factual" narratives reflecting all without distortion. I also argue that some modes of fiction, such as science fiction, can function as a diffracting lens for the narrator's eye and thus help us to generate stories which move educational inquiry beyond reflection and reflexivity towards making a difference in the world. I recognize that *reflection* and *reflexivity* have complex meanings that are not limited to the language of optical metaphors and discourses of seeing. However, in their common uses in educational inquiry, both terms connote self-referentiality, including the use of *reflection* to signify deep thought (as an inward gaze). I take *diffraction* to be a tactical reminder that light can be directed otherwise than back at oneself—especially at *one* self—that enlightenment can be other than self-referential. In some ways, this essay can be read as a lengthy embellishment on the introductory quotations, since together they encompass my key proposition—that fiction is useful in curriculum inquiry—and introduce two key referents *(reflection* and *diffraction)* for my elaboration of some of fiction's specific uses. These quotations are also pretexts for introducing two key characters in the genealogy of my own fictions and thus serve to position this essay intertextually (especially for readers who already have some familiarity with Le Guin's and/or Haraway's work).

Like a number of educational researchers in recent years, I have been strongly influenced by the emigration of narrative theory from literary studies to other disciplines. As Kenneth Knoespel (1991, pp. 100-1) writes:

> Narrative theory has challenged literary critics to recognize not only the various strategies used to configure particular texts within the literary canon, but to realize how forms of discourse in the natural and human sciences are themselves ordered as narratives. In effect narrative theory invites us to think of all discourse as taking the form of a story.

My initial response to this invitation was to examine the ways in which the discourses of curriculum specializations in which I have a particular interest—environmental education and science education—are configured as stories, with particular reference to poststructuralism's questioning of narrative authority in the sciences and other disciplines. Many of these inquiries are framed by my practical interests in appraising the adequacy of the conventional narrative strategies used by science and environmental educators in their work and with exploring ways of expanding their range and variety (see, for example, Gough, 1991b, 1993abcd, 1994c). More recently, I have been exploring ways in which the kinds of stories we usually classify as fiction—and the modes of storytelling that produce them—might inform reading and writing practices in curriculum inquiry (Gough, 1995) and educational research generally (1994b). It should be noted from the outset that I take "research" not only to signify an "endeavor to discover new or collate old facts etc. by scientific study of a subject, [or] course of critical investigation" (*Oxford English Dictionary*), but also to describe the means by which a discipline or art develops, tests, and renews itself (Reid, 1981b, p. 1). Within the wide range of textual practices to which the term "educational research" can thus be applied, I argue that many might usefully (and appropriately) be reconceptualized in terms of fictional storytelling, with particular reference to the reflexive narrative strategies of metafiction. Using the field of curriculum inquiry as an example, I also argue that certain kinds of postmodernist fiction— especially in such genres as cyberpunk science fiction and feminist fabulation—are particularly helpful in developing and renewing specific educational discourses and practices.

Reflection and Distortion in "True Stories" and Fiction

In much everyday speech, fiction is equated with falsehood, whereas "non-fiction" is taken to designate a "true" story. Indeed, the concept of narrative *per se* sometimes carries connotations of falsehood—I recall that in my childhood "telling stories" was a colloquialism for "telling lies." If we assume that research is primarily concerned with documenting "facts," without distortion, in "true" stories, then we might conclude that there is no place for fiction in curriculum inquiry. Rob Walker (1981, p. 147) raises a number of pertinent philosophical questions about these sorts of assumptions—such as, "is fiction the only route to some kinds of truth?"—but the issues he addresses in detail are for the most part pragmatic, prudential, and procedural. For example, he demonstrates that lightly fictionalizing case studies of curriculum evaluation and educational action research (by using pseudonyms, composite characters, places or events, and so on) may ameliorate some of the difficulties raised by issues of confidentiality. However, each of the fictions with which he illustrates this proposition is clearly based on extensive empirical data and "really changes the truth very little" (Walker 1981, p. 163).

Tom Barone (1992a) argues that moral imperatives, such as the desire for social justice, should drive qualitative researchers in education to include "critical storytelling" in their methodological repertoires.

Reflecting on his earlier experience (Barone, 1989) of documenting the life story of a potential school drop out, Barone (1992a, p. 143) describes storytelling as an artful practice which "eschews formal theory" (of either the scientific or philosophical type) and "systematic method." However, Barone (1992a, p. 143) also suggests criteria for the crafting of worthwhile stories, one of which is honesty:

> more specifically, a kind of honesty achieved through a heightened *empiricism*, a determined scrutinizing of the world around us. Like all good art, honest stories are powerfully observed, carefully detailed. They must tend to generate in the reader awareness of the locations of (actual or fictitious) characters' thoughts, beliefs, desires, and habits, in the webs of contingencies that constitute their life-worlds [emphasis in original].

Barone implicitly rejects the idea that fiction equals falsehood by asserting that stories characterized by honesty and heightened empiricism can also be fictitious. According to Barone (1992a, p. 145) "critical stories *par excellence*" include "nonfictional" works of investigative journalism like Norman Mailer's (1968) *Armies of the Night* and novels such as John Steinbeck's (1939) *The Grapes of Wrath*; of the latter he notes: "this novel's power to persuade... emanates from a careful and committed empiricism that is made manifest through such features of writing as powerfully 'thick' description and invented but convincing dialogue." Barone (1992a, p. 146) adds:

> Does it matter that this story...[is] fictional? Hardly. I would argue that the ultimate purpose of the critical storytelling I have described can be served equally well through journalistic or novelistic modes.... In that sense, critical storytelling moves qualitative researchers and readers not only beyond theory and method but beyond genre as well.

Novels and other forms of fictional writing have been used both to teach about social and educational phenomena and to study them.[1] However, as Barone (1992b, p. 32) writes:

> In the past, of course, a masterpiece of educational inquiry such as *Hard Times* [Dickens 1854/55] would not have sufficed as, say, a

doctoral dissertation. But in the new world view we see how dismissing literary works as "merely subjective" wildly misses the point.... In succeeding in their critical purposes, novelists such as Dickens have, in my judgment, earned entrance into the hallowed Citadel of Educational Inquiry.

Support for Barone's view does not yet seem to be widespread, although Elliot Eisner (1993, p. 9) is "optimistic" about the prospects of Stanford University one day accepting a novel as a doctoral dissertation in education.[2]

Realist fictions like *Hard Times* and *The Grapes of Wrath* clearly exemplify Richard Rorty's (1989, p. 141) proposition that novels can serve the purposes of socially critical inquiry by "help[ing] us to see how social practices which we have taken for granted have made us cruel." However, while fictions of this kind might well serve the moral interests of scholars engaged in emancipatory projects, many educational researchers are likely to share Walker's (1981, p. 163) fear that there could be "dangers inherent in the approach":

> Can fiction ever be as "good" as reality? What are the limits on the uses of fiction? How much of an account can be invented? How far can the data be altered, distorted or changed? Should the "story" emerge from the data (as in the examples I have given), or should the story control the use made of the data (as a serious fiction writer might feel) [?]

Accepting that such questions signal "dangers" depends to some extent on accepting the categorical distinctions they imply, although Walker (1981, p. 163) acknowledges that it is difficult to distinguish "pure fiction from fictional research styles."[3] Walker's questions assume that it is possible, at least in principle, to establish intersubjectively reliable distinctions between fiction on the one hand and particular constructions of reality on the other—namely, reality as represented by data that have *not* been "invented...altered, distorted or changed." But while it is defensible to assert that reality exists *beyond* texts, much of what we think of as real is—and can only be—apprehended *through* texts. For example, most of what we call history is inaccessible to us except in textual form. Furthermore, much of what we call "direct" experience is mediated textually and intertextually (see Gough 1993d). What is at issue here is not *belief* in the real but confidence in its representation. As Rorty (1979, p. 375) puts it, "to deny the power to 'describe' reality is not to deny reality" and "the world is out there, but descriptions of the world are not" (Rorty, 1989, p. 5).[4]

In other words, the conventional binary opposition of reality and fiction—and other binaries implied by this opposition, such as fact/ fiction and real/imaginary—does not mean that it is possible to distinguish clearly between textual representations of the world "out there" and other worlds constructed in texts. My own doubts about the referential adequacy of such binaries do not constitute an antirealist position but, rather, contribute to my distrust of storytelling practices that seem to be motivated by what Sandra Harding (1986, p. 193) calls "the longing for 'one true story' that has been the psychic motor for [modern] Western science." Desires for "one true story" have driven the construction of narrative strategies in which fact and fiction are mutually exclusive categories and particular kinds of facts, such as "scientific facts" and "historical facts," are equated with "reality"— claims to ontological status for the worlds that scientists and historians imagine.

Fact and fiction are much closer, both culturally and linguistically, than these narrative strategies imply. A fiction, in the sense in which it derives from *fictio*, is something fashioned by a human agent. The etymology of "fact" also reveals its reference to human action; a fact is the thing done, "that which actually happened," the Latin *factum* being the neuter past participle of *facere*, do (*OED*). In other words, both fact and fiction refer to human performance, but "fiction" is an active form —the act of fashioning—whereas "fact" descends from a past participle, a part of speech which disguises the generative act. Facts are testimonies to experience and, as Linda Hutcheon (1989, p. 57) asserts, are "events to which we have given meaning." Thus, for example, historical facts are the testimonies that historians make from their experiences of using disciplined procedures of evidence production and interpretation to *construct* meaning—to *produce* events that are mean- ingful within their traditions of social relationships and organization. Similarly, scientific facts are testimonies to the experiences of scientists as they use their specialized technologies to generate and inscribe data. Haraway (1989, p. 4) demonstrates how closely fact and fiction can be related in her description of biology as a narrative practice:

> Biology is the fiction appropriate to objects called organisms; biology fashions the facts "discovered" from organic beings.

> Organisms perform for the biologist, who transforms that
> performance into a truth attested by disciplined experience; i.e.,
> into a fact, the jointly accomplished deed or feat of the scientist
> and the organism.... *Both* the scientist and the organism are actors
> in a story-telling practice.

Doing educational research as "actors in a story-telling practice" means, in part, seeing fact and fiction as mutually constitutive—recognizing that facts are not only important elements of the stories we fashion from them but also that they are given meaning by the storytelling practices which produce them. Thus, for example, part of Patti Lather's (1991, p. 106) rationale for using experimental forms of textual construction to report an instance of feminist empirical research in education is her realization that "the so-called facts that one 'discovers' are already the product of many levels of interpretation." However, in contrast to Haraway's characterization of biology as a storytelling practice, Lather does not seek "*the* fiction appropriate to" *one* construction of the objects of her curiosity, but "fashions the facts" into several kinds of fiction, each of which narrates the production of "a truth attested by disciplined experience." Working from a data base of "interviews, research reports, journal entries, and [her] own insights/ musings collected over the course of a three-year inquiry into student resistance to liberatory curriculum in an introductory women's studies course," Lather (1991, pp. 83, 87) chooses to "craft four narrative vignettes, to tell four different 'stories' about [her] data" which she labels "a realist tale, a critical tale, a deconstructivist tale, and a reflexive tale." Lather self-consciously foregrounds the generative acts through which she produces these stories, and there is thus a sense in which all four tales are reflexive, but their juxtaposition in her multivoiced text demonstrates convincingly that no "one true story" can be fashioned from the data.[5]

Within a categorical framework defined by a binary opposition of fact and fiction, many researchers may be reluctant to refer to Lather's four tales as fictions, since they are quite clearly fashioned from empirical data (that is, while Lather provides suspicious and even perverse readings of her data, she does not appear to *invent* any). But this binary opposition is itself a fiction—part of a story which has been fashioned to rationalize the strategies used by researchers in the sciences and social sciences to produce facts. Rather than thinking in these terms, I suggest that there may be some virtue in reconceiving *all* the stories we tell in education as fictions—as stories fashioned for particular purposes—especially those that most resolutely proclaim that they are "factual." Like Le Guin (1989, p. 45), I am skeptical that there can be such a thing as "a totally factual narrative... a mirror reflecting all without distortion." As Malcolm Ashmore (1989, p. 198) asserts, we cannot pretend that any story "is not a *product* of *processes* which have a determinate *effect* on what it claims to be *showing*" (emphasis in original). If we think of all stories of educational inquiry as being fictions, we may be less likely to privilege without question those that pretend not to be, and more likely to judge each story on its particular merits in serving worthwhile purposes in education.

The tendency for educational researchers to be suspicious of apparently fictionalized accounts of experience is exemplified by Andrew Brookes (1995) in a review of Florence Krall's (1994) *Ecotone.* Brookes draws attention to Krall's (1994: 187) insistence that "personal narrative [is] the only honest way for researchers to express their views" and then raises his "concerns about Krall's authenticity claims":

> The second chapter [of *Ecotone*], 'Navajo Tapestry', rang a bell, and I found my copy of a paper with the same title and author in the *Journal of Curriculum Theorizing* (Krall 1981). I wanted to see if the two were the same, since no mention is made in the book of the earlier paper. The 1981 paper is longer, but draws on the same journal entries, italicized in the book. What I had assumed would be identical verbatim journal extracts turned out to be different. There were changes of tense, and some sections had been shortened, but I also found meanings altered.
>
> For example, a face that in 1981 'radiates warmth, friendliness, beauty' (p. 191) was no longer beautiful in 1994 (p.57) and 'long, beautiful hair' (p. 191) in 1981 is 'long, black hair hanging to her waist' in 1994 (p. 58). Perhaps feminine beauty is out, post-feminism. In the 1981 paper, Krall (p. 171) says: 'I began seeing the beauty that exists in nature that had somehow escaped me since my childhood on a sheep ranch where survival and hard times had transformed nature *into an enemy to be conquered.*' (my emphasis). In 1994 this becomes: 'Slowly the beauty and meaning that had surrounded me unacknowledged since childhood on that sheep ranch, where survival dominated our thoughts, emerged in a flood of recognition' (p. 41). The omission of nature-as-enemy makes sense, given that by chapter one in 1994 nature (presumably friendly) was 'calling' (p. 7), but where does this leave 'truth'? One more example: in 1981 Krall

applies a bandaid to a Navajo preschooler, Lenny, then: 'I search in my pack for my binoculars, take them out, and scan the hillside. What about me? asks Lenny. I place the strap around his neck. To my amusement, he mimics me, scans the hillside. Suddenly I am part of a pre-school organism. Plump, brown hands tug, pull, tap' (p. 190). By 1994, with the clarity of hindsight, serendipity has become crafty intentionality. Krall applies a bandaid to a Navajo preschooler, Danny, then: 'Needing something further to mediate interaction, I lifted my binoculars to my eyes and scanned the hillside. A small, plump, brown hand tapped me on the shoulder. "What about me?" asked Danny. I placed the strap around his neck. He mimicked my actions precisely, scanned the landscape. Suddenly I became a part of a preschool organism. Tugs, pulls, taps' (p. 56).

In narrative, meaning, if not God, dwells in the details. Krall's two versions of 'Navajo Tapestry' highlight some of the difficulties inherent in her insistence that narrative provides reliable access to truth.

While I am in sympathy with Brookes' concerns, I cannot entirely agree with his implied assumption that such terms as "honest," "authentic," "reliable," and "true" can be applied to personal narrative as though they were synonymous. I am not surprised that a memoir fashioned for publication in 1981 has been fashioned differently for publication in 1994. Krall fashions similar facts (testimonies to her experience) into different fictions (stories) at different times for (what I assume are) different purposes. Would recounting identical verbatim journal extracts in both stories have served her purposes any better? For some readers, the answer will clearly be "yes," but I suspect that might result in other distortions. To write an identical memoir of an incident after more than a decade of personal growth, development, and change might no longer seem to the author to be authentic or even true. For example, perhaps there was "crafty intentionality" in Krall's encounter with the Navajo preschooler, but in 1981 she did not recognize it as tacit pedagogical knowledge (and thus represented it then as "serendipity"), whereas in 1994 she admits to that possibility. However, I can only speculate on such matters and, unfortunately, Krall has left herself wide open to the kind of criticisms that Brookes levels—and has missed an opportunity to demonstrate the virtues of critical storytelling—by not drawing attention to her different versions of "Navajo Tapestry." Since nobody else can do it, Krall could have used her different stories to demonstrate how each is fashioned as an expression of situated knowledge—or (to repeat Ashmore's [1989, p. 193] formulation) "a *product* of *processes* which have a determinate *effect* on what it claims to be *showing*."

Reflexivity and Metafiction

If we agree with Reid (1981a, p. 182) that "reality is more complex than any account that can be given of it," then one sure way of falsifying stories of educational experience is to produce the illusion of a transparently clear reality in them without drawing attention to the narrative strategies through which that illusion is produced. For example, the "critical stories *par excellence*" identified by Barone (1992a, p. 145) may be "ideologically open" to the extent that they reveal their authors' moral and political commitments, but the storytelling modes they exemplify—investigative journalism and realist fiction—do not necessarily lend themselves to questioning the *ideology of representation* they embody. In this respect, many empirically based reports of educational research deploy similar narrative strategies to those found in mimetic novels like *Hard Times* or *Grapes of Wrath*. Both kinds of text sustain the illusion that they do not mediate between the reader and an exterior world but, rather, that they offer transparent windows onto that world. That is, the language of much empirical educational research and literary realism is similar insofar as descriptions are presented as if they were a selection from a whole which is the "real" world. A key difference is that authors of realist fiction are usually conscious of their own artistry in sustaining the reader's belief in the verisimilitude of the artificial world "revealed" by the text, whereas many authors of empirical educational research reports seem to assume—or want their implied audience to assume—that they have constructed a neutral transmitter of the real to the reader.

To avoid accusations of naïveté or deception, educational researchers who claim to be representing reality in their stories need to demonstrate that they are aware of the ways in which they have deliberately constructed their texts to work as generators of meaning and significance. As Wenche Ommundsen (1993, p. 19) writes, "true stories about the world, in order to be 'true', must be self-conscious, must acknowledge the story-telling process." This is not to say that all research reports must be reconstructed as fictions which self-consciously display every aspect of their own fictionality. Rather, in most circumstances, there will be limits to the extent to which such reflexivity is possible and desirable. David Caute's (1971, p. 212) warning is pertinent here: "total exposure of a process is never possible because the actor has to *act* his [sic] exposure of acting just as the writer has to *write* his [sic] exposure of writing" (emphasis in original).

We can write our "exposure of writing" in various ways. For example, Barone (1989, p. 147) begins his case study of a potential highschool dropout by declaring his own position in the narrative:

> Billy Charles Barnett...is a member of the rural 'disadvantaged,' a 15-year-old nominated by the vice principal as the student least likely to remain in Dusty Hollow Middle School. I am a middle-aged urban academic who, secure in a tenured university position, will *never* leave school.

With these words, Barone immediately invites suspicion of the narrative authority that academics usually take for granted by suggesting that, in telling Billy Charles' story, the author may be disadvantaged by his own privilege (from which he will *never* escape). Later in the story, Barone (1989, p. 148) quotes at length from Billy Charles' account of the arts of "jugging" for turtles, catfish, and bass, which ends with the boy asking: "do you know how to make turtle soup?" Barone continues:

> I find myself squirming in my seat. But why should I? Why should *I* be the one feeling inadequate and defensive? No, I didn't know—until Billy Charles told me—that the market was bearish on coon-skins this year, and that I could expect no more than $40 for a flawless one of average size. The topic had simply never arisen in any graduate course in curriculum theory. Moreover, E.D. Hirsch and his co-authors had included no such items in their *Dictionary of Cultural Literacy: What Every American Needs to Know.* So I take comfort: not only am I the better informed, but also apparently the better *American...* (Barone, 1989, p. 148).

Thus, Barone interrogates his own assumptions about the purposes of American schooling and, more pointedly, questions taken-for-granted notions of "cultural literacy" that ignore "the fundamentals of a world no longer honored in the dominant culture."

Barone (1992a) offers a further exposure of his writing when he retrospectively analyzes his story of Billy Charles Barnett as an example of critical storytelling and qualitative problem solving. In this later account, we are left in no doubt as to the kinds of stories and storytellers Barone admires and which of their qualities he attempts to incorporate in his own writing. If this information had been provided in the earlier story, it would have been more reflexive but, quite possibly, less effective. The particular purposes our stories are intended to serve, and the audiences for whom they are intended, are significant considerations in determining the appropriate level of reflexivity they should display. In this particular case, Barone's (1989, p. 151) purposes in arguing to an audience of American teachers and administrators that "we would not *necessarily* be better off were the dropout rate to decrease rapidly tomorrow" are different from his purposes (Barone, 1992a) in extolling the virtues of critical storytelling to an audience of qualitative researchers. For each argument, and each audience, different approaches to reflexivity are defensible. Of course, audiences are also fictions— discursive constructions fashioned by authors and the institutions that support the circulation of their texts. For example, John Hartley (1993, p. 166) argues that "audiences may be imagined empirically, theoretically or politically, but in all cases the product is a fiction that serves the need of the imagining institution."[6] The fictionality of the audiences we imagine for our stories presents us with further strategic choices about what to expose (or not to expose) in reflexive research writing.

Another approach to reflexivity is demonstrated by Alison Jones (1992) when she revisits a critical story (Jones 1989) she had previously written about the interaction of class, gender, and race in the school lives of adolescent girls in New Zealand. Jones' earlier story is ideologically open (a critical ethnography explicitly informed by feminist and neo-Marxist politics) but she later admits (Jones 1992, p. 19) that her stance is "authoritative and distanced" and that she is an "invisible, neutral, observing presence" in her written text. As she reflexively reconstructed her research in the light of postmodernist understandings of the constructedness of texts, Jones (1992, p. 21) found that "every sentence of [her] original text became suspect":

> I now confronted not a carefully observed scholarly account but a "story"—my own partial story of the girls in the classroom.... My "invisibility" mocked me. I needed to change my position from a presence hidden in the text, to a new visible entity. I needed to *decentre* myself. I was to become one partial observer, telling one partial story....

Jones (1992, p. 18) sees "the old distant voice of the objective observer/writer...as a fiction, and as a mechanism of power which, in the case of her earlier story, reinscribes power dynamics to which she was theoretically opposed. I regret Jones' implicitly disparaging reference to fiction here, since she admits "that our accounts of the world *can only be* constructions, made up from the language meanings and ideas historically available to us" (emphasis in original) and, in this sense, her new, self-consciously partial story is also a fiction. However, Jones is right to link the status of her earlier account as an *undisclosed* fiction with the way it functions as "a mechanism of power." To paraphrase Heide Ziegler and Christopher Bigsby (1982, p. 121), the power of fiction to coerce is never greater than when it falsely pretends to surrender that power.

A reflexive account of educational research in some ways resembles the literary form known as *metafiction*, which Patricia Waugh (1984, p. 2) describes as a story that "draws attention to its status as an artifact in order to pose questions about the relationship between fiction and reality." But whereas reflexive accounts of educational research are usually concerned with the production of meaning from empirical data, metafiction is not restricted to representations of "real" worlds. Indeed, metafiction demonstrates that it is not necessary for a story to be realistic or in any way truthful for it to be useful to us in exploring questions about "the possible fictionality of the world outside the literary fictional text" (Waugh 1984, p. 2). According to Waugh (1984, p. 18), "in showing us how literary fiction creates its imaginary worlds, metafiction helps us to understand how the reality we live day by day is similarly constructed, similarly 'written.'" Thus, for example, Marlene Barr (1992, pp. 7-8) argues that "the contrived nature of patriarchal reality, the fiction about women's inferiority and necessarily subordinate status, is best confronted by metafiction":

> sexist societies are artificial environments constructed by patriarchal language which defines sexist as normal.... Feminist SF [science fiction] writers create metafiction, fiction about patriarchal fiction, to unmask the fictionality of patriarchy. When these authors use language to construct nonsexist fictional worlds, they develop useful models for learning about how patriarchy is constructed.... Feminist SF metafictionally facilitates an understanding of sexism as a story authored by men who use their power to make women the protagonists of patriarchal fictions.

Metafiction is increasingly evident in popular media culture. For example, Douglas Rushkoff (1994, p. 160) writes of the attractiveness of metamedia to his "twentysomething" generation (also known to marketing-industry demographers as "Generation X" and/or "generation why?"): "we are particularly attracted to media that use bracketing devices to comment on media methodology. Built into our favorite shows are characters and narrative techniques that constantly remind us of our relationship to the program we are watching." Paralleling the feminist use of metafictional SF to "unmask the fictionality of patriarchy," Rushkoff (1994, p. 160) valorizes self-reflexive popular artists who "keep the audience aware of its relationship to media." These include the creators of characters like Bart Simpson who "demonstrate proper aloofness toward media iconography as well as the skills to dissect and reconstitute television imagery against its original purposes."

Such strategic uses of fiction are not restricted to social and cultural criticism. Sociologists of scientific knowledge also recognize the generativity of fiction in posing questions about the complex inter-relationships between reality—or, rather, the fictionality (the textual and intertextual construction) of what we experience as reality—and the stories we construct in texts of all kinds. For example, Ashmore (1989, pp. 66-7) describes how new literary forms are being used to inform approaches to reflexivity in this field:

> The idea is that the format of the standard empiricist research report inhibits the development of any serious and sustainable reflexive practice, and that therefore other alternative formats are to be preferred.... The various experimental forms include the play, the limerick, the parody, the parable, the dialogue, the antipreface, the anti-introduction, the parallel text—analytical and meta-analytical, the narrative collage, the lecture, the encyclopedia, the examination, and the press report. In addition to all of these, occasional use has also been made of such self-referential devices as the self-engulfing photograph and self-referring footnote....
>
> What characterizes many of these experiments is their use of explicitly fictional forms of writing. This aspect of these new literary forms implies a critique of the distinction between the fictional and the factual; a distinction which constitutes the most basic interpretative prop for the production of scholarly/scientific (nonfiction) discourse....

Of course, epistemologically sophisticated analysts of scientific knowledge are unlikely to accept the analytic validity of a crude disjunction between fact and fiction; however, the majority practice their trade as if the distinction held. The importance of experiments in fictionalizing in this area of discourse is, therefore, to show the inadequacy of the distinction in practice.

The inadequacy of the distinction between fact and fiction is not simply a matter of pointing to "borderline" stories like *Hard Times* or *The Grapes of Wrath* in which the distinction is blurred. As Barr's comments on feminist science fiction indicate, and as I discuss in more detail below, stories that are unequivocally made up can serve important purposes in social and educational inquiry.

Diffractive Fictions

Fiction may be particularly useful to us when we are attempting to reconceptualize or reconstruct some aspect of our work. Reading and writing fiction can help to move us beyond the naïve empiricist dream of representing "reality" without distortion, beyond the heightened empiricism of critical storytelling, and even beyond the reflexivity of texts that self-consciously display the narrative structures through which we produce realist, critical and reflexive stories. Fiction also provides potential discursive spaces within which new knowledge and understanding can be produced. This heuristic potential of fiction underlies the argument advanced by Gillie Rowland et al. (1990, p. 291) for writing fiction in research on professional practice:

[I]f we were asked why, as teachers, we encourage children to write stories, we would explain that writing stories is a way of "learning" about our experiences by ordering and exploring them.... In writing (and responding to) stories, we exercise our imaginations by playing with the relationships between experiences and with the ideas they evoke: the structure of a story is an implicit set of general ideas about a segment of life experiences. This, briefly, is the rationale for our proposal that writing fiction can be a valuable mode of inquiry into professional practice: we recommend it for children; why not for ourselves?
Writing in a fictional form enables familiar ideas and experiences to be brought into new relationships, and new ideas to be set alongside the familiar. Through fictional writing related to our professional context we can test out new ideas and explore the values upon which our practice is based...we can draw into our

narratives those crucial but subtle textures of thought and feeling which are not readily accessible to more standard forms of "research."

This rationale echoes Le Guin's (1989, pp. 44-5) claims that fiction "connects possibilities," poses "options and alternatives," and enlarges present reality "by connecting it to the unverifiable past and the unpredictable future."[7] Moreover, such speculative thinking is not just an intellectual exercise, since some of the new relationships and new ideas that are generated in fiction can become the kinds of cultural inventions that materially affect—and are part of—our social reality. For example, there is a sense in which George Orwell's phrase, "Big Brother is watching you," can be regarded as pure fiction. But in the forms in which it has been mobilized in arguments against bureaucratic surveillance or centralized information systems, it has clearly become part of our reality. When the Australian federal government attempted to introduce a national identity card in the late 1980s, both headline writers and those who opposed the idea of the Australia Card made frequent references to Big Brother.[8] The ways in which images, symbols and metaphors drawn from such fictions as Karel Capek's *R.U.R.* (in which the term "robot" was coined), Aldous Huxley's *Brave New World*, Orwell's *1984,* and Mary Shelley's *Frankenstein*, have been strategically deployed, over long periods of time, clearly demonstrate that made-up stories can both create and critique a real world. In terms of the optical metaphors to which Haraway (1994) refers, these fictions are diffractions rather than reflections of the social and material realities in and from which they were generated, and they are still making a difference in the world through their direct and indirect influences on successive generations of readers and authors.

The overlapping genres collectively signified by the umbrella term "SF" are among our richest sources of diffractive fiction. As Haraway (1989, p. 5) explains, SF designates "a complex emerging narrative field in which the boundaries between science fiction (conventionally, sf) and fantasy became highly permeable in confusing ways, commercially and linguistically;" SF also signifies "an increasingly heterodox array of writing, reading, and marketing practices indicated by a proliferation of 'sf' phrases: speculative fiction, science fiction, science fantasy, speculative futures, speculative fabulation." This broad conception of SF subsumes the category Barr (1992, p. 11) calls "feminist fabulation" which she describes as a "specifically feminist corollary to…structural fabulation" (yet another "sf" phrase). Barr takes her notions of "fabulation" and "structural fabulation" from Robert Scholes (1976, p. 47), who describes fabulation as "fiction that offers us a world clearly and radically discontinuous from the one we know, yet returns to confront that known world in some cognitive way." Scholes (1976, pp. 54-5) adds that

> in works of structural fabulation the tradition of speculative fiction is modified by an awareness of the nature of the universe as a system of systems, a structure of structures, and the insights of the past century of science are accepted as fictional points of departure…. It is a fictional exploration of human situations made perceptible by the implications of recent science.

Since I borrowed the idea of textual diffraction from Haraway, it is fitting to note that *Primate Visions* (1989), her critical history of the development and cultural effects of primatology, remains one of the finest exemplars of the scholarly work that can be done with SF. Haraway (1989, pp. 4-5) begins *Primate Visions* by acknowledging John Varley's (1978) SF story *The Persistence of Vision* as part of the inspiration for her elucidation of the ways in which the storytelling practices of science structure scientific vision and, in turn, construct myths of gender, race, and nature in our culture:

> monkeys, apes, and human beings emerge in primatology inside elaborate narratives about origins, natures, and possibilities. Primatology is about the life history of a taxonomic order that includes people. Especially western people produce stories about primates while simultaneously telling stories about the relations of nature and culture, animal and human, body and mind, origin and future. Indeed, from the start, in the mid-eighteenth century, the primate order has been built on tales about these dualisms and their scientific resolution.

One of the ways in which Haraway (1989, p. 5) reads primatology is "as science fiction, where possible worlds are constantly reinvented in the contest for very real, present worlds:"

> Placing the narratives of scientific fact within the heterogeneous space of SF produces a transformed field. The transformed field sets up resonances among all of its regions and components. No region or component is 'reduced" to any other, but reading and

writing practices respond to each other across a structured space. Speculative fiction has different tensions when its field also contains the inscription practices that constitute scientific fact. The sciences have complex histories in the constitution of imaginative worlds and of actual bodies in modern and postmodern "first world" cultures.

The results of using SF as a conceptual space within which to read the primatology story are particularly apparent in the final chapter of *Primate Visions* which alternates between reading primatology as science fiction and reading science fiction as primatology. Haraway begins this chapter by using one of Isaac Asimov's SF novels to recapitulate the themes of *Primate Visions*. She then reviews the work of several women SF writers in the light of her reconstructed narratives of primatology. Her reasoning (Haraway 1989, p. 370) is that

> mixing, juxtaposing, and reversing reading conventions appropriate to each genre can yield fruitful ways of understanding the production of origin narratives in a society that privileges science and technology in its constructions of what may count as nature and for regulating the traffic between what it divides as nature and culture.

Primate Visions testifies to the potential effectiveness of SF in helping to deconstruct and demystify contemporary orthodoxies. Clearly, SF mediated and facilitated Haraway's research in the social, textual, and material history of primatology in important ways. My own attempts to deploy a similar strategy in educational research and teacher education have been focused on reconceptualizing curriculum inquiry as a postmodernist textual practice (see, for example, Gough 1994c, 1995). Some of the work I am presently undertaking in this vein is described and discussed in the remainder of this essay.

Diffractive Storytelling in a Postmodernist *Currere*
One of the key themes in the reconceptualization of curriculum studies during the last two decades has been the effort to understand curriculum as "the collective story we tell our children about our past, our present, and our future" (Grumet, 1981, p. 115). Influential examples of research in this vein include *currere*—the name William Pinar (1975) coined for a distinctive autobiographical method of curriculum inquiry—and related methods of investigating storied lives such as Michael Connelly and

Jean Clandinin's (1990) "narrative inquiry."9 Both *currere* and narrative inquiry seek to understand and question the ways in which curriculum is constituted in the subjectivities of teachers and other curriculum workers by encouraging personal (and sometimes collaborative) reflection on stories generated through such procedures as autobiographical writing and journal-keeping. Both methods have conceptual and ideological antecedents in existential philosophy and phenomenology. However, these methodological grounds for using autobiography and narrative in curriculum inquiry have now been destabilized —irreversibly, I believe—by postmodernist skepticism about the assumption of a singular, fixed, essential self. As I argue elsewhere (Gough 1994a), phenomenology seems especially vulnerable to poststructuralist criticism.

While I can no longer justify *currere* by reference to its existential and phenomenological foundations, autobiography continues to provide postmodernist literary and cultural critics with a generative discourse through which to theorize human agency, constructions of the self and problems of self-representation (see, for example, Gilmore 1994). Thus, I have been experimenting—a better description might be *playing*10— with what I call a "postmodernist currere" by using postmodernist texts and textual practices to diffract the storylines produced by autobiographical writing and personal narrative. I still encourage my graduate students in curriculum to write autobiographies and other personal stories (and to reflect on them), but my revised pedagogical strategy (in very broad terms) is to invite a mutual interreferencing and deconstructive reading of personal *and* cultural texts—to read stories of personal experience within and against the manifold fictions of the world around us.

In facilitating this process, I explicitly privilege postmodernist forms of storytelling, including metafiction, graphic novels, cyberpunk SF, and feminist fabulation. My reasons for using these particular forms follow, at least in part, from wider-ranging explorations of the ways in which different modes of storytelling construct and question the world.11 For example, Brian McHale (1992, pp. 146-7) argues that modernist fiction is characterized by an "epistemological dominant," its plot organized as "a quest for a missing or hidden item of knowledge." Thus, in its structure and thematics, "a modernist novel looks like a detective story," centrally concerned with "problems of the accessibility and circulation of knowledge, the individual mind's grappling with an elusive or occluded reality." The detective is the archetype of the modernist subject—a quest(ion)ing "cognitive hero," an "agent of *re*cognitions...reduced synecdochically to the organ of visual perception, the (private) eye," seeking to understand the *uni*verse, a unified and objective world. Modernist fiction may offer multiple perspectives on the world, but does so without disturbing the essential unity of the self: "each perspective is lodged in a subjectivity which is itself relatively coherent, relatively centered and stable" (McHale, 1992, pp. 254).

McHale sees postmodernist fiction as being characterized by an "ontological dominant" in which neither the world nor our selves are assumed to be unitary. In contrast, postmodernist fiction explores the possibility that we function in an ontologically plural *multi*verse of experience—that selves and worlds operate in many modalities. According to McHale (1992, p. 247), the characteristic genre of postmodernism is SF, with its stock-in-trade of a potentially infinite variety of bodily forms, beings, and cultures:

> while epistemologically-oriented fiction (modernism, detective fiction) is preoccupied with questions such as: what is there to know about the world? and who knows, and how reliably? How is knowledge transmitted, to whom, and how reliably?, etc., ontologically-oriented fiction (postmodernism, SF) is pre-occupied with questions such as: what is a world? How is a world constituted? Are there alternative worlds, and if so, how are they constituted? How do different worlds, and different kinds of world, differ, and what happens when one passes from one world to another, etc.?

Many stories of educational inquiry still resemble detective fiction—a quest for *the* truth about some aspect of curriculum, teaching and/or learning. Indeed, I would argue that educational research has not even kept pace with developments in the methods of fictional detection that have accompanied the cultural changes of the late modern era. Scientific rationalism is still privileged even though its personifications in fiction—such as Sherlock Holmes and other heroes of the classic logic and deduction detective story—have long been displaced as models of how we can or should obtain reliable knowledge of the world. [12] During the 1920s and '30s the detachment and supposed objectivity of Holmes' method of inquiry began to give way to a variety of more involved and subjective approaches. For example, Agatha Christie's (1930) Miss Marple approached detection in the manner of an ethnographer: her detailed observations (thick descriptions) of life in the village of St.

Mary Mead provided her with a grounded theory of human behavior which she was able to deploy in solving mysteries both within that community and elsewhere. A different kind of involvement and subjectivity was displayed by hard-boiled detectives like Dashell Hammett's (1930) Sam Spade and Raymond Chandler's (1939) Philip Marlowe, who were often deeply implicated (as actors rather than spectators) in the mysteries they were called upon to explicate. In addition, Marlowe and his successors usually told their stories in the first person, a change in narrative perspective that further problematized the role of the participant-observer in the dialectic of truth versus deception decades before interpretivist styles of inquiry seriously challenged positivistic social science. More recently, fictional detectives have adopted a variety of critical standpoints, with feminist detectives like Amanda Cross' (1981) Kate Fansler and Sara Paretsky's (1993) V.I. Warshawski proving to be particularly popular. But, while fictional detectives now model more diverse approaches to epistemologically-oriented inquiry than their predecessors, they rarely grapple with the ontologically-oriented questions which preoccupy authors of postmodernist fictions.

I find cyberpunk SF—the term was initially coined to describe William Gibson's (1984) first novel, *Neuromancer*—particularly useful for raising ontologically-oriented questions in curriculum inquiry. Cyberpunk SF can be read as a vigorous imaginative response to the ontological questions generated by cultural postmodernism.[13] As Jenny Wolmark (1994, p. 110) writes:

> Cyberpunk narratives focus explicitly on the destabilizing impact of new technology on traditional social and cultural spaces: in so doing they provide a peculiarly appropriate response to the complex conditions of postmodernity, particularly the collapse of traditional cultural and critical hierarchies, and the erosion of the distinction between experience and knowledge which has provoked the decentering and fragmentation of the subject.

These are also key issues for curriculum inquiry as teachers, policy-makers, parents, and children struggle to respond to the destabilizing effects of new technology on schooling's "traditional social and cultural spaces," including the increasingly significant role of media culture (globalized and digitized networks of broadcasting, publishing, and computing) in socialization and identity-formation. Schooling can no longer claim a privileged position in the "traditional cultural and critical

hierarchies" of knowledge production and reproduction as new information and entertainment technologies provide readily available evidence of
the increasing gap between the ways the world is represented in the
global datasphere and in school curricula (even as the academy struggles
with the crisis of representation that dissolves meaningful distinctions
between experience and knowledge; see Green and Bigum 1993).

Cyberpunk SF brings a sense of immediacy and urgency to an
issue with a much longer history, namely, our acceptance of—and
resistance to—what we can now call cyborg subjectivity. Until
relatively recently, creatures that embodied the interface between human
and machine were restricted to imaginary worlds (Frankenstein's
monster was an early cyborg). Cyborgs now foreshadow the real
possibility of a posthuman condition—they are what humans might be
becoming in the late twentieth century. Unlike many of the other
creatures of SF, cyborgs are both narrative and material constructions.
Katherine Hayles (1993, pp. 152-3) suggests that this conjunction of
technology and discourse in the cultural production of cyborgs is part of
the explanation for their unprecedented impact on our cultural narratives
of (for example) evolution, reproduction, life cycles, and identity:

> Were the cyborg only a product of discourse, it could perhaps be
> relegated to science fiction, of interest to SF aficionados but not
> of vital concern to the culture. Were it only a technological
> practice, it could be confined to such technical fields as bionics,
> medical prostheses, and virtual reality. Manifesting itself as both
> technological object and discursive formation, it partakes of the
> power of the imagination as well as the actuality of technology.
> Cyborgs actually do exist; about 10 percent of the current U.S.
> population are estimated to be cyborgs in the technical sense,
> including people with electronic pacemakers, artificial joints,
> drug implant systems, implanted corneal lenses, and artificial
> skin. Occupations make a much higher percentage into metaphoric
> cyborgs, including the computer keyboarder joined in a cybernetic
> circuit with the screen, the neurosurgeon guided by fiber-optic
> microscopy during an operation, and the teen player in the local
> video-game arcade.

Scott Bukatman (1993, pp. 8-9) argues that much recent SF narrates
"new technological modes of being in the world" and constructs a new
subject position, "terminal identity,"[14] which he calls "an unmistakably
doubled articulation" that signifies both the end of the modernist subject

and the construction of a new subjectivity that can "occupy or intersect the cyberscapes of contemporary existence." Haraway (1985, 1991ab) draws on SF stories to theorize the cyborg as a new myth of feminist political identity, using it to challenge many of the most problematic dualisms of Western culture. But cyborgs do more than challenge *epistemological* dualisms. Like a number of other creatures of fiction— including angels, aliens, monsters, mutants, and superheroes—cyborgs are "realized metaphors of the violation of ontological boundaries" (McHale, 1992, p. 202)[15] and thus direct attention towards a plurality of worlds and worldviews. However, in order that they may breach ontological boundaries, many of these creatures are constructed according to the conceit that they exist independently of human imagination and desire, whereas cyborgs are explicitly human inventions. For example, by situating the origins of angels and aliens elsewhere—in supernatural or non-terrestrial worlds—each creature is imagined as having qualities that are in principle ineffable, unknowable, and beyond human emulation.[16] Thus, cyborgs not only violate ontological boundaries in a metaphorical sense but also *materialize and embody* the human capability to transform and transcend such boundaries with our own imaginative and material resources—without the intervention of Others or otherness.

As significant narrative experiments in ontology and subjectivity, cyborg fictions are useful textual resources for diffracting the stories we generate and encounter in curriculum inquiry.[17] My experience of using *currere* with graduate students suggests to me that such diffraction is desirable because reflection—a self-referential narrative strategy—is less likely to destabilize a conventional autobiography's narrative trajectory. Much autobiographical writing follows an implicit genre modelled by the works of Augustine, Rousseau, Henry Adams, and contemporary public figures whose autobiographies are given prominence by the mass media. This genre is modernist in constructing and reproducing an essentialized view of the self and, as Gilmore (1994, p. 5) observes, it "has naturalized the self-representation of (mainly) white, presumably heterosexual, elite men"; in conventional studies of autobiography the terms that are likely to shift within postmodernism—particularly history and subjectivity—are taken as stable elements in the story of one's life. Texts that affirm this stability, or that can be construed as affirming it, form the "tradition" of autobiography.

Currere, as practiced by Pinar (1994) and Grumet (1988), can be seen as an attempt to break with this modernist tradition of autobiography, and both writers demonstrate strategies for exposing and criticizing the ways in which personal narratives can reproduce a politics of identity that maintains social hierarchies of class, gender, sexuality, and race. They also demonstrate the ways in which fiction can illuminate autobiographical writing but, because they tend to choose modernist rather than postmodernist texts for this purpose, what is seen in this light may be a reflection of modernist fiction's stable subjects and histories rather than a diffraction of their autobiographical storylines. For example, in "Death in a Tenured Position," Pinar (1984) describes the difficulties and discouragements he and his colleagues experienced in working to reconceptualize curriculum studies during the 1970s and the threats to that work he saw emerging in the 1980s. Pinar depicts the reconceptualists' position as being analogous to that of the character who becomes the requisite corpse in a detective novel by Amanda Cross (1981)—also titled *Death in a Tenured Position*. The analogy allows Pinar (1984, p. 76) to warn of imminent dangers to the reconceptualist movement by using words like "murder" and "suicide" —terms that might otherwise be regarded as exaggerating (rather considerably) the hazards of curriculum theorizing.[18] It is an exemplary exercise in using fiction reflectively in phenomenological self-inquiry, but it also exemplifies Haraway's (1994, p. 63) point that reflection involves "displacing the same elsewhere." That is, the usefulness (and credibility) of Pinar's story depends on recognizing that it is "mirrored," in some non-trivial ways, by the story Cross tells—that elements of each storyline are sufficiently isomorphic for them to be reflected in (displaced into) the other. What Pinar (1984, p. 76) hopes to be able to see with the aid of such reflections is couched in terms of finding stable elements of his life story that might otherwise remain hidden, including "the self that exists outside the social and especially bureaucratic definitions of it... [the] self lost to social definition and role."

None of this is intended to be a criticism of Pinar's autobiographical method. Rather, I am suggesting that scrutinizing a personal story in the light of modernist fiction reveals something *different from* (not necessarily "better than") the new stories that may emerge from reading autobiography through the diffracting lenses of postmodernist fiction or SF. For example, after reading several of Gibson's (1988) cyberpunk short stories,[19] one of my students wrote a series of extended journal entries in the form of stories about a time-traveling Future Dog. Dog steps in and out of time, providing narrative links between the student's previous journal entries (including excerpts from the writing of some his ninth-grade students), historical material (such as versions of—and commentaries on—Chief Seattle's speeches on Native American relationships with the land), and contemporary events (including daily press reports and reflections on current reading and class activities). Towards the end of his Future Dog stories the student wrote:

> Unlike Dog, we cannot just step into a future—we can only dream it.
>
> The lives of all of us are marked by the tension between dream and drift, between pursuing the plums and letting the ripe fruit fall. The triumph of generativity over a sense of stagnation is, of course, a combination of dream and drift, a life so empowered by a vivid guiding vision of the possibilities that there is time and space throughout the life cycle for creative and re-creative drift.
>
> Reading SF text and dreaming about it while creating connections using Future Dog is to dream and drift with generativity in mind. The process becomes part of the living that adds to and restructures the "vivid guiding vision of possibilities" through which choices are faced. (Daniels, 1981, p. 301)

Much SF inspires hope for the "triumph of generativity over a sense of stagnation." If I now found myself in a situation similar to that which Pinar (1984) describes, I would be more likely to read my experience against, say, Marge Piercy's (1991) *He, She and It*—a near-future fiction which explores tensions between metaphors of cyborgs as, on the one hand, products of cybernetic and corporate control processes and, on the other, embodiments of resistance to those processes—rather than Cross's detective novel. In part, this would indicate my personal reading preferences, but it would also register my confidence in the generativity of diffractive storytelling. I find the dream of life as a cyborg a more "vivid guiding vision" than the prospect of death—or stagnation—in a tenured position.

Postscript

> I am well aware that I have never written anything but fictions. I do not mean to say, however, that truth is therefore absent. It seems to me that the possibility exists for fiction to function in truth, for a fictional discourse to induce effects of truth.... (Foucault, 1980, p. 193).

The strategic position to which all of the above reasoning—and the obligatory reference to Foucault—presently leads me is this: we can initiate and sustain worthwhile inquiries in education by taking seriously J.G. Ballard's (1985, p. 8) proposition that *if* "we live in a world ruled by fictions of every kind" *then* "the most prudent and effective method of dealing with the world around us is to assume that it is a complete fiction." By this I do not necessarily mean that Ballard's assertion is a hypothesis to be tested scientifically. Rather, I am suggesting that in practicing curriculum inquiry and teacher education as storytelling crafts, I have sufficient reason to believe that Ballard's formulation refers to "real" conditions, with particular reference to the conditions under which I might need to judge my own and others' actions to be prudent and effective (or not). Rather than struggling with popular distinctions between stories of the imagination and of reality, I prefer to situate myself in the world-as-fiction as a researcher-narrator whose subjectivity is author of (that is, authorizes) his methodology.

Acknowledgments

An earlier version of this essay appeared in the *Australian Educational Researcher* (Gough, 1994b). Much of the research which informs this essay was supported by internal grants from Deakin University. Its experiential basis was very largely generated in collaboration with students in the Masters Program in Curriculum Studies at the University of Victoria, British Columbia, Canada, during summer school sessions in 1992, 1993, and 1995—their willingness to share their stories is greatly appreciated, and they have been among my most creative and critical friends. For their constructive comments on drafts of this essay I thank Catherine Beavis and Annette Gough (Deakin University).

Notes

1. See, for example, Brieschke (1990, 1992, 1993), Gough (1993a), and various chapters in Willis and Schubert (1991).

2. Hofstra University (New York) has already accepted a novel as a doctoral dissertation (Sellitto, 1991) and the University of Victoria (British Columbia, Canada) has accepted a Master of Education (by research) thesis comprising a collection of short (fictional) stories (Hughes, 1993), but these are among the very few examples I have

found, to date, of explicitly fictional works meeting with such formal approval by the academy.

3. For example, Walker (1981, p. 163) cites Truman Capote's *In Cold Blood* and Tom Wolfe's *The Last American Hero* as works that elude categorization as either research reports or "pure fiction"—a blurring of journalistic and novelistic modes that Barone, as quoted above, refers to as moving critical storytellers "beyond genre."

4. For a variety of perspectives on problems of realism and representation see the essays collected in Levine (1993).

5. A complementary process is demonstrated by Cleo Cherryholmes (1993), who enacts alternative readings of a research report rather than alternative readings of the data it purports to interpret.

6. Hartley is referring here to the institutions that construct television and its audiences, but my experience of academic publishing suggests that his proposition is equally applicable to textual production in educational research.

7. See Convery (1993) for an explicit example of the approach advocated by Rowland et al. (1990).

8. More recently, an article by P.P. McGuiness *(The Weekend Australian* 15-16 September 1990, p. 2) on the uses of tax file numbers and the extension of government access to taxation records was headed "Spectre of Big Brother refuses to fade away."

9. For recent intellectual histories, genealogies and justifications of *currere* and its successor projects in North America, see Graham (1991, 1992), Pinar (1994), Pinar and Reynolds (1992), and Pinar et al. (1995).

10. I use "play" in a Derridean sense that likens the play of power a-cross discursive fields to "play" in a machine, a relative freedom of move-ment within limits; see, for example, McGowan (1991, pp. 103-5).

11. I recognize, however, that there are elements of retrospective rationalization in this reasoning, since my own autobiographical

writing reveals the long-standing influence of SF in my life and work (see Gough 1991a).

12. Umberto Eco (1983, p. 215) notes that "many of the so-called 'deductions' of Sherlock Holmes are instances of creative abduction"—"abduction" being the term used by Charles S. Peirce (he also used the term "retroduction") for the inclination to entertain a hypothesis (see also Sebeok and Umiker-Sebeok 1983). Slavoj Zizek (1992, pp. 48-66) also argues that "the Sherlock Holmes way" is not strictly analogous to scientific method, although this is a popular misconception. Zizek compares the evolution of detective fiction from classical to hard-boiled ("the Philip Marlowe way") with the evolution of psychoanalytic methods from Freud to Lacan. His illuminating readings of a wide range of epistemologically-oriented fictions testify to the internal diversity of modernist genres, and thus provide a useful counterpoint to McHale (whose rhetorical purposes may lead him to oversimplify these genres in order to highlight the complexities of postmodernist fictions).

13. The significance of cyberpunk SF is also indicated by the variety and quality of the literary and cultural criticism it has generated; see, for example, Bukatman (1993), McCaffery (1991), Slusser and Shippey (1992).

14. Bukatman takes this term from William Burroughs (1964, p. 19).

15. McHale is referring here to angels rather than to cyborgs. However, in his "postmodern angelology," McHale (1992, pp. 202-3) refers to "an enduring angel-function which is fulfilled in similar ways by different beings at different times" and notes that "in our own time,... the angel-function has been largely 'science-fictionized.'"

16. These qualities are shared by monsters and/or mutants that are created by accident (for example, the Incredible Hulk, Teenage Mutant Ninja Turtles)—and whose origins are thus to some extent mysterious—whereas those that are deliberate creations (for example, Frankenstein's monster, Black Orchid) have more in common with cyborgs. Black Orchid (Gaiman and McKean, 1991) is a particularly interesting variation on the "normal" conception of a cyborg (a creature that combines human with machine and/or animal qualities) in that she combines human qualities with those of plants.

17. For further examples of this generativity see Gough (1995).

18. It is not, however, the first time that the curriculum field has been characterized as a corpse. Some years previously Joseph Schwab (1969, p. 1) introduced the first of his seminal papers on the practical by declaring that "the field of curriculum is moribund."

19. A key story for this student was *Johnny Mnemonic*, recently reissued (Gibson 1995) to tie in with the release of the movie of the same name (for which Gibson also wrote the screenplay).

References

Ashmore, Malcolm. (1989). *The reflexive thesis: Wrighting sociology of scientific knowledge*. Chicago and London: University of Chicago Press.

Ballard, J.G. (1985). Introduction to the French edition of *Crash*. London: Paladin. (Original work published 1974).

Barone, Thomas E. (1989). Ways of being at risk: The case of Billy Charles Barnett. *Phi Delta Kappan* (71), 147-151.

Barone, Thomas E. (1992a). Beyond theory and method: A case of critical storytelling. *Theory into Practice, 31*(2), 142-146.

Barone, Thomas E. (1992b). On the demise of subjectivity in educational inquiry. *Curriculum Inquiry, 22* (1), 25-38.

Barr, Marlene S. (1992). *Feminist fabulation: Space/postmodern fiction*. Iowa City: University of Iowa Press.

Brieschke, Patricia A. (1990). The administrator in fiction: Using the novel to teach educational administration. *Educational Administration Quarterly, 26* (4), 376-93.

Brieschke, Patricia A. (1992). Reparative praxis: Rethinking the catastrophe that is social science. *Theory into Practice, 31* (2), 173-80.

Brieschke, Patricia A. (1993). Interpreting ourselves: Administrators in modern fiction. *Theory into Practice, 32* (4), 228-35.

Brookes, Andrew. (1995). Multiple stories or several flaws? Reflections on architecture, narrative, and place in educational research. *Australian Educational Researcher*, 22(3), 145-149.

Bukatman, Scott. (1993). *Terminal identity: The virtual subject in postmodern science fiction*. Durham, NC & London: Duke University Press.

Burroughs, William S. (1964). *Nova express*. New York: Grove Press.

Capek, Karel (1923). *R.U.R.* [Trans. P. Selver.] Oxford: Oxford University Press.

Caute, David. (1971). *The illusion.* London: André Deutsch.

Chandler, Raymond. (1939). *The big sleep.* New York: Alfred E. Knopf.

Cherryholmes, Cleo. (1993). Reading research. *Journal of Curriculum Studies, 25* (1), 1-32.

Christie, Agatha. (1930). *Murder at the vicarage.* New York: Dodd, Mead & Company.

Connelly, F. Michael, and Clandinin, D. Jean. (1990). Stories of experience and narrative inquiry. *Educational Researcher, 19* (5), 2-14.

Convery, Andy. (1993). Developing fictional writing as a means of stimulating teacher reflection: A case study. *Educational Action Research, 1* (1), 135-151.

Cross, Amanda. (1981). *Death in a tenured position.* New York: Ballantine.

Daniels, Pamela. (1981). Dream vs. drift in women's careers. In Barbara L. Forisha and Barbara H. Goldman (Eds.). *Outsiders on the inside: Women and organizations* (285-302). Englewood Cliffs, NJ: Prentice-Hall.

Dickens, Charles. (1955). *Hard times.* Oxford: Oxford University Press. (Original work published 1854)

Eco, Umberto. (1983). Horns, hooves, insteps: Some hypotheses on three types of abduction. In Umberto Eco and Thomas A. Sebeok (Eds.), *The sign of three: Dupin, Holmes, Peirce* (pp. 198-220). Bloomington and Indianapolis: Indiana University Press.

Eisner, Elliot W. (1993). Forms of understanding and the future of educational research. *Educational Researcher, 22* (7), 5-11.

Foucault, Michel. (1980). *Power/knowledge: Selected interviews and other writings 1972-1977* (Colin Gordon, Ed.). New York: Harvester Wheatsheaf.

Gaiman, Neil, and McKean, Dave. (1991). *Black orchid.* New York: DC Comics.

Gibson, William. (1984). *Neuromancer.* New York: Ace.

Gibson, William (1988). *Burning chrome.* London: Grafton.

Gibson, William. (1995). *Johnny Mnemonic: The screenplay and the story.* New York: Ace Books.

Gilmore, Leigh (1994). The mark of autobiography: Postmodernism, autobiography, and genre. In Kathleen Ashley, Leigh Gilmore and

Gerald Peters (Eds.),*Autobiography and postmodernism* (3-18). Amherst, MA: University of Massachusetts Press.

Gough, Noel. (1991a). An accidental astronaut: Learning with science fiction. In George Willis & William H. Schubert (Eds.), *Reflections from the heart of educational inquiry: Understanding curriculum and teaching through the arts,* (pp. 312-20). Albany, NY: State University of New York Press.

Gough, Noel. (1991b). Narrative and nature: Unsustainable fictions in environmental education. *Australian Journal of Environmental Education, 7*, 31-42.

Gough, Noel. (1993a). Environmental education, narrative complexity and postmodern science/fiction. *International Journal of Science Education, 15*(5), 607-625.

Gough, Noel. (1993b). *Laboratories in fiction: Science education and popular media.* Geelong: Deakin University Press.

Gough, Noel. (1993c). Narrative inquiry and critical pragmatism: Liberating research in environmental education. In Rick Mrazek (Ed.), *Alternative paradigms in environmental education research,* (pp. 175-197). Troy, OH: North American Association for Environmental Education.

Gough, Noel. (1993d). Neuromancing the stones: Experience, intertextuality, and cyberpunk science fiction. *Journal of Experiential Education, 16*(3), 9-17.

Gough, Noel. (1994a). Imagining an erroneous order: Understanding curriculum as phenomenological and deconstructed text. *Journal of Curriculum Studies, 26*(5), 553-568.

Gough, Noel. (1994b). Narration, reflection, diffraction: Aspects of fiction in educational inquiry. *Australian Educational Researcher, 21*(3), 47-76.

Gough, Noel. (1994c). Playing at catastrophe: Ecopolitical education after poststructuralism. *Educational Theory, 44*(2), 189-210.

Gough, Noel. (1995). Manifesting cyborgs in curriculum inquiry. *Melbourne Studies in Education, 29*(1), 71-83.

Graham, Robert J. (1991). *Reading and writing the self: Autobiography in education and the curriculum.* (Vol. 24). New York: Teachers College Press.

Graham, Robert J. (1992). *Currere* and reconceptualism: The progress of the pilgrimage 1975-1990. *Journal of Curriculum Studies, 24*(1), 27-42.

Green, Bill & Bigum,Chris (1993). Aliens in the classroom. *Australian Journal of Education*, 37 (2), 119-141.

Grumet, Madeleine R. (1981). Restitution and reconstruction of educational experience: An autobiographical method for curriculum theory. In Martin Lawn and Len Barton (Eds.), *Rethinking curriculum studies: A radical approach*, (pp. 115-130). London: Croom Helm.

Grumet, Madeleine R. (1988). *Bitter milk: Women and teaching*. Amherst, MA: The University of Massachusetts Press.

Hammett, Dashiell. (1930). *The maltese falcon*. New York: Alfred E. Knopf.

Haraway, Donna J. (1985). A manifesto for cyborgs: Science, technology and socialist feminism in the 1980s. *Socialist Review*, *15*(2), 65-107.

Haraway, Donna J. (1989). *Private visions: Gender, race, and nature in the world of modern science*. New York: Routledge.

Haraway, Donna J. (1991a). A cyborg manifesto: Science, technology, and socialist-feminism in the late twentieth century *Simians, cyborgs, and women: The reinvention of nature*, (pp. 149-181). New York: Routledge.

Haraway, Donna J. (1991b). The actors are cyborg, nature is Coyote, and the geography is elsewhere: Postscript to "Cyborgs at large." In Constance Penley and Andrew Ross (Eds.), *Technoculture* (pp. 21-26). Minneapolis: University of Minnesota Press.

Haraway, Donna J. (1994). A game of cat's cradle: Science studies, feminist theory, cultural studies. *Configurations: A Journal of Literature, Science, and Technology*, 2(1), 59-71.

Harding, Sandra. (1986). *The Science question in feminism*. Ithaca, NY: Cornell University Press.

Hartley, John. (1993). Invisible fictions. In John Frow and Meaghan Morris (Eds.), *Australian cultural studies: A reader*, (pp. 162-179). St Leonards NSW: Allen and Unwin.

Hayles, N. Katherine. (1993). The life cycle of cyborgs: Writing the posthuman. In Marina Benjamin (Ed.). *A question of identity: Women, science, and literature*, (pp. 152-170). New Brunswick, NJ: Rutgers University Press.

Hughes, Denny. (1993). *Narrative inquiry: The songs and silences of adolescent alienation*, unpublished Master of Education thesis, University of Victoria, Victoria, British Columbia, Canada.

Hutcheon, Linda. (1989). *The Politics of postmodernism*. London and New York: Routledge.

Huxley, Aldous (1932). *Brave new world*. London: Chatto and Windus.

Jones, Alison. (1989). The cultural production of classroom practice. *British Journal of Sociology of Education, 10*(1), 19-31.

Jones, Alison. (1992). Writing feminist educational research: Am "I" in the text? In Sue Middleton and Alison Jones (Eds.), *Women and education in Aotearoa 2*, (pp. 18-32). Wellington, NZ: Bridget Williams Books Ltd.

Knoespel, Kenneth J. (1991). The emplotment of chaos: Instability and narrative order. In N. Katherine Hayles (Ed.), *Chaos and order: Complex dynamics in literature and science* (pp. 100-122). Chicago: University of Chicago Press.

Krall, Florence R. (1981). Navajo tapestry. A curriculum for ethno-ecological perspectives. *Journal of Curriculum Theorizing, 3*(1), 165-208.

Krall, Florence R. (1994). *Ecotone: Wayfaring on the margins*. Albany NY: State University of New York Press.

Lather, Patti. (1991). *Getting smart: Feminist research and pedagogy with/in the postmodern*. New York: Routledge.

Le Guin, Ursula K. (1989). Some thoughts on narrative. *Dancing at the edge of the world: thoughts on words, women, places* (pp. 37-45). New York: Grove Press.

Levine, George (Ed.). (1993). *Realism and representation: Essays on the problem of realism in relation to science, literature and culture*. Madison WI: University of Wisconsin Press.

McCuffery, Larry (Ed.). (1991). *Storming the reality studio: A casebook of cyberpunk and postmodern science fiction*. Durham & London: Duke University Press.

McGuiness, P.P. (1990, 15-16 September). Spectre of Big Brother refuses to fade away. *The Weekend Australian,* p. 2.

McGowan, John. (1991). *Postmodernism and its critics*. Ithaca NY: Cornell University Press.

McHale, Brian. (1992). *Constructing postmodernism*. London and New York: Routledge.

Ommundsen, Wenche. (1993). *Metafictions? Reflexivity in contemporary texts*. Carlton: Melbourne University Press.

Orwell, George (1949). *1984*. [Trans.by Marc E. Heine.] London: Secker.

Paretsky, Sara. (1993). *Tunnel vision*. New York: Hamish Hamilton.

Piercy, Marge. (1991). *He, she and it.* New York: Alfred A. Knopf.

Pinar, William F. (1975). *Currere*: Towards reconceptualization. In William F. Pinar (Ed.), *Curriculum Theorizing: The Reconceptualists* (pp. 396-414). Berkeley, CA: McCutchan.

Pinar, William F. (1984). Death in a tenured position. *Curriculum Perspectives, 4* (1), 74-76.

Pinar, William F. (1994). *Autobiography, politics and sexuality: Essays in curriculum theory 1972-1992.* New York: Peter Lang.

Pinar, William F., and Reynolds, William M. (Eds.), (1992). *Understanding curriculum as phenomenological and deconstructed text.* New York: Teachers College Press.

Pinar, William F., Reynolds, William M., Slattery, Patrick, and Taubman, Peter. (1995). *Understanding curriculum: An introduction to the study of historical and contemporary curriculum discourses.* New York: Peter Lang.

Reid, William A. (1981a) The deliberative approach to the study of the curriculum and its relation to critical pluralism. In Martin Lawn and Len Barton (Eds.). *Rethinking curriculum studies* (pp. 160-87). London: Croom Helm.

Reid, William A. (1981b). The practical, the theoretic, and the conduct of curriculum research, *Annual Meeting of the American Educational Research Association.* Los Angeles, CA.

Rorty, Richard. (1979). *Philosophy and the mirror of nature.* Princeton NJ: Princeton University Press.

Rorty, Richard. (1989). *Contingency, irony, and solidarity.* Cambridge MA: Cambridge University Press.

Rowland, Gillie, Rowland, Stephen and Winter, Richard. (1990). Writing fiction as inquiry into professional practice. *Journal of Curriculum Studies, 22* (3), 291-293.

Rushkoff, Douglas (Ed.). (1994). *The genX reader.* New York: Ballantine Books.

Scholes, Robert. (1976). The roots of science fiction. In Mark Rose (Ed.), *Science fiction: A collection of critical essays* (pp. 46-56). Englewood Cliffs NJ: Prentice-Hall.

Schwab, Joseph J. (1969). The practical: A language for curriculum. *School Review, 78*(1), 1-23.

Sebeok,Thomas A. & Umiker-Sebeok, Jean (1983). "You know my method": A juxtaposition of Charles S. Peirce and Sherlock Holmes. In Umberto Eco and Thomas A. Sebeok (Eds.), *The Sign of three: Dupin, Holmes, Peirce* (11-54). Bloomington & Indianapolis: Indiana University Press.

Sellitto, P. (1991). *Balancing acts: A novel*. Doctoral dissertation, Hofstra University, Hempstead, NY.

Shelley, Mary (1992/1818). *Frankenstein: Or, the modern Prometheus*. London: Penguin.

Slusser, George and Shippey, Tom (Eds.). (1992) *Fiction 2000: Cyberpunk and the future of narrative*. Athens, GA and London: The University of Georgia Press.

Varley, John. (1978). *The persistence of vision*. New York: Dell.

Walker, Robert. (1981). On the uses of fiction in educational research—(and I don't mean Cyril Burt). In David Smetherham (Ed.), *Practicing evaluation*, (pp. 147-165). Driffiel: Nafferton Books.

Waugh, Patricia. (1984). *Metafiction: The theory and practice of self-conscious fiction*. London: Methuen.

Willis, George and Schubert, William H. (Eds.). (1991). *Reflections from the heart of educational inquiry: Understanding curriculum and teaching through the arts*, Albany, NY: State University of New York Press.

Wolmark, Jenny. (1994). *Aliens and others: Science fiction, feminism and postmodernism*. Iowa City: University of Iowa Press.

Ziegler, Heide and Christopher Bigsby (Eds.). (1982). *The radical imagination and the liberal tradition: Interviews with English and American novelists,* London: Junction Books.

Zizek, Slavoj. (1992). *Looking awry: An introduction to Jacques Lacan through popular culture*. Cambridge, MA: The MIT Press.

Chapter Six

Pinar's *Currere* and Identity in Hyperreality: Grounding the Post-formal Notion of Intrapersonal Intelligence

Joe L. Kincheloe

Taking his cue from the phenomenologists, William Pinar developed his notion of *currere* in the early 1970s. The publication of Pinar's *Autobiography, Politics, and Sexuality: Essays in Curriculum Theory 1972-1992* (1994) and *Understanding Curriculum* with Peter Taubman, Bill Reynolds, and Patrick Slattery provides a timely occasion to review the impact of *currere* and to analyze its possibilities in relation to the identity politics that have emerged in this postmodern era. In his attempt to analyze educational experience, Pinar connected his understanding of phenomenology to psychoanalysis and aesthetics to produce a unique analytical form. *Currere,* the Latin root of the word, "curriculum," concerns the investigation of the nature of the individual experience of the public. Utilizing this analytical synthesis, Pinar argued that we are better prepared to approach the contents of consciousness as they appear to us in educational contexts. Such exploration allows us, Pinar argued, to loosen our identification with the contents of consciousness so that we can gain some distance from them. From our new vantage point we may be able to see those psychic realms that are formed by conditioning and unconscious adherence to social convention.

In Latin the word, *currere,* means running the race course–a verb. Mainstream understandings in the field of curriculum have traditionally reduced the word to its noun form, the track. In this context Pinar's student Patrick Slattery (1995) argues that mainstream educators forget that curriculum is an active process; it is not simply the lesson plan, the district guidebook, the standardized test, the goals and milestones, or the textbook. The curriculum, Slattery continues, is a holistic life experience, the journey of becoming a self-aware subject capable of shaping his or her life path. As a perpetual struggle, the curriculum in Pinar's *currere* is never a finished product that can be finally mastered and passed along to an awaiting new generation. Such a perspective protects the curriculum from the all-too-common fragmentation of modernist pedagogies, as it focuses our attention on the lived realities, socio-political encounters, and the identity formation of individual human beings.

Of course, *currere* held implications for practitioners involved in various phases of educational activity. For those of us concerned with the political and economic dimensions of schooling, *currere* taught us to guard against the tendency to allow the realm of the theoretical to overwhelm and erase the realm of the personal. Pinar has for two decades correctly insisted that the discourses of social justice and individual justice as well as concerns with collectivity and individuality should not be in conflict—indeed, they are companion efforts. For classroom teachers *currere* insisted that the self should never be collapsed into subject matter, that self and identity should be cultivated in relation to the learning process. *Currere* introduced us to the concept of identity politics long before cultural studies made it fashionable. Long denying the Marxist charge that the exploration of self is merely the latest incantation of the narcissism of bourgeois individualism, Pinar maintained that grounded identity studies enable us to explain how the politics we located "out there" in society are lived "in here" in our minds, bodies, and everyday speech.

Before Its Time: *Currere* in Hyperreality
Currere also anticipated the debates over multiculturalism and the traditional canon of the 1980s and 1990s. Exploring the interior experience of the individual vis-a-vis multiculturalism, we begin to understand the human impact of culture's struggle for self-description. Who are we and who do we wish to become are central questions posed by *currere*. Continuing Pinar's line of questioning: how are we shaped by others' perceptions of us?; and, how does dominant culture contribute to the shaping of the identity of the marginalized? Anticipating the recent attention to the social construction of white identity in the public conversation about multiculturalism, *currere* insisted on the exposé of white "racialization." European Americans

cannot hope to gain a critical consciousness of their own identity until they gain insight into the ways that they construct the racialized "other." And, of course, as *currere* induced us to give up the safety of our points of view, whether they be empiricism, critical theory, or neo-Marxism, it induced both men and women to explore the gender dimension of their identities. Pinar's *currere*-based explorations of masculinization, heterosexual male-male relations, and the tacit gender politics of social and curriculum theory in the early 1980s have lost little of their original impact.

Conceived before the formal articulation of the postmodern critique, *currere* plays well in the expanding hyperreality of our new times. The condition of postmodernity's assault on identity induces us to speak of our "subjectivity" rather than the more Cartesian notion of "identity." The grounded and bounded Cartesian version of self has given way to the partiality and contradiction of the postmodern subject. The storm of imagery and the hidden ideology of language constructs our sense of self, revealing that subjectivity is not innate but socially produced. As forms of hegemony mutate and expand on the media-driven postmodern landscape, the attempt to address the social and personal malformations that result from power discourses and political structures grows more and more difficult. In such a context Pinar's original construction of *currere* takes on a new relevance in the socio-personal dislocation of the present with all of its race, class, and gender-based pathologies. A *currere* catalyzed by advances in feminist theory, post-structuralist deconstruction, and the sophistication of qualitative research strategies can provide a valuable point of departure in the study of the late twentieth century crisis of identity. Indeed, a reconstituted postmodern *currere* can help us promote a multicultural curriculum of identity that explores the genesis of our ways of seeing and the nature of our consciousness construction.

Currere, Post-Formal Thinking, and Intrapersonal Intelligence

This need to refigure the self vis-a-vis hyperreality demands a new form of thinking, a cognitive vision that transcends mainstream developmental psychology. It was this concern juxtaposed with an understanding of *currere* that led Shirley Steinberg and myself to our formulation of post-formal thinking (1993). In this cognitive context *currere* and post-formal thinking can be linked to questions of identity by a critical analysis of Howard Gardner's (1983) notion of intrapersonal intelligence. If intrapersonal intelligence involves the development of the internal aspects of a person, especially access to the way one feels and the awareness of one's continuum of affect or emotions, then Gardner would be well-served to acquaint himself with *currere*–not to mention a variety of other critical and postmodern discourses as well. Post-formal thinking would assume that a critical form of intrapersonal intelligence would involve not only the ability to discriminate among feelings, to isolate and define emotions, and to use such insight in the attempt to shape one's behavior, but also the ability to analyze the social and political dimensions of those emotions and feelings. As Steinberg and I formulate this notion of a critical intrapersonal awareness in the post-formal theory, we propose an etymological dimension of cognition that asks what are the psychological and *social* origins of my perceptions of the world, my understandings of my own identity.

Thinking about thinking in post-formalism induces students to deconstruct their personal constructions of the purpose of their schooling; it induces men to expose the ways the privileged position of masculinity has shaped their self-images; it induces heterosexuals to refigure their identities vis-a-vis confrontation with the dynamics of heterosexism and sexual preference; it induces workers to reconsider the workplace and its social dynamics as profound influences on identity formation. The postmodern condition's crisis of meaning and identity is also a crisis of thinking. As a culture, we have little idea how our identities are shaped by power relations and the impact of such a process on how we define intelligence. Post-formal thinking about thinking appropriates *currere's* ideological disembedding, pushing cognition into the complexity of self-production. Transcending Piagetian formalism with its disembodied abstraction and its concern for disinterested procedure, post-formal thinking about thinking encourages a running meta-dialogue, a constant conversation with self.

Revolutionary Pedagogy: Exploring Self-Production
Profound pedagogical implications emerge from this conversation between *currere* and post-formalism's thinking about thinking. In schools still organized around cultural standardization, Chester Finn's and Diane Ravitch's monoculturalism, *currere* (twenty years later) is still pedagogically revolutionary. As we engage students in their perceptions of themselves and the social construction of their subjectivities, they begin to demand a more challenging and world-connected curriculum. Antonio Gramsci was thinking in this context

when he argued that philosophy should be viewed as a form of self-criticism. The starting point for any higher understanding of self, he maintained, involves a consciousness of oneself as a product of socio-historical forces. Until teachers model and encourage a *currere-* grounded post-formal analysis of self, students are often paralyzed in the effort to explore the formation of their subjectivities. Few educational opportunities present themselves in contemporary society to prepare students for such a task (Reynolds, 1987; Mardle, 1984). Thus, a post-formal pedagogy provides students with the conceptual apparati needed for the exploration of self-production.

Pinar's conceptualization of *currere* focuses on educational experience in particular, as teachers and students are encouraged to reflect on their past lives in schools and their interactions, with teachers, books, and other education-related artifacts. Pinar urges students to remember, observe, and record; focus specifically, he advises, on present responses to what is remembered. At this point in Pinar's effort to induce students and teachers to think about their educational thinking, he induces individuals to ask "What do I do with what I have been made?" What happens when students and teachers find in this process that they are homophobic, racist, misogynist, or class-biased, he asks. Upon such discoveries the individual must begin to deal with such socially-constructed legacies, utilizing logic, emotional empathy, prayer, or whatever means that work to reform such tendencies. Unfortunately, in my observations of classrooms from elementary to graduate schools I rarely encounter such pedagogy.

Currere, **Action Research, and Autobiography**
Thus, Pinar through *currere* is asking us to become action researchers of ourselves. Teachers and students begin to systematically analyze how sociopolitical distortions have tacitly worked to shape their world views, perspectives on education, and self-images. With a deeper appreciation of such processes, practitioners recognize the insidious ways power operates to create oppressive conditions for some groups and privilege for others. Thus, a critical form of teacher research opens new ways of knowing that transcend modernist formalist analysis (May and Zimpher, 1986; Hultgren, 1987). Such teachers as researchers cannot help but turn to biographical and autobiographical analysis in their inquiry. Aware of past descriptions of higher order thinking, such teachers would be alert to connections between biography and cognition. In other words, teachers in this situation become researchers

of themselves, researchers of the formation of their own cognitive structures. Such inquiry produces a meta-awareness of an omnipresent feature of the role of critical postmodern teachers: They are always in the process of being changed and changing, of being analyzed and analyzing, of being constructed and constructing, of learning and teaching, of disembedding and connecting. Indeed, the purpose of a *currere*-aware action research is not to produce certified data and validated theories of education–it is to produce a meta-theoretical cognition supported by reflection and grounded in sociohistorical context (Carr and Kemmis, 1986; Schratz and Walker, 1995; May and Zimpher, 1986).

Thus, action research is connected to Pinar's *currere* and its concern with conceptual sophistication, with a more embedded form of knowledge produced by teachers and students, and with a discipline's relation to one's ever-evolving autobiography. Such concerns inform a post-formal conception of a deeper level of understanding or a higher order of cognitive activity. In this context teacher researchers must confront not only what they see but *why* they see what they see. Post-formal researchers want to "see" the classroom as opposed to just "looking" at it for the purpose of fitting it into categories. When we learn why we see what we see, we are thinking about thinking, analyzing the forces that shape our consciousness, placing what we perceive in a meaningful context. We come to learn that all seeing is selective, filtered by the ways that power has constructed our subjectivity. We learn that we see from particular vantage points in the web of reality, coming to realize that there is no value-neutral way of perceiving. The post-formal observer uses this media-awareness in combination with Pinar's instrumental concept of the self-application of disciplinary knowledge to tease out what is significant in a classroom situation. This recognition of significance emerges from a larger post-formal appreciation of context, an understanding of the history, philosophy, and sociology of education. For example, an observation might be significant in that it illustrates the contemporary embodiment of the postindustrialization purpose of schooling as a method of social classification, the influence of positivism in shaping the way student evaluation is conducted, or the power of androcentrism to shape the definition of a "successful" school administrator.

Currere: Teachers and Students as Knowledge Producers

After applying Pinar's method of *currere,* a post-formal teacher encounters a new dimension, an alternate universe of educational activity.

Buoyed by such insight teachers begin to reconsider familiar pedagogical faiths. They come to understand that much of what cognitive science and in turn the schools have defined as intelligence consists of uncritically committing to memory an external body of information. They become aware that the frontier where the information of the disciplines intersects with the understandings and experience that individuals carry with them to school is the point where knowledge is created (constructed). The post-formal teacher facilitates this interaction, helping students to reinterpret their own lives and uncover new talents as a result of their encounter with school knowledge. This view of cognition as a process of knowledge production presages profound pedagogical changes. If knowledge is viewed, however, as simply an external body of information independent of human beings, then the role of the teacher is to take this knowledge and insert it into the minds of students. Evaluation procedures which emphasize retention of isolated bits and pieces of data are intimately tied to this view of knowledge. Conceptual thinking is discouraged, as schooling trivializes learning. Students are evaluated on the lowest level of human thinking —the ability to memorize. Unless students are moved to incorporate school information into their own lives, schooling will remain merely an unengaging rite of passage into adulthood. Little doubt exists, the way we engage with Pinar's *currere* and the subsequent way we define a sophisticated cognitive act help shape the nature of schools, the role that teachers play, and ways we construct our personal/social identities.

In this context we develop a pedagogy and a teacher education that encourages teachers to develop their own self-knowledge, while learning how to teach students to do the same. Henry Giroux and Peter McLaren (1991) extend our thinking on this issue, as they envision a teacher education that provides teachers the skill to assist students in the analysis of their interpretations of events and cultural meanings. The critical illumination that grows out of such analysis allows participants to intervene into their own consciousness construction. The key aspect of the role of teacher education in this context involves prospective teachers learning how to engage student experience in a way that both affirms and questions it, all the time keeping alive the possibility of self- and social transformation. Such an idea can revolutionize the long-maligned methods course, as it transforms it into a subtle, academic, and practical pedagogical process of learning "how." Lesson plans, in this context, transcend their present form as technical blueprints used to facilitate administrative surveillance of teachers. As Pinar writes about lesson planning:

> Regularly I walk into class without a preconceived lesson plan. Although I have a general notion of what I am up to, I make no preliminary sketches. This last year, for example, in a ten-week introductory course on Existentialism I taught as part of a senior elective program, I walked in, sat at a student desk, and asked if there were any comments or questions concerning the film we have viewed the day before. There were, and some time was spent in exchanging observations, questioning each other's conclusions, and wondering aloud about the film's symbolic import. Finally, some moments of silence persuaded me that no one had anything more to say about the film. I began reading from Kierkegaard's *Either/Or*, but interrupted myself soon after to ask for comments, of which there were many. We did some textual analysis, but primarily students explained how a particular passage affected them, what it meant to them. One such explanation intrigued me; I responded, referring to my life history to express agreement with the student's observation. In the remaining time, various individuals responded to that particular point, and to each other, most disclosing elements of their life histories in doing so (Pinar, 1994, pp. 7-8).

Notice the emphasis on identity formation, on the relation between educational activity and student consciousness.

In the *currere*-guided classroom, Pinar argues, planning should be informal and personal, allowing teachers room to adjust to the idiosyncrasies and needs of students. If teaching involves adherence to pre-planned delineations of data and prescribed student activities, why not simply use a computer or a televised lecture accompanied by low-paid para-professionals to keep order and disperse materials? What is special about teaching, Pinar continues, is the moment-by-moment experience of specific teachers and students in a particular place at a particular time. In Pinar's words:

> There are always issues to be addressed, often not conscious for either students or teachers, which the aware teacher can help identify, and make use of in order to ground whatever the planned lesson is in the actual and immediate experience of everyone in the room. Much misbehavior, from one point of view, is related (although not caused in a simple-minded linear way) to the teacher

refusing, because she or he has become an automation teaching a standardized curriculum, simply trying to get through her or his day, to address the specific individuals in front of her or him, to acknowledge in any explicit way what is occurring at any specific time. Or if it is acknowledged—usually when there is misbehavior —it is to mold it into his or her plan. I do not want to follow this link of thinking further, as it begins to sound like "blame the teacher," easy enough to do, not entirely inappropriate, but useless in this context. However a teacher drones on, and there are many individual as well as bureaucratic and cultural reasons for it, we curriculum specialists can be accused of having contributed to it to the extent we have supported standardized curriculum and teaching procedures. To the extent we have standardized is the extent we have disallowed idiosyncratic behavior, which is the extent to which alienation must be said to characterize social relations in the classroom (Pinar, 1994, p. 126).

Taking our cue from *currere,* a form of post-formal intra-personal thinking can be considered. Like post-formalism in general this description of post-formal intrapersonal thinking is not an essentialized, fixed set of cognitive features. It is simply a device to encourage analysis, an elastic proposal with ever-shifting boundaries.

Post-Formal Intrapersonal Intelligence

1) *Meta-consciousness–expanding the capacity for self-reflection and the analysis of identity formation.* Post-formal self-reflection asks why we are the way we are, i.e., the etymology of self. As individuals explore personal meanings, the origins of their actions, they gain an awareness of alternatives, of possibilities in their lives. Meta-conscious individuals refuse to accept or reject validity claims of any body of information without considering its discursive nature, that is, where the information came from, what can be officially transmitted and what cannot, and who transmits it and who listens. Without such reflection individuals travel through life imprisoned by the prejudices derived from everyday existence or by what is often labeled common sense. The habitual beliefs of an individual's age become tyrants to a mind unable to reflect on its genesis. We often emerge from sixteen to twenty years of schooling without having been asked to think about our thinking. Such a formal education too often ignores the effects of the emergence of a social climate of deceit with its decontextualized and allegedly disinterested science. Such processes leave their fingerprints on our identities.

When *currere* and post-formal self-reflection intersect, teachers learn to generate self-reflection in both themselves and their students. In addition to journal writing assignments that explore "how I felt when...," post-formal teachers push the intra-personal cognitive boundaries with techniques that encourage student dialogue that evokes insight into one another's subjectivities. Such delicate introspective activities demand a critical metaperspective on the nature of classroom conversations (how do we talk to one another?), the nature of classroom learning (what do we call knowledge?), curriculum decisions (what do we need to know?), and assessment (is what we're doing working?). When thinking advances and the dialogues grow in sophistication, students come to reflect about the socio-political nature of their school experience, asking whose interest it serves for them to see themselves and the world in the way they do.

2) *Transcendence of egocentrism—the difficult journey outward.* The social climate created by the postmodern hyperreality with its constant commercial inducements to consume, to gratify the self contributes to an egocentric culture. In the context of personal intelligence this cultural egocentrism holds serious consequences. Egocentrism (as opposed to connectedness) reduces our awareness of anything outside our own immediate experience. In our self-centeredness we tend to reduce everything to an individual perspective that causes us to miss meanings of significance. Many would argue (often in a New Age context) that this self-absorption leads the way to an introspective self-knowledge that will move us to higher levels of experience, new dimensions of cognition. Post-formal intrapersonal intelligence does not accept the individualistic, anti-communitarian aspect of such analysis. While self-knowledge is extremely important, egocentrism tends to reduce our ability to critique the construction of our own consciousness—we cannot gain the meta-consciousness to recognize the social forces that have shaped us. Unless we learn to confront egocentrism, the possibility of gaining critical perspectives in regard to ourselves and the world around us is limited. In other words, we will fail to develop post-formal intrapersonal intelligence. While post-formal teachers must make sure that students have confidence in their own perceptions and interpretations, they must concurrently work to help students overcome the tendency to see the world only in terms of self. Such self-centeredness lays the foundation for ethnocentrism, racism, homophobia, and sexism. In a way post-formal thinkers must learn to cope with a lifetime struggle between the tendency for self-confidence

and the tendency for humility. We do not seek resolution, just a healthy tension between the impulses.

3) *The creation of integrated knowledge–understanding ourselves in relation to the way we make sense of the world, integrating personal knowledge into secular knowledge and vice versa.* Post-formal thinkers manifest their intrapersonal intelligence at the level of knowledge seeking and knowledge production. Such individuals no longer see themselves as passive receivers of expert produced information. The act of knowledge creation not only teaches us to think and make meaning, but it allows us to understand ourselves. At the intrapersonal level post-formal thinkers demonstrate the ability to use knowledge they've created about the world to make personal meaning. Knowledge, they understand, is never independent of human knowers. *The frontier where information about the world collides with personal experience is the point where integrated knowledge is created.* In other words, to be considered knowledge in this *currere*-grounded post-formal context information must be incorporated into one's own life. Post-formal teachers working in complex and ever-changing cultural and classroom learning situations must constantly emphasize and act upon this understanding–the process of knowledge production changes who we are. Thus, post-formal intrapersonal intelligence knows no precise boundaries–as post-formalism in general, it is elastic. Such intelligence expands in relation to what men and women make of themselves, what they can produce in new understandings.

4) *Recognition of non-hierarchical difference–connecting intrapersonal development with an understanding of other individuals.* Modernist scholars have long contended that the foundation of political and ethical thinking has rested on a close-knit community with a common set of precepts. Sharon Welch (1991) challenges such a perception, arguing from a postmodern perspective that heterogeneous communities with differing principles may better contribute to the cultivation of critical thinking and moral reasoning. A homogeneous community often is unable to criticize the injustice and exclusionary practices that afflict a social system. Criticism and reform of cultural pathology often come from the recognition of difference—from interaction with individuals or communities who do not suffer from the same injustices or who have dealt with them in different ways. We always profit in some way from a confrontation with another system of defining that which is important–indeed, our intrapersonal as well as our interpersonal intelligence is enhanced through such experiences.

Consciousness itself is spurred by difference in that we gain our first awareness of who we are when we gain a cognizance of our difference from another or another's ways.

Welch maintains that the concept of solidarity is more inclusive and transformative than the concept of consensus. Even if we perceive consensus to involve a common recognition of cultural pathology and the belief that we must work together to find a cure, we first have to accept the value of interpersonal solidarity. Welch claims that solidarity has two main aspects: (1) The ethic of solidarity grants social groups enough respect to listen to their ideas and to use them to consider existing social values, and (2) the ethic of solidarity realizes that the lives of individuals in differing groups are interconnected to the point that everyone is accountable to everyone else. No assumption of uniformity exists here—just the commitment to work together to bring about mutually beneficial social change (Welch, 1991). In the classroom, this valuing of difference and its political and cognitive benefits exhibit themselves in a dialogical sharing of perspective. In this process students slowly come to see their own points of view as one of many sociohistorically constructed ways of perceiving. As the classroom develops, students are exposed to more and more diverse voices in various texts and discussions, a process that engages them in other ways of seeing and knowing. Thus, their epistemological circle is widened, as difference expands their social imagination, their tolerance, their vision of a better world, their knowledge of themselves and the production of their identity.

5) *Developing self-reliance in the transcendence of authority dependence–confronting the culture of ethical and political passivity.* In regressive modernist teacher education and schooling both teachers and students are enculturated into a culture of passivity. In the worst modernist, technicist teacher education programs teachers are taught to tame their pedagogical imagination. They are barred from discussions of educational purpose or the social or economic context of teaching. As such teachers lose their autonomy, they become acculturated to an academic culture of passivity. It is a culture that teaches both teachers and students to conform, to adjust to their place (their particular rung of the status ladder) and to submit to authority. Teachers and students are induced to develop an authority dependence, a view of citizenship that is passive, a view of learning that means listening. The predisposition to question the authority structure of the school and the curriculum it teaches or to reject the image of the future that the structure presents to

teachers and students is out-of-bounds. The politics of authoritarianism rub democratic impulses the wrong way (Shor 1992).

Post-formal teachers and students have too much confidence emanating from their well-developed intrapersonal intelligence to accept such passivity. Drawing upon their ability to produce integrated knowledge, students and teachers study both the forces that forge their identities and the ways such forces can be resisted. In such a context students explore their place in the social hierarchy of their peer group, their romantic relationships, their vocational aspirations, their relationships with teachers, and their definitions of success. They become researchers, in other words, of their intrapersonal and interpersonal lives, in the process gaining a post-formal meta-consciousness of who they are and how they constantly change in the hyperspace of the contemporary era.

Armed with a meta-consciousness of their relationship to the culture of passivity, teachers and students begin to question the nature of civic courage, ethical interpersonal relations, and democratic forms of governance and administration. In this frame of mind they begin to challenge conceptually the administrative structure of schools and other institutions. Such students and teachers find it interesting that administration is taught only to people who serve at the head of administrative structures and not to people who are to be administered. A post-formal perspective thus begins to expand into various curriculums, exploring mutating power relations and their impact on the formation of identity. Pinar's *currere* is alive and well in these post-formal formulations. In an era overwhelmed by startling adolescent suicide rates (400,000 attempts per year) (Gaines 1990) intrapersonal understanding takes on an even greater importance. *Currere's* concern with individual consciousness and experience holds implications for a variety of educational fields not to mention postmodern psychology and cultural studies. The pedagogical, cultural, and political possibilities offered by *currere* have yet to be realized.

References

Carr, W., & S. Kemmis (1986). *Becoming critical.* Philadelphia: The Falmer Press.

Gaines, D. (1990). *Teenage wasteland: Suburbia's dead end kids.* New York: Harper Perennial.

Gardner, H. (1983). *Frames of mind: A theory of multiple intelligence.* New York: Basic Books.

Giroux, H., & McLaren, P. (1991). Language, schooling, and subjectivity: Beyond a pedagogy of reproduction and resistance. In K. Borman, P. Swami, and L. Wagstaff (Eds.), *Contemporary issues in U.S. education.* Norwood, NJ: Ablex Publishing Corporation.

Hultgren, F. (1987). Critical thinking: Phenomenological and critical foundations. In Ruth G. Thomas, *Higher-order thinking: Definition, meaning and instructional approaches.* Washington, DC: Home Economics Education Association.

Kincheloe, J. & Steinberg, S. (1993). A tentative description of post-formal thinking: The critical confrontation with cognitive theory. *Harvard Educational Review,* 63 (3), 296-320.

Mardle, G. (1984). Power, tradition, and change: Educational implications of the thought of Antonio Gramsci. In J. Codd (Ed.), *Philosophy, common sense, and action in educational administration.* Victoria, Australia: Deakin University Press.

May, W., & Zimpher, N. (1986). An examination of three theoretical perspectives on supervision: Perceptions of preservice field supervision. *Journal of Curriculum and Supervision,* 1, 2, 83-99.

Pinar, W. (1994). *Autobiography, politics, and sexuality: Essays in curriculum theory, 1972-1992.* New York: Peter Lang.

Pinar, W., Reynolds, W., Slattery, P., & Taubman, P. (1995). *Understanding curriculum.* New York: Peter Lang.

Reynolds, R. (1987). Einstein and psychology: The genetic epistemology of relativistic physics. In D. Ryan (Ed.), *Einstein and the humanities.* New York: Greenwood Press.

Schratz, M., & Walker, R. (1995). *Research as social change: New opportunities for qualitative research.* New York: Routledge.

Shor, I. (1992). *Empowering education: Critical teaching for social change.* Chicago: University of Chicago Press.

Slattery, P. (1995). *Curriculum development in the postmodern era.* New York: Garland.

Welch, S. (1991). An ethic of solidarity and difference. In H. Giroux (Ed.), *Postmodernism, feminism, and cultural politics: Redrawing educational boundaries.* Albany, NY: SUNY Press.

Chapter Seven

Psychoanalytic Feminism and the Powerful Teacher

Wendy Atwell-Vasey

History places a child and her teacher. History cares about the nation of the birth, the resources of the land, the section of the city, the earning power of the parent, the color of the skin, womanhood or manhood. People are thrown into dangerous historical intersections. As educators, we try to identify these vectors as standpoints from which students and teachers can express their experience of reality.[1] We also try to provide access to other experiences of reality and to play a part in the community to improve the conditions in which people live, and to offer reflective methodologies to empower people to change history.

But the power of learning is not just a question of sociology or history, of background, role, or neighborhood, or of expertise. It is also a question of status. *How powerful a teacher seems to her students is as important as who she is and what she knows.* Power is also about whether the students want the teacher and what the teacher has for them.

Cultural theorists refer to the status issue I am talking about by using the term, "representation." Reality does not come to us directly, objectively, or unproblematically; it is re-presented to us within meanings already made, which we may remake, but which we cannot wholly strip away. I have argued elsewhere that the representation of maternal relations and our representation of maternal life is crucial to our representation of reality.[2] What we experience with the one who has taken care of us, what we imagine we experience with her, and how we represent what we experience with her cannot be extricated from our understanding of how we know the world at all. As shared parenting becomes more prevalent, the maternal structures to which I refer will more meaningfully be analyzed as parental structures. But today we still need to honor the historical prevalence of females as primary caretakers, even though as Julia Kristeva has indicated, we need to analyze maternity as a structure of its own, and not as womanhood. Because of maternity's trans-societal and transhistorical presence, the function of the maternal must be examined, even as we reconceive and enhance relations with offspring by undoing stereotypical gendering and discriminating processes, by encouraging shared parenting, and by unburdening our institutions of the apparatus of domination. Here I want to argue further that students find themselves in a disabling predicament when schooling replicates paternalistic and not maternalistic cultural norms.

We see that schools reproduce traditional patriarchal structures, with the majority of administrators being men, and about two-thirds of teachers being women, and about 87% of elementary teachers being women as of the nineteen seventies.[3] We see that academic settings valorize standardization and align intellectual maturity with hierarchies, categorization, and abstract abilities over representations that are more visceral, phenomenological, imaginative, and relational.[4] I hope we see too that schools often operate primarily as a site for ensuring that our children meet the pressures of public accountability and conformity but exile from their curricula those sensual, semiotic, affiliative, narcissistic, and transitional phenomena which help people develop, and whose features have been traditionally linked to the mothering work of women.[5] As a means of bringing nourishment of the individual back to schools from exile, feminist psychoanalysis is helpful. In the psychoanalytic theorist Julia Kristeva's work, we see the "lost" maternal structures revived, and I draw on them for their application to linguistics and teaching, especially language arts teaching.

Kristeva offers a theory of linguistic development which stipulates that it is, through reduplication of maternal structure, that is identifying with the mother's body and what it does, that the infant assumes the ability to assimilate, repeat, and reproduce words, and becomes like the other: a subject (Kristeva, 1987, pp. 25-26). She connected the infant's incorporation of the breast (or bottle, which, to the child, comes from the mother's body) to the subsequent incorporation of "the speech of the other." (Kristeva, 1987, pp. 25-26) The "mum, mum, mum," noises coming from the lips are extensions of efforts to suck and substitutions for sucking, rather than imitations of sounds. Kristeva says that becoming linguistic by incorporation involves displacing the child's thirst to devour food; he or she "holds on to the joy of chewing, swallowing, and nourishing oneself...with words"(Kristeva, 1987, pp. 25-26). Words are like food and love. Language does not require giving up the mother's body, but being like it.

This theory suggests that children do not primarily take up language as imitation or by being threatened with something they lack, as we shall see the psychoanalyst Jacques Lacan argued. Rather, they take up language as a physical fulfillment of their own desire.

In summary, Kristeva offers a theory of *incorporation*, the child's movements and sounds taking the place of the body of the mother, and of *reduplication*, that is, the child identifying itself with what the mother's body is, a being with drive and intention. The mother's body is never just flesh–it is flesh intended for satisfaction. If the child's first sounds and words are like the mother's body, they have drive and intention as well.

Kristeva writes, "In being able to receive the other's words, to assimilate, repeat, and reproduce them, I become like him: One. A subject of enunciation. Through psychic osmosis/identification. Through love." (Kristeva, 1987, p. 26). Kristeva explains that through incorporation of the speech of the m/other, the infant incorporates the patterns of language and thereby identifies with the other. In fact, it is the incorporation of the patterns of language through the speech of the other that enables the infant to communicate and thus commune with others.

Kristeva calls this incorporation of the other "narcissism" because it involves becoming a speaking subject without learning to do so in the sense that one must acknowledge what one knows or doesn't have. A deficit or lack is not presented. One assumes the position of speaker without knowing the objects of speaking, that is, without knowledge of specific words. The next step is crucial. The child puts herself in the place of language or signs, just in the same way she put herself in the mother's position. At the point of speaking, the child is already positioned within language as a being with drive and intention mediating letters and words, (signifiers) and referents (signified).

This incorporation and reduplication theory of language as drive aimed at satisfaction challenges our views about confronting students with standards and grammars, and suggests the limits of building language competence from chunks of letters and propositions. It also suggests that syntactical competence is deep-seated in the body's rhythmic, directional, repetitive, and patterned structures. It suggests that pioneers in language-arts teaching like Sylvia Ashton-Warner and her organic reading methods, Nancy Atwell and her writing programs based on students' imagination and desire, and Madeleine Grumet and her theater-based pedagogies, are most theoretically sophisticated.

Kristeva also shows that the alterity which is part of mother/infant, self/other, body/language reduplication opens up a metaphysical space in which imagination comes to life (Oliver, 1993b, p. 73). Because the child will be allowed to assume the position of the mother, without threat, and to fill up the new space between them with *his* imagination, he experiences both stable love and difference at the same time.[6] The child assumes he can do like mother can do even though what the mother can do in reality is receding always out of his reach, sparking his imagination. Narcissism protects the child from what he doesn't know, what he lacks, so that the difference between himself and the other does not need to be closed by him; rather, he uses that space to imagine what he wants. This productive narcissism is a structure that teachers will want to preserve and protect. For example, Denny Taylor (1989) writes that we ought to keep literacy biographies of students which record how each enlarges his or her linguistic world day by day, rather than testing students' literacy against standards which emphasize deficits. This constructive model honors students' need for narcissistic protection.

Narcissism is not merely a developmental stage, but an *ongoing* structure of the ego that helps the child negotiate between the maternal body and the symbolic world. Kristeva calls this process a healthy kind of narcissism which "prefigures and sets in motion the logic of object identification in all object relations including both discourse and love" (Oliver 1993b, p. 72).

D.W. Winnicott's work reinforces the child's reliance on productive narcissism. He writes about how the material world first begins to get objectified by the child as an extension of the reduplication process going on with the mother. He describes the interplay "in the child's mind of that which is subjective (near-hallucination) and that which is objectively perceived (actual or shared reality)" (Winnicott, 1971, p. 52). Winnicott asserts,

> This intermediate area of experience, unchallenged in respect of its belonging to inner or external (shared) reality, constitutes the greater part of the infant's experience, and throughout life is retained in the intense experiencing that belongs to the arts and to religion and to imaginative living and to creative scientific work (Winnicott, 1971, p. 14).

Winnicott's conception of how we come to know the world challenges the notion of splitting reality between what is "inside" and what is "outside," and challenges the notion of keeping what is private separate from what is shared. He showed that the knower and the known cannot be separated and sought to understand how the self uses culture to expand his or her world.

Winnicott credits a "good-enough" mother with one who is able to steer this narcissistic and liberating transitional phrase, a departure from Freud's story.[7]

But what of the father? Mythologically, as a culture, we have always relied on a third influence to break open the mother-child dyad and to release the child to become autonomous. Freud's references to ancient patriarchs like Moses and Oedipus remind us of the omnipresence of the paternal law-giver and lawbreaker throughout history and serve as a marker for where we are as a culture. Freudian analysis suggests that a paternal figure must enter into a child's life to disrupt the dyadic fusion with mother by confronting the child with a third image, a paternal image.

Picking up on Freud's reference to a "mirror stage" as the symbol of this third intrusion into the child's life, the psychoanalyst Jacques Lacan uses the story of a child's viewing of a specular image of itself in a mirror to tell a story of a radical and painful move out of maternal relations, a reading that Kristeva perceives as a masculine fantasy.[8]

Lacan has re-read Freud to powerfully influence linguistic theory. He used the Freudian myth of the mirror as a metaphor for the symbolic order of language. Lacan associates the mirror with the phallic figure who captures the child's attention and diverts it from the earlier maternal connections by threatening the child with a look that goes beyond him and by reflecting an image back to the child different from his previous confused experience of himself–more whole and cohesive, but not familiar either. The cohesive image in the mirror makes the child feel that he has not been whole without the solidifying image offered by the phallus to replace who the child is. In Lacanian theory, the child suffers the threat of deficiency or "lack"– the child sees that he has been lacking and wants to make up for what is missing in him. If we follow Lacan's line that the mirror is a metaphor of the symbolic order for the child, then symbolic activity, language, is something that the child needs, but lacks or is always in threat of losing. Lacan believed that the child identifies with language as a "stand-in" for the gap between what he means and what others can know of what he means. He stresses that it is necessarily like the castration that Freud narrated. For Lacan, the alien, arbitrary and standard quality of language, suits the child's necessary alienation from what he thought he was (maternal earlier experience) and from what he wants to be (whole, complete, phallic).[9]

Language teachers have a stake in whether they believe Kristeva or Lacan, because one believes that language is attractive and the other believes it is essentially threatening. Linguistic practice, modeled on Lacan's theory, would stress submission to distance, structure, objectivity, and abstraction. However, Kristeva is not convinced that the child would be willing to leave the mother's body and intersubjective shelter because of a threat. She suggests that there must be an attraction for the child to go beyond the dyadic relationship with mother, or teacher, and to leave the fusion with her in order to become an individual. She sees a different function of the third term, or the "paternal" other, which implies something different for language theory and teaching, something positive.[10] I find her story more convincing because of her more careful consideration and theory of maternal relations, because of my experiences as an educator, and because of my reflection on my own language use and on the development of language in my children.

Agreeing that to individuate, the child must reject the mother's body, but not maternity, to which he is inseparable, Kristeva suggests that the child find a positive and energizing motive for language use and agency, not in a completely new relationship, but in the deepening complexity of the former maternal one. The third or "paternal" term, in Kristeva's view, plays an important part in support of maternal function, not in opposition to it.

Kristeva suggests that the third term, represented as the desired father in Freud, need not appear to the child as a new desire in opposition to mother, but as the fulfillment of her desire. The child need not imagine paternity as overtaking the mother to rule or obliterate her. It is more logical from the child's egocentric point of view that the paternal factor exists to help create the child. Logically, the father is there to fulfill the mother's desire to conceive the child, literally and figuratively. The child identifies on two levels with what has attracted and satisfied the child's mother. On one level the child's own conception attracted and fulfilled her, and on another level, a third term —something foreign and other attracted and fulfilled her.

The object of the desiring and caring mother's gaze is a place made for her and her loved ones, a conception. Her desire must continually recede as a horizon for the child, but it is not regressive since it searches for a place in which both she and the child can live. This ever-receding horizon must be in the domain of a world the two can inhabit; therefore, its creativity is situated within the possibilities of both consciousness and facticity in transformation. Her desire does not look beyond the child to the world. Rather, the way she handles the world includes the needs of the child, of the other, of others. Hers is an ethics and economy of love and agency.

The child's ego is strengthened by the mother's desire for the paternal function because the child can only recognize himself as "other" from her, if he realizes that he is not the only "Other." Kelly Oliver says we cannot take this paternal other too literally (Oliver, 1993a, p. 70). Other people, community, work, can divert mother's eyes away from the child and fulfill her, in order to make him realize that the child is not the only one. (These others, or third terms, are sometimes called imaginary fathers or maternal imaginaries in Kristeva's work.) For the child, being the only one for the mother threatens to be an identification with her–being the same as the mother, with no individuation. On the other hand, being one of "others" is a function of love, of a desire, and is liberating for the child. The child identifies with the object of mother's desire–the father, who fulfills desire–not solely with the mother from whom he must individuate. The child becomes not merged with the mother, but loved by her, and by being fulfilling for her, he can afford to individuate. If the desire of the mother is unrequited, ignored, or repudiated, it is hard for the child to imagine that he was conceived out of love and is cared for out of love. Instead he either has trouble separating from the mother to individuate (he has to continue to *be* her to have her), or he repudiates her nourishment as too weak to sustain him. The child must then bank on the paternal, symbolic, stern, masculine figures in society to identify with and save him from being engulfed by the mother. He may either mourn the long-lost mother in a kind of depressive nostalgia, pretend she never existed, or spend his life making her abject. He may develop the False Self of which Winnicott warns, to appear compliant to paternalistic authority. From this angle, Freud and Lacan's stern paternal third figure is a failure of support for maternal relations and for the child.

The child needs to know that he is loved by the mother, but not the same as her. This knowledge sets up the possibility that the child is a subject who has desires of his or her own. This relationship of love helps us see an alternative for the child to severing the ties to life with its drives and passions, as he or she tries to enter symbolic life. Remembering that the paternal represents symbolic achievement to the child, and that the maternal represents pleasure, Kristeva's triangle suggests that language can carry us back to the source of our pleasures and needs, not in regression, but as subjects doubling back with new tools. This is an alternative to being taken up by the look and law of the stern father in a chain of significations whereby the child doesn't feel herself or himself as a subject but only as an object of the father's wishes. The referral back to the mother's desires allows the child to keep his or her link to maternity, even through differentiation.

Let us steal a famous reading scenario to see how this referral back to the mother operates in reading. This scene from Sartre's autobiography, *Words*, is instructive when read from a Kristevan perspective:

> I did not yet know how to read, but I was pretentious enough to demand to have my books...I wanted to start the ceremonies of appropriation at once. I took the two little volumes, sniffed at them, felt them, and opened them casually 'to the right page' making them creak. In vain. I did not have the feeling of ownership. I tried to treat them like dolls, to rock them, to kiss them, to beat them. On the verge of tears, I finally put them on my mother's lap. She raised her eye from her sewing: 'What would you like me to read to you darling? The Fairies?' I asked incredulously: 'Are the fairies in there?'

> While she spoke, we were alone and clandestine, far from men, gods, and priests, two does in a wood, with those other does, the Fairies. I simply could not believe that someone had composed a whole book about that episode of our profane life, which smelled of soap and eau de cologne.

> My mother had gone off, not a smile, not a sign of complicity, I was in exile and besides, I didn't recognize her speech. Where had she got that assurance? A month later, I realize: it was the book that was speaking... Singing, nasal, broken by pauses and sighs, rich in unknown words, they were enchanted with themselves and their meanderings without bothering about me (Sartre, 1964, pp. 44-47).

Sartre is at first threatened by the difference in his mother when her voice changes and she goes off with the fairies. But eventually he identifies with what satisfies her—the charm and excitement of the characters, and he puts himself in their place:

> It seemed to me that a child was being questioned: What would he have done in the wood cutter's place? Which of the two sisters did he prefer? Why? Did he approve of Babette's punishment? But the child was not quite I, and I was afraid to answer. Nevertheless I did. My weak voice faded, and I felt myself become someone else.

In school teaching, traditionally a woman's profession, we must also be suspicious of customs that cut off the teacher's ability to connect herself and her students with the worldly authority and drive traditionally associated with men. Likewise, we must be suspicious of language arts teaching that separates structure from drive. If the mother is most efficacious for the child when she both meets his or her gesture and is attracted by someone or something else, *then the model for a powerful teacher is one who accepts the child's ego and reflects his interests back to him, and who has strong interests and ties to the outside world that are visible to the child.* It may be useful to review the implications of maternal theory for language teaching:

1) A teacher would be re-envisioned and would re-envision herself or himself as someone who provides the opportunity for the child to bring drives, passion, and intention to symbolic form through theatrical scores, journals, writing poetry, strong individual responses to reading and choosing his or her own writing topics.

2) A teacher would provide settings in which attraction to language takes place, rather than slavish conformity to threatening standards or formulas. She or he would protect linguistic narcissism by refraining from emphasizing ignorance or deficits in language. Accumulative accounts of language progress would be more productive, like literacy biographies, drafts, and portfolios.

3) He or she would encourage negation as part of any intersubjective and constructive process. Classes would provide plenty of opportunity for dialogue in which the reader or writer can project ideas elsewhere, introject ideas from elsewhere, and reject ideas in an effort to construct his or her own position. The importance and right to negation must be modeled by a teacher who has likes and dislikes, who holds positions that contest and can be contested, and who negotiates with others the boundaries of what can and should be done in school.

4) A teacher would see the value of making visible to students her

or his own worldly, political and literary interests and desires which extend beyond the class and his or her relationship to students. Students would see this "third term" for the teacher as a model for their own license and responsibility to go further than what is known between the student and teacher, and engage in the real problems of the world. The curriculum would not be assigned the teacher or students but constructed and negotiated with the worldly and academic community.

The status of the many female teachers for our students in a patriarchal system is a predicament. The student whose teacher's status is precarious is left with two choices in the end.

He or she can identify with the oppression of the domesticated teacher and place constraints upon himself or herself. The student can censor her own questions, avoid risks, make no plans. This is the depressive position of one who has no desire and no intention. Her fears may be masked by obsessive technique, like the technocratic teacher who has lost intention.

The other choice for the student is to rebel against the fate of the domesticated teacher and avoid identifying with her. We have seen from the problems of class resistance theory that the repudiation of teachers and schools is not only a heroic performance by working class students to refuse the economic stratification of themselves as objects in schools (Willis, 1981), it is the failure to have gotten the support they needed to become more powerful in society. This support should have come from a more maternalistic system of teachers who could have helped students connect with power by helping them identify with their own power. The repudiation of the teacher who seems weak leaves students on their own and vulnerable to becoming undisciplined, unfocused, restless, and hysterical. In the light of the psychoanalytic critique I have laid out, these traits surface not as mere personality traits, but as typical responses to the oppression of women in schools, an oppression many students also encounter at home.

Neither depressive identification with school limits nor repudiation of school constraints prepares our students to renew their culture with any vigor or to take their political, familial, and economic part in caring for others. And no matter what road she comes from, or in what section of the city she teaches, if the teacher must be ignored, transcended, or avenged, she cannot empower.

Kristeva argues that theoretical analysis can help us separate woman from mother, and woman and mother from our representations of both. But it would be hard to know which suffers most in our patriarchal schools, in which real women face glass ceilings in the hierarchy of jobs and responsibility, anyone in the role of teacher is denigrated, and powerful maternal pedagogical structures are misunderstood and underused.

Notes

1. See Hartsock (1983), The feminist standpoint: Developing the ground for a specifically feminist historical materialism. In S. Harding and M. B. Hintikka (Eds.), *Discovering reality,* D. Reidel Publishing Company, Boston, for foundational language on the notion of standpoint as derived from Marx and Engel's insistence that "The nature of individuals thus depends on the material conditions determining their production."

2. See W. Atwell-Vasey, *Nourishing words: Bridging private reading and public teaching*, from which material for this article has been taken.

3. See M. Grumet's *Bitter milk: Women and teaching,* (1988). Amherst, MA: University of Massachusetts Press, especially "Pedagogy for Patriarchy."

4. Besides Grumet, see J. Flax, (1983). Political philosophy and the patriarchal unconscious: Psychoanalytic perspectives on epistemology and metaphysics. In S. Harding and M.B. Hintikka (Eds.), *Discovering Reality.* D. Reidel, Holland, J. Benjamin's *The bonds of love*, N.Y.: Pantheon; E.F. Keller's *Reflections on gender and science,* New Haven: Yale University Press, and C. Gilligan's *In a different voice.* Cambridge, MA: Harvard University Press.

5. For a more expansive account of this exile as it is manifest in language arts and English education, see Atwell-Vasey, op. cit.

6. I use both "she" and "he" as pronouns throughout the text to reflect both sexes. In sentences in which one subject is a female caretaker, like the mother, I may more often use "he" or "him" to distinguish the child from the mother in the dyad and in the sentence.

7. See especially the footnote by Freud in his essay, "Beyond the pleasure principle," on page 599 of Peter Gay's (1961) *The Freud Reader.* In this footnote, Freud relates a true story of a child of eighteen

months with whom he was residing at the time and who Freud felt "confirmed" his interpretation of how children come to transcend separation through pleasure. Freud writes in the text that the boy was preoccupied with a game in which "What he did was to hold [a] reel by the string and very skillfully throw it over the edge of his curtained cot, so that it disappeared into it, at the same time uttering his expressive, 'o-o-o-o'," which the mother and Freud had recognized from other encounters as representing the German word, "Fort," meaning "gone." Freud continues, "He then pulled the reel out of the cot again by the string and hailed its reappearance with a joyful 'da,' " meaning "there." In the footnote Freud writes, "One day the child's mother had been away for several hours and on her return was met with the words, 'Baby o-o-o-o!' which was at first incomprehensible. It soon turned out however, that during this long period of solitude the child had found a method of making himself disappear. He had discovered his reflection in a full-length mirror which did not quite reach to the ground, so that by crouching down he could make his mirror-image 'gone.'" In this essay, as well as "The Ego and the Id," in the text, *Group Psychology and the Analysis of the Ego,* Freud (1961a) interprets the child as conquering the mother by replacing her with his own image and gaining control over it. He will develop this line of thinking in his theory that the child will master his fears about mother by moving toward an ego-ideal or super-ego (p. 641).

8.   Lacan will focus on how the image in the mirror in Freud's story represents this ego-ideal or super-ego, and he will see it as rivalrous and masculine. Anthony Wilden describes an important aspect of Lacan's view: "For the boy, the specular identification with an ideal, notably with the father, constitutes the subject in the *position* of the real father and thus in an untenable rivalry with him; what the subject must seek is the symbolic identification with the father–that is to say he must take over the *function* of the father in the normalization of the Oedipus complex. This is an identification with a father who is neither Imaginary nor real: what Lacan calls the Symbolic father, the figure of the Law." (Lacan, 1968, p. 164) Wilden states that for Lacan the mirror stage is not an occurrence, but a structural or relational concept (Lacan, 1968, p. 174). This structure is paternal for Freud, as well. Freud writes, (p. 639 in Gay), "This leads us back to the origin of the ego ideal; for behind it there lies hidden an individual's first and most important identification, his identification with the father in his own

personal prehistory." Freud also assumed that the child "cannot have possibly felt his mother's departure as something agreeable or even indifferent" and explains the child's pleasure in repeating the fort-da games as the pleasures of mastery and even revenge (p. 600 in Gay), although he has misgivings about how this interpretation can be compatible in a pleasure principle theory. Kristeva will offer the missing and powerful interpretation, to my mind, that the child gradually identifies with the mother's pleasure in going out to seek gratification beyond the child and that the child identifies with her desires and the satisfaction of her desires, and assumes, due to narcissism, that these gratifications have something to do with gratifying the child as well. These gratifications can be met by father, but certainly not the stern, potentially humiliating and threatening father of guilt and conscience alone. The gratifying father, for Kristeva, is one who refers the child back to his mother and the building-up of his world. The mother's sexual relations with the father suit this purpose of gratification, but so could her relationships to other women, work, the community, and the world in which she makes a place for the child.

9.   See Anthony Wilden's commentary in Lacan (1968).

10. See Freud and love: Treatment and its discontents. In Kristeva (1987).

References

Ashton-Warner, S. (1963) *Teacher.* New York: Simon and Schuster

Atwell-Vasey, W. (forthcoming) *Nourishing words: Bridging private reading and public teaching,* State University Press, Albany, NY.

Flax, Jane (1983). Political philosophy and the patriarchal unconscious: A psychoanalytic perspective on epistemology and metaphysics. In Harding, Sandra and Hintikka, Merrill (Eds.) *Discovering reality.* Boston, MA: Kluwer.

Freud, S. (1961a). The ego and the id. In Peter Gay (ed.), *The Freud reader.* New Haven, CT: Yale University Press. Also in J. Strachey (Ed. and Trans.), *The standard edition of the complete psychological works of Sigmund Freud.* (Vol. 19, pp. 3-66). London: Hogarth Press. (Original work published 1923)

Freud, S. (1961b). Psycho-analytic notes on an autobiographical account of a case of paranoia. In J. Strachey (Ed. and Trans.), *The standard edition of the complete psychological works of Sigmund*

Freud. (Vol 12, pp. 9-82). London: Hogarth Press. (Original work published 1911)

Freud, S. (1989). Beyond the pleasure principle. In Peter Gay (Ed.), *The Freud reader* (599-644). New Haven, CT: Yale University Press.

Gay, Peter (Ed). (1961). *The Freud reader*. New Haven, CT: Yale University Press.

Grumet, M. (1988). *Bitter milk: Women and teaching.* Amherst: University of Massachusetts.

Hartsock, Nancy, (1983). The feminist standpoint: Developing the ground for a specifically feminist historical materialism. In Harding, Sandra and Hintikka, Merrill (Eds.) *Discovering reality.* Boston, MA: Kluwer.

Kristeva, J. (1980). *Desire in language: a semiotic approach to literature and art* (L. Roudiz, A. Jardine, & T. Gora, Trans.). New York: Columbia University Press.

Kristeva, J. (1982). *Powers of horror: an essay on abjection.* Leon S. Roudiez (trans.). New York: Columbia University Press.

Kristeva, J. (1986). *The Kristeva reader.* Toril Moi. (Ed.) New York: Columbia University Press.

Kristeva, J. (1987). *Tales of love.* Leon S. Roudiez, Trans. New York. Columbia University Press.

Lacan, Jacques (1968). *The language of the self.* Trans. Anthony Wilden. New York: Dell Publishing.

Oliver, Kelly (ed.) (1993a). *Ethics, politics, and difference in Julia Kristeva's writing.* New York: Routledge.

Oliver, Kelly (1993b). *Reading Kristeva: unraveling the Double-bind.* Bloomington: Indiana University Press.

Sartre, J.P. (1964). *The words.* (B. Frechtman, Trans.). New York: George Braziller.

Taylor, Denny (1989, November). Toward a unified theory of literacy: Learning and instructional practices, " *Phi Delta Kappan*, pp. 184-193.

Willis, P. (1981). *Learning to labor.* Hampshire, England: Gower.

Winnicott, D.W. (1965). *The maturational processes and the facilitating environment.* New York: International Universities Press.

Winnicott, D.W. (1971). *Playing and reality.* London: Tavistock Publications.

Chapter Eight

Early Childhood Education: A Call for the Construction of Revolutionary Images

Gaile S. Cannella

A few years ago, I attended an AERA session in which the presenters were providing accounts of children from a variety of cultures and using the stories of those children to critique universalists' notions of child development. As the discussion progressed, the audience members became very disturbed by the idea that the child development knowledge base (Silin, 1987) was being questioned. The presenters were accused of "throwing out the baby with the bath water." The early childhood educators argued that much has been learned about children in the field of child development (i.e., developmental psychology) and this knowledge should not be ignored. The presenters argued that the child development perspective is a view of children that has been constructed within a particular sociocultural political context by individuals with a particular belief system.

Although both groups displayed concern for children, a shared discourse was never created. The early childhood educators spoke the language of deterministic research, the expectation that universal truths can be applied to all children. "What we know about children must be used to improve their lives." The presenters spoke the language of politics, social construction, oppression, privilege, marginality, emancipation, and possibility. "Are the voices of all (or any) children being heard?"

Western thought and developmental psychology have so grounded the field of early childhood education that we have most often accepted assumptions regarding children as "truth." We have not questioned the

social and political belief structures underlying that "truth." Critical
constructivist thought characterizes truth (e.g., reality, knowledge) as
subjective, created by human beings to best fit their perceptions of
particular social contexts, and dependent on the negotiation (or lack of
negotiation) of power relationships between various peoples (Lincoln
and Guba, 1985; Kincheloe, 1991). The field of early childhood
education cannot escape this power struggle. Questions must be asked.
How has our historical and political context served to construct the
values that have led the field? Do these beliefs lead to equity and social
justice for all children? Are groups of children (and their families and
communities) disenfranchised by the values that we have promoted in
the field? For researchers in early childhood education, critical
constructivist perspectives can provide avenues for the examination of
hidden ideological forces influencing our reality, shaping our constructions, and even molding our actions. Using critical research
methods and potential critical pedagogies that can emerge, the field can
be broadened to serve a greater number and variety of children.

As early childhood educators, we must examine how our "images"
of children and education have been constructed, how these images have
framed our consciousness, how language has been both constructed by
and serves to limit these images, and what these images have meant in
different situations for different children. My purposes in this chapter
are twofold. First, I identify those "images" in early childhood education
that have created the field, problematizing them within our present day
context. Second, I propose alternative images for the construction of a
field whose goals would become social justice and the creation of
revolutionary views in which children are seen as emancipatory agents
in their own lives.

Dominant Images
Three themes have dominated the field, each shaped by images that have
guided and controlled discourse and action. These themes include (1) the
construction of "childhood" and consequently "the child" as possessing
unique characteristics that are universal in the human condition, (2) the
construction of education for "the child," resulting in the creation of the
field of Early Childhood Education, and (3) the creation of a profession
that formulates and supports policy and practice.

Constructing the Young Child
The concept of childhood is a modern idea (Aries, 1962), indeed, a

modern western idea (Nsamenang, 1992). Perhaps the idea was conceptualized to counter times in which cruelty and brutality were part of the everyday lives of both young and old in Europe and the United States (DeMause, 1974). However, Nsamenang reminds us that in many cultures the characteristics and nature of the child are not considered separate or uniquely different from other cultural participants. Further, different notions of "childhood" appear to have been invented by different human cultures within different contexts and time periods (Kessen, 1981).

The modern framework (dominating western thought) for the construction of "the child" as unique and universal in the human condition has emerged from the beliefs and assumptions underlying the field of psychology, and especially developmental psychology. Burman (1994) analyzes power structures underlying key issues in developmental psychology that are applicable to early childhood education as a field grounded in the "human science." Using a deconstruction process, she unveils dominant discourses that structure the field. These moral/political discourses include: the use of human beings as research objects, subjugation of women as mothers in a deterministic environment, the construction of normative/pathological views of childhood, the scientific demand for control and prediction that underlies psychological perspectives, and the individualistic (context free) interpretation of human beings. Based on psychological constructions, children are abstracted and colonized as objects whose lives are determined and manipulated; women are regulated by a psychologically informed cultural climate that imposes particular mothering behaviors and constructs women's identities around the act of mothering. Individuals and groups are classified and stratified into oppressive hierarchies based on notions of "normality." Human beings, and especially young members of society, are viewed as context-free individuals, independent of time, culture, or condition.

Intertwined with these dominant discourses are dichotomous visions of "the child" constructed by those who are directly concerned with young children, those who have constructed childhood as pure, innocent, and needy (Silin, 1995). As opposed to adults who are worldly, sexual, intelligent, and strong, children are viewed as requiring protection from the world, vulnerable, fragile, asexual, ignorant, and weak. In the field of early childhood education, these psychological discourses have become connected to this dichotomous perspective and resulted in three distinct images of "childhood": the separate and distinct "whole child," childhood as progression through developmental stages, and the family as implicated in determining the life of the child.

WHOLE CHILD NARRATIVES. Education, and especially early childhood education, has always focused on the belief that the child is a whole and separate being, influenced by the environment, but ultimately an independent whole creature. The various whole-child narratives of the twentieth century begin with the perspective that childhood and adulthood are dichotomous. The two are qualitatively distinct, with the child depending on the adult, not only for food, nurturance, and caring, but to learn how to function in the adult world. Innocent and needy are examples of constructed views of childhood that are oppositional to the intellectual, competent descriptors more often associated with adults.

Silin (1995) examines the construction of childhood innocence, and therefore ignorance, as a romanticized response to Reformation notions of the sinful, morally corrupt child. Nineteenth-century writers created a literary child who was the symbol of innocence, contrasting the authors' dissatisfactions with society. This innocent child construction has supported a political order in which public intervention into the lives of children is considered appropriate. Adults concerned with social reform (Takanishi, 1978) have attempted to "save the children" (Silin, 1995, p. 122) by protecting them from the experiences and knowledges that characterize adulthood. Innocence is thus tied to ignorance, privileging older members of society. The knowledges constructed by society's children are denied voice, as if illegitimate and even non-existent.

The psychological construction of the child as needy has resulted in an environment in which adults determine child needs through extensive surveillance and empirical study (Woodhead, 1990). This perspective gives authority to the adult/expert while eliminating the child as an agent in his/her own life. Further, psychological surveillance assumes universal human needs, tied to universal behaviors and outcomes.

Any theory that purports to explain the nature of childhood shapes the ways in which we interpret the activities of children (Polakow, 1982). These theories can serve to limit and devalue the multiple ways in which we may learn to know children (Merleau-Ponty, 1964; Silin, 1987). No voice is given to the notion that childhood and even adulthood may be cultural constructions (Kessen, 1981). Dichotomous psychological theories create a distance between us and the children that we hope to know by constructing an ultimate "Other." Our constructions result in an opposition that is not necessary, concealing the realities of children's lives (Silin, 1995). Living within our psychological constructions, children are deprived of their own ways of making meaning.

Whole-child narratives are further constructed within a psychological context in which categorization and classification are taken for granted. Although posturing a whole-child perspective, the dominant discourse separates childhood into the various developmental domains –cognitive, social, language, emotional, moral, and physical. The child is considered a "whole" being, functioning within separate but interrelated domains of thought and development. Domains as constructions within a particular historical context with underlying value agendas are not questioned, even though the very creation of human domains of thought mirrors reasoned classification posed by proponents of logic and rationality.

Burman (1994) further describes how the social and moral orientations of a given time period are reflected in the categorizations of childhood. For example, the modern commitment to scientific production and technology has resulted in descriptions of the "child" as predisposed to logic, reason, and organization. Ambiguous, indeterminate characteristics exhibited during the early years are suppressed (Harris, 1987). Not only is a domain such as cognition constructed out of societal values, but the domain is privileged over other domains or forms of knowledge.

Finally, the psychologized human being is constructed as an individual, progressing through life as a free-standing whole (Kessen, 1981). This self-contained, isolated perspective mirrors American values that promote independence and self reliance. Although other individuals (parents, friends, teachers, siblings) may influence the child, the unit of concern remains the independent whole child. This individual focus masks social, educational, and economic inequities (Burman, 1994), fostering a perspective in which some children are judged as socially competent, ready for school, or intelligent wholes–and other children are not.

PROGRESSIVE DEVELOPMENT. Early childhood educators consider progressive child development to be foundational to the field, a clear example of a universal human process. "Forgetting" the value systems and political atmosphere that have fostered the notion, children are viewed as "progressing" toward a "higher level" of life as an adult. Posited by Rousseau (1933), the assumption that being an adult is

better and more advanced than being a child was given "scientific
legitimacy" with the publishing of *On the Origin of Species* by Darwin
in 1859. Darwin's evolutionary view has been adopted by child experts
as applicable to the lives of human beings. Children are conceptualized
as progressing through primitive stages, similar to the progress of
European cultures (Silin, 1995). Adults are privileged as those who are
more advanced, qualitatively more sophisticated than the unknowing,
developing child.

The progressive notion of development also removes children from
time, space, and the realities of their everyday lives. The notion that the
child is continuously moving toward a life that is more advanced denies
the power, reality, and agency of the present.

Finally, progressive development cannot be considered without
focusing on the assimilation/accommodation model of adaptation
constructed by Piaget. As early childhood educators, most of us will
continue to believe that Piaget's work has expanded our understanding
of possibilities for children. However, we cannot ignore the historical
and cultural assumptions underlying this work. Although he used new
and unique methodologies for the historical period, his model arose in a
late nineteenth/early twentieth century environment in which a
scientific commitment to truth, objectivity, and reason dominated. This
commitment is well illustrated in Piaget's description of the child as a
developing scientist, systematically examining problems in the real
world, hypothesizing about these problems, and learning how to solve
them through discovery (Piaget, 1957; Burman, 1994). An uphill
model of human change (similar to that of scientific discovery and
European views of cultural progress) is posited (Rorty, 1980), in
addition to a hierarchical model of cognitive structures (Burman, 1994).
While the model includes the notion of individual construction, the
developmental path, the way of coming to know, and what is to be
known are displayed as common to all, regardless of culture or life
history. These assumptions are normative, privileging masculine and
Western forms of reason. Within the context of a universal human
development, children and peoples who represent societies that are not
grounded in European cultural values are considered more primitive and
are by implication placed in the political and social margin (Cleverly
and Phillips, 1986; Gould, 1981), becoming objects for social control.
Finally, the notion of adaptation does not lead to viewing children as
revolutionaries who create new possibilities (Silin, 1995).

CHILD AND FAMILY. An image that dominates both talk and vision in early childhood education is the belief that the family determines (in one way or the other) the life of the child. This belief has arisen in an American scientifically-oriented context in which early life experiences are considered critical to the future functioning of the child. Psychoanalytic, behaviorist, psychometric, ethological, and constructivist developmental psychologies have all dogmatically and universally supported this belief in early experience (Kessen, 1981). While early educators and psychologists may use this notion to maintain support for early education and care, the idea must be understood as a multi-edged sword. Does the importance of early experience imply that certain culturally constructed experiences are better than others? When individuals have grown out of the early years, are they considered to be lost?

This focus on early experience has been used to hold the family, and especially the mother, responsible for the child's well-being throughout his/her entire life. (While this discussion of family does not focus on the concept of family as a social construction, the reader is referred to White and Woollett, 1992; Munn, 1991; Abbott, 1989; Brannen and Wilson, 1987; Gittins, 1985; Donzelot, 1979). As the expert has emerged in psychology, education, and other helping professions, an atmosphere of dependence has evolved (Kincheloe, 1991). While families are expected to provide quality early experiences for their children, the "what" and "how" of experiences are determined by experts outside the family, usually those who have studied psychologically grounded universal notions of early experience. Families whose experiences deviate from the expert perspective are considered deficient and in need of intervention. Diverse family experiences are not accepted or given voice.

Although children experience and thrive in a variety of social settings, the model of a heterosexual, nuclear family further dominates expert constructions of appropriate early experience. Within this context, developmental psychology has exhaustively studied the mother and young child (often because they were available in the home during working hours), creating a vision of child growth in which women bear the major responsibility. For example, Bowlby's (1951) construction of the good mother is one who is always available to the child. Not only does this increase the division between the public and private for both mother and child, but both identities are rendered meaningless without the other. Additionally, although expected to be privately at home with the children, mothers are held responsible for emotional disturbance and violence in the "outside" public world, a dichotomy created by the discourse of early experience (Singer, 1992). This blaming the mother perspective further promotes the notion that social problems originate within the individual. Political agendas, socioeconomic conditions, and hegemony are concealed (Tizard, 1991; Caplan, 1985).

Further, constructs such as attachment (Ainsworth, Bell, and Stayton, 1974) foster dominant gender perspectives. The child is expected to move from the stereotypic feminine "attachment" to the culturally determined masculine "detachment" (Burman, 1994). Advanced development is described as going beyond characteristics that have been culturally associated with being feminine. Girls and women are implicated as intellectually inferior (Gilligan, 1982).

Finally, discussions of attachment lead to class, culture, and gender privilege. Mothers are labeled as those most capable of forming healthy attachments, especially those who exhibit the sensitive, attentive behaviors most often displayed by women who do not work outside the home. This attachment perspective serves to regulate both middle-class and working-class women, one group pressured to bring forth active, productive children, the other chastised for failing to even know how to interact "appropriately" with their children.

I would not argue with the notion that children need early experiences in supportive, continuous human relationships. We all need those relationships throughout our lives. However, the idea that early experiences are more important than those that occur later in life and that these experiences must be of a particular type, with particular people, in a given context is a deterministic, power oriented view. Women and young children become objects of control; fathers are silenced; and anyone who deviates from predetermined expectations is condemned as ignorant and uncaring.

Constructing Early Childhood Education

The construction of the field of Early Childhood Education can, as with any other field, be traced historically using characters and events. This history includes an initiation in philosophy and religion with the pedagogical work of Comenius, Locke, Rousseau, and Froebel. The history of the field is grounded in child study and the psychological work of Hall, Gesell, Freud, Berlyne, and Piaget (Caldwell, 1984). Programs for the education and care of young children have emerged in the private sector, as part of government programs, and in public schools. We have provided experiences for our teacher education students that include integrated units, whole language, learning centers, discovery learning, and in some cases, even direct instruction. We explore models of education from Montessori and British Infant School programs to Head Start and Follow Through Models, to the recent craze, Reggio Emilia. Although recent openness to qualitative research perspectives and concern for cultural diversity may foretell change, the language of psychology has permeated educational discussions regarding curriculum content and practice. From this historical discourse dominated by psychological paradigms, images emerge that focus on the institutionalization of dominant perspectives, child-centered, play based instruction, and pedagogical determinism.

INSTITUTIONALIZING DOMINANT PERSPECTIVES. The image of institutionalization at first appears counter to the foundation of early childhood education. We are proud of our resistance to worksheets and large group instruction for young children. We insist on knowledge of child development to be used in understanding the individual young child. We focus on parents as the child's first teacher. However, as we analyze the knowledge base in our field, our philosophy toward curriculum, and program development and implementation, we cannot ignore the singularity of our perspectives.

Since the literature on psychological development has grounded our construction of the young child, and childhood in general, we cannot escape the influence of that same work on educational programs. Early childhood teaching models (e.g., behaviorist, cognitively oriented, developmental) are presented as philosophically distinct. Yet, all have been conceived within a sociopolitical context in which a psychological view of children is used to create learning experiences that are purported to result in particular outcomes. This perspective is linear and Tylerian, and assumes that the child is a psychological being. Regardless of psychological philosophy, the assumptions about education and learning are the same. Essentially, all models use the same knowledge base (Silin, 1987). The notion that we can *a priori* construct models that will lead to particular educational outcomes is reductionist. Linear, positivist, deterministic assumptions have lead to an unintended institutionalization of the field.

As early childhood education is increasingly implemented in the public school context, institutionalization cannot be denied. The narrow focus on behavior, logic, and literacy that can be measured in schools either directly or indirectly impacts early education programs. Early childhood education falls prey to the ideological configurations dominating schools in our society (Giroux and McLaren, 1989).

Finally, different forms of education and care have become institutionalized for different groups of young children. Wrigley (1991) has demonstrated that although programs remain grounded in psychological perspectives, differing assumptions regarding socioeconomic class have emerged. These belief structures were the foundation for the construction of custodial day nurseries and middle-class nursery schools in the early 1900s and remain part of Head Start and modern-day private nursery education. The assumptions are that poor families need help in raising their children. The dominant purpose for early education for middle-class children is to assist in the development of individuality. Community members with little training can work with poor children, but middle-class nursery schools should be staffed by teachers trained in child development. Through our assumptions regarding the needs of children from different socioeconomic levels, and with the assistance of government programs, we have constructed an early education system in which social segregation is institutionalized.

CHILD-CENTERED, PLAY-BASED INSTRUCTION. Rooted in the work of Rousseau, Pestalozzi, and Froebel, contemporary educators have advocated for education that is based on the interests, needs, and development of children. Emerging as a reaction to rote teaching methods and behaviorism, the image developed at a time in which women were being introduced to teaching and both love and nature were emphasized (Walkerdine, 1984). Romantic, child-centered instruction has become the expression in early childhood education of natural individualism; if the child's basic needs are met, he/she voluntarily learns through exploration and discovery. When child-centeredness is posited as the method appropriate for all children, a positivist perspective is inferred. Just as dogmatic use of rote memory learning presupposes a universal truth that is applied to all, child-centeredness as the privileged method leads to the assumption of one reality regarding children.

Child-centeredness assumes that human beings are rational, isolated individuals (Burman, 1994) with equal access to choice, socioeconomic privilege, and a shared value and experience base. This perspective tends to produce the cultural capital of the dominant group (Freire and Macedo, 1987; Delpit, 1993). For example, Delpit (1993) explains how children from middle-class environments are given multiple opportunities for exposure to dominant knowledge. Minority children are not exposed in their everyday lives to the knowledge and rules of the dominant culture. In educational environments, these rules must be directly explained because learning through romanticized, natural methods takes too long. Further, Walkerdine (1990) has demonstrated that females (and we might hypothesize, ethnically different young children) in child-centered environments face societal contradictions between notions of independence and action contrasted with negotiation and compromise. While the dominant societal view of woman is that of caregiver, the child-centered approach privileges pioneering behavior, exploration, and object-oriented experiences.

Play, a central tenant of child-centered instruction (Burman, 1994), is described as exploratory, voluntary, self-directed activity that naturally occurs and is needed by all children. Defended by early childhood educators as the young child's work, the distinction between play and work appears to collapse. The separation is, however, superficial. Beneficial play is described as productive or therapeutic, an orientation that leads to the judgment of play quality. The continued distinction can be traced to long-held practices of marginalizing the activities of children and the poor. Before the seventh century, games and play were considered part of the culture of all ages and groups. In the later part of the seventh century, the games of adults and the nobility were separated from the games of children and the poor. Subservience and dependence became characteristics that would be associated with the lives and activities of both children and those in lower socioeconomic levels (Hoyles, 1979).

The recent focus, for both home and school, is on play as the most valid way in which children are educated. Teachers and primary care givers (most often women and mothers) are expected to provide an idealized and continually stimulating atmosphere using exploration of materials and language interaction. These ideas are grounded in notions of privilege and middle-class values. Women are positioned as if they have no life commitments other than to respond to children. Education for young children advantages the play and language behaviors that are familiar to middle-class children and their families.

PEDAGOGICAL DETERMINISM. As discussed previously, our constructions of children as well as our educational practices have been conceived within a psychological perspective. The conceptualization of psychology as a field is both deterministic and reductionist. The underlying message is that science can discover and therefore determine the nature of the human mind (and that the mind is separate from the body). This psychological determinism has dominated our pedagogy in the form of lesson plans, units, management techniques, and whatever form our predetermined goals have taken (e.g., objectives, competencies, proficiencies, outcomes).

The image of pedagogical determinism is most recently illustrated in attempts to establish a standard for Developmentally Appropriate Practice (Bredekamp, 1987), particular methods of teaching considered appropriate to all children because the techniques are based on current knowledge of child development. O'Loughlin (September 1992) has clearly discussed the problems with the notion of methodological and content certainty implied by the creation of an appropriate versus inappropriate dichotomy. The creation of a dichotomous perspective unintentionally leads to a technical view. More importantly, the espoused child-centered pedagogy intrinsically creates an advantage for individuals who have gained mastery over white middle-class cultural capital and places children who are not part of the dominant culture at a disadvantage (Delpit, 1993). Creators and supporters of Developmentally Appropriate Practice (DAP) have constructed what Apple (1992) calls "official knowledge" by claiming universal application to all children, consensus of professionals in the field, and scientific legitimation (Lubeck, 1994). This official knowledge, actually the values and property of the dominant class, then serves to control and oppress those with different experiences and perspectives. DAP supports one particular cultural view.

The notion that we can describe appropriate practice immediately institutionalizes, reifies, and limits our views of learning for young children. We perceive their learning only through our predetermined lens. We begin to underestimate children's abilities and the importance of the societal context in which they and we live. The implementation of appropriate practice constructs a conservative environment in which critical pedagogies, emancipatory knowledge construction, and possibility are not supported (O'Loughlin, September 1992; Silin, 1995).

Constructing a Profession
The professionalization of early childhood education focuses on improving the status of the field, generating respect for teachers, and improving educational opportunities for children, a clearly warranted agenda. However, critical sociologists have demonstrated that professionalization can become a conservative act, preventing teachers from examining political assumptions underlying professional action (Grace,

1978; Larson, 1977). As professional expectations become institutionalized, professionalism supports the status quo, reifying particular beliefs, knowledges, and behaviors as "truth." Teachers have learned to view themselves as apolitical, attempting to address the needs of the "universal child," free from time, context, or power agendas. Professionalism thus supports class division and masks issues of race and gender. Images underlying attempts to professionalize the field include: the creation of a gendered professionalism based on control and public policy and the maintenance of power.

PROFESSIONALISM, GENDER, AND CONTROL. The field of early childhood education can be examined as emerging from within a context in which beliefs about women served as foundational. Beginning with the child study movement, women were seen as sentimental, lacking the objectivity necessary for rational child observation (Burman, 1994). Men were viewed as detached and capable of making scientific judgments. "Objective" males constructed a psychology based on rational, hierarchical theories, reflected in the power held by psychology over education in general. For example, the professional field is grounded in a knowledge base that is not ours and has not attended to the voices of the children with whom we work. Because early childhood education is considered the application of the theoretical field of developmental psychology (Caldwell, 1984), we function in a hierarchical relationship with a group of experts outside of our field. The knowledge base that we have accepted is linear, rational, and deterministic, the stages and learning theories proposed by psychology. We have not questioned the problems with the psychology/education relationship or the limitations of the knowledge base (Silin, 1988). Whose interests are served by the knowledge? Are there other individuals and groups whose knowledge should play an equal role in grounding the profession? Further, the technologies of measurement and comparison that dominate developmental psychology result in the construction of power roles, male over female, European over non-European, adult over child, child over child.

Attempts to construct a professional image can mask issues of power and control (Silin, 1988). The language of professionalism has different meanings depending on the interest group(s) to be served–psychologists, administrators, businessmen attempting to sell test instruments and curriculum materials. In the early part of this century, the unification of a profession was used to place women in teaching positions, with administration controlled by men. Women were described as patient, obedient, generous, and silent. Although recently challenged by the introduction of alternative teaching structures and professional perspectives (Pinar, 1994; Grumet, 1988), the field is not considered intellectual or requiring cognitive ability, a perpetual gender and power issue. Philosophical assumptions that focus on women as child caretakers have reified the field as "women's work" (Miller, 1992), yet, women's life experiences have been prohibited from the organization and practice of schooling (Grumet, 1988). Women are expected to provide warmth and caring without developing or expressing intellect or challenge.

"Educators," both male and female, who led the common school movement justified the use of female teachers as frugal and moral. Horace Mann openly contended that women could be paid less than men. Catherine Beecher, founder of the Central Committee for Promoting National Education and the daughter of a Calvinist minister, argued that the feminization of teaching would result in morally superior schools. Feminine submissiveness, self-sacrifice, and domesticity could be used to shape a national collective character of self-reliance and independence. As Grumet explains, "the good daughter had found a way to advance women into the public sphere without disturbing the dominance of the partiarchical authority" (Grumet, 1988, p. 40).

Women were felt to be ideal workers with children. Elizabeth Peabody, in her introduction to a collection of activities by Froebel (1878), describes the self-denial required of the ideal mother, the ultimate feminine role. The ideal mother leads her child's free activity by obediently controlling her own will. The kindergarten movement combined this submissive mother view with the sentimental notion that women become all things to all children: physician, artist, poet, philosopher, priest. This image of the ideal woman as the ideal mother was directly applied to teaching. The ideal teacher became one who was controlled by her superiors and could control her children (Grumet, 1988).

Women were invited into schools by male educators and were expected to educate children in the language, rules, and expectations of the patriarchy. The active, connected, nurturant life experiences of women were denied as they yielded to the partiarchical ethos of schooling. The integrity, status, and lived experience of family and community were exploited as women were taught to contribute to their own oppression and control and were complicit in the construction of environments and perspectives that objectify and control children. This image is reflected today as teachers continue to be managed by principals, superintendents, state departments, and predetermined curricula.

POLICY AND THE MAINTENANCE OF POWER. Finally, the image of public policy as an unbiased vehicle for the protection of young children is problematic. We create standards, policies, and programs with the assumption that differences are pathologies rather than alternative and respected ways of experiencing and perceiving the world (Silin, 1995). We have constructed a world in which we assume we must intervene into the lives of others in the name of individual and social welfare. Beliefs that children, their families, and their communities are substandard have been fostered. Our patriarchal stance has been one of superiority, a missionary zeal to save those who are different than ourselves and educate those who are ignorant.

Policies conceptualized with the best of intentions have not been analyzed for underlying biases and assumptions. We have come to function as if we can and must tell "other people" how to raise and educate their children (Delpit, 1993). Head Start is a prime example of this pathological intervention, constructed with the assumption that deficient parenting is the reason for poverty (Wrigley, 1991). Robert Cooke, the chair of Head Start's original planning committee, described the program as an "effort to interrupt the cycle of poverty, the nearly inevitable sequence of poor parenting" (Wrigley, 1991, p. 196). This view creates an environment in which we can ignore societal conditions that lead to marginalization and promote division by race, class, and gender.

Children of low-income families have been considered socially and intellectually incompetent and in need of intervention. This perspective denies the multiple positive ways in which parents may view the world and interact with their children and blames children and their families for societal conditions. The addition of children with disabilities to Head Start programs in the 1970s and the recent focus on the "at-risk" child (Swadener and Lubeck, 1995) further ghettoizes children (Mallory, 1994). Now all those who are different are either placed in one national early childhood program or have been (or will be) identified for social services. Our power structure is complete; we have developed a method to identify and control the "poor" and the "different."

In the United States, we voice a rhetoric of concern for our children, but we have not accepted public responsibility for the well being of all of society's children and families. Although we intervene into the lives of particular groups of children, insist on demonstrating that certain parents are unqualified and incompetent, and remove children from families that are expertly judged as inferior, we continue to reject measures that would support family and child possibility by increasing economic, social, and educational opportunity. For example, although large numbers of women have always needed to work and increasingly more women are choosing to work, we continue to reject national child care proposals. Policy continues to support the controlling position that mothers are responsible for raising the next generation. Community responsibility for family and child support is not seriously considered. Public policy has either maintained or increased societal control over children, women, people living in low socioeconomic conditions, and people identified as different. Possibilities have not increased; individuals have been isolated and damaged.

Revolutionary Images
In 1995, again at an American Educational Research Association Conference, I attended a debate on Developmentally Appropriate Practice. As the notion was critiqued, an early childhood educator again exclaimed "Why is there a problem with psychology? We can't throw the baby out with the bath water!" We are not "throwing the baby out with the bath water;" we must recognize that a psychological construction of the child is *not the actual child.* This psychological construction is not the baby. Broadened philosophical perspectives, recognition of cultural diversity, and even current discourse in developmental psychology (Rogoff, 1990) have lead to the realization that human development (known as the foundation for early childhood education) has been largely constructed from a monocultural perspective (Lerner, Winter, 1992) The psychologized vision of middle-class development and education may not be the vision that would empower diverse groups of children, female children, or even all of their teachers. Using psychology and a deficit human perspective, we have constructed a field in which children, their teachers, and their families are silenced, pathologized, disrespected, and controlled.

We can be proud of our work (however grounded in psychology, monocultural biases, and positivist thought) as attempting to place the child first, but we cannot separate our field from the political, historical, and cultural context from which it has emerged. As we have used human development theory to place the child first, the voices of children living their everyday lives have been systematically excluded. We have created a field by responding to the voices of "experts" from the dominant culture (Delpit, 1993). I therefore join with others (Kessler and Swadener, 1992) in proposing a reconceptualization of our field, a reconceptualization that is open to continuous thorough critique, recognizing that the child is not independent from larger forces in our society. This reconceptualization would require new images, perhaps revolutionary images, leading us to controversial and most likely revolutionary actions. We would be required to examine our personal and professional values and beliefs, our assumptions about life, society, and education. We would be forced to look at the hidden messages in our own history, acknowledging the political and moral agendas that underlie even the best of intentions. We would be forced to confront different philosophical and educational questions, as well as different forms of knowledge and different ways of knowing. Most likely, we would need to learn to live with ambiguity, the realization that any description of human beings (children) limits the possibilities that we as educators provide for them.

Reconceptualizing the Field
Critical reconceptualization (Pinar, 1994) is a continuous, never-ending process; the work is never complete, questions never fully answered. Reconceptualization begins with a critique of the field. However, the critique is carried forward, becoming a method of thought and the foundation for action. Reconceptualization is often ambiguous, involving not only the identification of what exists, but the construction of a collective vision. I do not believe that there is any one way, or one direction, in which we reconceptualize our field. I do believe that our reconceptualizations cannot be independent of our history, culture, time, or context. In a democratic society (and/or a world in which equity is a goal), reconceptualization would involve sharing our values and biases openly, respecting and valuing multiple realities and possibilities, and intersubjective collaboration through which values and realities are shared and action is taken. The following ideas are my attempt to contribute to our collective dialogue, our aspirations, our new beginning.

From within this democratic context, and with the help of others (Silin, 1995; Kincheloe, 1993; Kessler and Swadener, 1992), I propose the following themes for the field: (1) the achievement of social justice and equal opportunity for younger members of society, (2) education as hearing and responding to the voices of younger human beings in their everyday lives, and (3) professionalism as the development of a critical disposition in the pursuit of social justice. Perhaps these themes would be more appropriately identified as values that would serve as the foundation for the construction of images that guide the field, professional and personal language(s), and actions that are taken within practice.

Insuring Social Justice and Care
Focusing on childhood as distinct, separate, and psychological, we have denied our connectedness to the younger members of our society (and world) as human beings. We have controlled, oppressed, and limited them. Their voices have remained silent under the weight of our psychological, educational, and policy constructions of and for them. They are poor, hungry, dropping out of life, experiencing violence, and facing institutionalized assaults on their families, cultures and values. Our view of childhood is not improving the lives of younger human beings. I recommend that we place our construction of childhood into the historical and cultural context from which it has arisen, eliminating childhood as the foundation for our actions. Our new foundation should be to insure social justice and an ethic of care for younger human beings, a social justice that leads to greater possibility, liberation, and the development of a just and caring community (Giroux and Simon, 1989) without oppressing older human beings.

New and different questions would be asked. Are we truly hearing the voices of everyone involved? What are the underlying messages in our beliefs, goals, and actions? "How is human possibility enhanced/ diminished here?" (Giroux & Simon, 1989, p. 250) Power relations between sexes, socioeconomic groups, ethnic groups, and generations would be acknowledged for the oppressive states that they generate. Patriarchal values, so often presented as genderless and natural, would be continually evaluated. Goals for action would include decolonization, the elimination of inequity, injustice, and privilege, and the construction of a societal community that cares about and facilitates life-affirming emancipation for all of its members.

Social justice would include an "ethic of care" (Noddings, 1992) in which the human person (including the body) is respected. Knowledge would be viewed as indeterminate, mind/body dualisms eliminated as well as other forms of categorical determinism (e.g. intellect/emotion, social/individual). Being with other human beings would become a form of caring in which knowledge and interpersonal relationships were always integrated (Silin, 1995). Social justice would not (and most likely could not) exist without an ethic of care in which concern for others and human connection thrive (Martin, 1986).

Hearing Voices from Everyday Lives

Early childhood educators in the 1990s are constructing methodologies, guidelines, and policy recommendations that continue to privilege experiences most often found in middle-class environments and a form of logic that promotes both gender stereotypes and male domination. Excellent examples can be found in Piagetian constructivist programs and in the determinism and marketing (by NAEYC and others) of Developmentally Appropriate Practice. We continue to structure a field around models based on the psychologized child. Even when a somewhat non-psychologized model such as Reggio Emilia (Edwards, Gandini, and Forman, 1993) emerges, we ignore the context in which it was constructed and function as if universal application were possible. Not only have we not heard the voices of children, but our own voices (in the form of child development knowledge, best practices, child-centeredness, concern for the protection of children, etc.) have dominated their lives. I propose that psychological models, learning theories, and management and intervention models also be placed into the political and historical context from which they have arisen, that we acknowledge the role of these constructions in the creation of hegemony and oppression. I would recommend that we reconceptualize our field as one in which young human beings create their own voice(s), and we make every attempt to actually hear what is being said (Delpit, 1993).

To hear the voices of children, we must first accept as legitimate those who have been most often ignored and silenced. In our construction of childhood, younger human beings have become the ultimate "Other." This construction has to some extent legitimized children as having voices; however, these voices have been controlled and determined. We have continuously spoken for them. Further, we have not accepted the multiple voices impacting children in the world outside of our control except when we perceive them as forces that either support or inhibit our goals. The everyday lives of younger human beings must be viewed as legitimate, multidirectional, and multi-dimensional.

In the end, we can only hope to hear the voices of younger human beings through our joint participation in their world. We can only hope to share in their lives. However, we can work with them to explore and hear how they wish to create their own texts. "Radical" methods that have informed our own lives, such as body knowing (Dewey, 1959), phenomenological methods (Weber, 1984), and the arts (Coe, 1984), are possible constructions that can provide beginnings. We can share our own childhood experiences. We can offer a field in which hearing and experiencing the world with the younger members of our society is of utmost importance. There is/will be no set of methods that would give voice to all human beings. Identities, positions, and contexts will constantly shift as we explore our relationships to each other. Ultimately, we cannot speak for children. Our field must become one in which we continually search for ways to connect their lives to ours, ways to hear and respond to their voices.

Pursuing Social Justice

Early childhood educators can, in a traditional sense, be considered child advocates. Perhaps more than any other group, we have endeavored to stand for children. The current push for developmentally appropriate practice is an attempt to establish educational environments in which children are not damaged, in which they are not expected to sit at a desk all day completing worksheets (an activity that would be difficult for any of us, at whatever age). We have constructed a field whose professional actions are grounded in the best of intentions. However, these actions were based on psychologically biased knowledge that serves to support our patriarchal condition. Our professional actions have often supported the very structure that we would challenge for the sake of children. I would propose that we construct a new form of professionalism, grounded in the development of a critical disposition. The goals of this new professionalism would be social justice and care for younger members of society and the construction of education in which the voices of these younger human beings are heard.

The development of a critical disposition would require that we learn to ask new kinds of questions, that we learn to analyze the political, linguistic, cultural, social, and power context in which our own lives have been constructed. How have children been objectified by schools? by society? How can connections be made with younger members of society? How do we give voice to all of our views? What does social justice mean for younger members of society who are cared for by parents and others? How have our values and daily behaviors resulted in the continuation of oppression or privilege? How does a critical disposition impact identity? How can we build connections that support our efforts to attain social justice? The work of feminists (Pagano, 1990; and Grumet, 1980), critical theorists (Kincheloe, 1993; Giroux and McLaren, 1989), and queer theorists (Cruikshank, 1982; Garber, 1994) can provide guidance. The work of such scholars as Foucault (1965, 1970, 1977, 1978, 1980) can be used to assist us in understanding power relationships within our discourse, cultural representations, and hidden histories. Ultimately, we must construct our own critical dispositions, our own ways of coming to hear all voices, and our own ways of striving to attain social justice and care.

The discursive practices within our society and within the field of education have emerged from and promoted patriarchy and domination. We must learn to interrogate this form of language as well as construct languages that foster justice, liberation, and possibility. As critical theorists have suggested, a discourse of liberation is possible that would be grounded in notions of possibility, identity, emancipation, and life affirmation. Grumet (1988) and Pagano (1990) have suggested the language of domesticity and nurturance, the language of ordinary experience (Lortie, 1975). We must construct language(s) that foster connections (e.g., care, intersubjectivity, collaboration) rather than separation and patriarchal judgment (e.g., appropriate/inappropriate, adult/child, expert/novice, right/wrong).

This new professionalism would require that we accept the political nature of our views of the world and the actions that we take. We would admit that no one is politically neutral; when we perceive ourselves as neutral, we support the status quo, the dominant perspective. We would admit to our values, biases and agendas, but also attempt to critique those views as they relate to social justice and hearing the voices of young members of our society. Our actions would be based on this critical disposition with the realization that actions that would foster social justice may not be popular, traditional, or conform to dominant expectations. We would accept controversy, conflict, ambiguity, and even revolution if those conditions appear necessary for the attainment of social justice.

Revolutionary Images

Within a profession whose goals were social justice and hearing the voices of children, revolutionary images could provide a framework for action. The images that I propose here could actually apply to all human beings who want to be listened to, cared for, treated fairly, and given just opportunities. These images are: human respect, multiple realities, subjectivity/agency, radical democracy, and revolutionary action. They are revolutionary images because we have not listened to and cared for each other; we have oppressed, dominated, and controlled each other. They are revolutionary in that fostering these images would allow us to no longer support an ethic of domination and determinism. We would take action that would challenge patriarchal, reductionist, oppressive perspectives. We would be open to controversy and ridicule. However, we would not forget that our first concerns are the attainment of social justice and care for young human beings and to construct environments in which we attend to the voices of their lives.

HUMAN RESPECT. Respect for other human beings can of course take multiple forms. Yet, when placed in the context of social justice, our connections as fellow human beings would be placed at the forefront. The distinction between child and adult would be set aside in so far as the separation leads to the dehumanization of the younger members of our society. We all want to be valued and appreciated simply because we are human; we want to be equitably and fairly connected to other human beings.

MULTIPLE REALITIES. In order to share in the lives of others, to hear their voices, multiple forms of knowledge and multiple ways of knowing must be affirmed. We have all functioned (or tried to function) in a context in which truth and knowledge are upheld as predetermined, even sacred. This reductionism has silenced the younger members of society and even many adults. The acceptance of and appreciation for multiple realities would help us to understand that there are multiple "ways of being in the world" (Silin, 1995, p. 202). Knowledge is not necessarily separated from body or emotion. Doubt and uncertainty are legitimate and can be positive. We cannot hear and respond to the young members of society without accepting and appreciating the notion of multiple realities.

SUBJECTIVITY/AGENCY. Human beings are subjects in their own lives, yet our educational discourse treats children and, at times, teachers as if they are objects to be observed, controlled, protected, and manipulated. As we learn to make connections with younger human beings, we must foster democratic relationships. Human beings are not separate from the world or their everyday lived experiences. The younger members of our society (and all of us) must be affirmed as the subjects of their own lives, the agents or initiators of action, the force in their world.

RADICAL DEMOCRACY. A radical democratic perspective would not only be a voice for equity and justice, but would embrace difference, dialogue, and struggle. Democracy would be understood as more complicated than voting. Politics would be recognized as the struggle for power among various discourses. Young members of society would be encouraged to claim their own culture and history (Macedo, 1994), decolonizing dominant interpretations.

REVOLUTIONARY ACTION. We can all become revolutionaries in the pursuit of democracy. First, young human beings can themselves become active participants in the construction of an increasingly more democratic society. As early childhood educators, we can collaborate with children, their families, and communities to construct liberatory educational practices in both our everyday lives and in the unique educational opportunities that we work together to provide. We can all share in the recognition that democracy, education, and society are not separate. Our actions should not be confined to the walls of a school building or the homes of the people with whom we work. We, along with children, their families, and community members, must construct actions that lead to social justice and care for all of us.

Recently, one of my colleagues in early childhood education told my department chairperson that these ideas are too revolutionary. Ideas can cause trouble. I contend that we must cause trouble; our voices must be heard as advocates and activists for social justice and care, not only for the younger members of our society, but for everyone. When any of us must endure inequity or injustice, when there are those who are not heard, as human beings we are all diminished.

Portions of the first section of this chapter were presented at the American Educational Research Association Conference in San Francisco, CA, in April 1995.

References

Abbott, P. (1989). Family lifestyles and structures. In W. Stainton Rogers, D. Hevey, & E. Ash (Eds.), *Child abuse and neglect: Facing the challenge*. London: Batsford.

Ainsworth, M.D.S., Bell, S.M., and Stayton, D.J. (1974). Infant-mother attachment and social development: "Socialization" as a product of reciprocal responsiveness to signals. In M.P.M. Richards (Ed.), *The integration of the child into a social world*. Cambridge: Cambridge University Press.

Apple, M. (1992). The text and cultural politics. *Educational Review,* 21(7), 4-11.

Aries, P. (1962). *Centuries of childhood–A social history of family life.* New York: Knopf.

Bowlby, J. (1951). *Maternal care and mental health.* Geneva: World Health Organization.

Brannen, J., and Wilson, G. (Eds.). (1987). *Give and take in families: Studies in resource distribution.* London: Allen & Unwin.

Bredekamp, S. (Ed.). (1987). *Developmentally appropriate practice in early child programs serving children from birth through age eight.* Washington, DC: National Association for the Education of Young Children.

Burman, E. (1994). *Deconstructing developmental psychology.* New York: Routledge.

Caldwell, B. (1984). Growth and development. *Young Children,* 39(6), 53-56.

Caplan, P. (1985). Mother-blaming in major clinical journals. *American Journal of Orthopsychiatry,* 55(3), 345-353.

Cleverly, J., and Phillips, D.C. (1986). *Visions of childhood: Influential models from Locke to Spock.* New York: Teachers College Press.

Coe, R.N. (1984). *When the grass was taller: Autobiography and the experience of childhood.* New Haven, CT: Yale University Press.

Cruikshank, M. (Ed.). (1982). *Lesbian studies: Present and future.* New York: Feminist Press.

Darwin, Charles (1859). *On the origin of species by means of natural selection.* London: John Murray.

Delpit, L. (1993). The silenced dialogue: Power and pedagogy in educating other people's children. In L. Weis, and M. Fine (Eds.), *Beyond silenced voices: Class, race, and gender in United States schools* (pp. 119-139). Albany, NY: SUNY Press.

DeMause, L. (1974). *The history of childhood.* New York: The Psychohistory Press.

Dewey, J. (1959). The school and society. In M.S. Dworkin (Ed.), *Dewey on education* (pp. 33-90). New York: Teachers College Press. (Original work published 1899).

Donzelot, J. (1979). The *policing of families.* New York: Pantheon.

Edwards, C., Gandini, L., and Forman, G. (1993). *The hundred languages of children: The Reggio Emilia approach to early childhood education.* Norwood, NJ: Ablex.

Foucault, M. (1965). *Madness and civilization: A history of insanity in the age of reason.* New York: Pantheon.

Foucault, M. (1970). *The order of things: An archaeology of the human sciences.* New York: Vintage Books.

Foucault, M. (1977). *Discipline and punish: The birth of the prison.* New York: Pantheon.

Foucault, M. (1978). *The history of sexuality: Vol. I, II, III.* New York: Pantheon.

Foucault, M. (1980). *Power/knowledge: Selected interviews and other writings 1972-1977.* New York: Pantheon.

Freire, P., and Macedo, D. (1987). *Literacy: Reading the word and the world.* Westport, CT: Bergin & Garvey.

Froebel, F. (1878). *Mother-play and nursery songs.* F.E. Dwitht and J. Jarvis (Trans.). Boston: Lorthrop, Lee, and Shepard.

Garber, L. (Ed.). (1994). *Tilting the tower.* New York: Routledge.

Gilligan, C. (1982). *In a different voice: Psychological theory and women's development.* Cambridge, MA: Harvard University Press.

Giroux, H.A., and McLaren, P. (Eds.) (1989). *Critical pedagogy, the state, and cultural struggle.* Albany, NY: SUNY Press.

Giroux, H.A., & Simon, R. (1989). Popular culture and critical pedagogy: Everyday life as a basis for curriculum knowledge. In H.A. Giroux and P. McLaren, *Critical pedagogy, the state, and cultural struggle* (pp. 236-252). Albany, NY: SUNY Press.

Gittins, D. (1985). *The family in question.* New York: Macmillan.

Gould, S.J. (1981). *The mismeasure of man.* New York: W.W. Norton & Co.

Grace, G. (1978). *Teachers, ideology and control.* London: Routledge & Kegan Paul.

Grumet, M. R. (1988). *Bitter milk: Women and teaching.* Amherst: The University of Massachusetts Press.

Harris, A. (1987). The rationalization of infancy. In J. Broughton (Ed.). *Critical theories of psychological development.* (pp 31-60), New York: Plenum Press.

Hoyles, M. (1979). *Changing childhood.* London: Writers and Readers Publishing Cooperative.

Kessen, W. (1981). The child and other cultural inventions. In Kessel, F.S., and Siegel, A.W. (Eds.), *The child and other cultural inventions.* (pp 26-39), New York: Praeger.

Kessler, S., and Swadener, B.B. (1992). *Reconceptualizing the early*

childhood curriculum: Beginning the dialogue. New York: Teachers
College Press.

Kincheloe, J. L. (1993). *Toward a critical politics of teacher thinking.*
Westport, CT: Bergin & Garvey.

Kincheloe, J. L. (1991). *Teachers as researchers: Qualitative inquiry as
a path to empowerment.* New York: Falmer Press.

Larson, M. (1977). *The rise of professionalism.* Berkeley: University of
California Press.

Lerner, R.M. (Winter, 1992). *Diversity.* Newsletter of the Society for
Research in Child Development.

Lincoln, Y.S., and Guba, E.G. (1985). *Naturalistic inquiry.* Beverly
Hills, CA: Sage.

Lortie, D. (1975). *School teacher.* Chicago: University of Chicago
Press.

Lubeck, S. (1994). The politics of developmentally appropriate
practice. In B. Mallory and R. New (Eds.), *Diversity and developmentally appropriate practices: Challenges for early childhood
education.* (pp. 17-39). New York: Teachers College Press.

Macedo, D. (1994). *Literacies of power: What Americans are not
allowed to know.* Boulder, CO: Westview Press.

Mallory, B. (1994). Inclusive policy, practice, and theory for young
children with developmental differences. In B. Mallory and R. New
(Eds.), *Diversity and developmentally appropriate practices:
Challenges for early childhood education.* (pp. 44-62). New York:
Teachers College Press.

Martin, J. R. (1986). Redefining the educated person: Rethinking the
significance of gender. *Educational Researcher,* 15(6), 6-10.

Merleau-Ponty, M. (1964). *The primacy of perception.* Evanston, IL:
Northwestern University Press.

Miller, J. L. (1992). Teachers, autobiography, and curriculum: Critical
and feminist perspectives. In S. Kessler, and B.B. Swadener (Eds.),
Reconceptualizing the early childhood curriculum. New York:
Teachers College Press.

Munn, P. (1991). Mothering more than one child. In A. Phoenix, A.
Wollett, and E. Lloyd (Eds.), *Motherhood: Meanings, practices and
ideologies.* London: Sage.

Noddings, N. (1992). *The challenge to care in schools: An alternative
approach to education.* New York: Teachers College Press.

Nsamenang, A.B. (1992). *Human development in cultural context: A
third world perspective.* Newbury Park: Sage.

O'Loughlin, M. (September 1992). *Appropriate for whom? A critique of the culture and class bias underlying developmentally appropriate practice in early childhood education.* Paper presented at the Conference on Reconceptualizing Early Childhood Education: Research, Theory, and Practice, Chicago.

Pagano, J. (1990). *Exiles and communities: Teaching in the patriarchal wilderness.* Albany, NY: SUNY Press.

Piaget, J. (1957). The child and modern physics. *Scientific American,* 197, 46-51.

Pinar, W. (1994). *Autobiography, politics and sexuality: Essays in curriculum theory 1972-1992.* New York: Peter Lang.

Polakow, Suransky, V. (1982). *The erosion of childhood.* Chicago: The University of Chicago Press.

Rogoff, B. (1990). *Apprenticeship in thinking: Cognitive development in social context.* New York: Oxford University Press.

Rorty, R. (1980). *Philosophy and the mirror of nature.* Oxford: Blackwell.

Rousseau, J.J. (1933). *Emile.* B. Foxley (Trans.), New York: Dutton.

Silin, J.G. (1987). The early childhood educator's knowledge base: A reconsideration. In L. G. Katz (Ed.), *Current topics in early childhood education,* Vol. VII. Norwood, NJ: Ablex.

Silin, J.G. (1988). On becoming knowledgeable professionals. In B. Spodek, O.N. Saracho, and Peters, D.L. (Eds.), *Professionalism and the early childhood practitioner.* New York: Teachers College Press.

Silin, J.G. (1995). *Sex, death, and the education of children: Our passion for ignorance in the age of AIDS.* New York: Teachers College Press.

Singer, E. (1992). *Child-care and the psychology of development.* New York: Routledge.

Swadener, B. and Lubeck, S. (Eds.) (1995). *Children and families "at promise": Deconstructing the discourse of risk.* Albany: SUNY Press.

Takanishi, R. (1978). Childhood as a social issue: Historical roots of contemporary child advocacy movements. *Journal of Social Issues,* 34(2), 8-28.

Tizard, B. (1991). Employed mothers and the care of young mothers. In A. Phoenix, A. Wollett, and E. Lloyd (Eds.), *Motherhood: Meanings, practices and ideologies.* London: Sage.

Walkerdine, V. (1990). *Schoolgirl fictions.* London: Verso.

Walkerdine, V. (1984). Developmental psychology and the child-centered pedagogy. In J. Henriques, W. Hollway, C. Urwin, C. Venn, and V. Walkerdine (Eds.), *Changing the subject: Psychology, social regulation and subjectivity.* London: Methuen.

Weber, E. (1984). *Ideas influencing early childhood education.* New York: Teachers College Press.

White, D. and Woollett, A. (1992). *Families: A context for development.* New York: Falmer Press.

Woodhead, M. (1990). Psychology and the cultural construction of children's needs. In A. James and A. Prout (Eds.), *Constructing and reconstructing childhood* (pp. 60-78). New York: Falmer Press.

Wrigley, J. (1991). Different care for different kids: Social class and child care policy. In L. Weis, P.G. Altbach, G.P. Kelly., and H.G. Petrie (Eds.), *Critical perspectives on early childhood education* (pp. 189-209), Albany, NY: SUNY Press.

Chapter Nine

Beyond Eurocentrism in Science Education: Promises and Problematics from a Feminist Poststructuralist Perspective

Annette Gough

Introduction

Two quotations, among many others, encapsulate much of what has directed me in developing a new orientation in my research and practice.[1] The first, from Marion Namenwirth (1986, p. 29) states that "Scientists firmly believe that as long as they are not conscious of any bias or political agenda, they are neutral and objective, when in fact they are only unconscious." Such unconsciousness is, I will argue, what we need to move beyond in science education.

The second quotation, from Evelyn Fox Keller (1985, p. 12) reflects where I have come from and provides some of the framework for where I am going:

> As a woman and a scientist, the status of outsider came to me gratis. Feminism enabled me to exploit that status as a privilege. I began to see the network of gender associations in the characteristic language of science as neither natural nor self-evident, but as contingent, and dismaying. I began to see further that these were not just ornamental images on the surface of scientific rhetoric; they were deeply embedded in the structure of scientific ideology, with recognizable implications for practice.

In her more recent work, Keller (1992, 1995) has further developed her "linguistic turn," as have many other writers who have informed my research and writings in this area. However, I have taken an additional step, guided particularly by the work of Sandra Harding (1993abcd, 1994), and I am now exploring the possibilities for science education of going beyond Eurocentrism.[2] In this paper I am working from an acceptance of feminist critiques of modern science and only draw upon them when relevant to my arguments rather than discussing them in detail. My focus here is upon critiques of the Eurocentrism of modern science as the basis for a new direction for science education research and practice. As Harding (1993b, p. 1) argues,

> There are few aspects of the "best" science educations that enable anyone to grasp how nature-as-an-object-of-knowledge is always cultural: "In science, just as in art and life, only that which is true to culture is true to nature." These elite science educations rarely expose students to systematic analyses of the social origins, traditions, meanings, practices, institutions, technologies, uses, and consequences of the natural sciences that ensure the fully historical character of the results of scientific research.

Consistent with Harding's (1993b, p. 3) assertion that "around the world as in the West, new social movements have challenged the authority of the West to impose its values and standards on peoples with histories and present concerns that are opposed to those of privileged groups in the West," in this paper I first outline some of the postcolonial critiques of Western[3] science. I then outline some of the critiques that argue for a more democratic science and, in the final section, discuss some of the promises and problematics of these critiques for new directions in science education.

Postcolonial Critiques of Science

Postcolonial critiques of science, that is, critiques of the influence of modern Western science on other cultures, have been developed contemporaneously with feminist critiques (see, for example, Birke and Hubbard, 1995; Bleier, 1986ab; Haraway, 1989, 1991; Harding, 1986, 1991, 1993bd; Hardy, 1986; Hubbard, 1981, 1995; Keller, 1985, 1992, 1995; Merchant, 1980; Namenwirth, 1986). As with these critiques, postcolonial critiques are not so much concerned with "science bashing" but rather with "pointing out how better understandings of nature result when scientific projects are linked with and incorporate projects of advancing democracy; [and that] politically regressive societies are likely to produce partial and distorted accounts of the natural and social world" (Harding 1993d, p. ix). Many of these critiques have been mutually informative. For example, the works of Vandana Shiva (1989), Donna Haraway (1989) and Sandra Harding (1993d) have informed both feminist and postcolonial critiques of science.

Postcolonial critiques of science also fit within a broader framework of critiques of Eurocentrism, colonialism, and the construction of the non-West as "Other" developed by people such as Chinua Achebe (1960); Ashcroft, Griffiths, and Tiffin (1989); Homi Bhabha (1985, 1986, 1988, 1994); Ashis Nandy (1986); Ngugi Wa Thiong'O (1986); Edward Said (1978, 1985, 1993); Gayatri Spivak (1987, 1990ab, 1993); and those authors collected in Adam and Tiffin (1991); Ferguson et al. (1990), and Tiffin and Lawson (1994) to name but a few. According to these critiques, women and non-Europeans have been constructed as "Other" in the dualism that placed rational mechanistic men as masters of all nature, women and slaves. As Berman (1989, pp. 232-233) argues,

> Aristotelian dualism became the natural, and the ideal, precursor of the ideology of nature as a machine driven by immutable laws, the direct progenitor of our present-day mechanism.... His identification of the leisured male master with the rational, the mind, and the nonproductive (science for science's sake) and women and slaves with the irrational and the useful was patently self-serving.

Within science, the postcolonial critiques argue that Western science has resulted in partial and distorted accounts of nature and social relations, and that, as the Third World Network argues (1993, p. 485),

> Modern science and technology has dislocated Third World societies, destroyed traditional cultures and played havoc with the environment of Third World nations. It has also replaced a way of knowing which is multi-dimensional and based on synthesis, in Third World societies, with a linear, clinical, inhuman and rationalist mode of thought.

There is now widespread agreement that "nature-as-an-object-of-knowledge is always cultural" (Harding 1993b, p. 1); thus, the cognitive content of science claims is coherent with the cultural concerns of the society in which the knowledge is generated, and these cultural concerns have influenced the directions taken in the development of scientific knowledge.[4]

That there is a need for scientists "to learn to reconceptualize science, its methods, theories, and goals, without the language and metaphors of control and domination" (Bleier 1986a, p. 16) has also been noted by Merchant (1980), Keller (1985), and other historians of science. As an alternative which "may enable less partial and distorted descriptions and explanations," Harding (1991, p. 301) proposes the use of "metaphors and models that stress context rather than isolated traits and behaviors, interactive rather than linear relations, and democratic rather than authoritarian models of order in both research and nature."

Modern science has argued that the West is "progressive, rational and civilized...in contrast to the backward, irrational and primitive 'rest'" (Harding 1993b, p. 7) and the knowledge claims of the non-Western cultures have thus been denigrated and silenced. It is therefore important to analyze the Western, racist, gendered, and classist agendas which have directed Western science as a strategy for advancing a more democratic science. As John Dewey (Harding 1993b, p. 3) argued, "an effective pursuit of democracy requires those who bear the consequences of decisions have a proportionate share in making them." However, such democracy appears to be absent in the experiences of some writers in this area. Susantha Goonatilake (1984), for example, argues that Asian scientists are kept dependent on Western science, and their scientific creativity is stifled, while indigenous science traditions are overlooked. Shiva (1989) provides a critique of the two sacred categories of Western science's theory of progress: modern scientific knowledge and economic development. She argues that the imposition of this theory on the Third World is threatening to annihilate nature and humankind and she seeks to oppose and challenge it through asserting a non-violent, non-gendered, and humanly inclusive alternative. Harding (1993b, p. 8) argues similarly that "non-Western science traditions need to be evaluated in more objective ways, and that the Western traditions need to be more objectively situated in world history." Through examining Western science's complicity with racist, gendered, imperialist, and Eurocentric projects, we should "gain a more critical, more scientific perspective on an important part of that Western 'unconscious' and thus on the history some groups in the West and 'elsewhere' have been busy making" (Harding 1993b, p. 19). This is an enormous challenge for both science and science education research.

Toward a Democratic Science

A strong theme throughout the feminist critiques of science is concern with criticizing the objective, value-free claims made of science. As Hubbard (1981, p. 218) argues, "An era's science is part of its politics, economics and sociology: it is generated by them and in turn helps to generate them." Bleier (1986b, p. 63) similarly argues that "scientists cannot simply hang their subjectivities up on a hook outside the laboratory door.... [A]s is the case for everyone else, scientists bring their beliefs, values, and world views to their work" thus affecting their research questions, assumptions, interpretations, and activities. Building on the work of Berger and Luckmann (1966), Hubbard (1981, pp. 218-219) argues that to become conscious of the biases introduced by our implicit, unstated, and often unconscious beliefs about the nature of reality is more difficult than anything else we do, but "we must try to do it if our picture of the world is to be more than a reflection of various aspects of ourselves and of our social arrangements." Harding (1986, p. 27) further develops this notion by arguing that "objectivity never has been and could not be increased by value-neutrality. Instead, it is commitments to antiauthoritarian, antielitist, participatory, and emancipatory values and projects that increase the objectivity of science."

The relationship between science and democracy is an interesting one. For example, Needham (Harding 1993d, p. 432) argues that "democracy might...almost in a sense be termed that practice of which science is the theory." Other postcolonial critics, including those represented in Harding's (1993d) anthology, argue that modern science is very undemocratic. Yet there is a continuing search for re-establishing science in a democratic future.

As Ciencia para el Pueblo (in Harding 1993b: 431) writes,

> If we do know that there exists a science which is imperialist in its uses, its organization, its method and its ideology, there must exist, and in fact there does exist, an anti-imperialist science. It is still in its infancy, and it takes different forms, according to the conditions it is found in.

Alas, Pueblo does not provide much detail of this anti-imperialist science, except to "look for means to put our scientific knowledge at the service of the people." While some postcolonial critics of modern science are developing some concrete proposals (see, for example, Shiva 1989; Third World Network 1993), some possibilities worthy of serious consideration are forthcoming from discussions of feminist science. For me, such discussions have potential to be broadened to include other notions of a more democratic future for science and science education.

The questions of whether there should be a feminist science, what the term means, and whether it is an oxymoron, have been topics for discussion for some time: "the question...has been raised by virtually everyone who participates in or contemplates the feminist discussions of the sciences" (Harding 1991, p. 296). She also notes (1991, p. 297) that "traditions in the philosophy of science and sociology of science can encourage conflicting answers to the question of whether there can be feminist science," as both feminism and science are "contested zones." A variety of these answers are discussed in this section.

Bleier (1986a, pp. 15-16), for example, provides some distinguishing, but, she believes, "inadequate" principles for a feminist science:

- scientists acknowledge that they, like everyone else, have values and beliefs, and that these affect how they practice their science.

- scientists explore and understand in what ways these subjectivities specifically affect their perspectives and approaches, their actual scientific methods.

- scientists are explicit about their assumptions; honest, thoughtful and careful in their methods; open in their interpretations of each study and its significance; clear in describing the possible pitfalls in the work and their conclusions about it; and responsible in the language used to convey their results to the scientific and nonscientific public.

Bleier (1986a, p. 16) continues her argument by suggesting that in enacting these principles feminist scientists

> may wish to claim a feminist approach to scientific knowledge that in its language, methods, interpretations, and goals, acknowledges its commitments to particular human values and to the solution of particular human problems.... [This] would aim to eliminate research that leads to the exploitation and destruction of nature, the destruction of the human race and other species, and that justifies the oppression of people because of race, gender, class, sexuality, or nationality.

For Bleier (1986a, p. 16) this is a science of the future, or, as Harding (1991, p. 299) argues, it will happen "only after the revolution," as it requires profound changes "in a system that is based on power, control and domination and that recognizes and rewards those who support and reinforce its ideologies and aims." Elizabeth Fee reserves the term feminist science for a possible future science. She argues (1983, p. 22) that what is currently being developed "is not feminist science, but a feminist critique of existing science." According to Fee (1983, p. 22), our sexist society has developed a sexist science; however, a feminist society can be expected to develop a feminist science, although "for us to imagine [this] is rather like asking a medieval peasant to imagine the theory of genetics," nevertheless, "our inability to imagine a fully developed feminist science" should not be taken "as evidence that a feminist science is itself impossible."

Donna Haraway (1986, p. 81) similarly argues that feminist science is a radical project in that it

> construct[s] a different set of boundaries and possibilities for what can count as knowledge for everyone within specific historical circumstances.... Feminist science is not biased science, nor is it disinterested in accurate description and powerful theory. My thesis is that feminist science is about changing possibilities, not about having a special route to what it means to be human–or animal.

For Haraway, narratives and discourses are paramount in "what might problematically be named feminist science.... Both feminist and scientific discourses are critical projects built in order to destabilize and reimagine their methods and objects of knowledge in complex power fields" (1989, p. 324). She argues for altering the structure of a field through destabilizing it rather than "replacing false versions with true ones" (1986, p. 81).

There appears to be growing acceptance of the notion of such an approach to science, just as the dichotomies of science should be transcended. For example, Haraway (1989), Hardy (1986), and Small (1984) report that feminist primatologists have succeeded in re-directing their field, its methodologies, basic assumptions and principles, inter-pretations, and conclusions. As Haraway (1986, p. 80) argues, "Primatology is the scene of a feminist scientific revolution, one that has changed the way both men and women practice their science." Similarly, feminist psychologists, such as Gilligan (1982), have caused others in their field to question their methodologies, assumptions, interpretations, and conclusions. In both fields, the feminists have undermined the most influential theories which grounded present-day notions of interrelationships among primates, which served as models of our ancestors and of cognitive and moral development in humans. These effects reflect Keller's (1992, p. 31) argument:

> Different metaphors of mind, nature, and the relation between them, reflect different psychological stances of observer to observed; these, in turn, give rise to different cognitive perspectives–to different aims, questions, and even to different methodological and explanatory preferences.

It is not only important to question methodologies, assumptions, interpretations, and conclusions from a feminist perspective, however. We also need to raise questions from the perspective of other races, classes, and cultures.

Sandra Harding has written frequently on the theme of feminist science, relating it particularly to feminist epistemology. She argues that feminists need successor science projects–"they are central to transferring the power to change social relations from the 'haves' to the 'have nots'" (1986, p. 195). More recently she has argued that "there already are feminist sciences and that it is beneficial to both feminism and the sciences to continue developing them" (1991, pp. 296-297), and that those who argue that feminist sciences are not yet possible "appear to have only the natural sciences in mind" (1991, p. 305). Instead, she believes that scientific knowledge-seeking, directed by existing feminist theories and agendas, should be considered as "research traditions that compete with a plurality of theoretical approaches in their respective fields" (1991, p. 305), and that natural sciences "are a particular kind of social science and should be so conceptualized" (1991, p. 309). However, she cautions that such knowledge-seeking needs to be disloyal to conventional assumptions such as restricting the use of the term "science" to the natural sciences rather than including the social sciences. She argues that because feminist science is still disputing the foundations of the field it is not a real science. It does not accept metatheorizing as an integral part of science proper but accepts that "'real science' is only what the modern West has done or chooses to call science" (1991, p. 306). For Harding,

> the emergence of feminist science depends not on whether all
> fields of contemporary science can be transformed but only on
> whether some processes of seeking knowledge about the natural
> and social worlds can be developed which are directed by feminist
> rather than androcentric goals (Harding, 1991, p. 310, emphasis
> in original).

Such feminist sciences require transformation of the logics of science
and of feminism and shares much in common with the moves toward a
democratic science for the future.

Some writers on feminist science have been exploring the links
between feminism and postmodernism in science, although many are
ambivalent about the relationship between feminism and the Enlightenment. Jane Flax (1990) for example, argues that feminism is solidly in
the terrain of the postmodern, as does Haraway (1988, 1991), whereas
Christine Di Stefano (1990) argues that Western feminism is located in
the modern ethos and puts a feminist case against postmodernism.
Nancy Hartsock (1987, p. 191) also argues "that postmodernism
represents a dangerous approach for any marginalized group to adopt."
She is particularly concerned about the universalizing claims that creep
back into the work of postmodernists, even though they oppose such
claims. It is not an intention of this paper to resolve these discussions
but to note, as does Harding (1991, p. 183-4), that "many different
social groups are trying to think their way out of the hegemony of
modern Western political philosophy and the worlds it has constructed."
Such groups include feminists, the ecology movement, and
marginalized groups.

Harding (1991, p. 184) sees the tensions between Enlightenment
and postmodernist agendas in feminism as healthy: "The conflict
between our different and valuable political projects is just what is
creating in feminist thought a necessary ambivalence toward the
Enlightenment and toward the beliefs and politics of Postmodernists."
She concludes that "both feminist science and epistemology proponents
and also their Postmodernist critics stand with one foot in the
Enlightenment and the other in the present moment–or, rather, the
future.... At this moment in our history, our feminisms need both
Enlightenment and Postmodernist agendas" (1991, p. 187). This is a
position with which I am comfortable in this still emerging field. I find
particularly attractive her discussion about postmodernists assuming
symmetry between truth and falsity and her assertion that "feminist

thought can aim to produce less partial and distorted representations without having to assert their absolute, complete, universal, or eternal adequacy" (1991, p. 187), which she sees as bridging feminist science and epistemology and feminist postmodernism.

A concern raised by Haraway (1986, 1989, 1991), Harding (1986, 1991, 1993c) and Hartsock (1987) that has not been addressed by many others, but which is pertinent to this argument, is the intersection of feminist and postcolonial discourses in the sciences. Haraway (1986, p. 80) in particular writes of monkeys and apes having "been enlisted in Western scientific story telling to determine what is meant by human: what it means to be female, to be animal, to be other than man." Even a feminist perspective on primatology is a form of simian orientalism, remaining "deeply Western: deeply marked by the logics of nature and culture, by Western searches for the self in the mirror of a subordinated other, by the constantly repeating origin stories that ground Western political culture" (Haraway, 1986, p. 80). Harding (1991, p. 268, emphasis in original) discusses standpoint theories as strategy for correcting the dominant Western accounts by "moving from including others' lives and thoughts in research and scholarly projects to starting from their lives to ask research questions, develop theoretical concepts, design research, collect data, interpret findings." Hartsock (1987, p. 191), another proponent of feminist standpoint theories, also discusses ways of including the voices of marginalized people, and in doing so argues against postmodernist theories because they "merely recapitulate the effects of Enlightenment theories–theories that deny marginalized people the right to participate in defining the terms of their interaction with people in the mainstream." I disagree with Hartsock in that I believe that a promise, rather than a problematic, of adopting a feminist poststructuralist perspective in science education is that such an approach can give equal voice to both dominant and marginalized peoples' accounts in moving toward a more democratic science.

Beyond Eurocentrism in Science Education
Postcolonialism and feminism have developed as parallel discourses which have much in common, and some writers are starting to draw the two together (for example, Spivak, 1987, 1990). Feminist and post-colonial discourses both seek to re-instate the marginalized in the face of the dominant (the former colonizer), and both are oriented to the future, "positing societies in which social and political hegemonic shifts have occurred" (Ashcroft et al., 1989, p. 177). Postcolonialism

provides a possible approach, for it "challenges how imperial centers of power construct themselves through the discourse of master narratives and totalizing systems; they contest monolithic authority wielded through representations of 'brute institutional relations' and the claims of universality" (Giroux, 1992, p. 20). Feminist critique provides another, yet similar, approach from the perspective that "[w]omen in many societies have been relegated to the position of 'Other', marginalized and, in a metaphorical sense, 'colonized', forced to pursue guerrilla warfare against imperial domination from positions deeply imbedded in, yet fundamentally alienated from, that imperium" (Ashcroft et al., 1989, p. 174). The experiences of India's Chipko movement (see Merchant, 1992; Shiva, 1989), and the Kenyan Green-belt Movement (see Merchant, 1992) are examples of women pursuing ecological guerrilla warfare as attempts to maintain or achieve sustainability. As Merchant (1992, pp. 200, 206) argues, "many of the problems facing Third World women today are the historical result of colonial relations between the First and Third Worlds," but Third World women "are making the impacts of colonialism and industrial capitalism on the environment and on their own lives visible."

In this, there is both a challenge and a dilemma (or two or three) for science educators. The politics of difference goes beyond being "simply oppositional in contesting the mainstream (or maelstrom) for inclusion," and beyond being "transgressive in the avant-gardist sense of shocking conventional bourgeois audiences" and aligns itself "with demoralized, depoliticized and disorganized people in order to empower and enable social action and, if possible, to enlist collective insurgency for the expansion of freedom, democracy and individuality" (West, 1990, p. 19). We need to be aware that there are ways other than those to which we are accustomed of looking at science and science education. In the light of these feminist and postcolonial critiques of modern science, and the movements toward a more democratic science, what are the implications for science education research and practice?

For me, a major implication is that we need a different approach to science education—one which problematizes both the view of science content that science educators assume and the methodologies they use. Both content and methodologies need to take account of the critiques of modern science and strategies for achieving a more democratic science. Recognizing that there are links between language and power in the discourses of science, it would seem important to examine the multiplicity of meanings in these discourses and to provide less partial and distorted descriptions and explanations using language which stresses context, interaction, and democratic models of order. A methodology for doing this arises out of feminist poststructuralist analysis which is "a mode of knowledge production which uses poststructuralist theories of language, subjectivity, social processes and institutions to understand existing power relations and to identify areas and strategies for change" (Weedon, 1987, p. 40-41). Cleo Cherryholmes (1988, p. 177) provides further explication: "[p]oststructural analysis points beyond structure, utility, and instrumentality. Our ability to shape and design the social world can be enhanced, I hope, if we outline, examine, analyze, interpret, criticize, and evaluate the texts and discourse-practices that surround us." While my original interest grew out of feminist post-structuralist analysis, and continues to be informed by its discourses, the following discussion is informed by the broader constructions (and deconstructions) of poststructuralist analysis per se.

Working from the frames suggested by Weedon (1987) for feminist poststructuralist analysis, and by Cherryholmes (1988) and Davies (1994) for poststructuralist analysis, to date I have drafted four guiding principles for science education research which I am exploring in my own work. These principles, which are still being developed and which are all grounded in an opposition "to the longing for 'one true story' that has been the psychic motor for Western science" (Harding, 1986, p. 193), include:

- to recognize that knowledge is partial, multiple, and contradictory

- to draw attention to the racism and gender blindness in science education

- to develop a willingness to listen to silenced voices and to provide opportunities for them to be heard

- to develop understandings of the stories of which we are a part and our abilities to deconstruct them.

In proposing these principles, I recognize that there are inherent promises and problematics in their practice, some of which I now discuss.

Promises

As a way of exemplifying these principles, and illustrating how less partial and distorted descriptions and explanations may become part of the content of our science education research and pedagogical practices, I provide an example which comes from a teacher education module concerned with using indigenous knowledge, practices, and perspectives in environmental education that I have developed for a regional UNESCO project (Gough, in press). In this example of how people speak of and experience time, various texts are analyzed poststructurally to develop awareness of the domination of Western perspectives in scientific accounts and appreciation that other equally valid perspectives exist. The use of poststructuralist theory as a tool is equally appropriate for science education research methodology as it is for use by students in classroom activities on science content.

An Example:

Time, according to Dick White (1988, pp. x-xi) is a very basic concept, but it is one that is spoken of differently in different cultures:

> The universe impinges on us, and we are aware of it through our senses. From the sensations we receive we construct objects and incidents and determine causes for effects. Each of us builds a world.... Since the concepts are invented and..mean different things to different people, models are constructions. Not only are they constructions themselves, they influence further constructions–the ways we interpret the world.
>
> To give an example, consider the very basic concept of time, which is spoken of in most cultures as if it were a regular continuous progression in one direction along one dimension. It is represented mathematically in that way in our science, and we are so imbued with it that it is hard to appreciate that there are other ways of looking at it. The Hopi Indians experience time just as we do, of course, but think and speak about it in a very different way. "Among the peculiar properties of Hopi time are that it varies with each observer, does not permit simultaneity, and has zero dimensions; i.e. it cannot be given a number greater than one. The Hopi do not say 'I stayed five days,' but 'I left on the fifth day'" (Whorf 1940, p. 216). Whorf has called Hopi a timeless language. He points out that although the Hopi can describe the universe quite adequately, their non-dimensional view of time means that they do not share our concepts of velocity and acceleration. They are not wrong in their view, nor are we; it is just that our

constructions differ. Even within cultures that follow modern science, time may be seen differently. Mori, Kitagawa and Tadang (1974) demonstrate that religious beliefs affect Thai and Japanese conceptions of time. The Buddhist Thai tended to think of time as a circular succession, infinitely recurring with no beginning or end; Japanese from Christian schools more often thought of it as linear, with a beginning and an end; and Japanese from public schools tended to think of it as linear with a definite beginning but infinite in extent.

However, despite his acknowledgment (from Whorf) that different groups of people construct time differently, White seems to be caught in his own need for a universal argument: "[t]he Hopi Indians experience time just as we do, *of course*" (my emphasis). Although he recognizes that understandings, such as of time, are culturally dependent –"religious beliefs affect Thai and Japanese constructions of time"–he still seems intent on presenting a universal "rules are the same everywhere" principle of us all experiencing time in the same way (which is a very imperialist notion) and that "most cultures" have a linear understanding of time. As well as sliding between ontological understandings (experiences of being "in time") and epistemological understandings (intellectual concepts and constructions of time), White seems intent on developing a notion that most cultures' experiences and constructions of time follow modern science. However, his examples illustrate that such a universalism is unfounded–and undemocratic–because there are different ways of experiencing/understanding/constructing time in different cultures. Indeed, if we are going to understand "time" as a concept, then we need to understand it from the perspective of other's lives, not by imposing a Western modern science concept on all peoples.

Peter Høeg provides some support for this argument in his portrayal of time from a Greenlander perspective. Here, time and distance are mixed together in developing a combined ontological and epistemological understanding (Høeg, 1994, p. 278):

> In North Greenland distances are measured in sinik, in "sleeps," the number of nights that a journey requires. It's not a fixed distance. Depending on the weather and the time of year, the number of sinik can vary. It's not a measurement of time, either. Under the threat of a storm, I've traveled with my mother non-stop from Force Bay to Iita, a distance that should have required two nights.

Sinik is not a distance, not a number of days or hours. It is both a spatial and a temporal phenomenon, a concept of space-time, it describes the union of space and motion and time that is taken for granted by Inuit but that cannot be captured by any European everyday language.

The European measurement of distance, the standard meter in Paris, is something quite different. It's a concept for reshapers, for those whose primary view of the world is that it must be transformed. Engineers, military strategists, prophets. And mapmakers. Like me.

The metric system didn't become part of me until I took a course in surveying at Denmark's Technical College in the autumn of 1983. We surveyed the Dyrehaven. With theodolites and tape measures and normal distribution and equidistances and stochastic variables and rainy weather and little pencils that had to be sharpened constantly. And we paced off areas. We had a teacher who repeated over and over that the alpha and omega of surveying is that the geodesist must know the length of his [sic] own stride.

I knew my own pace measured in sinik. I knew that when we ran behind the sleigh because the sky was black with pent-up explosions the space-time around us would be half the number of sinik required when we let the dogs pull us over smooth new ice. In fog the number would double, in a snowstorm it might be tenfold.

A third perspective on time comes from an Australian society, and here, once again, time is experienced and constructed differently from White's universal conception. In Stephen Davis' (c.1988, pp. 26-27) description of the seasons as a basic organizing principle of Aboriginal societies, he is providing yet another way of thinking and speaking about, and experiencing, time:

The simplest learning principle is at the crux of this issue.... [S]tart teaching from where the learner is. In Aboriginal schools in places like the Northern Territory, the school program must start with what the Aboriginal child knows about the environment and proceed in tandem with traditional structuring of learning about the environment.

To proceed in such a way it would first be necessary to document Aboriginal traditional knowledge of the local environment and identify the major organizational principles (such as seasonal variations). The simple seasonal calendar is an ideal framework from which one may develop and integrate such information.

A problem which has faced Aboriginal schools in outlying communities since time immemorial has been the lack of equipment. A program which relies to a reasonable extent on Aboriginal knowledge of the environment will not, at least in the early years, necessitate a high level of technical resources and equipment. Rather, the emphasis will be upon the thoughtful use of local resources which may change as the emphasis on Aboriginal life changes throughout the seasons of the year.

Thus, while Western cultures (and those cultures which have been affected by Western science and religion, such as Christian Japanese people) generally speak of time "as if it were a regular continuous progression in one direction along one dimension" (White, 1988, p. x), there are obviously many other ways of experiencing and representing time in other cultures. These ways should be equally valued and sought to be understood, as they could help provide insights into other ways of understanding the scientific beliefs of particular cultures and moving toward a more democratic science which challenges master narratives and totalizing systems. I see poststructuralist analysis as a promising tool for moving toward such a more democratic science, where more than one story is regarded as valid.

Problematics

Two great problematics for moving beyond Eurocentrism in science education research and practice at the present time are the search for national and international standards in science education and the renewed emphasis on traditional content in science curriculum frameworks in Australia, and in other countries, in the pursuit of developing a scientifically literate citizenry.

Although there was a content emphasis in the national curriculum statement on science for Australian schools (Curriculum Corporation, 1994), it did at least have some overarching principles which were consistent with moving toward a more democratic science. For example, it encourages teachers and students

- to develop critiques of developments in science.

- to examine the social implications of science ideas and applications.

- to tolerate different world views.

- to recognize the gendered nature of the selection and presentation of knowledge in science curricula in schools.

- to recognize that scientific understanding is not the only way of making sense of the world.

While not totally consistent with them, these principles are at least heading in the direction of those I have proposed here. They are also consistent with those proposed in the American Association for the Advancement of Science, Project 2061 publication, *Benchmarks for Scientific Literacy* (1993), although the principles herein do omit an acknowledgment of the gender bias of science in *Benchmarks* (Cross, 1995, p. 453).

Unfortunately, dramatic changes were made to the Australian national statement's successors and relatives such that the more recent documents (such as the 1995 Curriculum and Standards Framework: Science from the Victorian Board of Studies) tend to be content-driven and neglectful of research findings from science and science education of the past thirty years such as gender and science education, the STS (science, technology, and society) movement, and the role of history and philosophy of science.

A content focus is also to be found in New Zealand's science and technology curriculum reforms. For example, according to Malcolm Carr ("Students Must Embrace Understanding," 1994, October 6-12, p. 19), who was intimately involved in reforming New Zealand's science and technology curriculum in schools, such a curriculum should be content based: "Teaching and learning about science should be absolutely focused on where the students are, what they already know about, what they can develop their knowledge and skills from–and this means using contexts that are familiar to them." Such a curriculum would seem to be the very opposite of one that is encouraging of moving beyond modern science and toward a more democratic future.

In contrast, in their re-examination of school science in America, Project 2061, the American Association for the Advancement of Science (such as reflected in their 1993 *Benchmarks for Scientific Literacy*) recommended a reduction in the amount of content covered and in curricula which weakened or eliminated rigid subject matter boundaries; paid more attention to the connections among science, mathematics and technology; and presented the scientific endeavor as a social enterprise that strongly influences–and is influenced by–human thought and action. The focus is on whether the proposed content is likely to help citizens participate intelligently in making social and political decision(s) on matters involving science and technology. However, one concern in these trends is summed up by Jenkins (1995, p. 447) in his comments with respect to *Benchmarks for Scientific Literacy* (1993)–that the focus is on what scientific literacy is *about*, but contains little discussion of what that literacy might be *for*. There is a large body of research which indicates that simply acquiring seemingly relevant scientific knowledge provides no guarantee of later involvement in scientific decision making, and this then raises questions about the actual likelihood of achieving scientific literacy through a focus on scientific content in the curriculum. Carlsen, Cunningham, and Lowmaster (1995) also focus on "Who will teach it?," albeit from a different perspective. Such aspects are yet to be considered in the Project 2061 process, and in the interim, the focus is more likely to be on the "benchmarks" (the "knowing thats") that are specified at particular levels in both the American and Australian documents. In this, there are also problematics in that the "knowing thats" privilege one particular view of science knowledge–a universal Western view–rather than supporting notions that knowledge is partial, multiple, and contradictory, and that in the construction of such universal views other voices are silenced.

In many ways, the recommendations from the US Project 2061 and the Australian national school science curriculum are consistent with a more feminist approach to science education. Such an approach argues that, "if science subjects continue to be presented as 'factual, with abstract laws and concepts to be learnt,' they will remain unattractive to many girls. Alternatively, if they were presented in a more integrated mode, as 'enmeshed in a complex of inter-relations,' this would be more attractive to girls" (Yates, 1993, p. 65). The recommendations from Project 2061 (as spelt out in *Benchmarks*) include demands that students (and therefore teachers)

- develop deeper understandings of the nature of science

- grapple explicitly with the values and attitudes that underlie science

- study the history of science

"and do all of this and much more in an interdisciplinary context that not only provides a common core of scientific literacy, but does so in ways that are attentive to local needs and opportunities" (Carlsen, Cunningham, and Lowmaster, 1995, p. 449). While these requirements are laudable, they also raise a number of problems. For example, Jenkins (1995, p. 448) points out that instead of being concerned with science content, the focus should be on the science teachers: "[s]tandards in science teaching ultimately reside in the practice, discourse, assumptions and aspirations of science teachers." However, the preparedness of teachers to teach in an interdisciplinary manner and their acceptance of the problematic nature of science are also limiting factors.

There would seem to be many arguments for moving toward a more democratic science, coming from many directions, including scientists and philosophers as well as educators. This provides science educators with a challenge to investigate and encourage more democratic science education research and practices in schools. I remain optimistic in that policy documents are often overlooked, and even within the constraints of the new policies it is possible to explore less partial and less distorted accounts of the particular science content. There is no directive that other ways of knowing are not allowed to be considered; it is just that it is not overtly encouraged. The challenge for science education researchers and practitioners is to encourage the valuing of these other ways of knowing.

Conclusion

Moving beyond Eurocentrism in science education will not be easy. Yet there are increasing challenges to the West imposing its values and standards on others, and these need to be both acknowledged and taken into account in future developments in science education. The challenges posed in the discussions around the 1994 United Nations Population Conference in Cairo are a case in point (see, for example, Elliott and Dickey, 1994; Jiggins, 1994). The papers collected by Harding (1993d), and the plethora of postcolonial literature and critiques, provide further support for such challenges. We need to be working toward less partial and less distorted accounts of nature and social relations in science education content and we need to be working toward pedagogies and research methodologies that are not in pursuit of "one true story." The principles I have proposed here, which are grounded in feminist and postcolonial critiques of science and science education and in feminist poststructuralism, are where I am starting on my work toward encouraging more democratic science content and science education practices. As a science educator I am trying to stop being unconscious.

Acknowledgment
An earlier version of this paper was presented at the annual conference of the Australian Association for Research in Education, Newcastle, NSW, December 1994. I would like to thank Noel Gough of Deakin University and Lyn Yates of LaTrobe University for their (de)constructive comments on earlier drafts of this paper.

Notes
1.   These quotations are also cited in the opening of the chapter from my dissertation which is the origin of parts of this paper (Gough, 1994, p. 56).

2.   Following Harding (1993b, p. 2) "Eurocentrism" means "the assumption that Europe functions autonomously from other parts of the world that Europe is its own origin, final end, and agent; and that Europe and people of European descent in the Americas and elsewhere owe nothing to the rest of the world."

3.   By "Western" I mean not only Europe and North America but anywhere else that follows the canons of Enlightenment science. I recognize that by using "Western" I am reinstating the West-East contrast that postcolonial writers are trying to undermine, but this is the construct in use and readily understood so I will continue to use it with the understanding that it should always be read in "scare" quotation marks.

4.   This argument has been advanced by writers such as Haraway (1989), Harding (1993c), Keller (1985), Merchant (1980), Needham (1969) and the authors represented in Harding (1993d).

References
Achebe, Chinua (1960) *No longer at ease.* London: Heinemann.
Adam, Ian and Tiffin, Helen (Eds.), (1991). *Past the last post: Theorizing post-colonialism and post-modernism.* Hemel Hempstead, U.K: Harvester Wheatsheaf.
American Association for the Advancement of Science, Project 2061

(1993). *Benchmarks for scientific literacy.* New York/Oxford: Oxford University Press.

Ashcroft, Bill; Griffiths, Gareth; and Tiffin, Helen (1989). *The empire writes back: Theory and practice in post-colonial literatures.* New York/London: Routledge.

Berger, Peter and Luckmann, Thomas (1966). *The social construction of reality.* New York: Doubleday.

Berman, Ruth (1989). From Aristotle's dualism to materialist dialectics: Feminist transformation of science and society. In Alison M. Jaggar and Susan Bordo (Eds.), *Gender/Body/Knowledge: Feminist reconstructions of being and knowing.* New Brunswick, NJ/London: Rutgers University Press, pp.224-255.

Bhabha, Homi K. (1985). Signs taken for wonders: Questions of ambivalence and authority under a tree outside Delhi, May 1817. *Critical Inquiry* 12(1): 144-165.

Bhabha, Homi K. (1986). The other question: Difference, discrimination and the discourse of colonialism. In Francis Barker et al. (Eds.), *Literature, politics and theory.* New York: Methuen, pp.148-172. (Original work published in 1983.)

Bhabha, Homi K. (1988). The commitment to theory. *Formations* 5: 5-23.

Bhabha, Homi K. (1994). *The location of culture.* London/New York: Routledge.

Birke, Lynda and Hubbard, Ruth (Eds.), (1995). *Reinventing biology: Respect for life and the creation of knowledge.* Bloomington: Indiana University Press.

Bleier, Ruth (1986a). Introduction. In Ruth Bleier (Ed.), *Feminist approaches to science.* New York: Pergamon Press, pp. 1-17.

Bleier, Ruth (1986b). Lab coat: Robe of innocence or klansman's sheet? In Teresa De Lauretis (Ed.), *Feminist Studies/Critical Studies.* Bloomington, IN: Indiana University Press, pp. 55-66.

Carlsen, William S., Cunningham, Christine M., and Lowmaster, Nancy E. (1995). But who will teach it? *Journal of Curriculum Studies* 27(4): 448-451.

Carr, Malcom (1994). Students must embrace understanding. (October 6-12, 1994). *Campus Review,* p. 19.

Cherryholmes, Cleo H. (1988). *Power and criticism: Poststructural investigations in education.* New York/London: Teachers College Press.

Cross, Roger (1995). A vision of scientific literacy. *Journal of Curriculum Studies* 27(4): 452-455.

Curriculum Corporation (1994). *A statement on science for Australian schools.* Carlton: Curriculum Corporation.

Davies, Bronwyn (1994). *Poststructuralist theory and classroom practice.* Geelong, Australia: Deakin University.

Davis, Stephen (c.1988). Aboriginal perception of the environment and the implications for environmental education. In Stuart Traynor (Ed.), *Sailing on an inland sea.* Proceedings of the 5th National Conference. Alice Springs: Australian Association for Environmental Education, pp. 21-28.

Di Stefano, Christine (1990). Dilemmas of difference: Feminism, modernity, and postmodernism. In Linda J. Nicholson (Ed.), *Feminism/Postmodernism.* New York/London: Routledge, pp. 63-82.

Elliott, Michael and Dickey, Christopher (1994). Body politics. *The Bulletin with Newsweek* 13 September: 56-60.

Fee, Elizabeth (1983). Women's nature and scientific objectivity. In Marian Lowe and Ruth Hubbard (Eds.), *Woman's nature: Rationalizations of inequality.* New York: Pergamon, pp. 9-27.

Ferguson, Russell, Gever, Martha, Trinh T. Minh-ha, and West, Cornel (Eds.), (1990). *Out there: Marginalization and contemporary cultures.* New York: The New Museum of Contemporary Art and Cambridge, MA: The MIT Press.

Flax, Jane (1990). Postmodernism and gender relations in feminist theory. In Linda J. Nicholson (Ed.), *Feminism/Postmodernism.* New York/London: Routledge, pp. 39-62.

Gilligan, Carol (1982). *In a different voice: Psychological theory and women's development.* Cambridge, MA/London: Harvard University Press.

Giroux, Henry A. (1992). *Border crossings: Cultural workers and the politics of education.* New York and London: Routledge.

Goonatilake, Susantha (1984). *Aborted discovery: Science and creativity in the third world.* London: Zed Books.

Gough, Annette (1994). *Fathoming the fathers in environmental education: A feminist poststructuralist analysis.* Doctoral dissertation, Deakin University, Geelong, Australia.

Gough, Annette (in press). *Using indigenous knowledge, practices and perspectives in environmental education.* A module for the UNESCO-ACEID Project on Learning for a sustainable environment–innovation in teacher education. Bangkok and Brisbane: UNESCO and Griffith University.

Haraway, Donna J. (1986). Primatology is politics by other means. In Ruth Bleier (Ed.), *Feminist approaches to science.* New York: Pergamon Press, pp. 77-118.

Haraway, Donna J. (1988). Situated knowledges: The science question in feminism and the privilege of partial perspective. *Feminist Studies* 14(3): 575-600.

Haraway, Donna J. (1989). *Primate visions: Gender, race and nature in the world of modern science.* New York: Routledge.

Haraway, Donna J. (1991). *Simians, cyborgs, and women: The reinvention of nature.* London: Free Association Books.

Harding, Sandra (1986). *The science question in feminism.* Ithaca, NY: Cornell University Press.

Harding, Sandra (1991). *Whose science? Whose knowledge? Thinking from women's lives.* Ithaca, NY: Cornell University Press.

Harding, Sandra (1993a). *After Eurocentrism: New directions in social studies of science.* Audiotape of presentation to the Annual Meeting of the American Educational Research Association, Atlanta, Georgia, 12-16 April.

Harding, Sandra (1993b). Introduction: Eurocentric scientific illiteracy– a challenge for the world community. In Sandra Harding (Ed.), *The "racial" economy of science: Toward a democratic future.* Bloomington: Indiana University Press, pp. 1-29.

Harding, Sandra (1993c) Rethinking standpoint epistemology: "What is strong objectivity?" In Linda Alcoff and Elizabeth Potter (Eds.), *Feminist epistemologies.* New York/London: Routledge, pp. 49-82.

Harding, Sandra (Ed.), (1993d). *The "racial" economy of science: Toward a democratic future.* Bloomington: Indiana University Press.

Harding, Sandra (1994). Is science multicultural? Challenges, resources, opportunities, uncertainties. *Configurations: A Journal of Literature, Science, and Technology* 2(2): 301-330.

Hardy, Sarah Blaffer (1986). Empathy, polyandry, and the myth of the coy female. In Ruth Bleier (Ed.), *Feminist approaches to science.* New York: Pergamon, pp. 119-146.

Hartsock, Nancy (1987). Rethinking modernism: Minority vs. majority theories. *Cultural Critique* 7: 187-206.

Høeg, Peter (1994). *Miss Smilla's feeling for snow.* London: HarperCollins.

Hubbard, Ruth (1981). The emperor doesn't wear any clothes: The impact of feminism on biology. In Dale Spender (Ed.), *Men's studies modified: The impact of feminism on the academic disciplines.* Oxford: Pergamon Press, pp. 213-235.

Hubbard, Ruth (1995). *Profitable promises: Essays on women, science and health.* Monroe, ME: Common Courage Press.

Jenkins, Edgar W. (1995). Benchmarks for scientific literacy: A review symposium. *Journal of Curriculum Studies* 27(4): 445-448.

Jiggins, Janice (1994). *Changing the boundaries: Women-centered perspectives on population and the environment.* Washington, D.C.: Island Press.

Keller, Evelyn Fox (1985). *Reflections on gender and science.* New Haven/London: Yale University Press.

Keller, Evelyn Fox (1992). *Secrets of life, secrets of death: Essays on language, gender and science.* New York and London: Routledge.

Keller, Evelyn Fox (1995). *Refiguring life: Metaphors of twentieth-century biology.* New York: Columbia University Press.

Merchant, Carolyn (1980). *The death of nature: Women, ecology and the scientific revolution.* New York: Harper and Row.

Merchant, Carolyn (1992). *Radical ecology: The search for a livable world.* New York/ London: Routledge.

Namenwirth, Marion (1986). Science seen through a feminist prism. In Ruth Bleier (Ed.), *Feminist approaches to science.* New York: Pergamon Press, pp. 18-41.

Nandy, Ashis (1986). *The intimate enemy.* Delhi: Oxford University Press.

Ngugi Wa Thiong'O (1986). *Decolonizing the mind: The politics of language in African literature.* London /Nairobi: Heinemann.

Said, Edward W. (1978). *Orientalism.* New York: Pantheon.

Said, Edward W. (1985). Orientalism reconsidered. *Cultural Critique* 1: 89-107.

Said, Edward W. (1993). *Culture and imperialism.* London: Chatto & Windus.

Shiva, Vandana (1989). *Staying alive: Women, ecology and development.* London: Zed Books.

Small, Meredith F. (1984). *Female primates: Studies by women primatologists.* New York: Alan R. Liss.

Spivak, Gayatri Chakravorty (1987). *In other worlds: Essays in cultural politics.* New York: Routledge & Kegan Paul.

Spivak, Gayatri Chakravorty (1990a). Explanation and culture: Marginalia. In Russell Ferguson, Martha Gever, Trinh T. Minh-ha and Cornel West (Eds.), *Out there: Marginalization and contemporary cultures.* New York: The New Museum of Contemporary Art and Cambridge, MA: The MIT Press, pp. 377-393.

Spivak, Gayatri Chakravorty (1990b). *The post-colonial critic: Interviews, strategies and dialogues.* (Sarah Harasym, Ed.) New York/London: Routledge.

Spivak, Gayatri Chakravorty (1993). *Outside in the teaching machine.* New York/London: Routledge.

Third World Network (1993). Modern science in crisis: a Third World response. In Sandra Harding (Ed.), *The "racial" economy of science: Toward a democratic future.* Bloomington: Indiana University Press, pp. 484-518.

Tiffin, Chris and Lawson, Alan (Eds.), (1994). *De-scribing empire: Post-colonialism and textuality.* London/New York: Routledge.

Victorian Board of Studies (1995). *Curriculum and standards framework: Science.* Carlton, Victoria: Victorian Board of Studies.

Weedon, Chris (1987). *Feminist practice and poststructuralist theory.* Oxford: Blackwell.

West, Cornel (1990). The new cultural politics of difference. In Russell Ferguson, Martha Gever, Trinh T. Minh-ha and Cornel West (Eds.), *Out there: Marginalization and contemporary cultures.* New York: The New Museum of Contemporary Art and Cambridge, Mass: The MIT Press, pp. 19-36.

White, Richard T. (1988). *Learning science.* Oxford: Blackwell.

Yates, Lyn (1993). *The education of girls: Policy, research and the question of gender.* Hawthorn, Victoria: ACER.

Chapter Ten

Is There a Queer Pedagogy?
Or, Stop Reading Straight [1]

Deborah P. Britzman

The rather mundane question, "What are you working on?" is one academics ask each other, involving routinely the discussion of a problem, a course of study, and the sketching out of some theory. It is when I name the theory that some of these conversations get awkward. When I pronounce "Queer Theory" more than a few times, it is as if the listener cannot believe her or his ears, it is as if I had spoken in another language. One difficulty that borders these conversations is that for many of my colleagues, questions of gay and lesbian thought are, well, not given any thought. But this, after all, is part of my problematic, that is, accounting for the relations between a thought and what it cannot think.

Why is it unthinkable to work with gay and lesbian writing when one thinks about experiences like friendship, community, research methodology, curriculum theorizing, and educational theory? Can gay and lesbian theories become relevant not just for those who identify as gay or lesbian but for those who do not? What sort of difference would it make for everyone in a classroom if gay and lesbian writing were set loose from confirmations of homophobia, the afterthoughts of inclusion, or the special event? What is required for gay and lesbian scholarship and demands for civil rights to exceed its current ghettoized and minor identity? More interestingly, what if gay and lesbian theories were understood as offering a way to rethink the very grounds of knowledge and pedagogy in education? Conceptually speaking, what is required to refuse the unremarked and obdurately unremarkable straight educational curriculum?

At first glance, these problems may seem situated solely in the small spaces of classrooms and educational studies. The stakes, however, are raised when the absence of gay and lesbian theorizing in education is set in tension with crucial cultural and historical changes that concern the constitution of bodies of knowledge and knowledge of bodies. Throughout this essay, I will be working through some of these issues, but by way of introduction, I want to reference briefly two distinct yet often collapsed political experiences that defy the certitude and indeed the very possibility of education. One is the global pandemic known as AIDS, what Paula Treichler has termed "an epidemic of signification" in her analysis of how discourses meant to contain the pandemic as understandable work as contagion.[2] But just as significantly, while the pandemic known as AIDS references more about the transposition of bodies, geographies, and identities than, say, their capacity to assert stable boundaries, the problem is, as Paul Morrison insists, that "the cultural logic that structures the epidemic tends toward the opposite."[3] It is precisely this centripetal force, a cultural insistence to put back into place boundaries at all costs that education is obligated to exceed. The pandemic known as AIDS makes radically insufficient the categories education has historically offered.

The other political experience I bring to bear on education is gay and lesbian demands for civil rights, for the redefinition of family, for public economies of affection and representations, and for the right to an everyday not organized by violence, exclusion, medicalization, criminalization, and erasure. More specifically, gay and lesbian demands for civil rights call into question the stability and fundamentalist grounds of categories like masculinity, femininity, sexuality, citizenship, nation, culture, literacy, consent, legality, and so forth–categories that are quite central to the ways education organizes knowledge of bodies and bodies of knowledge. This movement as well might be constituted as an epidemic of signification if what is also understood by the phrasing is that these demands both force redefinitions of what counts as anyone's sociality and already shape how communities choose to be communities and accord themselves and others, whether understood or not, what Levinas terms, "the dignity of intelligibility."[4]

To work within the terms of gay and lesbian theories, then, allows for the consideration of two kinds of pedagogical stakes. One has to do with thinking ethically about what discourses of difference, choice, and visibility mean in classrooms, in pedagogy, and in how education can be thought about. Another has to do with thinking through structures of disavowal within education, or the refusals–whether curricular, social, or pedagogical–to engage a traumatic perception that produces the subject of difference as a disruption, as the outside to normalcy. Given these stakes–a sort of universalizing discourse that I will explore a bit later in this paper–what does education need to learn from the pandemic known as AIDS and from the political demands of those who live at or beyond the sexual limits? In these contexts, I wonder, to echo Spivak, "What is it to learn and to unlearn?" [5]

Throughout this essay, and in this rather long introduction, I want to raise some issues allowed when Queer Theory is brought into tension with education in general and pedagogy in its specificity. The questions I raise about the possibility of articulating pedagogies that call into question the conceptual geography of normalization–what the writer and director Tina Landau describes in her play *1969* as "the vast map of normalcy"–requires something larger than an acknowledgment of gay and lesbian subjects in educational studies. At the very least, what is required is an ethical project that begins to engage difference as the grounds of politicality and community.

I think of Queer Theory as provoking terms of engagement that work both to recuperate and to exceed the stereotypes that contain and dismiss gay and lesbian subjects. But as a doubled gesture, Queer Theory signifies improper subjects *and* improper theories, even as it questions the very grounds of identity and theory. Queer Theory occupies a difficult space between the signifier and the signified, where something queer happens to the signified–to history and bodies–and something queer happens to the signifier–to language and to representation. Whether one hears Queer Theory as figurative or as literal, as a provision or as a condition, may depend on what can be imagined when queer is brought to bear upon theory and when theory is brought to bear upon queer. The term is defiant but can be heard as accusatory. But the "queer," like the "theory," in Queer Theory does not depend on the identity of the theorist or the one who engages with it. Rather, the queer in queer theory anticipates the precariousness of the signified: the limits within its conventions and rules, and the ways these various conventions and rules incite subversive performances, citations, and inconveniences. The name, as D.A. Miller suggests, is "not a name, but the continual elision of one...[that disrupts] a system of connotation."[6]

Now, in these first conversations, some of my colleagues ask why such a disparaging term (at least for their ears and if not, for the ears they imagine) should be claimed. Some view it as too angry–too oppositional–for what can only be imagined as the general public. These folks assume teachers would never be able to pronounce such a term. They wonder if another term could be employed, one more easily exchanged, one that does not boomerang between the utterance and the utterer. Others view it as a new centricity, an attempt to reverse the binary of hetero/homo and to valorize, for a while, the latter term. For still others, it is not polite to call anything queer. Those who seem uncomfortable think the term queer as a noun or an identity. But the queer and the theory in Queer Theory signify actions not actors. It can be thought of as a verb, or as a citational relation that signifies more than the signifier.

My point in rehearsing these conversations and the various social anxieties produced there is not to posit a case of what Michael Warner calls, "Fear of a queer planet."[7] In fact, Queer Theory is an attempt to move away from psychological explanations like homophobia, a term that individualizes heterosexual fear of and loathing toward gay and lesbian subjects at the expense of examining how heterosexuality becomes normalized as natural. The subject of Queer Theory is more impertinent and more labile. Queer Theory offers methods of critiques to mark the repetitions of normalcy as a structure and as a pedagogy. Whether defining normalcy as an approximation of limits and mastery, or as renunciations, as the refusal of difference itself, Queer Theory insists on posing the production of normalization as a problem of culture and of thought. In its positivity, Queer Theory offers methods of imagining difference on its own terms: as eros, as desire, and as the grounds of politicality. It is a particular articulation that returns us to practices of bodies and to bodies of practices.

Queer Theory offers education techniques to make sense of and remark upon what it dismisses or cannot bear to know. This theory insists, using psychoanalytic method, that the relationship between knowledge and ignorance is neither oppositional nor binary. Rather, they mutually implicate each other, structuring and enforcing particular forms of knowledge and forms of ignorance. In this way ignorance is analyzed as an effect of knowledge, indeed, as its limit, and not as an originary or innocent state.[8] Perhaps the more curious insistence is the study of what hegemonic discourses of normalcy cannot bear to know. In this way, Queer Theory can think of resistance as not outside of the subject of knowledge or the knowledge of subjects but, rather, as con-stitutive of knowledge and its subjects.

Protests about the usefulness and provisionality of bringing the term queer to bear upon theory is part of the conversation in the theory itself. But perhaps it is more useful to think of competing queer theories, being refashioned in academic fields like sociology, literary and cultural criticism, education and, within cultural practices like video production, reading popular culture, and the reconceptualization of memory.[9] Another fashioning of queer is performed in political street activism (Groups like Queer Nation, ACT-UP, Queer Kids, The Lesbian Avengers, and so on). In commenting upon the use of queer to connote a style of politics, Michael Warner posits queer as "thoroughly embedded in modern Anglo American culture and does not translate easily.... As a politically unstable term...'queer' dates from the Bush-Thatcher-Mulroney era."[10] As used in street activism and cultural production, queer politics is meant to disturb and to provoke pleasure.

In an academic context, Judith Butler's essay "Critically Queer" examines how the term queer has been used to mobilize hatred and repressive legislation against gays and lesbians. Discourses, of course, have a history, and the history of the term "queer" is one that both enables and disables an everyday. Butler's questioning of the term is worth exploring as a reply to the kinds of discomforts expressed by some colleagues in education: "How is it that the apparently injurious effects of discourse become the painful resources by which a resignifying practice is wrought?.... [H]ow is it that the abjected come to make their claim through and against the discourses that have sought their repudiation?"[11] But along with this question, I want to hold the hope that in resignifying the signifier queer, in attempting to grab hold of meanings that refuse to be held because the term queer signifies first and foremost a social relation and not a sheer positivity–that is, a problem with conceptual orders injuring bodies–one might work with the provision queer without recourse to ontological debate. One might suspect the very limits of intelligibility that allow some ontological claims to be more natural than others.

In this essay, then, I am trying to imagine specific techniques of queer theory and what these might offer to the rethinking of pedagogy and the rethinking of knowledge. To do so I will be following Queer Theory's insistence upon three methods: the study of limits, the study of ignorance, and the study of reading practices. Each method requires an impertinent performance: an interest in thinking against the thought of one's conceptual foundations; an interest in studying the skeletons of learning and teaching that haunt one's responses, anxieties, and categorical imperatives; and, a persistent concern with whether pedagogical relations can allow more room to maneuver in thinking the unthought of education. I am trying, then, to imagine Queer Theory along the lines of what Sue Golding calls technique, "a 'route,' a mapping, an impossible geography–impossible not because it does not exist, but because *it exists and does not exist exactly at the same time.*"12 Moreover, following the advice of Lee Edelman, this essay refuses to secure Queer Theory to a fixed content, to a set of guidelines one might apply to automatize a queer logic and to a stable and singular body of knowledge that supposes a medicalized or minor identity. Rather, my discussion of Queer Theory is an attempt to articulate a thought of a method rather than a pronouncement of content, to bring to pedagogical spaces consideration of, what Edelman terms, "unstable differential relations."13

On the Study of Limits

The study of limits is, in a sense, a problem of where thought stops, a problem of thinkability. It begins with the question, "what makes something thinkable?" as opposed to explaining how someone thinks. The strategy attempts to get at the unmarked criteria that work to dismiss as irrelevant or valorize as relevant a particular mode of thought, field of study, or insistence upon the real. It is meant to move beyond essentialist/constructivist debates that have been necessary to rethinking questions of social difference, identity risks, and politics but that tend to stall in stories of origin, arguments of causality, and explanations of conditions. To engage the limit of thought–where thought stops, what it cannot bear to know, what it must shut out to think as it does–allows consideration into the cultural conditions that, as Judith Butler writes, make bodies matter, not as sheer positivity, but as social historical relations, forms of citation that signify more than individuals or communities need or want.14

As a method, questions of thinkability that question the grounds of thought follow from what Foucault examines as "structures of intelligibility," or regimes of truth that regulate–in a given history–the thinkable, the recognizable, the limits, and the transgressions discursively codified through legal, medical, and educational structures.15 But these limits, in order to be recognized as limits, require the presence of the dismissed, the unworthy, the irrelevant. In educational discourse, for example, one requires the individual who lacks self esteem in order for the category of self esteem to be installed into the body. In discourses of science, the homosexual as an identity is required for the heterosexual as an identity to enter the stage of history. The dynamic, however, turns back on itself. McLaren's study of the Eugenics Movement in Canada, for example, details the historical shift from the governmental preoccupation with defining and containing deviancy through institutionalization and immigration law to the fashioning of normalcy in compulsory education through such progressive measures as the introduction of school nursing, social hygiene movements, sex education, and pedagogies directed at white racial improvement.[16] A similar shift is noted by Foucault in his introductory volume on sexuality.[17]

Given that exclusion sets the limits of inclusion and hence constitutes both the included and the excluded, we might turn to Eve Sedgwick's discussion of two forms of discourse–minoritizing and universalizing–as a method of implication. Whereas minoritizing discourses close down–to the small space of minor subjects–the question of whether a particular experience is relevant or not, universalizing discourses begin with a view of identity as a category of social relations, or again, to return to Edelman's formulation, as "unstable differential relations." A universalizing discourse attempts both to study these relations and the refusals to recognize the relational and to provide techniques that might pose as a problem, the differential responses to a condition, experience, or technique. Sedgwick offers the following question that works to interpellate the addressee of whatever positionality: "In whose lives is homo/heterosexual definition an issue of continuing centrality and difficulty?"[18] With this question, we are back to the everyday as both a conceptual and a material space, a space where, as Gary Wickham and Bill Haver argue, "violence against queers is installed...in that ideological 'lived relation' [is] termed 'daily life' itself, as well as in the objectification, thematization and valorization of everydayness (as in 'family values,' for example)."[19]

As a study of limits, Queer Theory proposes to examine differential responses to the conditions of identities on terms that place as a problem the production of normalcy and on terms that confound the intelligibility that produces the normal as the proper subject. These are bothersome and unapologetic imperatives, explicitly transgressive, perverse, and political: transgressive in their attention to the regulations, repressions, and effects of binary categorical conditions such as the public and the private, the inside and the outside, the normal and the queer, and the ordinary and the disruptive; perverse in their turn against the proper and their claim of deviancy as a site of interest; and, political because as a method, queer theory attempts to conceptualize strategies that confound–through the very refusal of subjects to properly normalize themselves–the logic of institutional laws and the social practices that sustain these laws as normal and natural.

With these imperatives, Queer Theory constitutes normalcy as a conceptual order that refuses to imagine the very possibility of the other precisely because the production of otherness as the outside is central to its own self recognition. This orientation to normalcy as the pernicious production of such binaries as the self/other and the inside/outside may be quite significant to the conceptualization of education if part of this conceptualization is concerned with studying what students and teachers cannot bear to know. [20] And, within contexts of education, the pointing to normalcy as exorbitant production allows one to consider simultaneously "the unstable differential relations" between those who transgress the normal and those whose labor is to be recognized as normal. At the same time, difference can then be constituted, following Jonathan Rutherford, "as a motif for that uprooting of certainty. It represents an experience of change, transformations, and hybridity, in vogue because it acts as a focus for all those complementary fears, anxieties, confusions, and arguments that accompany change." [21]

In Queer Theory, then, talk about identity has moved well beyond the old formulas of accepting experience as telling and transparent and as supposing that role models are the transitional object to self esteem. Something far less comforting is being put into place: namely, identity is examined as a discursive effect of the social and as constituted through identifications. Douglas Crimp, in his essay on AIDS activists and the question of making a political community, makes this shift clear:

> Identification is, of course, identification with an other, which means that identity is never identical to itself. This alienation from the self it constructs...does not mean simply that any proclamation of identity will only be partial, that it will be exceeded by other *aspects* of identity, but rather that identity is always a relation, never simply a positivity.... [P]erhaps we can begin to rethink identity politics as politics of relational identities formed through political identifications that constantly remake those identities. [22]

This conceptualization of identity as made possible through identifications allows a way to think through the limits of curricular reform if curriculum is thought of as offering some grounds for identity by way of identifications. It is an orientation that requires curriculum to be thought of as a problem of ethics, if the grounds of curriculum are understood as offering students and teachers the stuff of identifications and hence the possibility of exceeding selves through new modes of sociality. In this way, the problem of curriculum becomes one of proliferating identifications *not* closing them down.

But in thinking beyond the limits of curriculum, more is required than a plea to add marginalized voices to an overpopulated site. Inclusion, or the belief that one discourse can make room for those it must exclude, can only produce, as Judith Butler puts it: "that theoretical gesture of pathos in which exclusions are simply affirmed as sad necessities of signification."[23] The case of how gay and lesbian studies has been treated in a sentimental education that attempts to be anti-homophobic serves as my example of where arguments for inclusion produce the very exclusions they are meant to cure. Part of the tension is that in discourses of inclusion, there tends to be only two pedagogical strategies: techniques for attitudinal change and provisions for information.[24] These two strategies are emblematic of the limitations produced when gay and lesbian subjects are reduced to the problem of remedying homophobia, a conceptualization that stalls within a humanist psychological discourse of the individual fear of homosexuality as abject contagion and shuts out an examination of how the term homophobia as a discourse centers heterosexuality as the normal.

The normal view on techniques of attitudinal change via provisions of information is that one should attempt to recover authentic images of gays and lesbians and stick them into the curriculum with the hope that representations–in the form of tidy role models–can serve as a double remedy: on the one hand for hostility toward social difference for those who cannot imagine difference, and, on the other, for the lack of self esteem in those who are imagined as having no self. But this formula cannot address the very problems–"the unstable differential relations," and the different forms of ignorance–unleashed when students and teachers are confronted with gay and lesbian representations.[25] Many in education who work in their classes with gay and lesbian representations have argued that normal techniques of attitudinal change via provisions of information cannot address the problem of identification:

how affective investments in identity as a means through which the self and the other can be secured actually work to dismiss gay and lesbian perspectives. Additionally, these cultural representations cannot be reduced to correct information about gays and lesbians. Imaginative works have a very different and unwieldy function and to treat fiction–or indeed, any representation–as if it were a realistic mirror is already to shut out the work of the unconscious. Pedagogical thought must begin to acknowledge that receiving knowledge is a problem for the learner and the teacher, particularly when the knowledge one already possesses or is possessed by works as an entitlement to one's ignorance or when the knowledge encountered cannot be incorporated because it disrupts how the self might imagine itself and others. These dynamics, quite familiar in contexts where multiculturalism is constituted as a special interest, are not resistance to knowledge. Rather, they are knowledge as a form of resistance.

The problem is that this liberal desire for recovery and authenticity that takes the form of inclusion in the curriculum, perhaps as an add-on, certainly in the form of a special event, attempts two contradictory maneuvers. On the one hand, the strategy constructs an innocently ignorant general public. Here, I want to signal how the normal of the normative order produces itself as unmarked sameness and as if synonymous with the everyday, even as it must produce otherness as a condition for its own recognition. For those who cannot imagine what difference difference makes in the field of curriculum, the hope is that the truth of the minority might persuade the normative folks to welcome the diversity of others and maybe in allowing the presence of the other, transform–at the level of these very transferable feelings–their racist, sexist, and heterocentric attitudes. But how, exactly is identification with another to occur if one is only required to tolerate and therefore confirm one's self as generous? In other words, what has actually changed within the ethical imperatives of one's identity? On the other hand, this strangely estranged story of difference requires the presence of those already deemed subaltern. Here, the recovery being referenced is the recovery of what the norm supposes these different folks lack, namely the self esteem of the same. The installation of the need for self esteem works to individuate the sufferer from what the same can only imagine as the tyranny of the historical and the social. In this way, identification is still impossible, for what exactly does one identify with here if the grounds of identification–history, culture, sociality–are already deemed irrelevant?

These liberal hopes, these various narratives of affirmation that are lived, however differently, are about the production of sameness, and oddly, of marking its limits. The problem is that the lived effects of inclusion are a more obdurate version of sameness and a more polite version of otherness. David Theo Goldberg puts it this way: "The commitment to tolerance turns only on modernity's 'natural inclination' to *in*tolerance; acceptance of otherness presupposes as it once necessitates the 'delegitimation of the other.'"[26] Pedagogies of inclusion, then, do not facilitate the proliferation of identifications necessary to rethinking and refashioning identity as more than a limit of attitude. In an odd turn of events, curricula that proport to be inclusive may actually work to produce new forms of exclusivity *if* the only subject positions offered are the tolerant normal and the tolerated subaltern.

On the Study of Ignorance

The study of limits of educational strategies does not, however, get at the twists and turns of pedagogical attempts or the experiences of the detours of discourse. Such detours–call it the lived everyday–are queer spaces that Samuel Delany, in his study of street and straight rhetoric on the subject of AIDS, imagines as "the margin between claims of truth and the claims of textuality [a space where] all discursive structures are formed."[27] How are pedagogical discourses lived within such a space? And, what of the queer turns where discourse no longer makes sense? In thinking about these questions, I offer two stories of ignorance. The first is drawn from the work of Cindy Patton who analyzes how U.S. governmental provisions of information both construct and eliminate subjects. The specific crisis of education Patton addresses is how AIDS education becomes organized when there is no direct relation between acquiring the facts about viral transmission and fashioning safer sexual practices. Patton questions some central assumptions of education, that good knowledge leads to good conduct and that receiving information is no problem for the learner.[28]

Patton examines how purportedly inclusive governmental campaigns of information actually work to produce the basis of exclusion, discrimination, social policing, and moral panic. The addressee of these facts is actually two: the general public who might get the virus and the risky communities who spread the virus. She argues that the general public is positioned as having *the right to know* whereas communities who are imagined as at risk of transmitting the virus have *the obligation to know* not to spread the virus and to confess their relation to HIV status. Precisely because such discourse claims are tied to varying contexts of self-knowledge, or identity, all that can be produced are identities that are either guilty or innocent. The general public is thus constructed as innocent bystanders who, with facts in hand, might be able to protect themselves. The belief is that this information discourse, in and of itself, is anti-discriminatory: if safety can be constituted as the capacity to be outside the epidemic because of possessing information, then there is nothing to fear. With nothing to fear, the general public has no reason to discriminate and is safely positioned within the realm of rationality. This self-protective gesture shuts out any thought of identity as an ethical relation.

Such dynamics of subjection become even more elaborate in recent AIDS campaigns of "No One Is Safe." While ostensibly producing inclusivity, at the level of social effects, new forms of exclusivity are being discursively produced. In Patton's words:

> Far from breaking down the sharp dichotomy between 'risk groups' and the 'general public,' the rhetoric of "no one is safe" produced a policing of identity borders as well as community borders: "no one is safe" because you can't tell who is queer.[29]

The campaign "No One Is Safe" supposes queerness as the social virus and heterosexuality as being at risk. What can happen to anyone is that anyone can be queer. Two kinds of social policing, then, are provoked. The normal must suspect both the self and the other. And in a queer turn, one might consider that far from being an originary state, the normal, too, requires a surveillance and pedagogy. But while, as Patton suggests, the campaign works to set in motion a policing of identity borders, something anxious is also produced. In part, this campaign unleashed the unthinkable: no place of safety, no stable comparisons, and the struggle with the fear of being mistaken, of not knowing or being known. Sometimes, something queer happens when the categories of Us/Them scramble for articulation.

A second story of ignorance, the flip side of "no one is safe," is described by Eve Sedgwick as it is lived in a graduate seminar composed of men and women reading gay and lesbian literature. Sedgwick reports her own discomfort in the course: originally, she and the women of the seminar situated the discomfort "to some obliquity in the classroom relations between [women] and the men. But by the end of the semester it seemed clear that we were in the grip of some much more intimate dissonance." And this had to do with the differences between and within women.

In discussing gay and lesbian literature, readers–from whatever position–were confronted with their own self-knowledge. They were, at the same time, subjected to someone else's control, even while they scrambled to become tied down to their own identity. This description harkens back to Foucault's troubling formulation of the subject: subject to the control of others and tied to self-knowledge.[30] In Sedgwick's words:

> Through a process that began, but *only* began, with the perception of some differences among our mostly explicitly, often somewhat uncrystallized sexual self-definition, it appeared that each woman in the class possessed (or might, rather feel we were possessed by) an ability to make one or more of the other women radically doubt the authority of her own self-definition as a woman; as a feminist; as a positional subject of a particular sexuality.[31]

The problem is not that no one was safe because, in this case, one could tell who was queer. Rather, telling queerness in the context of identity politics seemed to set up new forms of authority and new hierarchies of knowledge and identity that called into question old forms of authority, namely categories like "woman," "feminist," and "sex." At the same time, newly inverted forms of Us/Them emerged from reading gay and lesbian texts, and consequently, the boundaries of the inside and the outside were maintained. Evidently, many of the students might have read gay and lesbian literature as a vicarious means to learn something about the other or perhaps for the other to affirm their otherness. And yet when a discussion ensued about the texts themselves, the unremarked reading practices of these individuals actually worked to shut down identifications because they read as if to confirm or to catalog identities. No one was safe not just because anyone can be called queer, but because something queer can happen to anyone.

Now Patton's reading of governmental AIDS information discourses shows how the normal subject-presumed-to-know and the deviant subject-obligated-to-confess became discursively produced. Both positions require boundary policing, although such policing work is differential and demand different degrees of subjection. But these networks of power–discursively lived at the level of bodies and

disciplined by normative educational practices–depend upon an insistence of stable and hence predictable identities that can then be
contained. This, of course, is the authorship of normalization. Then we
have Sedgwick's description of her seminar, where differences within,
say, the category of woman disrupt the impossible promise of
sameness, the promise of a community whose very basis depends upon
subjects who presume, but cannot know, the same. In Sedgwick's
seminar, the identity hierarchy is upset, although epistemological
privilege as the grounds of knowledge is still dependent upon the
fashioning of bodies into stable identities whose knowledge is thought
to spring from identity. In both kinds of examples, then, the categorical
interpellation of identity stalls the very possibility of doing more with
identity, namely, fashioning–through the social–political practices that,
as Giorgio Agamben suggests, allow for "the idea of an inessential
commonality, a solidarity that in no way concerns an essence."[32] It is
this allowance that makes room for ethical possibilities.

These two instances point out divergent directions provoked by the
same problem, namely, the social effects of identity when identity
claims take on an aura of verisimilitude and hence are taken as if they
can exist outside of the very history and the very differential relations
that provoke such claims and their attendant feelings in the first place.
But if a pedagogical project is to move beyond the repetition of identity
and the only two subject positions allowed when identity is enacted as
one of self versus others, then, pedagogy itself–the production of
knowledge, ignorance, and subjects who presume to know–must rethink
its methods of how to read that queer space where such discursivity
occurs, namely, strategies that can acknowledge the "margins between
the claims of truth and the claims of textuality." [33]

On the Study of Reading Practices

Shoshana Felman's exploration of the pedagogical practices of Lacan's
re-reading of Freud offers a way to rethink reading practices beyond the
impulse to reduce identity to a repetition of sameness. Felman's
interests in techniques of thinking the limits, thinking beyond one's
means, are like those of Queer Theory. She notes three analytic
practices: practices of reading for alterity; practices of engaging in
dialogue with the self as the self reads; and practices of theorizing how
one reads. While I will briefly outline these techniques, they will be
elaborated by re-reading some of the issues raised earlier by my reading
of Patton and Sedgwick.

Reading for alterity begins with an acknowledgment of difference as the grounds of identity. One begins not by constructing resemblances with the text or with another but, as Felman writes: "[T]he reading necessarily passes through the Other, and in the Other, reads not identity (other or the same), but difference and self difference."34 For interpretations to exceed the impulse to normalize meaning and certify the self, reading must begin with an acknowledgment of difference as identity and not reduce interpretation to a confirmation of identity. The question a reader might ask is: Who am I becoming through the interpretive claims I make upon another and upon myself? The exploration becomes one of analysis of the signifier, not the signified, and hence, an analysis of where meaning breaks down for the reader. Reading, then, as an interpretive performance may be a means to untie self knowledge from itself if the self can be examined as split between recognition and misrecognition and if one can expose that queer space between what is taken as the real and the afterthought of recognition.

A second reading practice is provoked in dialogue. Here, Felman borrows Freud's recognition of dialogue as a "structuring condition of possibility." 35 To read is automatically to make a dialogic relation with a self and with a text. The reader, then, is obligated to ask, "What is it that I am responding to?" The text and the self perform differential replies, perhaps in the form of a question, perhaps an argument, perhaps a refusal. In acknowledging this relation–reading as provoking a dialogue–reading practices begin with the supposition of difference, division, and negotiation. When reading practices are privileged over the intentions of the author or the reader, the concern becomes one of thinking through the structures of textuality as opposed to the attributes of the biography. This makes possible the disruption of the interpreter and the interpreted hierarchy. To displace the subject, then, is to insist upon the dialogic of implication, not the problem of application.

Finally, as a practice, reading provokes a theory of reading, not just a reworking of meaning. How one reads matters. In Felman's words: "There is a constitutive belatedness of the theory over the practice, the theory always trying to catch up with what it was that the practice, or the reading, was really doing."36 Such belatedness, where the recognition of how one reads drags behind the investment in the immediacy of gathering meanings or getting meaning straight, might allow the reader to theorize the limits of her practices, or what she or he cannot bear to know.

If the interest is in how subjection is made from any body and with what reading practices have to do with confinement, then the limits of both AIDS education described by Patton and the hierarchies of identity that Sedgwick worries over might be exceeded. There might be a decision, on the part of those positioned as outside of the AIDS pandemic, to refuse the proffered grounds of innocence and rationality –and hence refuse to identify as a member of the general public. What might become suspect are the categorical imperatives and attendant inequalities produced within this campaign. Then, no one is safe from these governmental campaigns. As for Sedgwick's seminar, where the grounds of identity are still confined to mastery and certitude, there might be a decision to refuse these very grounds. Reading might then be one of theorizing why reading is always about risking the self, about confronting one's own theory of reading, and about theorizing difference without gathering the grounds of subjection. Then, thinking itself, in such classroom spaces, might take the risk of refusing to secure thought and of exposing the danger in the curious insistence of positing foundational claims at all costs.[37] So that no one is safe because the very construct of safety places at risk difference as uncertainty, as indeterminacy, as incompatibility. The problem, then, becomes working out ethical relations and not asserting identity hierarchies.

These reading practices point to the fact that there are no innocent, normal, or unmediated readings and that the representations drawn upon to maintain a narrative or a self as normal, as deviant, as thinkable are social effects of how discourses of normalization are lived and refused. Reading practices might well read all categories as unstable, all experiences as constructed, all reality as having to be imagined, all knowledge as provoking uncertainties, misrecognitions, ignorance, and silences. Then the problem becomes one of thinking through how readings might open the question of ethical relations. So given these queer theories, identities and the self-knowledge that render them intelligible and unintelligible suggest more about the social effects of the political than they do about essential selves.[38] The point is that part of what is at stake when discourses of difference, choice, and visibility are at stake is the capacity of the educational apparatus and its pedagogies to exceed their own readings, to stop reading straight.

In my work on pedagogy, what I want to call my queer pedagogy, I am attempting to exceed such binary oppositions as the tolerant and the tolerated and the oppressed and the oppressor yet still hold onto an analysis of social difference that can account for how structural dynamics of subordination and subjection work at the level of the historical, the conceptual, the social, and the psychic. And, at the same time, my interest is in unsettling the sediments of what one imagines when one imagines normalcy, what one imagines when one imagines difference. So I wonder whether identity categories will be helpful in this work if identity depends upon the production of sameness and otherness, dynamics that anchor modes of subjection. And I am thinking that maybe, given the desire for knowledge of difference to make a difference in how social subjects conduct themselves and in how sociality might be imagined and lived so that anyone can live there, the new questions that must be addressed concern what education, knowledge, and identity have to do with the fashioning of structures of thinkability and the limits of its thought, with what education has to do with the possibilities of proliferating identifications and critiques that exceed identity yet still hold onto the understanding of identity as a state of emergency. Such desires are partly made from my identifications with Queer Theory as a method.

These identifications I take as the beginnings of a queer pedagogy, one that refuses normal practices and practices of normalcy, one that begins with an ethical concern for one's *own* reading practices, one that is interested in exploring what one cannot bear to know, and one interested in the imagining of a sociality unhinged from the dominant conceptual order. In the queer pedagogy I am attempting, "the inessentially common" is built from the possibility that reading the world is always already about risking the self, and about the attempt to exceed the injuries of discourse so that all bodies matter.

Notes
1. This chapter first appeared in *Educational Theory* 45(2), 1995: 151-165. The author thanks the journal for permission to reprint.

2. Paula Treichler, "AIDS, Homophobia, and Biomedical Discourse: An Epidemic of Signification," in *AIDS: Cultural Analysis, Cultural Activism*, ed. Douglas Crimp (Boston:MIT Press, 1988), 31-71.

3. Paul Morrison, "End Pleasure," *Gay and Lesbian Quarterly* 1 (1993): 55.

4. Emmanuel Levinas, *Outside the Subject* (Stanford: Stanford University Press, 1993), 1-2.

5. Gayatri Chakravorty Spivak, "Acting Bits/Identity Talk," *Critical Inquiry* 18, no. 4 (1992), 770.

6. D.A. Miller, *Bringing Out Roland Barthes* (Berkeley: University of California Press, 1992), 24.

7. Michael Warner, "Introduction," in *Fear of a Queer Planet* (Minneapolis: University of Minnesota Press, 1993).

8. See Shoshana Felman, *Jacques Lacan and the Adventure of Insight: Psychoanalysis in Contemporary Culture* (Cambridge: Harvard University Press, 1987); and Eve Kosofsky Sedgwick, *Epistemology of the Closet* (Berkeley: University of California, 1990) and *Tendencies* (Durham: Duke University Press, 1993).

9. While Queer Theory often exceeds disciplinary boundaries, and this list is far from exhaustive, in sociology, see Warner, ed. *Fear of Queer Planet.* In literary and cultural criticism, see Judith Butler, *Bodies that Matter: On the Discursive Limits of "Sex"* (New York: Routledge, 1993); Teresa de Lauretis, "Queer Theory: Lesbian and Gay Sexualities, An Introduction," *Differences* 3, no.2 (1991): iii-xvii; Teresa de Lauretis, *The Practice of Love: Lesbian Sexuality and Perverse Desire* (Bloomington: Indiana University Press, 1994); Lee Edelman, *Homographies: Essays in Gay Literary Theory and Cultural Theory* (New York: Routledge, 1994); and, Diana Fuss, ed, *inside/out: Lesbian Theories, Gay Theories* (New York: Routledge, 1991). In education, see Deborah Britzman, "Not a Special Section: Gay and Lesbian Studies in Education," *Educational Studies* 24, no. 3 (1993): 225-231; Deborah Britzman, "The Ordeal of Knowledge: Rethinking the Possibilities of Multicultural Education," *The Review of Education* 15 (1993): 123-135; Mary Bryson and Suzanne de Castell, "Queer Pedagogy: Praxis Makes Im\Perfect," *Canadian Journal of Education* 18, no. 3 (1993): 285-305; Kathleen Martindale, *Unpopular Culture: Theorizing Lesbian Readings* (Albany: State University of New York Press, forthcoming); Cindy Patton, *Inventing AIDS* (New York: Routledge, 1990); William Pinar, *Autobiography, Politics and Sexuality: Essays in Curriculum Theory 1972-1992* (New York: Peter Lang, 1994); and, Simon Watney, "School's Out," in Fuss, 387-404. In cultural practices like video production, see Martha Gever, John Greyson and Prathibha Parmer, eds, *Queer Looks: Perspectives on Lesbian and Gay Film and Video*

(Toronto: Between the Lines, 1993); Bad Object-Choices, ed., *How Do I Look: Queer Film and Video* (Seattle: Bay Press, 1991). In reading popular culture, see Alexander Doty, *Making Things Perfectly Queer: Interpreting Mass Culture* (New York: Routledge, 1993); Mandy Merck, *perversions: deviant readings* (London: Verso, 1993); Arlene Stein, ed., *Sisters, Sexperts and Queers: Beyond the Lesbian Nation* (New York: Penguin, 1993). And, in the reconceptualization of memory, see Gloria Anzaldua, *Borderlands/ La Frontera: The New Mestiza* (San Francisco: Aunt Lute, 1987); Alexander Garcia Duttman, "What will have been said about AIDS: Some Remarks in Disorder," *Public* 7 (1993): 95-115; Essex Hemphill, *Ceremonies: Prose and Poetry* (New York: Plume Books, 1992); and David Wojnarowicz, *Close to the Knives: A Memoir of Disintegration* (New York: Vintage, 1991).

10. Michael Warner, "Something Queer About the Nation State," *Alphabet City* 3 (1993), 14.

11. Butler, *Bodies That Matter,* 224.

12. Sue Golding, "Sexual Manners," *Public* 8 (1993), 166.

13. Edelman, *Homographesis,* 3.

14. Butler, *Bodies That Matter.*

15. Michel Foucault, "A Preface to Transgression," in *Language, Counter Memory and Practice: Selected essays and interviews by Michel Foucault,* ed., Donald Bouchard (Ithaca: Cornell University, 1977), 29-52.

16. Angus McLaren, *Our Own Master Race: Eugenics in Canada, 1885-1945* (Toronto: McClelland and Steward, 1990).

17. Michel Foucault, *The History of Sexuality: An Introduction, Volume 1* (New York: Vintage Books, 1990).

18. Sedgwick, *Epistemology of the closet,* 40.

19. Gary Wickham and William Haver, "Come Out, Come Out,

Wherever You Are: A Guide for the Homoerotically Disadvantaged" (Paper delivered at the Conference on Comparative Fascisms, Cornell University, Ithaca, New York, 7 November 1992), 5.

20. See Shoshana Felman and Dori Laub, *Testimony: Crises of Witnessing in Literature, Psychoanalysis and History* (New York: Routledge, 1992).

21. Jonathan Rutherford, "A Place Called Home: Identity and the Cultural Politics of Difference," in *Identity: Community, Culture, Difference* (London: Lawrence and Wishart Limited, 1990), 10.

22. Douglas Crimp, "Hey girlfriend!" *Social Text* 33 (1992), 12.

23. Butler, *Bodies That Matter*, 53.

24. See Patton, *Inventing AIDS*.

25. To glimpse how gay and lesbian representations rethink pedagogy, see, for example, the following discussions of pedagogical practices in: Peter Bowen, "AIDS 101," in *Writing AIDS: Gay Literature, Language and Analysis,* eds. Timothy Murphy and Suzanne Poirier (New York: Columbia University Press, 1993), 140-160; Bryson and de Castell, "Queer Pedagogy"; Annie Dawid, "The Way We Teach Now: Three Approaches to AIDS Literature," in *AIDS: The Literary Response,* ed., Emmanuel Nelson (New York: Twayne Publishers, 1992), 197-203; Linda Eyre, "Compulsory Heterosexuality in a University Classroom," *Canadian Journal of Education* 18, no.3 (1993), 273-284; Madiha Didi Khayatt, *Lesbian Teachers: An Invisible Presence* (Albany: State University of New York Press, 1992); and, Martindale, *Unpopular Culture.*

26. David Theo Goldberg, *Racist Culture: Philosophy and the Politics of Meaning* (Oxford: Blackwell Publishers, 1993), 7.

27. Samuel Delany, "Street Talk/Straight Talk," *Differences* 5, no. 2 (1991), 28.

28. Patton, *Inventing AIDS.*

29. Patton, *Inventing AIDS,* 28.

30. Michel Foucault, "The Subject and Power," in *Art After Modernism: Rethinking Representation,* ed. Brian Wallis (New York: New Museum of Contemporary Art, 1984), 417-434.

31. Sedgwick, *Epistemology of the Closet,* 61.

32. Giorgio Agamben, *The Coming Community,* trans. Michael Hardt (Minneapolis: University of Minnesota Press, 1993), 18.9.

33. Delany, "Street Talk/Straight Talk," 28.

34. Felman, *Jacques Lacan and the Adventure of Insight,* 23.

35. Ibid., 23.

36. Ibid., 24.

37. See William Haver, "Thinking the Thought of That Which Is Strictly Speaking Unthinkable: On the Thematization of Alterity in Nishida-Philosophy," *Human Studies* 16 (1993): 177-192.

38. See Deborah Britzman, Kelvin Santiago-Valles, Gladys Jimenez-Munoz, and Laura Lamash, "Slips that Show and Tell: Rethinking Multiculture as a Problem of Representation," in *Race, Identity and Representation in Education,* eds. Cameron McCarthy and Warren Crichlow (New York: Routledge, 1993), 188-200.

Chapter Eleven

Don't Ask; Don't Tell:
"Sniffing Out Queers" in Education

Suzanne de Castell and Mary Bryson

> The word in language is already half someone else's.
>   M.M. Bakhtin

So we get the other half, right?

What about the word "queer," then, in educational discourse? What does it mean to speak it in classrooms, the faculty lounge, the district administration boardroom, the research office, the academy, under such a severe prohibition against naming queerness, that even queers who are actively working on queer theory, pedagogy, curriculum, dare not ("I see no need to...") speak Its Name. And under such a prohibition on naming, acknowledging, what *acts* are able to be engaged in, there being "nothing" they are about?

We are interested in trying to understand the way speaking and silence are structured and managed in educational theory and practice, and this means trying to get at the discursive and representational strategies by means of which positions in discourse are and can be taken up. Perhaps this can help us understand, among other things, why so "*un*important" a disclosure ("I see no need to...") seems to be so important *not* to "disclose."

This is a paper about location, identity, and signification. Its purpose is to try to move outside normal "regimes" of academic/professional academic discourses, in search of less-well-colonized spaces, where Other things can be said...where things can be said Differently. That there is a need for this is here taken as axiomatic, so as a rhetorical "place holder" for a developed argument to that effect, we proffer some admittedly polemical caricatures of official educational discourse as a species of "Lying Game," in which (just as in the movie of a similar name) the aim is *not* to see that which is in front of your face. Stumbling towards a conclusion, we pursue the supposition that there is a significant relationship in educational practice between form and function, and that what we cannot represent at all in certain forms can at least be gestured at in others, albeit forms less precise, and far less well-developed. There being few other identities to which it is forbidden in education to lay claim, the question, raised by anti-gay legislation in education, of representational practice as recruitment is pursued in the form of a video project briefly described here.

An Unten(ur)able Discursive Posture...

Members of the Academy are expected to adopt an institutional voice–a distinctive discourse and a set of discursive practices, whose function is to privilege–and to legitimate–the role of the professional academic in constructing intellectual capital. The discursive practices of the traditional academician are, by definition, exclusive–for this is a discursive tradition which silences women, people of color, the differently abled, lesbians and gay men, and all those other "deviant" members of educationally marginalized groups, those positioned "out of bounds" in relation to the ground-rules of schooling. So it is not really surprising to discover that many queers working in heterosexist academic environments find ourselves waging an ongoing battle to keep our sexuality *out* of the closet, and having to adopt an assertively radical position in order to do so.

The fact is, we (alongside other Others) are academics who can never really *be* Academics. We can never really *be* Academics because we can never speak *as* Academics without in that very utterance, speaking against ourselves, against our very existence. The same point has been developed in relation to race, class and other "differences" (Hoodfar, 1992; Ng, 1993; de la Luz Reyes, in press). The discourse which authorizes us to speak is precisely the same one which denies any authority to our utterances, to our lives, to lives like ours.

Thus to occupy the position of the "Professor," to "profess," is, inescapably to profess against ourselves, to speak our own illegitimacy, so long as we speak in the language, the tones, the cadences of the academy which has spawned us as impossible beings, as monstrous, aberrant, eternal Outsiders who nevertheless dare to speak publicly about the *being* of being queer, knowing that we disqualify ourselves in the very act of speaking, that we dig our own ontological graves in this simplest of act of naming. Speaking *as* queers, we disqualify ourselves from speaking *as* the professors we can, therefore, never actually be. "The Professor," as a position in discourse, is not what the queer is, indeed, "The Professor" is what the queer is not.

Educators are supposed to be interested in the creation of knowledge, and in its transmission. Where we want to begin as "queer" educators, *inversely*, is with a very different interest, an interest in the *destruction* of knowledge, rather than in its creation. There is a long history to look at here, from the destruction of libraries to the burning of books (and, on occasion, their authors and even their readers), to censorship, a study of the forbidden, of what has been disallowed, the unspeakable–in the field of education, this appears an odd, not to say heretical, perspective from which to do one's work. But our long-standing interest in the destruction of knowledge is not a frivolous one.

It is born, first, not out of any spectacular postmodern theory, but much more mundanely, out of a frank amazement at the capacity of official discourse, which means, in particular, textual discourse, the written word in all its "normal" or authorized forms, to conceal entire worlds from existence, and to bring into existence in their place entire universes of ignorance and deception. Historical studies of the origins and development of literacy in the West (Graff, 1982; Olson, 1994; Goody, 1977) tell a long and elaborately illustrated story of how the written word has enabled the creation, enlargement, and dissemination of human knowledge and understanding; a good deal less attention, predictably enough, has been paid to the admittedly far less numerous studies of its equally significant role in creating and maintaining ignorance in the textually structured production (see esp. de Castell, 1995; Smith, 1987) of silences, omissions, eradications, and erasures–a role official documentary practices play no less well today.

Dorothy Smith writes: "[E]ducation, like other institutions functioning nondemocratically in a democratic society, depends on ignorance. The professional and administrative structures as well as the practices of professional and academic discourse interlock to prevent knowledge leaking out to...those who do not participate in the relations of ruling" (1987, p. 219) It is our hope that by turning in our weapons, handing our traditional tools–conventional academic/textual forms– back to the authorities, by changing tools, trying to learn how to use an entirely new set of non-textual media in every aspect of our work, from pedagogy, theory-construction, and research methods to finding alternate, image-based ways of reporting and recording our research findings and conclusions, we may learn how to penetrate the structured ignorances upon which the edifice of education depends—what might begin as little more than a trickle of forbidden knowledge, prohibited understanding, may in time and with much luck become something more, a rivulet, a stream. We really dare not hope for any more—though of course what we long for is a flood, a breaking through of forbidden knowledges, a tumultuous, uncontrollable release of what has been blocked, held back, dammed up for far too long. As Smith explains, "[a]n educational system is in the business of producing...inequalities of race, class and gender in the normal (though not the official) course of doing its business...." How threatening it would be to the stability of that institution, should the knowledge of the schools, normal-but-not-official business of producing inequality be permitted to "leak out" to parents, to students, to teachers, to the taxpaying public-at-large. And so the great need for reliable, effective strategies—most typically, textual strategies—for the production and preservation of ignorance.

Smith, whose extensive critical investigations of the role of texts in designing, constructing, and maintaining what she names "relations of ruling" (Smith, 1994), has spoken powerfully about the ways in which textual forms shape, constrain, and limit what can be expressed in and by them, bringing a new, more tightly regulated and managed textual world into official existence, and eradicating the irregular, un-manageable world of everyday, everynight lived actuality. She speaks of the need to understand how official texts and textual practices act upon readers and writers in the service of maintaining and strengthening the "relations of ruling," containing and neutralizing potential disruptions to the orderly management of individuals and collectivities by the state.

The shift from text-based to image-based intellectual practices may enable, we believe, a significant shift in the economy of communicative exchange. This new territory will doubtless be no less treacherous than the old, particularly given the ever-closer relationship between image-based media and corporate capitalism (Penley and Ross, 1991). But of course this is no less true of the university in its most traditional form, which is today little more than a shell concealing a thriving shopping mall of corporate-sponsored academic "product," so there's no escaping that particular danger, in any case.

Moving away from an exclusive reliance on written texts, and towards an increasing utilization of image-based media, we think (or perhaps only hope) takes us into territory far less familiar, but far more promising as a place from which to make change. [1] But this is a move in which we set aside what we have learned how to do in order to relocate to a context in which we know almost nothing, in which we have to begin again, to learn from the start, all over again.

Why would anyone want to do this?

> The word is already half someone else's.... The word does not exist in a neutral and impersonal language (it is not, after all, out of a dictionary that the speaker gets his words!), but rather it exists in other people's mouths, in other people's contexts, serving other people's intentions: it is from there that one must take the word, and make it "one's own" (Bakhtin, 1981, pp. 293-294).

The Lying Game

> In speaking of lies, we come inevitably to the subject of truth. There is nothing simple or easy about this idea. There is no "the truth," "a truth"–truth is not one thing, or even a system. It is an increasing complexity.... This is why the effort to speak honestly is so important. Lies are usually attempts to make everything simpler–for the liar–than it really is or ought to be (Rich, 1982, pp. 187-8).

Participation in contemporary educational discourse–research, scholarship and practice–seems increasingly to involve a kind of "lying game." Is this because (as Ghandi said), "To participate in injustice is a form of lying?" The educational lying game, as in the movie similarly named, is about how *not* to see or to acknowledge, nor, therefore, to *act* upon the complexities and contradictions staring you straight in the face.

Education: a field of discourse governed by the obligation to "be positive," a field in which, increasingly, no one dares to speak of obstacles, impediments, difficulties without in the same breath expounding on "solutions." A categorical imperative to remain "positive" at all costs reigns here, even at the cost of willful blindness, misrepresentation, a kind of *studied* ignorance which cannot be other than intentional, where full-grown "men of good will" speak unashamedly of the "wonderful world of education," disregarding utterly Cornel West's (1987) reminder to us that there are certain things in this "wonderful world" we cannot any longer be permitted *not* to know, things which we may no longer claim not to have seen, not to have understood, things which are endlessly "deferred" by demands for "further evidence."

It is by means of these deceits that we have come to the point at which–in educational institutions and no less in educational discourses/ practices, even as cries of "Fag," ring through virtually every school corridor, as students are assaulted and sometimes killed in their schoolyards, where racism flourishes as productively in staffrooms and professional journals (B.C.T.F., 1991) and board offices as in the classroom and in the curriculum, as female students and teachers who dare to contest male privilege are greeted with catcalls of "man-hating dyke" or, only slightly less awful, "feminist"–a label not so long ago invoked as a warrant for fourteen murders but since celebrated and parodied in "entertaining" university skits–it is obligatory to intone liberal and post-critical mantras about pedagogic possibilities to be located in contestation and resistance, about the pursuit of empower- ment and excellence. This "wonderful world of education" is one, let us just this once not refuse to see, where students are instructed to plan the "perfect rape" as a learning strategy, where school cops patrol the halls in order to protect classrooms in which, after all, the very same patterns of privilege and deprivation, of educational success and failure, continue unabatedly to reproduce what Porter (1965) so long ago referred to as the "vertical mosaic"–a "design"–another richly evocative term–in which racial and class-based differences are played out as disadvantage notwithstanding our purportedly multicultural public policies. In these sites of discursive and physical violence, of persisting inequality, of aggressively policed strategies enforcing "normalization" at all costs, including as acceptable losses is the educational project itself–for let us just this once actually *look* at what nowadays passes for knowledge and competence in so many of the schools we visit where–paradoxically– nothing but the good news may enjoy any hope of being heard, let alone listened to.

Where institutional commitments to equity and empowerment are nowadays increasingly being forged–and the term is used advisedly here, fully intending its conceptual echoes of fabrication, artifice, fraudulence to be heard–what *actualities* greet those educators, researchers, theorists who take up the challenges and who seek in their actual daily practice to redeem the promises of these policies and institutional commitments?

Queer (adj/noun)- sexual deviate, homosexual

Pedagogy (noun)- from pedagogue; *paidos*- boy; *agogos*- lead origin: the slave who escorted children to school.

Queer (verb)- to spoil, put out of order, to put into an embarrassing or disadvantageous situation.
(*The Concise Oxford English Dictionary*, 1964, pp. 895, 1007)

"A certain smell..." Notes from the Field

When C. Wright Mills argued that the political purpose of sociology should be the transformation of private troubles into public issues, you can bet he didn't have queers in mind...

Waited far too long to share this fieldnote.... It's dated November 30, 1993, and records a final meeting with a couple of high-ranking school district administrators, as they proceeded–inexplicably–to retract all agreements between us, both written and verbal, thus putting an end to our research project, which was to have begun that fall in a local high tech and therefore high-profile secondary school nearby the university where I work.

I have to tell you that we're not feeling comfortable about this project.... I can't really say what it is right now.... But you get so you can sense these things after so many years in the business. It's just a certain feeling...a certain taste.... *A certain smell....* I don't know what it is about you people.... I just can't put my finger on it.... Something just isn't quite right.

Those were the words spoken by the superintendent of a large British Columbia school district in a monologue about our un-suitability as researchers. That is to say, our *new-found* unsuitability despite the fact that we (1) had already been given the OK to conduct research on gender, educational equity, and uses of new technologies in a school in his district, (2) had been awarded a substantial research grant to conduct that study, and (3) had been meeting with the district research committee over several months leading up to this, our final, and most inauspicious meeting. And how unexpected this all was... unexpected and yet so familiar (It's like the superintendent said, you just get to recognize that old gender-trouble feeling...).

During our first meeting, in the boardroom surrounded by school administrators, every one of them male, despite the fact that the research proposal they'd come to appraise was explicitly focused on gender equity (an oversight, perhaps?), the superintendent had fired at us point blank, "So, are you here to court us?" "Absolutely," we had countered, not really knowing what to say. The implausibility of it all. Two dykes wearing matching Gap pants, Doc Martins, and jackets courting the superintendent and his henchman, the Director of Instruction. After our first meeting, they were jubilant–effusive about how well we had done– that in their books we were in a league with IBM and a select few others who had been able to withstand their intense scrutiny and tough questioning. They loved our research proposal and were ready to sign on the dotted line. If the number of arm-pumping handshakes by jovial men in suits was anything to go by, they even loved *us*! We were astonished...but we were *in*!

Dear Dr. Bryson and Dr. de Castell:

Further to our meeting of 1993-09-16, this is to advise you that the School District is interested in participating in the SSHRC Project as you described at our meeting. We are looking forward to receiving a copy of the written proposal and to further discussions about this partnership.

In the meantime, good luck with your application. Please let me know if there is anything else that we can do to assist.

Or so we thought. Our strategy had been a clever one–we'd imagined at the time. Because our proposal was not to study failure and exclusion, but *success*, to study "what works" in relation to girls and new technologies by taking our cue from communities of practice where gender was being articulated with greater agency and equity than was the case in more typical school contexts. We had federal funding, we had provincial funding. It was a good proposal. But the super-intendent couldn't put his finger on it, and so we were *out*.

Oddly enough, when we'd left that meeting, we'd managed to secure their agreement that we could, notwithstanding the super-intendent's discriminating nose, start work in the school. But first thing next morning, there was the fax, telling us exactly the opposite story.

Subject: "Gender, Educational Equity, and New Information Technologies" Project

Upon reflection of the issues and concerns that were raised at our meeting of November 30th, we feel that this is not an opportune time to initiate a research project of this magnitude at.... This is to advise you, therefore, that we do not wish to participate in this research project at this time.

I am aware that this decision will have implications with respect to funding arrangements. If there is anything that we can do to assist you to retain your grant while you seek an alternative context in which to pursue this research, we would be pleased to do so.

We took the pink slip, returned the research grant, abandoned the project, and spent the next year just kind of reeling from the horror of it all. You know, the usual emotional reverb, trying to understand what happened, just replaying over and over the sight of that room, the faces, the words, the barely repressed rage, the white knuckles, nearly-shaking hands holding a copy–almost entirely highlighted, and in two different colors to boot–of yesterday's fax from us asking when we might get to talk to the teachers, explaining that we were long past due the agreed time to start research, that our funding agency needed a report in just two months, so could we please be permitted to get started now. And, on the face of the other one, the "old hand," a half-smile, more like smirking, really, then the drawled-out insults, the bare-faced lies–and with all that, the impossibility of speaking to most of our colleagues– who of course continue to work with these people—about what happened because of the impossibility of simply being believed. *"Your paranoid "hermeneutics of suspicion"* as one such colleague kindly put it to me.

Straight–Synonyms:

unbent
unbroken
upright
honest
fair
authentic
good
honorable
orderly
ship-shape
unmixed
pure
unadulterated

Getting the Pink Slip

I am teaching a course on special students and inclusive education this term in the Teacher Education Program. In the second class, students were asked to choose from amongst a randomly mixed set of colored slips mixed in a cardboard box. There were seven color choices, representing seven topics, including gay and lesbian students, First Nations students, Race/Ethnicity issues, ESL [Teaching English as a Second Language] issues, gender issues, deaf culture, Identification as LD [Learning Disabilities]. Their color choice would determine to which small group they would belong in doing a collaborative project. A group of three male students seated at the back of the class chose pink slips, wanting to work together, and unaware of the fact that in this case, pink represented Gay and Lesbian issues. I continued my "waiter of knowledge" trek through the classroom, giving each student a chance to draw a colored slip. I hear a noise at the back of the room, and one of the group of three strides over. He looks raw, confused, distraught. "Ah, Dr. Bryson, we made, ah, an error." He throws the pink slips back into the box, and selects three green slips. An "error?" I ask. By the time the box is nearly empty, I look down to see what's left. None of the pink slips have been chosen. The most popular slips, those that disappeared first, were yellow–LD issues. The least obviously linked to systemic discrimination. The young man from the back of the class comes to chat while the rest of the class gets to work in their small groups.

"I want to know, why would it be relevant to study gay and lesbian issues as an elementary teacher? I mean, kids that age don't even have a sexuality yet."

I respond that in fact, lots of kids are quite aware of sexuality, but that the real point here is that homophobia is learned, and so if we want to produce inclusion, we have to pay attention to all forms of significant barriers to inclusion. That the intermediate years mark the arrival in school corridors and the playground of "fag" and "lezzie" as major put-downs, and that the early adolescent years mark a time of high suicide risk for children marked as sexually anomalous.

He is not persuaded. He says that the kids don't even know what words like "fag" mean.

But why, then, I respond, do they choose "fag" and "lezzie" as specifically derogatory?

He is not persuaded. I've seen the look before. He goes and sits down–vindicated. He didn't get the pink slip after all.

Knowledge, after all, is not itself power...

Ignorance and opacity collude or compete with knowledge in mobilizing the flows of energy, desires, goods, meanings, persons...

Such ignorance effects can be harnessed, licensed, and regulated on a mass scale for striking enforcements, perhaps most especially around sexuality (Sedgwick, 1990, p. 415).

"They don't even know what it *means*...!"

Tired from a late afternoon volleyball game, or "netball," as I knew it back then, aged 12 and in my third year at a British all-girls boarding school, I dragged my sweaty body into the residence house, on the alert, as always, for the sadistic Mrs. Doktor, the house mother, who would have relished yet another opportunity to impugn my messy appearance and, therefore, my lack of attention to the necessary attributes of a "proper young woman." Heading for the back staircase, I was faced with a sight of impending loss, the likes of which I have never experienced again to the same degree. All of the girls from the house were lined up and down the front stairs–the "front staircase," which we were expressly forbidden to use, except on days of parent visits. And that day was not a day of parental visits, yet the residents were draped over the banisters and lined up and down the stairs singing "Auld Lang Syne" and weeping into dripping handkerchiefs clutched in small fists. This was a mourning ritual usually reserved for the end of the year, when some girls were leaving the school for good. But who was leaving today, in the middle of the term?

Then I saw her face–that handsome face that I had explored, night after night, hiding under the sheets of a lumpy single bed.

It was Wendy coming down those stairs, hunched over, her parents following, eyes downcast, carrying her two small suitcases. Wendy, whom the other girls actively loathed, was the inspiration for this public wailing. Wendy was the school's lone scholarship student, placed in the "practical arts" stream simply because her working-class background made it, according to the headmistress, unlikely that she would benefit from chemistry and physics.

Wendy, a Welsh coal miner's daughter–a tomboy whose performance of the "proper young woman" routine was decidedly less persuasive even than my own. Wendy–whose warm body I curled into during the most special time of the day for those placed in residential schools–the night–a private time when forbidden lives and forbidden loves could be, albeit cautiously, entertained.

Wendy and I were roommates. We were also lovers and in love. It was Mrs. Doktor who had found us together. She said that we were disgusting, that we were immoral, that she would make sure that we were separated. Mrs. Doktor got her wish. Wendy got the pink slip. She had, according to the headmistress, violated the terms of her scholarship. Mrs. Doktor wrote a letter to my parents, in which my conduct was characterized as "depraved." As it happens, they didn't mention the letter for several years. Comfortably liberal, they were unperturbed. It was, "a phase."

Twenty-five years later, I still miss her. Sometimes, and especially at night, when I crawl into bed, I wonder where Wendy is–who she loves, what she remembers.

Silences...are an integral part of the strategies that underlie and permeate discourses. (Foucault, 1980, p. 2)

It is important to develop a theory of the epistemological significance of ignorance, and an understanding of the richness of its content. Ignorance represents a kind of knowing. Just like, as Foucault has argued, silence represents a kind of speaking–an active engagement with the production of what is considered normal and acceptable–in his words, a technology of normalization. From this standpoint, in order to determine how ignorance becomes a central mechanism through which lesbian and gay issues, lesbian and gay students, teachers and other Others are effectively marginalized in a given context of public schooling, the most productive analytical method entails a careful examination, not of what it *is* that we *do*–those "special signs" that mark us as deviant and by which our deviance can be recognized–but what it *isn't,* a study of what we *don't* do, what we *won't* do–such as the refusal, for instance, to participate in the active construction of an acceptably heterosexual public persona. An examination of the generative power of ignorance would involve the investigator in studying, not what *is* done *against* us (in the manner of explicit human rights violations, for instance which–surprise surprise!–can almost never be "proven") but what *is not* done *for* us, through it may be freely available to "all," (like spousal benefits). Such a study of the ethics and politics of ignorance would require us to investigate what is *not* said on our behalf, when teachers fail to defend gay students, or each other, and what is *not* named, specifically, our very existence in these places.

These silences, and the enforcement of them with respect to

lesbians and gays represent what Eve Kosofsky Sedgwick (1990) has called "the epistemology of the closet."

Sedgwick has powerfully argued that these systematic "ignorances," false "aporias," are not mere "absences," (Foucault,1980; Sedgwick, 1990; Britzman,1995; Lewis, 1992, Leach, 1992; contra Burbules and Rice, 1991) but *active constructions of alterity,* of otherness, of marginality, of deviance. Working from Foucault's terms, understanding the construction of homophobia in educational (and other) institutions entails undertaking an *archaeology of the silences* that have been erected in the service of this powerful and devastating social organization for the production of inequality, stigmatization, and exclusion.

> About one third of teen suicides are by lesbian and gay youth. (Remafedi, 1990)

Silence = Death

Wittgenstein, who was himself a gay man, as well as being the greatest philosopher of the twentieth century, had this to say about the unsayable: "Whereof we may not speak, Thereof we must pass over in silence." He spoke of the bedrock assumptions which pre-structure our life-world, assumptions about which we are usually completely unaware, unconscious. He speaks of philosophical investigation as a kind of excavation and says that when we hit bedrock, "This is where my spade is turned"–we cannot dig any deeper, for we have dug to our limits–we have found a "bedrock assumption" which tells us about the very foundations of our socio-cultural world view.

When we discover, as of course many before us have done, that education rests upon a rock-solid foundation of prohibition–the prohibition against naming queerness–except as the name of horror–in any of its manifestations, in any of its subjects, even those who immediately surround us, those to whom we speak, (and even she who may herself be speaking that very prohibition) we need to take notice. Because silence *does* equal death, and because in not speaking we are ourselves complicit in very real acts of violence, very real assaults against very real people. There is legislation which obliges us, if we are aware that children are being abused, to report that suspicion to the authorities–the police, the child welfare office. But when a mother says to her son after he discloses that he is gay, "God I wish you had never been born, I wish I were dead, I want to kill myself," when a gym teacher calls an already targeted student "FAG!" in front of his entire class, why is it that no one steps in to call a halt? It's just like in *Animal Farm*, when Orwell (1946) has the pig-rulers instruct the animals to recite that "All animals are equal; but some animals are more equal than others." In schools, in society, all violence is deplorable, but "some kinds of violence are much less deplorable than others." It's long past time to understand and to acknowledge there is complicity in violence against human bodies and human spirits whenever anyone stands silently by and allows queer subjects to be harmed, simply because silence, for them, is easier, simply because they themselves are afraid. Guilt by association cuts both ways, though. You may be called a queer if you are an ally and defender of queers. But you *are* contributing to violence against queers if you don't. Schools are sites of continuous aggression against gays and lesbians, they are battlegrounds upon which every day, teachers, students, workers, parents, walk every step in trepidation, knowing full well they are fair game for hatred, assault, for losing their jobs, their friends, their families, their future. And knowing that this is an abuse they must suffer without naming–because at school, gender, specifically heterosexual normativity, is "bedrock," what we must pass over in silence, because "this is where my spade is turned."

Well, our response to this is to remind ourselves that there are other tools besides the spade, and what might never submit to the shovel is like butter to a high-powered hydraulic drill. It's time to change tools.

BE GAY in a COTTON PRINT

Kamikaze Theory? From Utterance to Image

> The only reason for moving,
> And the reason why I roam
> Is to move to a new location
> And find myself a home.
> -Ry Cooder, "Into the Purple Valley"

To suggest that a "change of tools" might enable us to represent the "unspeakable" in what (and not only for queers) is always a "pedagogy of the repressed," what we have not yet said much about is *this very medium*–institutionally authorized forms of reading and writing as privileged means of representation. Nor, relatedly, about the shrinking audiences for and participants in traditional textual communities. By dramatic contrast are the very differently regulated media of television, film, and video, perhaps imminently to be overshadowed by new channels of access to information, but this time (or rather, in this space) information now far, far more extensive in its diversity and its epistemological "reach" than television ever was or could be.

There is an extent to which, in the discourses of any discipline, its very apparatus of articulation come gradually to overtake its capacity to carry new meanings. Like a replicator run amok, the discursive apparatus of educational theory exhausts itself in an endless repetition of structures–redemptive narratives of experience, ventriloquated in speech genres ranging from reassurances about "caring" to exhortations about change and challenge and excellence, riddled throughout with formulaic utterances invoking, less as concepts than as proper names, empowerment and oppositional consciousness and moments of possibility. In this carnivalesque theoretical midway of rigged games and loaded dice, it becomes increasingly apparent to many would-be critical theorists that the discourse virtually speaks itself. Hence, a new species of discursive ethics of textual production is called for, and a new "rhetorical responsibility" comes increasingly to require serious reconsideration of the forms and media in which educational theorists elect to represent themselves and the subjects of their attention. We need, then, to call into question our professional fascination with, absorption by, and somewhat myopic devotion to generic written language forms that, increasingly over time, and with what Benjamin (1969) called the "weight of tradition" (p. 256), come to write themselves, and to write us in the process (and for some of "us," it's more often "out" than "up")

Briefly and very preliminarily, this is why we are trying to work with images in place of text. It's about access and what can't be thought, what can't be said; what can't, therefore, be done.

Such a shift from text-based to image-based forms of representation may, accordingly, also offer a "queerer" pedagogy (Britzman, 1995; Bryson and de Castell 1993), especially insofar as, as Simon Watney (1991) has pointed out, the representation of queer existence, in and of itself, has come to be officially constituted as "recruitment" and prohibited as such. This is most readily apparent in the notorious "section 28" legislation in the UK, prohibiting "the promotion" of homosexuality.

As part of our ongoing research into gender/equity/technology, and in the attempt to learn to use new tools, we shot and edited a twenty-four-minute videotape concerned with technologies for the formation of lesbian identity (Sexed Tetes, 1994). Our intention in this project was not to contest but enthusiastically to *embrace* the charge that any representation of queerness constitutes its promotion, and, from that standpoint, to proclaim a fundamentally educational role for (and a complementary educational obligation to produce and promote) representations of queer identities. These are relatively unexplored tools for people to feel and respond to and remember with, to think with, *differently*, especially now that both "thinking" and "acting" are being reconfigured in startlingly new (Stone, 1991) constitutive relations to "virtuality." At a time when retreat to the body itself has become a chief contemporary semiotic domain, and this in particular for youth and other socially disenfranchised groups for whom the prospect of rights to/control over physical space appear remote, image-based media offer an additional, substantially broader territory, less-well colonized than "legitimate" academic genres. These new cultural spaces, whose "ownership" remains at this point still relatively undetermined, may perhaps be differently informed, and, the hope, therefore, is, that they will offer some possibility of being differently (pre)figured.

In their argument for the significant epistemic and expressive functions of non-linguistic forms, in this case, drawings, Weber and Mitchell (1996) invoke Suzanne Langer's (1971) reminder of a vast range of profound human experiences that "are generally regarded as irrational because words cannot give us clear ideas of them–namely [the view] that anything language cannot express is formless and irrational." For "Others" in discourse who have recourse only to tactics in the ongoing contest over meanings, however, such non-linguistic forms/

genres provide potential locations within which speaking "otherwise" becomes possible. Moreover, in alternative semiotic spaces, Weber and Mitchell explain, "Much of what we have seen of known, thought or imagined, remembered or repressed, slips unbidden..., revealing unexplored ambiguities, contradictions and connections. That which we have forgotten, that which we might censor from our speech and writing, often escapes into our drawings" (Weber and Mitchell, 1996, p. 34). New resources, then, in addition to new structures–these are the enticements to migrate to less well-charted locations from which to articulate new identities for theory and praxis in education.

Extroduction: Your Place or Mine?

> Roy: Your problem Henry, is that you are hung up on words, on labels, that you believe they mean what they seem to mean. AIDS. Homosexual. Gay. Lesbian. You think these are names that tell you who someone sleeps with, but they don't tell you that.

> Henry: No?

> Roy: No. Like all labels, they tell you one thing and one thing only; where does an individual so identified fit into the food chain, the pecking order. Not ideology or sexual taste, but something much simpler: clout. Not who I fuck or who fucks me, but who will pick up the phone when I call, who owes me favors. This is what a label refers to. Now to someone who does not understand this, homosexual is what I am because I have sex with men. But really this is wrong. Homosexuals are men who, in 15 years of trying cannot get a pissant antidiscrimination bill through City Council. Homosexuals are men who know nobody and who nobody knows. Who have zero clout. Does this sound like me, Henry? (Kushner, 1992, *Angels in America*, Act 1, Scene 9)

Well this, folks, is where we are. And from *that* position, can we get a pissant queer curriculum through the University?

Cheers,
Sz/M

Note
1.   de Certeau's analysis (1984) of the ownership of space/place as requisite to strategic action, with tactics being what is left to the

"landless," that is to say, those without rights to control territory, can here be productively read alongside Bakhtin's (1981) discussion of the history of utterances, and the notion that we as individual speakers at particular moments can only "rent" meaning. We are reminded though, that in a host of forms of "institutionally bound" (Habermas, 1984)) speech genres, with/in discourses more "authoritative" than "internally pursuasive," some speakers "own their own homes"–renting out their basement suites to Others. The move from controlled to unorganized (or at least as yet *less* organized) territory is a "tactical" move to a more "strategic" location.

References

Bakhtin, Mikhail. (1981). *The dialogic imagination.* Austin, TX: University of Texas Press.

B.C.T.F. (British Columbia Teachers' Federation). (1991). *Teacher,* 3(7), 2-3.

Benjamin, Walter (1969). *Illuminations.* [Trans. Harry Zohn.] New York: Schocken Books.

Britzman, Deborah P. (1995). Is there a queer pedagogy?: Or, stop reading straight. *Educational Theory* 45 (2), 151-165. [Reprinted in this volume.]

Bryson, Mary, and de Castell, Suzanne. (1993). Queer pedagogy: Praxis makes im/perfect. *Canadian Journal of Education.* 18(3), 285-305.

Burbules, Nicholas, and Rice, Suzanne. (1991). Dialogue across differences. *Harvard Educational Review,* 61, 393-416.

de Castell, Suzanne. (1995). Textuality and the Designs of Theory. pp. 241-257 In W. Kohli (Ed.) *Critical Conversations in Philosophy of Education.* New York and London: Routledge.

de Certeau, Michel. (1984). *The practice of everyday life.* Berkeley: University of California Press.

de la Luz Reyes, M. (in press). Chicanas in academe: An endangered species. In S. de Castell and M. Bryson (Eds.), *Radical in<ter>ventions: Identity, politics and difference in educational praxis.* New York: SUNY Press.

Foucault, Michel. (1980). *The history of sexuality: Volume 1.* New York: Vintage Books.

Goody, Jack. (1977). *The domestication of the savage mind.* Cambridge: Cambridge University Press.

Graff, Harvey. (1982). *Literacy and social development in the west.* Cambridge, Cambridge University Press.

Habermas, Jurgen. (1984). *The theory of communicative action. Volume One.* Thomas McCarthy (Trans.), Boston: Beacon Press.

Hoodfar, H. (1992). Feminist anthropology and critical pedagogy: The anthropology of classrooms' excluded voices. *Canadian Journal of Education,* 17, 303-320.

Kushner, Tony. (1992) *Angels in America, Part 1: Millennium Approaches.* New York: Theater Communications Group.

Langer, Suzanne.(1971). The cultural importance of the arts. In R. Smith (Ed.), *Aesthetics and the problems of education* (pp. 86-96). Chicago: University of Illinois Press.

Leach, Mary. (1992). Can we talk? A response to Burbules and Rice. *Harvard Educational Review,* 62(2), 257-263.

Lewis, Magda. (1992). Interrupting patriarchy: Politics, resistance and transformation in the feminist classroom. In C. Luke and J. Gore (Eds.), *Feminisms and critical pedagogy* (pp. 167-191), New York: Routledge.

Ng, Roxanna. (1993). "A woman out of control": Deconstructing sexism and racism in the University. *Canadian Journal of Education,* 18(3), 189-206.

Olson, David. (1994). *The world on paper.* Cambridge: Cambridge University Press.

Orwell, George (1946). *Animal farm.* New York: Harcourt, Brace and Company

Oxford Concise Dictionary (1964). Oxford: Oxford University Press.

Penley, Constance and Ross, Andrew. Eds. (1991) Introduction, *Techno-culture* (pp. viii-xvii). Minneapolis: University of Minnesota Press.

Porter, John. (1965). *The vertical mosaic.* Toronto: University of Toronto Press.

Remafedi, Gary. (1990). *Death by denial: Studies of suicide in gay and lesbian teenagers.* Boston: Alyson.

Rich, Adrienne. (1982). *Lies, secrets and silence.* New York: Norton.

Sedgwick, Eve Kosofsky. (1990). *Epistemology of the closet.* Berkeley: University of California Press.

Sexed Tetes Collective. (1994). *Deviance by design: A Queer pedagogy* (videotape, 24 min.). Simon Fraser University, Burnaby, B.C.

Smith, Dorothy. (1987). *The everyday world as problematic.* Toronto: University of Toronto Press.

Smith, Dorothy. (1994). *The documentary practices of power.* Toronto: University of Toronto Press.

Stone, Allequerre Rosanne. (1991). Boundary stories about virtual cultures. In M. Benedikt (Ed.), *Cyberspace: First steps* (pp. 81-118). Boston: MIT Press.

Watney, Simon. (1991). School's out. In Diana Fuss (Ed.), *Inside/out: Lesbian theories, gay theories.* (pp. 387-401). New York: Routledge.

Weber, Sandra and Mitchell, Claudia. (1996). *That's funny, You don't look like a teacher.* London: Falmer Press.

West, Cornel. (1987). Postmodernism and black America. *Zeta Magazine,* 1, 27-29.

Chapter Twelve

The Uses of Culture:
Canon Formation, Postcolonial Literature, and the Multicultural Project

Cameron McCarthy

> For those who really made the break through, it was Eliot's voice–
> or rather his recorded voice, property of the British Council–
> reading "Preludes," "The Love Song of J. Alfred Prufrock," *The
> Waste Land* and the *Four Quartets*–not the texts–which turned us
> on. In that dry deadpan delivery, the riddims of St. Louis (though
> we didn't know the source then) were stark and clear for those of us
> who at the same time were listening to the dedications of Bird,
> Dizzy and Klook. And it is interesting that the whole establish-
> ment couldn't stand Eliot's voice–far less jazz! (Edward
> Brathwaite, *The History of the Voice*, 1984, pp. 310-314)

> To establish his own identity, Caliban, after three centuries, must
> himself pioneer into regions Caesar never knew... (C.L.R. James,
> *Beyond a Boundary,* p. xix).

> In Latin America, epic events (terrible and wonderful) are
> commonplace (Carpentier, 1995, p. 163).

Introduction

This essay seeks to promote a rethinking of constructs such as culture,
identity and the relations between centers and peripheries. I want to
argue that these concepts and relations are far more dynamic than the
ways in which we normally conceptualize them in educational research.
I suspect that the dynamism and heterogeneity of everyday life of the
myriad human encounters that produce and reproduce cultures and

identities are thwarted in education because even the most radical research continues to be overburdened and weighed down by the legacy of behavioral social science and behavior psychology. Against the latter, much is still measured in the educational field. I want to suggest that by contrast, it is in literature and in popular culture that the dynamism and contradictions of identity, community, and so forth are restored and foregrounded. Specifically, this essay seeks to critique the gratuitous opposition of Western canonical literature and traditions to the literary traditions of the Third World. It looks specifically at examples of radical cultural hybridity foregrounded in postcolonial literature. And I argue that the latter constitute a space for the exploration of difference, not simply as a problem, but as an opportunity for a conversation over curriculum reform and the radically diverse communities we now serve in the university and in schools. This essay is a part of a larger project to bring a cultural studies perspective to bear on the theory and practice of multiculturalism by foregrounding historical variability, shifting social contexts and environments, and the inevitable trestles of association between the canon and the quotidian, the empire and the postcolony.

This essay challenges the easy opposition of the canon to non-Western and Third World literature and the curricular project of content addition and replacement that now guides some multicultural frameworks. This opposition is illegitimate, and furthermore, it is not empirically based. Indeed, as Edward Said (1993) points out, even a cursory glance at the literature of the Latino, African, African American, Asian, and Caribbean writers reveals a very different picture: that of a buoyant play of ideas and a vigorous dialogue over themes of authority, privilege, freedom, and culture. I agree with Said and Homi Bhabha (1994) that postcolonial literature, particularly with respect to the novel, involves a rewriting and a re-deployment of characterization and subjectivity of the nineteenth-century genre. I believe that the deconstructive critique of the West undertaken in postcolonial fiction has not yet been fulfilled, and has certainly not exhausted itself. Emergent discourses of multicultural education could profit from a closer look at the complex ways in which literature treats issues of culture, identity, and knowledge production. This essay aims at a long overdue intervention in the raging debate over postcolonial and minority literatures, canon formation, and multicultural curriculum reform. This essay is intended as a caution against the tendency toward cultural exceptionalism and cultural purity that informs current Eurocentric and ethnicity-based curriculum reform platforms now rampant in education. Instead, I seek to call attention to the radical cultural hybridity that is the historically-evolved reality of human encounters in the modern and postmodern world. By cultural hybridity, I am not talking about some happy process of integration of differences. Instead, I am talking about what Homi Bhabha (1994, p. 112) calls the "return of the gaze on the eye of power" itself. I am talking about the interactive, developmental, bricolage of postcolonial knowledge production that produces discontinuity and disquiet for the colonizer. This hybridization asserts itself in a triple-play, a radical excess of desires and interests. This hybridizing movement in aesthetics and politics chooses as its preferred strategy of resistance humor, satire, and parody, and it more importantly chooses to engage with the canonical tradition as if it were its own–reworking, reordering historical ruins with the dispassion of what Walter Benjamin (1977) calls, in his *The Origin of German Tragic Drama,* "melancholy." Melancholy is understood, here, not as sadness and despondency but as a liberating skepticism toward cultural hierarchies and historical ruins. This hybridizing development is a central force in peripheries and metropolises alike; and postcolonial literature, particularly postcolonial fiction, offers the most vocal announcement of the new multicultural age coming into itself.

Postcolonial Literature

In a 1984 interview, the Cuban novelist and music historian Alejo Carpentier talked extensively about the fact that the Latin American novel of magical realism draws on baroque, poetic, and culturally-hybrid impulses that continue to emanate from a cultural stream constantly replenished by the folkways of the Latin American people themselves. To illustrate this point about cultural hybridity, Carpentier tells the story of an intriguing encounter he had while visiting the remote forest community of Turiamo, on the Caribbean coast of Venezuela. Here, the villagers introduced Carpentier to "the Poet"–an illiterate Afro-Latin griot, who was regarded as the keeper of communal history, the people's poet. In meeting this illiterate, itinerant peasant, Carpentier came face to face with the multiaccented, polyphonic voice of these anthropologically defined "natives." At a late-night communal gathering, which Carpentier attended, this Afro-Latin griot, "the Poet," recited for his fellow forest dwellers gathered by the sea extensive passages of eighth-century French Epic verse in the indigenous Aztec language of Nahuatl. Carpentier tells the story this way:

Let me tell you an anecdote which illustrates the poetic tradition in Latin America. More than twenty years ago, when I was living in Venezuela, my wife and I went to stay in a small fishing village on the Caribbean coast called Turiamo. There were no hotels, no bars, and you got there by crossing kilometres and kilometres of virgin forest. All the inhabitants of the village were black, there were no schools and almost everyone was illiterate. We soon got to know the village people and they told us about the Poet, a person who enjoyed a great deal of prestige there. He hadn't been to the village for about two months and the people missed him. One day he reappeared, bringing news from other areas. He was a colossal negro, illiterate and poorly dressed. I told him I'd like to hear his poetry. "Yes," he replied, "Tonight, by the sea."

And that night all the village people, children, old folk, every one, gathered on the beach to wait for the Poet. He took off his hat with a ritual gesture and, looking out to sea, with his deep, somewhat monotonous voice, began in quite acceptable octosyllables to recite the wonderful story of Charlemagne in a version similar to that of the Song of Roland.

That day I understood perhaps for the first time that in our America, wrongly named Latin, where an illiterate black descendant of Yorubas could recreate the Song of Roland–in a language richer than Spanish, full of distinctive inflections, accents, expressions and syntax–where wonderful Nahuatl poetry existed long before Christopher Columbus was born, even before Alfonso the Wise and San Isidoro's *Etymologies,* in our America, there were a culture and a theatrical disposition which gave poetry an importance long lost in many countries in Europe (Carpentier, 1985, p. 160).

In a similar manner, the St. Lucian poet, Derek Walcott (1993), in his 1992 Nobel Lecture, "The Antilles: Fragments of Epic Memory," talks about taking some American friends to a peasant performance of the ancient Hindu epic of Ramayana in a forgotten corner of the Caroni Plain in Trinidad. The name of this tiny village is the happily agreeable, but Anglo-Saxon, "Felicity." The actors carrying out this ritual reenactment are the plain-as-day East Indian villagers spinning this immortal web of memory, of ancientness and modernity. Here, again, Walcott, like Carpentier, is "surprised by sin" at the simple native world unfurling in its utter flamboyance:

Felicity is a village in Trinidad on the edge of the Caroni Plain, the wide central plain that still grows sugar and to which indentured cane cutters were brought after emancipation, so the small population of Felicity is East Indian, and on the afternoon that I visited it with friends from America, all the faces along its road were Indian, which as I hope to show was a moving, beautiful thing, because this Saturday afternoon Ramleela, the epic dramatization of the Hindu epic of Ramayana, was going to be performed, and the costumed actors from the village were assembling on a field strung with different-colored flags, like a new gas station, and beautiful Indian Boys in red and black were aiming arrows haphazardly into the afternoon light. Low blue mountains on the horizon, bright grass, clouds that would gather color before the light went. Felicity! What a gentle anglo-Saxon name for an epical memory (Walcott, 1993, p. 1).

Carpentier and Walcott's vividly reported vignettes point us toward the complex flow of humanity across presumptive borders. What these authors have chosen to highlight is the radical encounter of ancient and modern peoples in postcolonial cultures, and the unanticipated trestles of affiliation that link up disparate populations. These writerly stories highlight the difficulty, indeed the futility, of atavistic attempts to maintain group purity, neonationalist-inspired attempts to separate cultural traditions as the basis of some new cultural or social regime.

But the founding of postcolonial literature is not simply to be located in the periphery, it most certainly must be located in the metropole as well. The complex humanity of an already culturally ruined, half-made Third World people has spread its tentacles into the first. The postcolonial novel is, then, ultimately a creation of forces of cultural modernization...huge dually destabilizing and integrative logics at home and abroad. The postnational travelers of Mexico, Nigeria, or Bombay greet London or Paris or Toronto or New York City with loudly announced intentions to hang round for awhile.

Latin American and postcolonial literatures, in the words of Octavio Paz (1990), have therefore often been "a reply" to European traditions. Postcolonial literature exists in a critical dialogue with First World literature. In this sense, George Lamming's *The Pleasures of Exile* (1984) is a direct response to William Shakespeare's *The Tempest*. Here, Lamming calls central attention to issues of language and identity and the master-slave relationship. For Lamming, Caliban's ensnarement by Prospero's gift of language reveals the mask that covers the face of language. Language is not a system of nomenclature in which words innocently name things that are already out there in the world. Instead, language is deeply wrapped up in the reproduction of social power, the coordination of hierarchies of identity, and the project of colonial subordination and its neocolonial variations. In the seductions and impositions of Prospero's language, Caliban is constrained to see the world through Prospero's motivated categories. But this encounter between Caliban and Prospero allows for Caliban's rearticulation and reinvention of imposed tradition–Caliban has the capacity to curse.

In a similar way, Chinua Achebe's *Things Fall Apart* (1969) is a reply to Joseph Conrad's *Heart of Darkness* (1988). In this novel (the title of which is borrowed from W.B. Yeats' poem, "The Second Coming"), Achebe responds to the moment of aporia in Conrad's construction of Africa as featureless, as a vast expanse of blankness. Achebe's fiction provides an historical account of colonial expansion in Nigeria and its destructive, corrosive effects on the Yoruba people and culture. At another level, Achebe's central character Okonwo is like a Michael Henchard in Thomas Hardy's *The Mayor of Casterbridge* (1994) caught between tradition and change, unable to grasp the future. In a similar manner, Toni Morrison's Jadine in *Tar Baby* (1981) is a liminal character caught between two worlds: one white, one black. When she visits the down-home Southern black community, Eloe, with her lover, Son, she is unable to connect with the stifling traditional values and folkways of the people of Son's origins. The loud kaboom which she hears when she is left alone in the Eloe community indicates her alienation from the place. This noise alludes to the echo that Adela Quested hears in the Malabar Caves in E. M. Forster's *A Passage to India* (1984). Finally, in *The Dragon Can't Dance* (1979), a novel written by the Trinidadian writer Earl Lovelace, one of the characters, a lunatic called Taffy, announces his own fake-crucifixion as a modern day Christ. He is the self-appointed messiah, a martyr, unrecognized, willing to die the classical death by stoning. But when he feels the first impressions of real stones pelted by his jeering friends, he hastily abandons his project and literally hurries down from the cross:

> This is the hill tall above the city where Taffy, a man who say he is Christ, put himself up on a cross one burning midday and say to his followers: "Crucify me! Let me die for my people. Stone me with stones as you stone Jesus, I will love you still." And when they start to stone him in truth he get vex and start to cuss: "Get me down! Get me down," he say. Let every sinnerman bear his own blasted burden; who is I to die for people who ain't have sense

enough to know that they can't pelt a man with big stones when
so much little pebbles lying on the ground" (Lovelace, p. 31).

The mock-religious chiding here is all good fun. But like Jamaica
Kincaid, in her travel book, *A Small Place* (1988) and V.S. Naipaul in,
The Mimic Men (1969), Lovelace intends to launch an attack on the
idea of the necessary centrality of the hero-figure in Western literature,
and his real life postcolonial counterpart, the self-deluded, pretentious
politician who almost never delivers on his promises.

Implications for the Curriculum

The postcolonial proposition that culture is radically hybrid has sharp
implications for the dominant curriculum and the emergent discourses
of multiculturalism that continue to represent culture and identity in
static and atheoretic terms.

First of all, the cultural hybridity registered in the new postcolonial
literature brings into view the subaltern gaze on the eye of power–the
West as deconstructed in the carnavalesque, the laughter, and excess
buried in the remains of empire, historical ruins, and opulent traditions
elaborated in the encounters between Europe and the rest of humanity.
Educational and cultural theorists often talk about identity and identity
politics as though only minority groups, particularly, African Americans and Latinos, practice and benefit from the deployment of identity
construction; and as if they are the only ones who experience the
consequences of such identity construction: namely, group fragmentation, hybridity, entropy, and so forth. But what the deconstructive
project in Third World literature points us toward is the radical instability within Western traditions themselves. This is particularly true
with respect to canon formation. As writers such as Michael Berube,
Gerald Graff, John Guillory, Dominic LaCapra, Gauri Viswanathan and
Cornel West have pointed out, canon formation is itself a strategy of
interpretation of historical crisis–a massive effort to coordinate
dominant identities by pasting over breaks and contradictions within
hegemonic cultural form. For instance, the canonization of British
literature occurred after World War I, in the 1920s and 1930s, at a time
when Europe was in disarray and the British empire was on the wane.
British canonization of its literature played a critical role, along with
the British Broadcasting Corporation, in cultivating a sense of national
identity and a recoding of empire as the "Commonwealth of Nations."
While the universities worked toward the canonization of literature, the

British Broadcasting Corporation helped to draw the line between high and low-brow cultural form and served to coordinate the standardization of spoken English at home and overseas. All of this, of course, would not prevent the empire from striking back as the migratory waves of postcolonial souls–the hybrid masses from the ends of the earth–descended on England in the '60s and '70s to collect long-overdue colonial debts.

A second consideration is the implications of postcolonial literature for the development of new methodologies in the multicultural project of curriculum reform. Multicultural education proponents must move beyond present Manichean notions of cultural form. The static models of content addition and content replacement that now drive some multicultural approaches to curriculum reform must be rethought. We need to get beyond the idea of teaching multiculturalism as corrective bits of knowledge–the fallout of a curricular truce with the textbook industry in which the good realism of the multicultural text is counter-posed to the bad fiction of stereotypes. We need to let the complexity of the world foregrounded in postcolonial literature into the classroom. This would mean, in the area of language arts, for instance, teaching literature contrapuntally, teaching Conrad's *Heart of Darkness* along with Achebe's *Things Fall Apart*, Shakespeare's *Tempest* along with Aime Césaire's *Tempe Noire*, and so forth.

And, finally, haven't we been here before? Didn't we visit this precipice with the great debates between John Dewey and Robert Maynard Hutchins in the 1930s over the Liberal Arts curriculum–perennialism versus pragmatism, absolute truth versus historical contingency and socially recognizable evidence? And haven't we been here before in the socially extended philosophy of W.E.B. Du Bois, C.L.R. James, and Walt Whitman? The last, in "Democratic Vistas," argued against the hegemony of what he called the "literature of the court," and had this to say about the role of literature in the education of the people:

> The great poems, Shakespeare included, are poisonous to the idea of the pride and dignity of the common people, the lifeblood of democracy. The models of literature, as we get it from other lands, ultra marine, have had their birth in courts, and bask'd and grown in castle sunshine; all smells of princes' favors.... Do you call those genteel little creatures American poets? Do you term the perpetual, pistareen, paste-pot work, American Art American drama, taste, verse?... We see the sons and daughters of The New

World, ignorant of its genius, not yet inaugurating the native, the universal, and the near, still importing, the distant, the partial, the dead (qtd. in Jordan, 1980, p. xx).

Maybe we are all exiles in a dehumanizing educational process. And maybe some modicum of redemption will begin in the first recognition of our inadequacies and our critical involvement in the plight of those others that we demonize in our theories every day. It is these demons, these cyborgs, that now inhabit postcolonial literatures in the periphery and in the center alike. In announcing their hybridity, they raise new possibilities of community, conflicted but bounded together for better or worse–in the multicultural world that rages into the twenty-first century.

References

Achebe, C. (1969). *Things fall apart*. New York: Fawcett Crest.

Benjamin, W. (1977). *The origin of German tragic drama*. (John Osbourne Trans.). London: New Left Books.

Bhabha, H. (1994). *The location of culture*. New York: Routledge.

Brathwaite, E. (1984). *The history of the voice*. London: New Beacon.

Carpentier, A. (1985). The Latin American novel. In *New Left Review* 154, pp. 159-191.

Conrad, J. (1988). *Heart of darkness*. New York: Norton.

Forster, E.M. (1984). *A passage to India*. New York: Harcourt Brace Jovanovich.

Hardy, T. (1994). *The mayor of Casterbridge*. London: Wordsworth Editions Limited.

James, C.L.R. (1983). *Beyond a boundary*. New York: Pantheon.

Jordan, J. (1980). For the sake of people's poetry: Walt Whitman and the rest of us. In, J. Jordan (Ed.), *Passion* (pp. ix-xxvi). Boston: Beacon.

Kincaid, J. (1988). *A small place*. New York: Plume.

Lamming, G. (1984). *The pleasures of exile*. London: Allison & Busby.

Lovelace, E. (1979). *The dragon can't dance*. London: Longman.

Morrison, T. (1981). *Tar baby*. New York: Plume.

Naipaul, V.S. (1969). *The mimic men*. London: Penguin.

Paz, O. (1990). *In search of the present*. New York: Harcourt Brace Jovanovich.

Said, E. (1993). *Culture and imperialism*. New York: Knopf.

Walcott, D. (1993). *The Antilles: Fragments of epic memory.* New York: Farrar Straus and Giroux.

Chapter Thirteen

Engendering Curriculum History

Petra Munro

That history produces subjects rather than subjects producing history might seem a poststructural "fact."[1] Yet, how the discourses of curriculum history collude in producing normative assumptions of gendered, raced, and sexed subjects remains relatively unproblematized. The primary focus of this essay is on the ways in which the discursive practices of curriculum history make particular subject identities thinkable. However, to interrogate the "subject of history" at the same time that the death toll of "history" and the "subject" has been rung is a seemingly contradictory position. It is this site of dis-ease, doing history while simultaneously being suspicious of it, which I embrace. What does it mean to do history if there is no longer a subject? What are the implications of history being in flux at the very moment that the histories of those traditionally marginalized are being articulated? As a woman curriculum theorist I ask, "Can I give up a history before I even have one?" When history has functioned as a primary form of oppression, "Do I even want one?" What does it mean to do curriculum history at this particular juncture?

Rather than abandon history as a "relic of humanist thought" (Scott, 1989), I seek a feminist poststructuralist reading of curriculum history which attempts to disrupt the search for origins and to decenter the unitary heroic subject, either male or female. I also want to challenge the myth of progress by conceiving of history as the confluence of processes so interconnected that it cannot be reduced to a unitary storyline (grand narrative). Rejecting a compensatory approach to re/writing history, which leaves dominant historical categories and periodization intact, I examine how the narrative structures of curriculum histories are implicated in the construction of gendered subjects. To problematize the notion of the subject, without giving up the political work of "recovering" women's history, is the feminist post-structuralist challenge which I take up. I maintain that we must become comfortable with a more complex, less tidy, nonlinear understanding of the history of curriculum theory which disrupts the very categories that make "history" intelligible.[2]

History as Memory Work

> History as celebrated by memory is a deciphering of the invisible,
> a geography of the supernatural.... It brings about an evocation of
> the past..." (Vernant, 1983, p. 80).

History has always provided me a way to reshape the future through reimagining the past. As a young girl it was history, rather than literature, science, or art, that provided me a way to understand who I was and more importantly who I was not. History held extraordinary power. As a young girl this was a profound insight. Having learned my history lessons well, I knew I was to be seen, not heard. This silencing was not the result of explicit sanctions. There was no need to cut my tongue out, to gag me, or to banish me from public places. Unlike the women in history books, this was not necessary. Astonishingly enough, I had already learned to silence myself–bite my tongue, hold my peace. This repression is the history that has no voice. My knowledge that women's experiencing of the world is invisible is a painful reminder that history, and in this case specifically curriculum history, is predicated on subjugation and erasure.

Consequently, I begin with the premise that to conduct history in these poststructural times is to recover from the "epistemic violence" (Spivak, 1988) which has been history. Put more simply, "history is what hurts, it is what refuses desire and sets inexorable limits to individual as well as collective praxis" (Jameson, 1981, p. 102). These limits are the consequence of the modernist obsession with objectivity and rationality which function to make "natural" the concepts of the subject as unitary; temporality as linear, continuous and coherent; and progress as the inevitable consequence of history. By problematizing the very nature of knowledge as objective and corresponding to any reality, the deconstructionist turn has been central to problematizing modern forms of knowledge, like history, that seem natural but are in fact contingent of sociohistorical constructs of power (Foucault, 1977; Polkinghorne, 1988; Young, 1990).

According to Jane Flax (1990), modernist history's "appearance of unity presupposes and requires a prior act of violence" (p. 33).[3] The subject of traditionalist history–unitary, male, heterosexual, white–is made possible through the de-construction of its other.[4] History's appearance of unity, of coherence, of order is predicated not on any direct correspondence to a reality but on the suppression of contradictory stories, those of women, people of color, the working class. History as we know it is not possible without this silencing. This suppression is the "epistemic violence" upon which the myth of a unified and fixed subject, which functions to "universalize" history and make it gender-less, is contingent (Smith, 1995). History as we know it limits contra-diction, multiplicity, and difference. Remembering this suppression is the memory work which must be done.

"Righting" or "Writing" History

My dis-ease in "doing history" is the result of the tension between the need to write/right the histories of "women," "African Americans," and other marginalized groups into curriculum theorizing while simultaneously deconstructing those categories of history which have made possible the violence of erasure and subjugation. Rather than see these views as incommensurate, I will try to avoid the binary sim-plicity of either/or arguments. I maintain that one sickness of contemporary theorizing is to continue to seek unitary theories despite our acknowledgment that knowledge is multiple, contradictory, and always in flux. To envision both of these standpoints as compatible and, in fact, necessary, I will briefly review their theoretical histories.

To write women back into history has been a primary aim of feminist scholarship. However, "doing history" which adds the stories of women, blacks, and marginalized others does little to disrupt history as usual. Merely adding the names of women would be to ignore Joan Kelly's (1984) salient reminder that "what we call compensatory history is not enough" (p. 2). To merely include women heroines would be to perpetuate the often silent and hidden operations of gender in shaping historical analysis. For example, although we include women–like Margaret Haley or Ella Flagg Young or Ida B. Wells–in the story of progressivism, the very concept or periodization of the "progressive movement" as gendered and gendering remains unproblematized.[5] In essence, the classic formation of narrative history as suggested by

Susan Paddle (1995)–a unified subject and a plot predicated on the unfolding of a tale with implicit motifs of progression, development, and growth–remains the same. As a consequence, history retains the illusion of a seamless narrative written by an omniscient, invisible narrator. In other words, history remains grounded in an epistemology based on objectivity, and the very categories of history which have functioned to make women invisible remain intact.

Ironically, then, this compensatory view of history can contribute to reinforcing the notion of objectivity by claiming to make "better" history or at least a more rigorous, complete history. Susan Friedman (1995) reminds us that "this search to discover the 'truth' of women's history that could shatter the 'myths' and 'lies' about women in the standard histories operates out of a positivist epistemology that assumes that the truth of history is objectively knowable" (p. 14). Consequently, this kind of compensatory or oppositional history has been deeply problematic for many feminists (Riley, 1989; Scott, 1987) because it constitutes "women" as an essentialized and fixed category. The diversity of women's experiences is not only ignored, but what becomes obscured is that "woman" itself is a social construction, a product of discourse. Events or selves, in order to exist, must be encoded as story elements. What compensatory history makes invisible is that there is no identity outside of narrative. Narrative, as Paul Ricoeur reminds us, imposes on events of the past a form that in themselves they do not really have. Because events and selves are reconstructions, original purity of experience can never be achieved.[6] For feminists concerned with writing women back into history, this is a profound theoretical as well as political concern.

History as Discourse or History as Anorexia?

To give up the concept of "woman" or even "women" because it is a fiction–a product of language or discourse–is potentially to delegitimate any concern for the "real" and "experience." Gayle Greene (1993) refers to this lack of a referential as a kind of "professional/pedagogical anorexia" in which endless deferral functions as a form of self-erasure, "an analogue to our obsession with thinness, a way of assuring ourselves and others that we'll take up less space" (p. 16-17). This "disappearing act" raises serious concerns regarding not only the ability to write women back into history but also about the ability to make any feminist knowledge claims.[7] The invisibility and silencing of women precedes as usual. Thus, the deconstructive turn potentially allows the subject to "stand free of its own history...and the depoliticization of knowledge can proceed more or less at will" (Said, 1989, p. 222). To be free of history is to sever the memory of inscription. Thus, despite my discomfort with a positivist epistemology, I am reluctant to give up the notion of "real women." If we abandon a representational view of history do we set ourselves up for erasure, do we in fact become complicit in the modernist dream of history as universal, objective, and, in essence, genderless?[8]

Of course, the binary of whether history is fact or fiction is part of the dis-ease (Margolis, 1993). History is always a fiction (White, 1978), but this does not make it less real. How the story is told–why and at what point the fictions are conceived (Adams, 1990; Portelli, 1991), the discrepancies between what is told and what is experienced–are themselves theoretical constructs (Pagano, 1990). To re-cover from history is in part, dependent on reconceptualizing and re-member-ing the suppression, the contradiction, the pain, the fiction that is history.

History is not the representation of reality, it never has been. For the early Greeks, memory was not a means to situate events within a temporal framework but to understand the whole process of becoming. History, as a function of time, loses the poetic, the imaginative and the power to evoke. History as an evocation of memory becomes our relationship to, and experiencing of, the identities made possible or impossible through historical narrative. In other words, history is the evocation of what makes invisibility possible. The Popular Memory Group (1992) suggests that memory is a dimension of political practice. As Gramsci has argued, a sense of history must be one element in a strong popular socialist culture (Popular Memory Group, 1992). History is the means by which a social group acquires the knowledge of the larger context of its collective struggles and becomes capable of a wider transformative role in society. This "recovery of history" is not intended to function as a corrective, to make history right, but as a process through which a group may "consciously adopt, reject or modify" history (Popular Memory Group, 1992, p. 214).

To remember our experiencing of ourselves as objects is to "witness" or "testify" to the trauma of silencing, distortion, and invisibility. To testify, according to Shoshana Felman (1992), is to "vow to tell, to promise and produce one's own speech as material evidence for truth" (p. 5). This, according to Felman, is not a statement of fact but a speech act. Drawing on the autobiographical life accounts given by

Holocaust survivors, Felman suggests that testifying

> enable[d] them for the first time to believe that it is possible,
> indeed, against all odds and against their past experience, to tell
> the story and be heard, to in fact address the significance of their
> biography–to address, that is, the suffering, the truth, and the
> necessity of this impossible narration–to a hearing "you," and a
> listening community (p. 41).

To make "something lasting out of remembrance" is the task of both
the poet and historiographer as Hannah Arendt reminds us (1954, p.
45).[9] To remember, to conceive of history as memory work, is to
confront the myths of what can and cannot have a history. How the
narrative of curriculum history genders is the memory work which must
be done.

Myth #1: The Line History Draws

Like a fairy tale, the story of curriculum history produces and
reproduces a narrative as soothing as a bedtime story–the lone scholar in
the wilderness (colonial school master) is confronted by the threat of
industrialization and urbanization. This struggle between the old and the
new is the site for rebellion and transformation. The narrative is a
familiar one–an age of innocence, crisis, and enlightenment. Embedded
within this plot is a deeply gendered tale. It is the quintessential hero's
tale predicated on separation (lone schoolmaster), individuation (common school movement), and control (reforms-progressivism, technical
rationalism, and professionalization are conspicuously masculine
discourses that focus on individuality and autonomy). It is a tale of repression and fear that has little to do with a "real" sequence of events
and everything to do with how gender is produced through the narrative
we call "history."

Narrative authority in Western culture is, according to Charlotte
Linde (1993), predicated on the ability of the narrator to create a sense
of continuity (cause and effect), coherence (connection of past and
present), and individuation (sense of a separate self). These narrative conventions are not constraints on the historian; rather, they create the
possibility of narration (Martin, 1986). Thus, locating how continuity,
coherence, and individuation are inscribed in history as "real" provides
ruptures and possibilities for interrogating how history is central to the
production of subject identities. In the case of the tale of schooling,

what identities/subjects are made possible or impossible when curriculum history presents itself as an apparently unified, linear story of the one-room school house, common school movement and pro-gressivism? And, how might we disrupt the tidiness of curriculum history to allow for the complexity of gender and history?

Curriculum history usually begins with the tale of the emergence of public schooling. [10] Horace Mann and Henry Barnard are most often credited with this democratization of education.[11] To view this sequence of events–from the one room schoolhouse to the public common school–as a natural culmination of events or process of development is to make real what is the product of narrative. Made invisible in this tidy sequence of events is the re-construction of gender necessitated by this shift of education from the private to the public realm. To construct education as public/male required reinscribing the home or schoolhouse as private/female. The emergence of the discourse of the "cult of domesticity" and its corollary, "teaching as women's true profession," suggested that women's role as educators, as knowers, was to be in-direct, it was to represent influence, not actual power, and it was to be exerted through others and for others. Not only was the task of edu-cating understood as the domain of men, but knowledge itself was gendered as public, as male. Separation from the private to identify with the common/public/male realm provides the mark of male gendered identity.

This redefinition of gender, and thus, education, was also a consequence of social changes resulting from America's emergence as an industrial nation which required the repression of the individual (private) to the state (public). Central to the regulation of the individual, as Valerie Polakow (1993) has suggested, was the emergence of "pedagogy" and "pediatrics" as a means of fashioning identity. These arenas of social life, traditionally associated with the private realm and appropriated simultaneously with "democratizing" the nation suggest not historical progress or development but what Foucault has termed "episodes in a series of subjugations."

The irony of this is that the construction of "pedagogy" as grounded in women's natural nurturing capacities functioned in complex ways to both valorize and sabotage women. Curricular history most often portrays women curriculum theorists at this time–Catherine Beecher, Emma Willard, and others–as complicit in participating in the "pedagogy for patriarchy" (Grumet, 1988). Most curriculum histories present these women educators as the dutiful daughters who joined the fathers in the quest to expand democracy through public schooling. In fact, their supposed complicity contributes to essentializing these emerging gender roles. This is particularly the case with Horace Mann and Catherine Beecher (1800-1878). Mann is commonly represented as the father of the "common school movement" and Beecher is credited with the feminization of teaching, and thus, a willing participant in the inscription of gender norms as unitary and fixed. However, when we acknowledge that there is nothing natural or fixed about these discourses, this opens spaces to explore how identities were being taken up, negotiated, and resisted.

To suggest that Beecher participated in this "pedagogy for patriarchy" is to deny legitimacy to Beecher's complex analysis of nineteenth-century gendered social relations and her vision of the role women teachers should play as active agents in shaping culture (Sklar, 1973). Confident that women were better suited than men to facilitate human development, she argued that the duties of home, child rearing, and education should be placed in the hands of women. Appropriating the "cult of domesticity," Beecher was able to argue for women's roles as teachers at the very moment when education and pedagogy were becoming specifically gendered as male and public. To take up the discourse of the "cult of domesticity" as a site of knowing, as an epistemological site, not only interrupted this engendering but simultaneously functioned to secure a place for women in the public sphere as well as ensuring a rationale for the education of women. In effect, Beecher challenged the values that placed the public/political above the domestic and the assumption that the domestic was not political (Martin, 1985). By embracing essentialist gender roles, she was able to advance women into the public sphere in spite of the dominance of patriarchal authority.[12]

By beginning curricular histories with Horace Mann and the "rise" of public education and the eventual "fall" through the feminization of teaching, the history of education becomes the story of public schooling. In constructing education as public, this plot excludes education in the home (parenting, domestic knowledge), education through aesthetic forms (slave quilts, spirituals, folklore), and through other "informal" (although certainly not considered such by those persons involved) institutions such as women's study clubs, settlement houses, etc. Obscuring education in "other" spheres outside of the public, erases womens', African Americans' and other marginalized groups' forms of knowing and being as a source for theorizing curriculum.

The neutrality implied in the natural progression of curriculum history from private to public also obscures the presence of large numbers of women teachers in colonial and pre-industrial communities, thus "reinforcing women's invisibility in the more distant past" (Prentice and Theobald, 1991, p. 23). Prentice and Theobald (1991) suggest that a more appropriate redefinition of the period, in which women became the majority of teachers, is the masculinization of teaching. The "feminization of teaching," as they suggest, ignores the ways that despite the increased numerical presence of women, teaching as well as education was increasingly controlled by men.

Discourses like the "common school movement" and the "feminization of teaching" thus function not as historical facts but as part of a narrative of coherence and continuity that genders knowledge and subjects. I would maintain that this focus on the feminization of teaching effectively obscures the ways that despite numerical dominance, what constituted knowledge and subjectivity was being deeply gendered as male. The very concept of the periodization of the "common school movement" and the "feminization of teaching" become incredible feats of fictions which function to ensure the maintenance of normative gender practices, and which, for the male, necessitates separation from, and continual repression (i.e., individuation) of, the feminine. This repression continually manifests itself in the need to control through ongoing reforms embodied in "progressivism," technical-rationalism (with its focus on objectivity), and "professionalization" (with its focus on individuality and autonomy). This narrative of curricular history situates individuation, separation, and control as central to education and, as a consequence, history as we know it functions to gender understandings of knowledge. When the story of curriculum history begins with the emergence of public schooling, it not only obscures other ways of coming to know, but it predicates education on separation from the private. I wonder what desires and fears are thus contained in these curricular fictions? History performs incredible epistemological acts. Central to this is the myth of origins on which linearity, continuity, and coherence are predicated.

Myth #2 Origins: Disrupting the "Seminal" Plot and Other Ovarian Twists

Historical narrative works to suppress contradictions (multiple stories) through constructing the illusion of origins (the source of existence, derivation). Origins imply beginnings and endings. The history of curriculum, predicated on this search, guarantees a unitary tale that can be traced. And yet, this obsession with origins is essentially a patriarchal one. It is the story of control and suppression. Origins implies roots, certainly a phallic symbolism. Who is the father? Where did the seed originate? Whose is the seminal work? Who has carried on the work of the father?

The concept of genealogy, the tracing of origins, is, according to Sarah Westphal (1994), stored with meanings arising from the "history of the patriarchal family: the 'traffic in women,' the severance of the bride's ties of kinship and the loss of the mother's name, all to ensure the orderly transmission of property and title through the legitimate paternal line" (p. 155). To conceive of history as the tracing of origins–Mann/Common School Movement; Hall/Child Study Movement; Dewey/Progressivism; Tyler/Technical Rationalism–of establishing lineages, is to secure the exclusion, the invisibility of women. How might we write this story without the search for origins which inevitably obscures women's and other's experiences? More importantly, how do we write in a fashion which acknowledges the continual production of gendered bodies through historical discourse?

The Traffic in Women: Dutiful Daughters and Spinster Sisters
The "traffic in women" is what makes curriculum history as we know it possible. Women, if they appear at all, are the "good daughters." They carry out the ideas of the father, thus securing his position as the originator. Catherine Beecher carries out the ideas of Horace Mann; Annie Julia Cooper of Frederick Douglass; Elizabeth Peabody of Froebel; Jane Addams, Ella Flagg Young, Mary Bethune McCleod of Dewey, and today the ideas of Foucault, Freire, and Derrida.[13] The dutiful daughter reproduces but is never generative in her own right. Women educators constructed as dutiful daughters ensure the orderly transmission of property (knowledge) and title through the paternal line. Daughters are never constructed as "seminal" thinkers; the severing of maternal kinship, through their positioning as dutiful daughters, guarantees reproduction through the paternal. The separation from and erasure of the maternal is complete. Consequently, the identities made thinkable through this origin myth are limited to the heterosexual, gendered discourses of the normative family plot.

Ironically, it is often the well-intentioned attempts to "include" women into the "story" of curriculum which further essentializes gender identities and perpetuates this family drama. David Tyack in the *One*

Best System describes Ella Flagg Young as "one of Dewey's strongest advocates...a woman of great intelligence, and compassion, she taught teachers about Dewey's new education" (1974, p. 178). Young teaches about Dewey's ideas. Her work is derivative. Rarely is she portrayed as an intellectual or social critic in her own right.[14] Her body of scholarship has been largely ignored, as well has her intellectual contributions to pragmatism and commitment to feminism.[15] As the dutiful daughter she is the conduit through which other's ideas are trafficked.

The standard tale of Young's life (1845-1918) goes something like this–a dutiful teacher, she makes her way "up" the ladder from teacher to principal, studies with John Dewey at the University of Chicago, becomes the first superintendent of a large urban school district and eventually the first women president of the National Education Association (NEA). Her roles as the "first" female superintendent of a large urban school district and the "first" female president of the NEA are compensatory in the sense that they focus on accomplishments that are deemed important by traditional history, those which are male, public, individual, and thus defined as political. Young only becomes a "subject" of history because her life is fashioned to "fit in" with the male plot–the male career ladder, the story of the paternal, the story of fathers, of origins. In effect, the inclusion of this particular version of Young's story into history reifies essentialized notions of male/female identity. Although Young gets "included" in history, the gendered plot of the text remains the same.

Making gender boundaries appear natural through reifying the male plot obscures how the very tale of progressivism constructs gender. By focusing on the public and political, Young's subjectivity is coded as male (active/public) as well as unitary, making invisible not only her agency as a woman but her ongoing negotiation of gender discourses. This negotiation occurs within the complex intersections of two supposedly polar discourses–progressivism and social efficiency. Although conceiving of the purposes of education very differently, both progressivism and social efficiency were predicated on the assumption that women's influence on education should be indirect. In the case of "progressivism," women's agency was to be subjugated to the child, and in the case of "social efficiency," it was to be subjugated to the "expert" and "principal." By positioning Young as the "dutiful daughter" carrying out the ideas of Dewey, the contradictory and discontinuous ways in which Young negotiated, subverted, and appropriated these curricular discourses remains obscured.[16] To remember this negotiation and its erasure as a site for curriculum theorizing is the memory work which must be done.

Rethinking Origins: Discontinuities, Dispersions, and Difference
When the origin story functions to construct a unitary tale predicated on essences, the multiplicities of factors constitutive of an event, in this case the "progressive era," are rendered invisible. Foucault's "genealogical" method attacks the notion of a founding subject and a continuous history. Poststructuralist thinkers have posited alternative metaphors–Deleuze and Guattari's notion of rhizomes rather than roots disrupts the phallic,[17] yet Derrida's notion of "dissemination" while striving for displacement and disruption remains embedded in a masculinist narrative (Flax, 1990, p. 39). Although "history" is rein-visioned outside the discourses of origins and linearity, each of these methodologies conceives of gender as a discourse or a technology of power. As Sarah Westphal (1994) maintains, to assume that gender is just another discourse is to neglect that we still don't know what gender is and to neglect the analytical power of gender in and of itself. How the discourses of progressivism and social efficiency shaped and were shaped by gender remains hidden when history relies on stories of origins that reinscribe and produce subjectivities that are unitary and fixed. Like Denise Riley (1989), I am concerned with understanding the conditions under which women "take up" identities of "women" and how and why they do this. To engage in this particular kind of memory work is to remember that the discourses of "progressivism" and "social efficiency" have no essence or origin, nor are they either inherently liberatory or oppressive, but they were and continue to be a site through which we can remember how we are gendered in complex and contradictory ways. I turn once again to Young's story to seek the discontinuities, dispersions, and play of dominations.

Young's work as an educator coincides with what Lynn Gordon (1990) has described as a period of female separatism, social activism, and belief in the special mission for educated women. As an active participant at Hull House, Young was engaged in the work of social reconstruction with other leading intellectuals and activists of the progressive era including Jane Addams, John Dewey, and George Herbert Mead. Young, Dewey, Addams, and Mead worked together in a variety of projects aimed at social reform including women's rights, labor unions for women, the extension of suffrage, and higher education for women (Deegan, 1990).[18] Like other progressives, she believed that schools played a central role in social change. For Young, women's work as teachers was central to social reform because it functioned as a form of democratic practice. In order to be democratic, teachers needed full participation in decisions affecting their work. By focusing on the democratic practices embodied in teaching, Young argued for radical reforms which took seriously the experiences of women teachers as central to social reconstruction. As President of the NEA she advocated not only increased teacher autonomy but "higher salaries, equal pay for equal work, women's suffrage, and advisory teachers' councils" (McManis, 1916, pp. 156-57). Her work centered on developing participatory forms of leadership in which teachers (women) would have a central voice in the development of administrative and curricular policies.

At the same time, education historians (Ravitch, 1974; Kliebard, 1986; Tyack, 1974) have described this period as one of centralization and bureaucratization which emphasized increased efficiency, standardization, and reliance on experts which reduced the teacher to a mere "factory hand." Young's dissertation (completed in 1900 under Dewey at the University of Chicago) entitled "Isolation in School Systems" was an analysis and critique of the ideology of social efficiency. She claimed that the isolation of teachers resulting from centralization and bureaucratization functioned to disempower teachers (women), by removing their decision making power over curriculum and school policy and placing it into the hands of supposed "experts" (male). When teachers were denied participation in decision making, Young warned that schools would develop a system comparable to a "great machine" (Reid, 1982, p. xxi).

These conflicting discourses/ideologies which signaled, on the one hand, a special mission for educated women through the discourse of teaching as women's true profession, and, on the other hand, the deskilling of teachers through increased control of education by experts, provides the context in which to understand Young's complex negotiation of conflicting gender ideologies. On the one hand, advocating teacher autonomy subverted the hierarchy of social efficiency. On the other hand, advocating teacher autonomy took up the discourse of professionalism, a subtext of social efficiency, as a means to argue for teacher independence. However, her focus on securing teachers' autonomy through decentralizing power and on securing teacher retention of curricular decision making were in direct contrast to the gender roles inscribed in *both* progressivism and social efficiency, which maintained that women teachers were to be facilitators of knowledge, not active agents in making knowledge claims.

By claiming women teacher's right to be active agents in decision making and central to shaping democracy through their work in schools, Young contested the control of education by experts (either progressives or those advocating social efficiency) through asserting that women's experience as teachers was a site for generating knowledge. Claiming women's experience as an epistemological site threatened the normative gender ideologies embedded in both discourses, which required the subjugation of women's knowledge. The degree of Young's threat can be registered by the fact that in 1915 she became the subject of an Illinois state investigation in which her policies as school superintendent were decried as "Frenzied Feminine Finance" (Murphy, 1990, p. 82) According to Murphy, critics depicted Young as "virtually giving away the store to public school teachers out of her feminist sentimentality, her Catholic sympathies and her alleged near-senility" (1990, p. 82). Young was accused by the Chicago school board of breeding rebellion and lack of respect for the school board authority. Although supported by Dewey, Mead, and Addams, Young stepped down as superintendent.

To brand Young as senile and feminist was to police the gender boundaries she was challenging through constructing her as a spinster. It is perhaps no coincidence that the image of the "spinster," often embodied in representations of teachers, emerged at the very moment when women teachers were contesting the gendered nature of the discourses of both social efficiency and progressivism. The spinster is represented as the sexless, manless, unmarried creature whose image embodies the consequences of women's refusal to comply with and be the subject of men's social and sexual power.[19] This sexually neutral social type, as, Jill Conway (1971) suggests, is often identified with the professional expert or the scientist as compared to the woman sage who relied on women's special nature for knowledge. Young, drawing on her pragmatist tradition, did not claim that women's knowledge was the result of an essentialized feminine nature. However, she claimed that women teachers' experiences, reflected upon (using the scientific method), could provide a site of knowledge and was in fact a way of coming to know. Claiming women's experience as a site of knowledge, Young contested the discourse of social efficiency which claimed bureaucratization as the site of knowledge and the discourse of progressivism which claimed experience as gender-neutral and the providence of the child.

As the dutiful daughter, Young's understandings of and nego-
tiations of gender are made invisible, as are the modes of subjugation
that they elicited. The relying on a tale of origins effectively obscures the
discontinuities and dispersions of gender central to shaping ideologies of
progressivism and social efficiency, and ultimately a richer and more
complex understanding of these ideologies. That these discourses are
inconceivable without their investment in maintaining normative
gender boundaries is the curriculum of control and separation that
becomes hidden. The memory work that must be done is to remember
that this erasure and subjugation proceeded under what has traditionally
been termed as the "progressive" era. This myth of liberation embedded
in the progressive era, and as experienced by women curriculum
theorists, is what must be remembered.

**Myth #3: Where's the Progress in the Progressive Era?:
Disrupting the Family Plot**
Modernist history is predicated on the premise that change is equivalent
to progress. History is told as a sequence of singular and inevitable
events in which humanity progresses from ignorance to enlightenment,
barbarity to civilization, oppression to freedom. And yet, we have been
reminded that the narrative of historical change is an enlightenment
myth which obscures the succession of one mode of domination by
another (Foucault, 1977). The notion that change is inherently progressive is, as Chet Bowers (1987) reminds us, deeply embedded in
most educational thinking where "enlightenment foundations...con-
tribute to thinking of liberal discourse as on the side of truth and
progress, and only engaged in a power struggle for the purpose of
liberation" (Bowers, 1987, p. 8).[20]

The writing of curriculum history is deeply invested in the myth of
progress as liberation through struggle. Curricular history is often
described as a "problem of warring educational doctrines" or "warring
extremes" or a "call to arms."[21] As Bonnie Smith (1995) suggests,
history has traditionally been a "celebatory saga of male fantasies
stressing combat and dominance" (p. 203). Liberation is contingent on
a rebellion narrative of conflict, separation, and control. In the tale of
progressivism, conflict first emerges in the competing factions of the
humanist/child-study/social efficiency and social reconstructionist
camps. The history of curriculum is told as a war between these competing theories. It is the conflict between W.T. Harris, G. S. Hall, F.
Bobbitt and E.L.Thorndike, and L.F. Ward. This contest signifies not

merely a dispute over the aim of education, but delineates the normative boundaries of what can be known, how we come to know and who can be a knower. These boundaries constitute normative cultural identities that are inevitably classed, raced, and gendered. Women (Addams, Beecher, Peabody) and African Americans (Du Bois, Bond, Cooper) who are curriculum theorists do not even enter into the conversation.

The focus on the struggle for the "right" curriculum reinforces the notion of progress, which ultimately situates the succession of progressivism, and its prodigal son, John Dewey, as the victor. Resisting social efficiency, he is the "rebel" son.[22] The story continues as Dewey is followed by Tyler as the rebel son promoting technical rationalism, to be followed by the neo-Marxists (Apple, Giroux), and so on. Ironically, the position of the father, as well as the dutiful daughter, is guaranteed through the resistant son (Pinar, 1983). Women, culturally situated as "dutiful daughters," make possible the "rebel son." Their supposed complicity (and thus erasure) enables the signification of the "rebel son," whose rejection of the father supposedly guarantees progress and change.

Mirroring the oedipal father/son plot, this focus on conflict reproduces the story of male gender identity. Progress is the result of separation, individuation, and control. In the story of progressivism, this gender drama manifests itself through the ongoing struggle between a "conventional narrative" and a "liberation narrative." Whose knowledge is of most worth–the father (reproduction) or the son (resistance)? The irony is that the focus on "whose knowledge?" (traditionally a question asked by critical and neo-Marxist theorists), functions to suppress the knowledge of others. This oedipal drama engenders a curricular master narrative bounded by the reproduction/ resistance binary that results in situating individuation and repression of connection as central to the curricular plot (Pinar, 1983). When the history of progressivism is articulated as the struggle between social efficiency and social reconstruction, father and son, this story is gendered in ways which necessarily exclude the experiences of women curriculum theorists. Although these curricular discourses are presented as genderless, and thus natural, the power of gender and gender oppression to structure historical thought is evident in the ongoing family plot of the father, "rebel" son, and dutiful daughter.

What, then, makes it thinkable or possible to conceive of the progressive era as progressive? Why is progressivism naturally understood as an advancement over an authoritarian approach to education based on social control (Marshall, 1995)? The fact that progressivism continues to function as a liberatory discourse despite current postmodern/poststructural critiques of its ideological embeddedness in enlightenment notions of change (Walkerdine, 1990), progress (Bowers, 1987), and the unitary individual (Aronowitz and Giroux, 1985) suggests the hegemony of this discourse. In fact, current attempts to reinterpret Dewey as "a postmodernist before his time" (Rorty, 1991, p. 201) suggest the deep investment in maintaining the category and myths of progressivism. This investment continues to obscure the ways in which the ideologies of progressivism work simultaneously as liberatory and oppressive by rendering invisible the ways in which the discourses of progressivism are implicated in regulating normative gendered and raced identities. That the history of curriculum theorizing is complicit in reproducing a male, Eurocentric and heterosexual subject is the forbidden "fruit" hidden under the guise of liberatory/emancipatory discourses. How might we imagine a history of curriculum theorizing not trapped within a narrative of struggle, which depends on unitary notions of gender to construct its subject?

Progress for Women?: Child-centeredness as the Regulation of "Woman"
Change in the case of progressive ideology was not necessarily progress for women. Progressive ideology required that a teacher subjugate her experience to that of the child. If left to unfold naturally (through activity-oriented approaches that released students' interests), without any imposition, the child would develop into an independent, free-thinking individual and thus democratic citizen. Of course, there is much debate over what progressives, especially Dewey, really meant by "child-centered" or "experience."[23] What is clear though is that teachers were not to impart or transmit knowledge, but were to draw it out of children.

What is obscured in the tale of progressivism is that this ideology was predicated on the already gendered construction of teaching. However, the assumption that this type of pedagogy was naturally suited to women because of their natural nurturing abilities is misleading. Dewey was quite clear that the realm traditionally associated with the female–the home–was not a site of knowledge. He suggested

> the occupations and relationships of the home environment are
> not specially selected for the growth of the child; the main object
> is something else, and what the child can get out of them is

incidental. Hence the need of a school. In this school the life of
the child becomes the all-controlling aim. (1900, p. 36)

The "child-centered curriculum" was predicated on the removal of the
child from the home, where learning was "incidental" to the school. In
effect, the "child-centered" curriculum functioned to displace the pri-
vate/domestic/female as a site for learning or knowledge. The role of the
female teacher in the progressive classroom mirrored this displacement
by situating women teachers as "facilitators" of knowledge rather than
as creators of knowledge. The teacher's primary role was passive–she
was to "help" the child release his or her inner self. Valerie Walkerdine
(1990) has argued that the

> liberation of children conceived in progressive terms did not mean
> the liberation of women. In some ways, it actually served to keep
> women firmly entrenched as caregivers. Women teachers became
> caught, trapped inside a concept of nurturance which held them
> responsible for the freeing of each little individual, and therefore
> for the management of an idealist dream, an impossible fiction.
> (p. 19)

She questions here the concept of liberation as freedom from overt
coercion. As Michel Foucault (1980) suggests, liberation opens up new
relationships of power, which have to be controlled by practices of
liberty. In the case of "progressive" teachers, they were to allow
individuals to unfold and grow according to their own needs by
providing maternal nurturance.

For Walkerdine, the suppression and control of rebellion through
maternal nurturance guarantees the rational subject precisely because
children who were not coerced would not need to rebel, thus guaran-
teeing the status quo. Thus, "they ensure the production of individuals
who are self-regulating through the power of rationality" (Walkerdine
1990, p. 32) and highlight what Foucault has described as the shift
from overt sovereign power to invisible power through technologies
and apparatuses of social regulation. The subject identities inscribed
through "progressive" discourses essentially reproduced and regulated
unitary gender norms through dichotomies like public/private and
reason/emotion (Kohli and Munro, 1995). What, I continue to ask, is
so "progressive" about that?

The Repressive Myths of Social Reconstructionism

What is obscured in the tale of the "progressive era" as inevitably liberatory is that this ideology worked in complex and contradictory ways. On the one hand, child-centeredness drew on and reinforced traditional gender norms of female nurturance, making it an acceptable ideology from which women could operate in the public sphere. At the same time, this ideology erased women's agency by further essentializing women's supposed maternal submissiveness and passivity. How the discourse of "child-centeredness" functioned to regulate gender norms to keep women in their place is revealed in the primary "battle" of the progressive era between the child-centered and social reconstructionist factions.

Despite the currency of child-centeredness as an alternative to social control, Dewey (1928) and Counts (1932) worried that those advocating child-centeredness lacked social and political direction. The reluctance on the part of those advocating a child-centered curriculum to use education as a form of political socialization was in part because they saw democracy and political indoctrination as antithetical (Pinar et al., 1995). As Stanley (1992) suggests, "most of these child-centered educators, reacting against the formalism of the past, tended to oppose any form of imposition or indoctrination" (p. 7).[24] Ultimately, child-centered progressives (usually women–Margaret Naumburg, Marietta Johnson, Jane Addams, Patty Smith Hill, Lucy Gage, Lucy Sprague Mitchell, Caroline Pratt, Laura Zirbes, Mary McCloud Bethune and Alice Miel) were reluctant, and in some cases ambivalent, daughters who resisted articulating a fixed and unitary theory of social reform.[25] Interpreted as a lack of political theorizing, commitment, and vision by Dewey, Counts, and others, the rejection of those advocating "child-centeredness" signifies the ongoing necessity to maintain gender boundaries through the repudiation and repression of the maternal.

However, despite the dominant perception that those engaged in child-centeredness were not concerned with social issues and lacked a political vision, the meanings these women attributed their work often tells a different story. For example, the work of Patty Smith Hill's Manhattanville project (an urban renewal program she directed in the 1930s in her retirement) situated itself as part of George Counts's call for social reconstruction by acknowledging that the teacher played a large part in the building of a new social order (Association of Early Childhood Education, 1972). Other examples of women who saw their work as political, despite the assumptions that those advocating child-centeredness were apolitical, were Lucy Sprague Mitchell (founder of Bank Street College, originally known as the Bureau of Educational Experiments) and Caroline Pratt (an avowed socialist who taught in the settlement homes in New York and worked for the Women's Trade Union League) who collaborated in establishing the Play School. According to Antler (1987), although the school drew on the progressive philosophy of Dewey, the mainspring of its pedagogy was political, and both Pratt and Mitchell preferred the term "experimental" to "progressive" because "progressive" was considered "too vague, snooty and restrictive" (1987, p. 243). Ironically, these two women (as well as others) rejected progressivism because it wasn't political enough (especially its lack of gender analysis). That many of these women educators saw their work as political and central to social change has not only been obscured by gendered assumptions embedded in the term child-centeredness, but by the exclusion of gender as a central analytical concept in theorizing progressivism. Because women were, and continue to be, situated differently in social relations, their theorizing about social relations, especially notions of change, agency, and power, have taken different forms from universal positions claimed by patriarchy.

The reluctance to embrace social reconstructionism was also in some cases a critique of the gender-neutral analysis of social reconstructionist theories. For example, Jane Addams rejected naming herself a socialist not because she was apolitical, but because she opposed the class struggle advocated by Marxist theory and its truncated analysis of women's status and values (Addams, 1902; Munro, 1995a, 1995c). For Addams, class struggle was a form of militarism which ultimately functioned to undermine the building of community that was necessary to democracy. Drawn to the cooperative philosophies of Tolstoy and Kropotkin, Addams embraced the concepts of non-resistance and pacifism as central to defining and changing class exploitation. The reluctance of many women progressives to put forward a comprehensive theory of social change has rarely been explored as a form of resistance to the gendered nature of progressive ideologies.[26] By reducing the history of the progressive era to the struggle between the social reconstructionist and the child-centered factions, gender binaries are essentially reproduced and normalized. The subject identities made available are restricted to the family plot in which the struggle between the father and "rebel" son defines what counts as power, resistance, and change. What would a history of the "progressive" era look like, I wonder, that was not dependent on interpreting women progressives as the dutiful daughters, whose ideas were extensions of, misreadings, or derivations of the progressive fathers?

How the theories of women progressives were framed by and were a response to the androcentric bias of progressive ideology is the memory work which must be done. The theorizing of progressive women educators must take account of the restrictive and normative gender subjectivities inscribed in the discourses of progressivism. How might their theories be a specific response to the limited gendered roles and subject identities made available through progressive ideologies? How were their theories a response to the degendering (or gendering) of knowledge through the discourses of rationality and child-centeredness? How was the taking up of the discourse of "child centeredness" by some women progressives in fact a form of resistance to the erasure of gender? In acknowledging that no discourse is "innocent," we must simultaneously ask what forms of domination women's theories and ideas perpetuated. That women educators actively negotiated the erasures and silences of gender implicit in progressive discourses, simultaneously appropriating and disrupting them, is the complexity I seek. To make visible these complexities, discontinuities, and contradictions would be to disrupt the father/son plot of reproduction and resistance by telling a messy, more complex story.

Progress as Reform as Castration Fear

To claim the progressive era as progressive is to obscure the ways in which this ideology deeply genders notions of teaching, curriculum, and education by excluding women's experiences. In fact, to claim the progressive era as progressive is to forget that in the 1930s (simultaneously to the critique of child-centeredness), gender ideologies like the spinster emerged to invoke and regulate gender. Geraldine Clifford (1989) maintains that despite the rhetoric of teaching as women's true profession, during the 1930s the "woman peril" in education led to concerns about the feminizing effects on boys due to the large number of female teachers. The influx of women into teaching, both numerically and in the form of the threat of the child-centered movement, necessitated control and reform. Consequently, supposed reform efforts like progressivism can in fact be read as fear of the feminine (castration fear) which necessitates separation, control, and repression. This regulation of gender continues in current reform movements through the discursive formation of teacher identities as either "professionals" (reproduction) or as "intellectuals/activists/cultural workers" (resistance)

(Munro 1995b; Goodman, 1995). The father/son plot remains the under-lying structuring of the narrative and continues to exclude women's agency, subjectivity, and knowledge that women have constructed. What desires, then, I wonder, are fulfilled by constructing a unitary tale of the progressive era as progressive? What continues to be rendered invisible by the telling of this myth? I would maintain that the telling of "progressive history" as the battle between "child-centeredness" and "social reconstructionism" has little to do with "actual" history and everything to do with policing dominant gender boundaries.

In Collusion with Conclusions

Despite the supposed postmodern turn, the narrative strategies of curriculum history remain deeply embedded in the myths of history as linear, as the search for origins, and as inevitably progressive. As a consequence, although history is a myth, it continues to operate as fact. Of course, I remain concerned about reducing complex political questions to the simplistic question of whether history is fact or fiction. To frame the "problem of history" as the choosing between history as fact or fiction is to ignore the complexity of "narrative" as a way of knowing. To write in these postmodern times is to acknowledge the textual nature of curriculum history—its construction through narrative, its mythical nature.

Myth is considered by many the "sacred" narrative. Sacred in the sense that myth is worthy of our reverence, our respect. Myth's sacredness lies not only in its explanatory power but in its role in justifying institutions and rights. Myth tells us how something came to be as it is. The fashioning of curricular myths—the democratization of education through public schooling, the plot of curriculum history driven by the struggle between reproduction or resistance, the triumph and tragedy of progressivism, and the heroes and their dutiful daughters—are narrative sleights of hand deserving our respect.

Engendering curriculum history is to interrogate the ways in which narrative makes particular subject identities possible or impossible. What, I continue to ask, would a narrative of history look like that did not depend on linearity, coherence, or a unitary subject as the organizing tropes of history? The purpose of the memory work I undertake is to incite my imagination to envision history in less dis-eased ways—where plot has no beginning, middle, or end, but is re-cursive and discontinuous; where historical texts induce contradictions, rather than unitary story lines; and where paradoxes, rather than cause and effect, evoke action. It is the complex and contradictory ways in which curricular history silences, distorts, and makes invisible that is the ongoing memory work which must be done.[27]

Notes

1.   Foucault's notions of archaeology and genealogy undertake to dismantle the hold of humanism on history by positing the unitary subject of traditional history as a product of discourse.

2.   I would like to delineate the history of curriculum theory from the history of teaching and education. Although these fields are interrelated, the history of teaching and education is primarily concerned with the history of the profession itself and its role in shaping what we consider the institution of schooling. The history of curriculum theory is more specifically concerned with the question of how education (more general than schooling) shapes and is shaped by ideology and culture. Women's symbolic relegation to nature versus culture (Rosaldo and Lamphere, 1974) has necessarily excluded them from being taken seriously as curriculum theorists. In other words, although much is written about the history of women and teaching, little consideration has been given to women curriculum theorists or how the history of curriculum theory itself constitutes gender.

3.   As Hannah Arendt (1954) maintains, history is itself a concept that must be historicized. Thus, modernist history with its emphasis on development and progress and objectivity is distinct from ancient history in which the poet and historian were not distinguished. Martin (1986) reminds us that until the end of the eighteenth century, history was considered part of literature and drew its methods primarily from classical rhetoric.

4.   I draw here on the work of Said (1989) and Spivak (1988), who show how identities in the West are always dependent on the construction of binaries–colonizer and colonized, white and black, male and female, etc.

5.   I do not want to dismiss the importance of historical work done on these individual women; without it we would not even be having this discussion. However, to "add" them as exemplars of women progressives without deconstructing the dominant historical narrative is

to potentially reproduce the very categories of subjectivity and agency that contributed to their exclusion in the first place (Munro, forthcoming).

6.   However, although experience can never be achieved, I am reluctant to give up a material world. Like Mark Freeman (1993) suggests, furniture only exists through language, but that doesn't keep him from bumping up against it.

7.   For further discussion of this "paralysis" of poststructuralism due to the loss of the subject and consequently agency see Nancy Harstock (1990). My concern with these critiques is that agency, and subjectivity, continue to be embedded in notions of power as unitary and graspable (Bloom and Munro, 1995; Munro, forthcoming). When power continues to be conceptualized in these ways, the multiplicities of ways in which agency and power are enacted are obscured.

8.   Like Jameson (1981), I am skeptical of whether the popular notion that history is text means that the "referent" does not exist.

9.   Remembrance, mnemosyne, was regarded with such reverence by the Greeks, since it guaranteed their immortality, that it was made the mother of the Muses. Mnemosyne was a Titan Goddess, the sister of Kronos and Oceanus, the mother of the Muses, she presided over the poetic function. In Homer, the narrator of the mythoi was the poet, the aoidos, who was society's bearer of tradition and educator.

10. Several curriculum histories (Schubert, 1986) do situate curriculum within a larger historical perspective by tracing curriculum history back through the Greeks, etc. However, this tracing is conspiciously male, white, and Western.

11. That this is called the democratization of education is a misrepresentation when we consider that at the end of this time period blacks and women were still severely restricted in their access to public education. What, then, makes it possible for us to tell this story, why are we so invested in this fiction?

12. I do not want to romanticize Beecher as a new heroine. Beecher engaged dominant ideologies in complex ways which functioned in

contradictory ways. Her engaging of dominant racial ideologies to support the influx of women into teaching certainly functioned in oppressive ways.

13. There are several exceptions to this genre of "good daughter" history–the work of Ellen Lageman (1985) on Jane Addams, K. Sklar (1973) on Catherine Beecher, Joyce Antler (1987) on Lucy Sprague Mitchel,Carolyn Steedman (1989) on Margaret McMillan, and Jane Roland Martin (1985) on Charlotte Perkins Gilman. However, this work is rarely analyzed in relation to the history of curriculum.

14. The work of Mary Jo Deegan (1990) and Smith and Smith (1994) are an exception, yet most discussions of pragmatism do not include Young (Stanley 1992; Kleibard, 1992). Cremin (1961) also notes that Young was not merely carrying out the ideas of Dewey but was, in fact, central to crystallizing Dewey's ideas.

15. The following are only an example of her work: *Scientific method in education* (1903). Chicago: The University of Chicago Press; *Some types of modern educational theory.* Chicago: The University of Chicago Press; *Ethics in the school* (1902). Chicago: The University of Chicago Press; Democracy and education (July 6, 1916). *Journal of Education.*

16. Constructing history as the tale between social efficiency and progressivism is reductionist in the sense that it obscures the micropractices of power and resistance. The work of Reese (1986), *Power and promise of school reform,* provides a more complex, dialectic portrayal of progressivism.

17. Deleuze and Guattari (1987). *A thousand plateaus.* Terms like–schizoanalysis, rhizamatics, pragmatics, diagrammatism, cartography, micropolitics–are used in order to prevent their position from stabilizing in an ideology, method, or single metaphor. Privileging botanical metaphors, they employ the term rhizome to designate the decentered lines that constitute multiplicities. Rhizomatics seeks to extirpate roots and foundations, to thwart unities and brake dichotomies, and to spread our roots and branches, thereby pluralizing and disseminating, producing differences and multiplicities, making new connections. Rhizomes are nonhierarchical systems of deterritorialized

lines that connect with other lines in random, unregulated relationships.

18. In fact, Young led the campaign for women's suffrage in Illinois. In June 1913, she was pictured with Jane Addams and Julia Lathrop, two other Chicago social reformers, with a caption that read "Three reasons why Illinois women won the vote" (Smith and Smith, 1994, p. 307).

19. When heterosexuality is one of the ways in which men's power over women is maintained, the spinster or lesbian functions as a threat to that power. See A. Oram (1989). Embittered, sexless or homosexual: Attacks on spinster teachers 1918-1939. *Current Issues* (pp. 183-302); M. Khayatt. (1992). *Lesbian Teachers: An invisible presence.* New York: SUNY.

20. Bowers (1987) maintains that the discourse of liberalism is part of a political lineage going back to John Stuart Mill, Jeremy Bentham, John Locke and Thomas Hobbes.

21. The phrase "warring extremes" is used by Kliebard (1992, p. 154) to describe the tension between Dewey and Tyler. Pinar et al. (1995, p. 127) use the term a "call to arms."

22. Recent curriculum theorists have critiqued the monolithic and idealistic view of Dewey as a social reconstructionist and,in fact, argue that Dewey's views were representative of an effort to maintain the status quo. See Hlebowitsh and Wraga (1995) for a review of these critiques.

23. According to Prawat (1995), Dewey rejected the either/or nature of the child-centered versus subject-centered debate. In fact, Prawat argues that Dewey has been misread as an advocate of child-centered or project-based approaches to education.

24. Stanley's only reference to a specific "child-centered" educator is Marietta Johnson. Dewey, however, is distanced from the child-centered faction of progressivism when Stanley suggests that the social reconstructionists "posed a direct challenge to the child-centered progressives who tended to dominate the Progressive Education Association (PEA) through the 1920's" (1992, p. 7) Stanley points out that Dewey

himself spoke out against the child-centered contingent of the PEA, because of the wide range of social problems that this approach tended to ignore (pp. 6-8).

25. Many of these women progressives were students or professors at Teacher's College throughout the 1920s and '30s and actively involved in the Progressive Education Association (PEA) as well as researchers, scholars, and founders of experimental schools. However, in-depth analysis of the meanings they gave to the discourse of child-centeredness, in other words, when and how they took up this discourse, remains rare. Without this kind of analysis the dominant assumptions based on gender stereotypes of child-centeredness as sentimental, apolitical, atheoretical, and individualistic will continue to pervade curriulum history.

26. In fact, taking up the discourse of child-centeredness might have functioned as both a political and theoretical move to counter-act the gender-neutral ideologies of progressivism. Taking into account prevalent gender norms and expectations, the child-centeredness discourse also provided many women an acceptable way to enter the public sphere of education as a way to reshape it. Thus, taking up this ideology probably worked in complex and contradictory ways.

27. I would like to thank Philip Bennett and Wendy Kohli for their thoughtful readings of ongoing drafts of this work. A special thanks to Douglas McKnight for his comments and careful editing.

References

Adams, T.D. (1990). *Telling lies in modern American autobiography.* Chapel Hill: The University of North Carolina Press.

Addams, J. (1902). *Democracy and social ethics.* New York: Macmillan Company.

Antler, J. (1987). *Lucy Sprague Mitchell: The making of a modern woman.* New Haven: Yale University Press.

Arendt, H. (1954). *Between past and future.* New York: The Viking Press.

Aronowitz, S. and Giroux, H. (1985). *Education under siege.* South Hadley, MA: Bergin and Garvey Publishers.

Association of Early Childhood Education. (1972). *Dauntless women in education.* Washington DC: Association of Childhood Education International.

Bloom, L. and Munro, P. (1995). Conflicts of selves: Non-unitary subjectivity in women administrators' life history narratives. In A. Hatch and R. Wisniewski (Eds.), *Life history and narrative* (pp. 99-112). London: Falmer Press.

Bowers, C. (1987). *Elements of a post-liberal theory of education.* New York: Teachers College Press.

Clifford, G. (1989). Man/woman/teacher: Gender, family and career in American educational history. In D. Warren (Ed.), *American teachers: Histories of a profession at work* (pp. 293-343). New York: Macmillan.

Conway, J. (1971). Women reformers and American culture, 1870-1930. *Journal of Social History,* 5(2), pp. 164-177.

Counts, G.S. (1932). *Dare the schools build a new social order?* New York: John Day.

Cremin, L. (1961). *The transformation of the school.* New York: Alfred A. Knopf.

Deegan, M. (1990). *Jane Addams and the men of the Chicago School. 1892-1918.* New Brunswick: Transaction Books.

Deleuze, G. and Guattari, F. (1987). *A thousand plateaus.* Minneapolis: University of Minnesota Press.

Dewey, J. (1900). *The school and society.* Chicago: University of Chicago Press.

Dewey, J. (1928). Progressive education and the science of education. *Progressive Education,* 5(3), pp. 197-204.

Felman, S. (1992). Education and crisis, or the vicissitudes of teaching. In S. Felman and D. Laub (Eds.), *Testimony: Crisis of witnessing in literature, psychoanalysis, and history* (pp. 1-56). New York: Routledge.

Flax, J. (1990). *Thinking fragments: Psychoanalysis, feminism, and postmodernism in the contemporary west.* Berkeley: University of California Press.

Foucault, M. (1977). *Language, counter-memory, practice: Selected essays and interviews by Michel Foucault* (D.F. Bouchard, Ed.). Oxford: Blackwell Press.

Foucault, M. (1980). *Power/knowledge: Selected interviews and other writings, 1972-77.* New York: Pantheon.

Freeman, M. (1993). *Rewriting the self: History, memory, narrative.* New York: Routledge Press.

Friedman, S. (1995). Making history: Reflections on feminism, narrative and desire. In D. Elam and R. Wiegman (Eds.), *Feminism beside itself* (pp. 11-53). New York: Routledge.

Goodman, J. (1995). Change without difference: School restructuring in historical perspective. *Harvard Educational Review, 65* (1), pp. 1-29.

Gordon, L. (1990). *Gender and higher education in the progressive era.* New Haven: Yale University Press.

Greene, G. (1993). Looking at history. In G. Greene and Coppelia Kahn (Eds.), *Changing subjects: The making of feminist literary criticism.* London: Routledge.

Grumet, M. (1988). *Bitter Milk.* Amherst: University of Massachusetts Press.

Hartstock, N. (1990). Foucault on power: A theory for women? In L. Nicholson (Ed.), *Feminism/Postmodernism.* (pp. 157-175). New York: Routledge.

Hlebowitsh, P. and Wraga, W. (1995). Social class analysis in the early progressive tradition. *Curriculum Inquiry, 25* (1), pp. 7-21

Jameson, F. (1981). *The political unconscious: Narrative as a socially symbolic act.* Ithaca: Cornell University Press.

Kelly, J. (1984). *Women, history and theory.* Chicago: The University of Chicago Press.

Khayatt, M. (1992). *Lesbian teachers: An invisible presence.* New York: State University of New York.

Kliebard, H. (1986). *The struggle for the American curriculum: 1890-1958.* London and Boston: Routledge and Kegan Paul.

Kliebard, H. (1992). *Forging the American curriculum.* New York: Routledge.

Kohli, W. and Munro, P. (1995). *Poststructural interrogations and interrogating poststructuralism: Two feminist tales.* Paper presented at the annual Conference of Curriculum Theorizing.

Lagemann, E. (1985). *Jane Addams on education.* New York: Teachers College Press.

Linde, C. (1993). *Life stories: The creation of coherence.* New York: Oxford University Press.

Margolis, J. (1993). *The flux of history and the flux of science.* Berkeley: University of California Press.

Marshall, J.D. (1995). Putting the political back into autonomy. In W. Kohli (Ed.) *Critical conversations in philosophy of education* (pp. 364-378). New York: Routledge.

Martin, J.R. (1985). *Reclaiming a conversation.* New Haven: Yale University Press.

Martin, W. (1986). *Recent theories of narrative.* Ithaca: Cornell University Press.

McManis, J. (1916). *Ella Flagg Young and a half-century of the Chicago public schools.* Chicago: A.C. McClurg and Co.

Munro, P. (1995a). Educators as activists: Five women from Chicago. *Social Education,* 59 (5). pp. 274-278.

Munro, P. (1995b). Speculations: Negotiating a feminist supervision identity In J. Jipson, P. Munro, S. Victor, K. Froude Jones, and G. Freed-Rowland, *Repositioning feminism and education: Perspectives on educating for social change.* (pp. 97-114). Westport, CT: Bergin and Garvey.

Munro, P. (1995c). *"Widening the circle": Jane Addams, gender and the definition of social education.* A paper presented at the National Council for the Social Studies. Chicago.

Munro, P. (Forthcoming). Resisting resistance: Stories women teachers tell. *Journal of Curriculum Theorizing.*

Murphy, M. (1990). *Blackboard unions: The AFT and NEA, 1900-1980.* Ithaca: Cornell University Press.

Oram, A. (1989). Embittered, sexless or homosexual: Attacks on spinster teachers 1918-39. In A. Angerman, G. Bennema, A. Keunen, V. Pucls, and J. ZirkZee (Eds.), *Current issues in woman's history* (pp. 183-202). London: Routledge.

Paddle, S. (1995). Writing against the clock: theorizing current feminist histories. *Melbourne Studies in Education,* 29 (1), pp. 1-11.

Pagano, J. (1990). *Exiles and communities. Teaching in the patriarchal wilderness.* Albany, NY: State University of New York Press.

Pinar, W.F. (1983). Curriculum as gender text: Notes on reproduction, resistance and male-male relations. *Journal of Curriculum Theorizing,* 5(1).

Pinar, W., Reynolds, W., Slattery, P., and Taubman, P. (1995). *Understanding Curriculum.* New York: Peter Lang.

Polakow, V. (1993). *Lives on the edge: Single mothers and their children in the other America.* Chicago: The University of Chicago Press.

Polkinghorne, D. (1988). *Narrative knowing and the human sciences.* Albany, NY: State University of New York Press.

Popular Memory Group. (1992). Popular memory: theory, politics, method. In R. Johnson, G. McLennan, B. Schwarz, and D. Sutton

(Eds.), *Making Histories* (pp. 205-252). Minneapolis: University of Minnesota Press.

Portelli, A. (1991). *The death of Luigi Trustulli and other stories.* Albany, NY: State University of New York Press.

Prawat, R.S. (1995). Misreading Dewey: Reform, projects, and the language game. *Educational Researcher,* 24 (7), pp. 13-22.

Prentice, A. and Theobald, M. (1991). *Women who taught: Perspectives on the history of women and teaching.* Toronto: University of Toronto Press.

Ravitch, D. (1974). *The great school wars: New York City, 1805-1973.* New York: Basic Books.

Reese, M. (1986). *Power and promise of reform: Grassroots movements during the progressive era.* Boston: Routledge and Kegan Paul.

Reid, R. L. (1982). *Battleground: The autobiography of Margaret Haley.* Urbana: University of Illinois Press.

Riley, D. (1989). *"Am I that name?": Feminism and the category of women in history.* Minneapolis: University of Minnesota.

Rorty, R. (1991). *Essays on Heidegger and others. Philosophical papers, Vol. II.* Cambridge: Cambridge University Press.

Rosaldo, M., and Lamphere, L. (1974). *Women, culture and society.* Stanford: Stanford University Press.

Said, E. (1989). Representing the colonized. *Critical Inquiry,* 15, pp. 205-225.

Schubert, W. (1986). *Curriculum: Perspective, paradigm, and possibility.* New York: Macmillan Publishing Company.

Scott, J. (1987). Women's history and the rewriting of history. In C. Farnham (Ed.), *The impact of feminist research in the academy,* pp. 34-52. Bloomington: Indiana University Press.

Scott, J. (1989). Gender: A useful category of historical analysis. In E. Weed (Ed.), *Coming to terms: Feminism, theory, politics.* New York: Routledge.

Sklar, K. (1973). *Catherine Beecher: A study in American domesticity.* New Haven: Yale University Press.

Smith, B. (1995). Gender, objectivity, and the rise of scientific history. In W. Natter, T.R. Schatzki, J.P. Jones III (Eds.), *Objectivity and its other* (pp. 51-66). New York: The Guilford Press.

Smith, G. and Smith, J. (1994). *Lives in education: A narrative of people and ideas.* New York: St. Martin's Press.

Spivak, G. (1988). *In other words. Essays in cultural politics.* New York: Routledge.

Stanley, W. B. (1992). *Curriculum for Utopia.* Albany, NY: State University of New York Press.

Steedman, C. (1989). *Childhood, culture and class in Britain: Margaret McMillan, 1860-1931.* New Brunswick, NJ: Rutgers University Press.

Tyack, D. (1974). *The one best system.* Cambridge: Harvard University Press.

Vernant, J.P. (1983). *Myth and thought among the Greeks.* London: Routledge and Kegan Paul.

Walkerdine, V. (1990). *Schoolgirl fictions.* New York: Verso.

Westphal, S, (1994). Stories of gender. In C. McDonald and G. Wihl (Eds.), *Transformations in personhood and culture after theory: The languages of history, aesthetics, and ethics* (pp. 153-164). University Park: The Pennsylvania State University Press.

White, H. (1978). *Metahistory.* Baltimore: The Johns Hopkins University Press.

Young, R. (1990). *White mythologies: Writing history and the west.* New York: Routledge.

Chapter Fourteen

Curriculum and Concepts of Control

William E. Doll, Jr., assisted by Al Alcazar

Control, and by that I mean imposed control, has been a main–
sometimes overt, sometimes hidden–aspect of American organizations
in the twentieth century. In a sense, Frederick Taylor (1911-1947) found
the beauty and power of this sort of control in his time-and-motion
studies on pig-iron handlers at Bethlehem Steel Company in 1896.
Through control of their motions, done with the precision of his stop-
watch, Taylor (1911-1947, p. 43) not only increased their production
almost 400% (from 12 1/2 tons to 47 tons per day) he also established
a paradigm–that of "scientific management"–which dominated American
social, industrial, managerial, and organizational thought for the next
six or more decades, and continues to remain a force today.[1] It is not too
much to say, as authors have done (Callahan, 1962; Kliebard, 1986,
1992; Doll, 1993), that this concept of control became a major factor in
the Progressive Movement in general and in the progressive educational
movement in particular–albeit with a degree of camouflage under the
rubric of "child-centeredness." American industry has used this concept
of control to make our nation the most productive society the world has
ever known. A by-product of this emphasis has been that what was
overt in the 1890s, 1900s, and 1910s has now become "natural" to our
way of thinking, actually buried deep within our understanding of what
organization should be. Organization and control (overt, top-down,
centralized) are virtually synonymous. In terms of educational organization, this sense of control has become, as I say elsewhere (Doll,
n.p.), "the ghost in the curriculum."

In this chapter I will look briefly at the role this sense of
(industrial) control has played in the curriculum, at a deeper sense of

control as methodization, at John Dewey's attempt to find a sense of control neither externally imposed nor internally developed, and will conclude with a new view of control–one which does not represent imposition nor self-development but rather emerges from the dynamic interaction that constitutes all life. This sense of control is oxymoronic in that it is control which depends upon change; it is control which operates not from a central locus but across a system as that system changes. Without the system changing, this sense of control does not emerge (no change, no control). This view of control lies at the heart of process thought and complexity theory. I believe this view has much to offer curriculum thought, both as a challenge to the way we have conceived of curriculum and as an opportunity for new directions. Explicating this view–no easy task–will be my personal challenge.

Control has been a central feature in American school organization ever since, as Herbert Kliebard (1986) points out, our educational focus, in the 1890s, "shifted from the tangible presence of the teacher to the remote knowledge and values incarnate in the curriculum" (p. 2). In the next century, "curriculum became a national preoccupation" (p. 3). A look at the writings of Ellwood Cubberley (1916) or Franklin Bobbitt (1918) reveal such:

> The kind, amount, and order of the subject-matter to be learned, by all pupils, in all parts of the city, regardless of age, past experience, future prospects, or physical or mental condition, is uniformly laid down for all (Cubberley, 1916, p. 281).

A statement like this shows that in these writers there is no hiding of the concept of control; it is recognized, accepted, honored. However, during the ensuing decades, control became glossed over as American educators became mesmerized with the ideological myths of schools as democratic institutions, of science as value-free inquiry, and of social problems as solvable through schooling. There is, of course, just enough truth in all these myths to make them myths. The result of all this was that, as a people, we began to see education, brought forth through curriculum, as a liberating, empowering force.

In the 1960s, we were quite surprised, in studying *On What Is Learned in School* (Dreeben, 1968), to find students not learning what we explicitly thought they were learning, that the formalized curriculum was not all we were teaching, and that anti-democratic control was evident. To use Philip Jackson's (1968) felicitous phrase, there were within the schools two curricula–one stated, one "hidden" (p. 33). The stated curriculum, of course, was that published by state education departments, school boards, principals, teachers in their syllabi and lesson plans. These all espoused values of democracy, free inquiry, and personal choice; the hidden curriculum, rarely discussed in public and certainly not printed for distribution, taught conformity, fear of reprisal, obedience to others. Needless to say, the dichotomy between these curricula was disturbing to many–Paul Goodman (1964), Ivan Illich (1971), Colin Greer (1972), and John Goodlad and Frances Klein, (1974), to name but a few.

Probably no one has done more to heighten our curriculum consciousness as to what is being taught and learned through the hidden curriculum than Michael Apple. Apple first raises the issue of the hidden curriculum in William Pinar's *Curriculum Theorizing: The Reconceptualists* (1975). There, Apple argues (pp. 95-119) that the hidden curriculum tacitly (and of course hiddenly) "legitimates the existing social order" (p. 114). Put another way by another curriculum theorist, Peter McLaren (1989): The hidden curriculum forces or at best induces students "to comply with the dominant ideologies and social practices related to authority, behavior and morality" (p. 184). Today these insights about the nature of schooling and the political-social role the curriculum plays seem almost too obvious to mention. This is a tribute to the work Michael Apple (1975, 1990), Herbert Bowles and Samuel Gintis (1976), Henry Giroux (1983), Linda McNeil (1986), Peter McLaren (1989), Patti Lather (1991) have done over the past few decades in raising our consciousness about the nature of schooling and curriculum design.

Unfortunately, along with this much-needed consciousness raising about schools and political power (my, we were naive in the 1960s!) came an acrimonious, intense, scholarly, arcane, and indeed "too precious" debate (argumentation might be a better word) about the nature of ideology, hegemony, reproduction, and resistance theories. A good summative history of this debate can be found in Pinar et al. (1995), Chapter 5, "Understanding Curriculum as Political Text." A personal account by one of the combatants can be found in the "Personal Biography" section of Michael Apple's *Official Knowledge* (1993).

I wish not to disparage the work these theorists have done, for we all are indebted to them; and indeed I am supportive of their own criticism of their earlier work as too narrow, too deterministic, and not human-agency enough oriented (see Apple, 1993; Pinar et al. 1995).

But I do wish to point out that in the esotericism of their debates they missed a key point, one Michael Apple (1975) made in his first essay on the hidden curriculum. There, he says, prior to his statement about the curriculum legitimating "the existing social order," that the curriculum in its hidden form also "serves to reinforce basic rules" by positing "a network of assumptions that...establishes the boundaries of legitimacy" (p. 99). All societies need rules; they are, again as Apple says, "the fundamental patterns which hold society together" (p. 98). However, when the legitimacy of these rules and patterns is shrouded in mist, then indeed control becomes a ghost. Light has been shed on that ghost, even if the ghost has not been exorcised,[2] but we have not given the attention I believe we must to the nature of and relationship between boundaries and networks. *All legitimacy, indeed all learning and knowledge, occur within temporally bounded networks.* The control that lurks as the ghost in the curriculum will never be truly illuminated or exorcised until we wrestle with this fundamental fact.

So far the concept of control discussed is that of control in a political and social realm, particularly as such relates to our present society–capitalistic, democratic, industrial, patriarchal. Important as these aspects (and their inherent contradictions) are, there are also other aspects of our society and its educational system worth investigating, aspects which pre-date the industrial movement and which let us see that control lies deep within Western educational thought.

David Hamilton (1989, 1990, 1992, n.p.) has done us all an immense service in resurrecting the educational origins of the word curriculum and its relation to the concept of "methodization," a movement which began in the latter sixteenth century and certainly received much attention in the seventeenth before it became a natural (and indeed "man-made") part of Western intellectual thought. Having "a method"–John Dewey devoted a whole chapter to it in *Democracy and Education* (1916/1966)–seems so natural to us, underlying as it does both Frederick Taylor's and Ralph Tyler's work, that even to mention it is to bring up the trite, the true, and the trivial. Such was not the case in the sixteenth century when the concept of uniform method was accused of going against the very essence of education. The idea of God's method, the *telos* of the universe, was, of course, a linchpin in Western thought. But this was His method, at best hazy to man [sic] and well outside the province of man's thought. The Protestant Reformation (really Revolution), influenced by the humanism of the Renaissance, changed this medieval relationship of man to God–now "every man became his own priest," no longer dependent on the religious interpretations of the (Catholic) Church hierarchy.3 Method, especially the hermeneutic method of biblical interpretation, became paramount. It was method that lay at the heart of the disagreement between Galileo and the Roman Church: he advocated a scientific/ experimental method founded on the use of the telescope; it advocated a philosophical/theological one founded on interpreting the writings of Aristotle. The apocryphal but illuminating story contrasting these methods is that of a discussion between Galileo and the Bishop. Galileo encouraged the Bishop to look through the telescope to watch movement in the heavens, but the Bishop declined, saying he had no need of such an activity or instrument, having read Aristotle on the point three times. Of more substance is Galileo's own writings (from his *Opere,* VII, p. 341) that while "in every hypothesis of reason error may lurk...a discovery of sense [sensory experience] cannot be at odds with the truth. How could it be otherwise?" (quoted in Burtt, 1967, p. 67). This is a dramatic pitting of the experimental/experiential against the rational, and in this contest a new method was emerging—the scientific. Control now began to shift from the authoritative interpretation of scripture to each person's own "eyewitness" account.

John Calvin was a man of method. Imbued with the protestant humanism of Desiderius Erasmus and Martin Luther,4 he advocated that each person read the Bible individually. But he also wrote copiously–*Institutes* (1536 and 1559) and *Commentaries* (1540-1565)– on how the Bible in all its simplicity was to be interpreted, especially regarding how it was to be influential in, indeed a model for, life. In short, he wanted his followers, his flock (to use a biblical metaphor), not to wander too far from the true and simple path he believed Christ trod. Throughout these writings and in his preachings, Calvin often referred to life as a "race" or "racecourse"–*cursus* and *stadium*. In the final (1559) edition of the *Institutes,* he did appropriate, maybe from Cicero, *curriculum* (a racecourse similar to that at the Circus Maximus)–to describe a path, course, way of life his followers were to follow. *Vitae curriculum* and *vitae curriculo* are the phrases he used, albeit not often (Hamilton 1989, pp. 48-49).

The sixteenth century had its share of turmoil–Martin Luther did nail his Ninety-five Theses to the church door in Wittenberg in 1517, the peasants revolted in Germany, Rome was sacked with thousands dying, the Reformation began earnestly in Scotland and France, Ignatius of Loyola founded the Jesuits as an order loyal and subservient to the

Pope, Pope Paul III established the Inquisition, the Counter-Reformation began, and on St. Bartholomew's Day, two thousand Huguenots were slaughtered in Paris. Along with political and social turmoil, it was a century in which intellectual thought began its shift from a medieval-Aristotelian-geocentric paradigm to a modernist-scientific-heliocentric one. The posthumous publication of Nicolaus Copernicus' *De Revolutionibus* (On the Revolutions of the Heavenly Spheres, 1543) may be considered a transition point in this shift. It was also a time when, as one observer has phrased it "the mother Church of Rome...gave birth to several daughter churches" (Bratt, 1964, p. 63). Toward the end of the century was also the beginning of the methodization movement and the first introduction of the word curriculum in educational literature. The birth of the daughter churches–those of a Protestant bent–was not an easy or natural birth; rather, it was "quite unnatural...awful, painful, bloody" (p. 63). These daughter Churches had hoped to remain within the mother fold, albeit they wished mother to reform her ways–break her unholy alliance with secular princes, give up papal superstitions, mechanical ceremonies, and scholastic traditions (p. 12). Reformation was "in the air" but the Council of Trent (1545-1563) failed to reconcile mother with her daughters; so an irrevocable split occurred, bringing Protestantism into direct conflict with Catholicism. Later in the century, Henry of Navarre (the IV) tried in his Edict of Nantes (1598) to give political and spiritual recognition to both Protestants and Catholics. But his assassination in 1610 by a frustrated candidate to the Jesuit order changed all that (Toulmin, 1990, p. 49). Shortly thereafter, John Donne penned his famous lines, which could apply to the social as well as intellectual situation:

> And new Philofophy cals all in doubt,
> The Element of fire is quite put out;
> The Sun is loft, and th'earth and no mans wit
> Can well direct him, where to looke for it.
> ∗∗∗∗∗∗∗∗∗∗∗∗∗∗∗∗∗∗∗∗∗∗∗∗∗∗∗∗∗∗∗∗∗∗∗∗∗∗∗
> 'Tis all in peeces, all cohaerance gone;
> All juft fupply, and all Relation:
> Prince, Subject, Father, Sonne, are things forgot,
> For every man alone thinkes he hath got
> To be a Phoenix, and that then can bee
> None of that kinde, of which he is, but hee.
> (Donne, 1633/1968, lines 205-218)

This sense of individualism (extreme for the time) of which Donne speaks and which both the Protestant Reformation and a spirit of rising commercialism encouraged was frightening to many, including Donne, who penned the famous phrase "no man is an islande." During this time of lost "cohaerance" when both the scientific and social worlds were seeking "light," there was felt to be a need for methodological procedures. Uniform procedures were needed not only for commercial trade; they were also needed for scientific study and most of all for a sense of intellectual comfort in a time of chaos. Comfort is a somewhat odd word to use here, for certainty (as Dewey points out, 1929/1960) was sought. Yet it was certainty, in the form of Romish doctrine and Aristotelian scholasticism, that humanism challenged and "dissenters and protesters" rejected. While no "man" was an island, each was an individual reader and interpreter of the Bible. This crisis in intellectual thought and personal being drove René Descartes from the passions and paradoxes of Paris into his solitary and visionary meditations where he developed the method of "Rightly Conducting Reason for Seeking Truth in the Sciences" (1637/1950). As I have already pointed out (Doll, 1993) the correlation between Descartes' "Four Rules" and Tyler's "Four Questions" is quite astonishing (pp. 30-31). Thus, I argue, America's penchant for scientific efficiency was an offshoot (or sub-set) of a larger methodization movement which began in the early sixteenth century, and was led by or at least received support from commercial interests, scientific advancement, and protest (ultimately Protestant) theologians. At the time, this methodization movement which eventually turned into the process we now call schooling was considered anti-educational. As the saying goes, *"plus ça change, plus c'est la meme."*

The origin of universal schooling–systematic instruction, applied to a broad class of people–can be traced to Pope Gregory's order in 1078 that all bishops have "the arts of letters" taught in their churches, followed by the Third and Fourth Lateran Councils' mandates in 1179 and 1215 that "every cathedral church shall maintain a master to give free instruction to clerics in the church and to needy scholars" (Wertheim, 1995, p. 41). From these church or cathedral schools–male-only, since clerics were male-only–came the first European universities, Bologna (1190), Paris (1200), and Oxford (1210), also male-only.[5] The method of instruction in these schools and universities was skill-driven to acquire competence in Latin, Greek, and Hebrew and then tutorial-driven in the reading and interpreting of the classic and biblical texts written in these languages. How long a student or scholar spent in these endeavors depended on how long one wanted to so spend his time, what scholars one wished to read with or "study under," and how serious one was regarding eventual mastery of the material presented in order to stand before the university scholars and receive one's degree–bachelor of arts, master of arts, or doctor of philosophy, law, literature, or theology. Martin Luther's experiences are not uncommon for the day. He studied first at nearby Erfurt, a thriving medieval university town (maybe of 20,000 souls) known as both "a beer chamber" and a "house of prostitution" but one that also possessed "2 endowed churches, 22 cloisters, 23 cloister churches, 36 chapels, and 6 hospitals" (Schwiebert, 1950, p. 130). While there in his late teens, he read the Latin classics, struggled with Greek and Hebrew, acquired the skill of playing the lute "quite well" (p. 137) and was influenced by Humanistic thought through one of his masters, Trutvetter, who had him read widely in physics, metaphysics, and the Bible. At the age of twenty-two, after receiving both his bachelor's and master's degrees and beginning his study of law, Luther applied "for admission to the 'Black Cloister' of the Hermits of St. Augustine," whose cloister house was at Erfurt. He remained a monk for the next nineteen years. While so, he became first a priest (1507, age 24), then a lector in Bible studies. This latter was the first step toward receiving a doctorate in theology, which Luther did in 1512 (p. 149) at the age of 29. Although racked by doubts and much influenced by "New Way" thinking, which emphasized faith alone in matters of Biblical interpretation, Luther did, at the University of Wittenberg in the fall of 1512, stand for his doctorate, pay his fee, swear fealty to the Roman Church, and on October 19th, was sworn in as a Doctor of Theology with a chair at the University (p. 195).

The length of time it took Luther to become a doctor was short for the day, certainly not long for our doctorates today. But the frame was quite different–the whole time (from the early twenties on) Luther was a monk, cloistered, celibate, studying (he rose at 4 am), and praying. Not all scholars, of course, were monks, nor were all so studious (although as a working language Luther seems to have mastered only Latin). The big difference, though, was that Luther, as representative of his time, did not follow a curriculum (a set course of study)–there was none.[6] Rather, Luther, and those like him, studied with masters for as long as either party wished or until the master felt the student was ready to stand before the faculty for his disputation. As a scholar, Luther studied Aristotle–the pillar of the scholastic tradition–with additional readings from Augustine, Aquinas, Boethius, and others. As a theologian he read, memorized, and interpreted the Bible. Then a student could and often did spend decades "studying" but never standing for a degree. The relationship was very personal–all students at Erfurt had to spend a year living in cloistered arrangements with a master; then, for a degree, they were tested on their knowledge and appraised on their moral and spiritual values. Control was definitely present, but it came through personal relations, institutional rules, loyalty, and tradition–it did not come in the form of a set curriculum. [Again, prior to the Calvinist universities of Leiden (1582) and Glasgow (1633) there was no curriculum as we know the word or concept.] The social-political control we call hidden in the twentieth century was open and overt (and theological) in the sixteenth.

The rise of Protestantism with its individualism, commercialism, with its formation of a middle class, and scientism with its new methodology brought a new sense to education, a sense interested in and committed to simplicity and method. As Grafton and Jardine (1986) say:

> The individualism, verging on hero-worship of [the great teachers], of early humanism gave way in the early sixteenth century to an ideology of routine, order, and above all, "method." (p. 123)

Two of the great methodizers of this time were Peter Ramus and John Comenius. With their methodizing they were, as I've said, accused by the traditionalists of vulgarizing the noble "art" of dialectic and of virtually ignoring the "arts" of grammar and rhetoric (these three formed the *trivium*) in favor of the more content ("letter") oriented subjects of the *quadrivium* (music, arithmetic, geometry, astronomy). In all this, the traditionalists believed the methodizers were going against the very essence of learning. The battle between the traditionalists and the methodizers was indeed bloody–Ramus lost his life in the St. Bartholomew's Day Massacre (1572) but his teachings lived on, for no less than 250 editions/adaptations of his *Dialectic* were published in the 100 years between the mid 1500s and the mid 1600s (Hamilton, 1992, p. 9). [This averages to two and one-half editions per year for approximately a century.] Teaching, under the Ramist method, changed from being a personal, dialogical art to a lettered, methodological, uniform, and almost commercial process. Curriculum now appeared (1576) as an educational word. Thomas Fregius of Basle, a Protestant professor-printer-publisher, used the word in presenting a Ramist "map of knowledge" (Hamilton, 1989, pp. 26-27; 1992, p. 9).[7]

Peter Ramus, hired-fired-hired professor at the University of Paris in the sixteenth century, is probably a good bifurcation point to mark the change from the traditional, scholastic, Aristotelian teaching to the new methodized teaching. Indeed, Ramus' own name means "branching" in Latin, and the word ramification (to break into branches, or spread out) came into use in the sixteenth century during Peter Ramus' lifetime (Hamilton, 1990, p. 26; O.E.D., 1989, vol. xiii, p. 156). It was ramification or branching which characterized Ramus' methodology, "furnishing students with a 'universal skeleton key' which, if 'properly applied,' could unlock any of the arts or sciences" (cited in Hamilton, 1990, p. 26). [No wonder Ramus' *Dialectic* sold so well.]

Strange as it may seem to us, imbued with the naturalness of both linear and categorical order with their implicit forms of control, prior to Ramus and his method, knowledge (as that which we teach) was not curricularized. It was not put into a set, sequential form. Nor was it handled comprehensively. Authors had listed subjects they felt were important, and Boethius' *trivium* and *quadrivium* were prominent, especially with the Jesuits. But how these were to be studied or whether they actually constituted a full course of something was not addressed. Curriculum, as a full course to be run, was not yet existent. Ramus changed all this, he provided a "map" of all knowledge (we would call it a chart, with categories and branching subcategories) and this map was carefully and definitely ordered in such a way that, "that enunciation is placed first which is first in the absolute order of knowledge, that next which is next and so on: and thus there is an unbroken progression" (Hamilton, 1989, p. 46). This is Ramus' "Method," and it swept Europe in the latter sixteenth and early seventeenth centuries, giving us a method still in use today.[8]

Two points stand out, I believe, in this quote. The first is the (implied) belief in ordering knowledge comprehensively. Ramus' method is to apply to all knowledge at all times. Ramus was not dealing with his or generic man's view of knowledge, he was dealing with all knowledge. In short, he had a method for all times–a universal methodology. This same sense of a universal methodology–still extant to a great degree in our curriculum "methods courses"–surfaced in Descartes' method for "rightly conducting reason for seeking truth." The second point, an offshoot of the first, is that there is "an absolute order of knowledge." What we have here is a metaphysical assumption about epistemology. Knowledge is organized in a logical form, hence Ramus' belief in the value of "mapping" this knowledge (in our parlance, building a chart or spread-sheet). Since knowledge is organized logically, Ramus played up the art of dialectic (which he turned into logic) and played down the art of rhetoric (communication). This emphasis on the value of clear presentation of ideas rather than the effective communication of these–the former subsuming the latter–is with us today. If we have taught an idea well (how can one teach an idea?), they, the students, will have learned it well. In fact, as absurd as this sequitur (or non-sequitur) is, this is *precisely* what Ramus believed. Looking at Ramus' reforms, Hamilton (1990) comments:

> In proposing these educational reforms, Ramus included two additional, and sweeping, claims about his method: first, that it could be used not only in philosophy but also in all other fields of human endeavor [it was indeed a "skeleton key" to all knowledge]; and secondly, that it was nothing less than the externalization of the mental processes of human cognition (p. 26).

This second point essentially asserts that learning is done best logically and uniformly, not experientially and personally. The history of learning theory from the sixteenth through the twentieth century is replete with this assumption–it shapes the logicalness and uniformity of our teaching, methods of presentation, and curriculum design. This methodology, of course, is an oversimplification of a most complex process but like all oversimplifications appeals because of its simplicity. Only now, through the development of neural research (Freeman, 1991; Triche and St. Julien, 1996) are we beginning to see the chaotic complexity of learning–a complexity Dewey, in his marvelous paper on "The Reflex Arc" (1896/1972), saw was highly interactive, requiring attention not only to the clarity of presentation but also to the natural organizational powers of the learner. Those enmeshed in "constructivist curriculum" design (see *NCTM, Monograph, No. 4,* 1990; *Educational Researcher,* 1994) are much aware of the importance of this point. In terms of control, this means a curriculum shift in focus from the relatively simple, logical organ-ization of knowledge to a complex interaction between and among text, teacher, taught. This shift will be explored more in this paper's concluding section on complexity theory.

As has been said, the word curriculum, as a course to be run, first appeared in educational literature as part of one of Ramus' maps printed in 1576. In school settings, it appeared in the university catalogues of Leiden (1588) and Glasgow (1633); again, both Protestant universities, indeed Calvinist ones.

Johann Amos Comenius, born two decades after Ramus' death, was not only a great methodizer but probably the one we know best as developing the ideas behind our modern concept of schooling. As Hamilton points out (1992; n.p.), Comenius–a Protestant preacher and schoolmaster–played a direct role in moving education from a sense of study to a sense of teaching and learning, or from pedagogics to didactics. In a wonderful, pithy statement, another history of schooling researcher has remarked "Comenius cared naught for study; teaching and learning were his thing" (McClintock, 1972, p. 178). To understand this statement, we need to remember that prior to the methodization movement (Hamilton calls it "methodologising," n.p., p. 17), education was essentially studying (reading, reflecting on, interpreting) the great biblical and classical texts. This was done individually or with others, but it was not done in a schooling situation. Schooling, with its sense of an ordered curriculum and a uniform instructional methodology, was concerned with "getting learning into the child" or learner, and with "keeping the learner present before such knowledge" (p. 13). Our "time on task" is but a variation [dare I say ramification] of this methodization-schooling movement. The whole purpose of the movement was to provide a "short-cut" to learning[9]–again, one is reminded of the teacher in Joseph Mayer Rice's book (1893/1969) who shouted to her student "Don't think. Tell me what you know" (p. 175). As Hamilton (1992) accurately and succinctly says:

> Human beings learned long before they were taught, or even taught themselves. They learned with the aid of their sense organs and their minds, not with the help of their textbooks and their teachers. (p. 161)

But with the advent of curriculum-methodization-didactics, "learning gradually became associated with, and shaped by, the external activity we know as teaching.... [T]eachers gradually became schoolteachers and learners gradually became schooled" (p. 161). "Learning" now appeared as a direct effect of methodized teaching while control, as a ghost, appeared in the form of curriculum and instruction–narrow, confining, limiting.

The use of the word didactics here has an interesting history to it, one much aligned with the concept of instruction as a part of, not apart from, curriculum. The curriculum/instruction debate–united versus separate–is an American, not a European "thing." This cultural distinction is due mostly to the influence Johann Amos Comenius has had in Europe but not in America. Comenius was both a preacher and a schoolteacher. In a sense, he was the methodizer who most brought the movement into the school field[10]–Ramus being more an academic than a schoolmaster. Comenius' great methodizing work in curriculum is called *The Great Didactic* (1657/1896). It definitely addresses school issues–i.e., how a teacher is to teach a class. In Chapter Nineteen, "The Principles of Conciseness and Rapidity in Teaching," Comenius laments that under current conditions, "no fixed landmarks were set up, which might serve as goals to be reached," nor "no method was known by which instruction could be given to all the pupils in a class at the same time" (pp. 313-314). He then goes on to offer remedies: (1) only one teacher in each school, (2) only one author for each subject, (3) the same exercise given to the whole class, (4) all subjects taught by the same method, (5) everything taught be done so "thoroughly, briefly, and pithily, that understanding may be, as it were, unlocked by one key" (p. 316). *Indeed, here we do have the origins of modern-day schooling.*[11] Infused into these school issues, though, is Comenius' metaphysical philosophy of *pansophie*[12]–an interconnection of all things through education. Through education, all people–women as well as men–would come to see and recognize "all points of view" (Comenius, 1967, p. 6). As a theologian-metaphysician, this sense of harmony that pervaded the universe was Comenius' own cosmology. As a preacher-teacher he believed awareness of this harmony could, indeed would, come through education–education which had a definite didactic bent to it. As a preacher he wished to use rhetoric to help others see "God's light"–here, as Hamilton (1992) points out, Comenius is being pietist, neo-humanist, and prescient of the coming Enlightenment (p. 168). As Ramus had emphasized the dialectical-logical aspects of the *trivium,* believing education should be curriculum-oriented in the way fields of knowledge were ordered, so Comenius emphasized the rhetorical-didactical aspects of the *trivium,* believing that instruction should be included with curriculum (á la Ramus) and that for instruction, a preacher's ability to declaim rhetorically and didactically was needed by the schoolmaster. To this day, in the north European and Scandinavian countries, curriculum and didactic are seen as one, curriculum *and* instruction.[13]

In American education, no one has been more concerned with "and" –curriculum and instruction, child and curriculum, experience and education, democracy and education–than John Dewey. [14] Regarding the sense of a uniform methodology for all, Dewey (1916/1966) says:

> Methods...authoritatively recommended to teachers, instead of being an expression of their own intelligent observations....have a mechanical uniformity [and are] assumed to be alike for all minds. (p. 168)

He goes on:

> Nothing has brought pedagogical theory into greater disrepute than the belief that it is identified with handing out to teachers recipes and models to be followed in teaching. (p. 170)

And concludes:

> Probably the chief cause of devotion to rigidity of method is, however, that it seems to promise speedy, accurately measurable, correct results. (p. 175)

Dewey's suggestion, of course, is to integrate methods with subject matter and to allow both the teacher and the student to use their own "native tendencies," "acquired habits and interests," and "intelligent observations." In short, Dewey is suggesting that control in method shift from a pre-set pattern or even from the teacher *per se* to an interaction (really a transaction) between and among teacher, taught, text.[15] Regarding the other main point in the methodists' emphasis, that of transferring directly the logical ordering of knowledge (as shown in a Ramist map of knowledge) to a learning subject, Dewey says:

> [N]o thought, no idea, can possibly be conveyed as an idea from one person to another.... Only by wrestling with the conditions of the problem, at first hand, seeking and finding one's own way out, does one think. (pp. 159-160)

But as has already been stated, the Ramist method was interested in teaching and learning, not in thinking. One of the subtle controls which has operated in our modernist-methodized concept of curriculum is that it limits thinking.

All his life Dewey worked to develop a pedagogy and a practice which enhanced, not limited, thinking. He actually wrote his book *How We Think* (1971) twice, in 1911 and again in 1933. Enhancing thinking, Dewey knew, required control, direction, or guidance. Of these three words, guidance, he says, "best conveys the idea of assisting through cooperation the natural capacities of the individual" (1916/1966, p. 23). However, it is with the word control that he works most and comes very close to positing the type of control now starting to emerge in complexity theory. [As Alfred North Whitehead, with his emphasis on nonlinear relations and process, has been called a forefather of mathematical chaos theory, so it may be posited that John Dewey, with his emphasis on interaction, transaction, emergence and with hints at self-organization, is a forefather of complexity theory.]

Control, Dewey (1916/1966) says, subordinates a person's "natural impulses" to another's end; indeed, control as we use the term, has "a flavor or coercion or compulsion about it" (p. 24). To operate in such an impositional manner is neither good nor practical; it does not lead to growth, it is too restrictive. Yet a type of control is needed; Dewey calls this "the other more important and permanent mode of control" (p. 27). This other mode is not the self-control of mere imitation. In fact self-control is probably not a good word to describe the control Dewey calls "intellectual not personal" (p. 33), that which is "a *guiding of activity* to its own end" (p. 24, emphasis added). While this guiding is partly our own doing from our habits of action-reflection-action, it is also true much of the control lies beyond us individually. To quote Dewey: "the basic control resides in the nature of the situations" developing (p. 39).[16] In this sense of *control residing in the situations themselves*–in the betweens and amongs, in the dynamic inter/transactions–Dewey gives a hint of self-organization.

Complexity, Curriculum, and Cosmology

Complexity theory is the study of order, obviously of complex order–of order that is dynamic, changing, emerging; finally, order that is self-generating or self-organizing. If complexity theory is about anything, it is about the development of self-organizing structures. In a very real sense, it is about how life at the cosmic, evolutionary, cultural, human, molecular levels occurs. For centuries it was believed (and by many still is believed) that human life was a gift from God–humans made by God in Her image, as it were. Darwinism offered a rather devastating alternative to this scenario–natural selection acting on random variation.[17] In this view, we become a mere historical accident–for evolution is no more than "randomness caught on the wing"–to use Jacques Monod's (1971) "sweet, lyric phrase" (p. 98; Kauffman, 1995, p. 97). Obviously, a number (a goodly number) were not happy with this conclusion nor with the dilemma of choosing between external creation and random chance. In Deweyan terms, this sense of either-or extremes is limiting. Are these the only choices available? Is this really the way the universe was constructed?

Evolutionary biologists–particularly C.H. Waddington and Jean Piaget–searched for a "third way," a *tertium quid,* to use Piaget's phrase. Philosophers such as Alfred North Whitehead and theologians Charles Hartshorne, John Cobb, and David Griffin proposed a different cosmology–one that either posited or allowed for creativity as a prime process. Physicists, too, joined in–Paul Davies probably being the most notable. It is, though, the chemist-metaphysician Ilya Prigogine who has brought self-organization to the fore and begun talk of a new type of order–complex order or chaotic order, if one wishes to be playful.[18]

A literature is developing about complexity theory: Roger Lewin and Michael Waldrop have written popular books, (both are titled *Complexity,* and both were published in 1992). The Santa Fe Institute, founded by the atomic scientists at Los Alamos, New Mexico, has devoted the most time and scholarly attention to complexity theory and of this group it is Stuart Kauffman (1993, 1995), I believe, who is doing the most to investigate and speculate on the origins of order. This investigation-speculation draws heavily on and integrates the fields of evolutionary biology, nonlinear mathematics (chaos mathematics, it is usually called), thermodynamic chemistry, and speculative metaphysics (or process philosophy). Kauffman is the individual on whom I will base my analysis and speculations.[19]

Currently a MacArthur Fellow working at the Santa Fe Institute, Kauffman has always been a bit of a maverick in his thinking, challenging the conventional. He began college (Dartmouth) wanting to be a "Great Playwright" but then switched to being a "Great Philosopher" (B.A. in Philosophy and a year at Oxford–Lewin, 1992, pp. 23-26). Convinced greatness for him did not lie in philosophy, he decided to enter medical school and work on embryology–the development of living organisms. With a background in poetry, literature, philosophy, he felt the randomness of Darwinian selection–the accidentalness of all life–was just too simple. Not wrong, just too simple. The phenomenal order in nature, often expressed mathematically as in the Fibonacci sequence, was too pervasive to be accidental.[20] Something else had to be present in the cosmos. Natural selection had to have a "companion." He found "that something" in the creativity of self-organization: which he has explored in computer-generated mathematics via Boolean networks, has applied to embryology in regard to cells self-forming, and has speculated on in social systems. At the cosmological or metaphysical level, Kauffman is looking for a "new marriage of self-organization, selection, and accident" (1995, p. 150). There is a spiritual but not necessarily a religious quest to Kauffman's search. In some ways, Kauffman is taking for study Alfred North Whitehead's (1929/1978) remark, "It lies in the nature of things that the many enter into complex unity" (p. 21).[21] Kauffman is studying both the "complex unity'" and the "entering into" of this statement.

A Boolean network, named after the mathematician George Boole, is a dynamical system of interconnecting parts. That is, it is a system or network of parts wherein the system as a whole changes as the parts undergo change. A simple example would be a square board with anywhere from 1,000 to 100,000 light bulbs interconnected in a random manner–one does need computers to make this example work. Each light bulb would be connected to one or more other light bulbs. On a random basis, some light bulbs would go on when its connecting bulb(s) is/are lit; others would not go on or would receive "mixed signals," switching back and forth between on and off. Since each bulb is connected with other bulbs, one might well expect that a switch of the current to "on" would produce a random maze of blinking bulbs–chaos would reign as the bulbs get "mixed signals." This is a fine modernist prediction, and a true one, sometimes. The interesting feature is that *under certain conditions* the blinking bulbs settle down to a pattern of change–i.e., order and harmony emerge at the system level as the bulbs cycle through change from one state to another. Kauffman calls this "order for free" (1995, Chapter Four), as it is an order neither imposed nor random but rather *emerging under certain conditions* from the interactions going on within the system itself. Here lies the key concept of his cosmological thesis–the organization of life is the natural result (neither imposed nor random) of a dynamical system acting under certain conditions. It is these "certain conditions" which Kauffman continues to explore and which hold heuristic value, I believe, for curriculum thought and theory.

I will not go into the leap Kauffman makes from the operations of Boolean networks with computers to the origins of life in the universe, except to say that he finds remarkable correspondences between the operation of such networks and the embryological problem of how cells are able to both differentiate and reproduce. As he poetically says: How "can a single cell, merely some tens of thousands of kinds of molecules locked in one another's embrace, know how to create the intricacies of a human infant?" (1995, p. 93). Those interested in this issue I refer to his Chapters Five, Six, Seven. Instead, I will concentrate on the conditions or circumstances needed for order (and control) to emerge. What methods, what sense of control are needed to have this occur?

The conditions for emergent order are really quite simple, almost naively so. But they are extremely important: without the conditions present, order (as we recognize as such) does not emerge. These conditions–all combined in an integrated and interactive manner–are a critical mass (light bulbs for the computer model used), a few connections (each light bulb connected with only two or so others), and simple rules (light bulbs connected in either an *and* relationship or an *or* relationship–i.e., both light up, only one lights up).[22] This integration of critical mass (fairly high) and connections (few) with rules (simple) produces what Kauffman and others refer to as order emerging at or near the "edge of chaos." In Kauffman's (1995) own words:

> What we have found for the modestly complex behaviors we are requesting is that the networks do adapt and improve, and that they evolve, not to the very edge of chaos, but to the ordered regime, not too far from the edge of chaos. It is as though a position in the ordered regime near the transition to chaos affords the best mixture of stability and flexibility (p. 91).

It is this "mixture of stability and flexibility" which Kauffman believes may "emerge as a kind of universal feature of complex adaptive systems in biology and beyond" (p. 91).

Systems that are "stable and flexible!" On the one hand this sounds almost trite–hardly worthy of a book or even of a chapter. Yet the curriculum model we have inherited from Calvin-Ramus-Comenius does not include *both* stability *and* flexibility; nor, indeed, do most teachers think of these two as a *necessary* combination. But this is just Kauffman's point, regarding the origins of life, and mine, regarding an alternative way to view curriculum. We have viewed stability-flexibility in either-or terms. As Dewey (1938/1963) says: Humankind, with its penchant for extreme opposites, "is given to formulating its beliefs in terms of *Either-Ors*" (p. 17). The uniqueness of a complexity theory approach (its radicalness from a modernist perspective) is that it replaces either-or with both-and.[23] The dynamic integration of stability and flexibility sends us "not to the very edge of chaos, but to the ordered regime, not too far from the edge," very close to the "transition to chaos." Our curriculum challenge, if we wish complexity theory to be heuristic and generative, is to combine stability with flexibility, flexibility with stability, in such ways that we operate near but neither on nor over the "edge of chaos."

There are, of course, many ways to accept this challenge. Personally, I look at my 4R's of a good curriculum (Richness, Recursions, Relations, Rigor) and try to set a framework that is rich in interconnections and problematic ways of viewing but has the flexibility of letting groups decide how the material presented is handled. There is no linear, atomistic, simple syllabus. Presently, master's level students in one of my courses are reading three books–by myself, by William Pinar, by C.A. Bowers. How they are handling the material in the books is a decision each group is making. How the groups will interact with each other and how I and a graduate assistant will interact with both the class and the groups is still forming. Control is present but it is not imposed, it emerges from the interactions present. This is but one example. In California, a few years back, frustrated in using a linear approach to help sixth-graders "solve math problems," I (with the advice of a colleague, Samuel Crowell) had the students make up their own problems and hand them to another group. The ability to do the math problems they could not solve before improved dramatically. In Dewey's terms, the learning occurred naturally and indirectly as a result of active involvement.[24] These are but two examples of my working with a framework (complex and nonlinear) that is *both* stable *and* flexible.

Summary

In this essay I have had two foci. One, I have looked at the history and origins of that which we call curriculum; two, I have explored a bit the relevance complexity theory (and its attendant notions of chaos) might have for a view of curriculum different from the modernist one we now embrace. Regarding the first, I have argued that the "naturalness" of our curriculum and instructional methods–their embedded sense of order and

control–is an historical artifact. There is nothing *necessary* about these
methods, they are the result of particular people operating in a particular
culture with particular ideologies. Alternatives are allowable. Regarding
the second, complexity theory and its usefulness, the time is yet too
soon for us to make an assessment. Such an assessment, of course, will
need to be made on its curricular successes/failures, not on its mathematical or biological ones. Presently, though, I am excited enough by
its implications to try organizing my classes in a manner that allows
for, indeed depends on, "stability *and* flexibility."

Notes:
1. It is interesting to note that as a social reformer and practical
businessman, Taylor believed that "all classes of men are not only
willing, but glad to give up all ideas of soldering, and devote all their
energies to turning out maximum work possible, providing [sic] they
are sure of a suitable permanent reward." The reward Bethlehem Steel
gave Schmidt (Taylor's "first class man") was an increase in pay from
$1.15 per day to $1.85 per day (Taylor, 1911/1947, pp. 45-46). Once
this new production schedule was established, Taylor, as a progressive,
considered it his moral duty to be certain the pig-iron was now loaded at
the new rate with the men "paid extra premium" (p. 43; Doll, 1993, p.
40). [With progressive thinkers like that it is no wonder the union
movement spread.]

2. Along these lines it is interesting to read Jacques Derrida's *Specters
of Marx* (1994), a fascinating reappraisal of Marx and the role of
Marxism in the history of intellectual thought.

3. "Every *man* his own priest" is important in Margaret Wertheim's
(1995) argument that women's exclusion from the new mathematics
and physics arising in the scientific revolution of the sixteenth and
seventeenth centuries was due to the Catholic Church's reforms from
the eleventh and twelfth centuries on (and certainly intensified by the
Protestant challenge), which followed Pope Gregory's decree that "all
bishop's were to have the 'the arts of letters' taught in their churches"
followed by the Third and Fourth Lateran councils, a century and
century and one-half later, decreeing that "every cathedral church shall
maintain a master to give free instruction to clerics in the church" (p.
41). Clerics were males. Women were categorically excluded from the
Renaissance of knowledge in the late Middle Ages and the following

scientific revolution of the sixteenth and seventeenth centuries. In fact, women were not allowed into the colleges of Oxford until late in the nineteenth century. It is not too much to say that from the twelfth century through the nineteenth, the control of Western knowledge lay in male minds.

4.   I am using a small p with Protestant here for in its early stages this movement was indeed a reform from within the Roman Church–both Erasmus and Luther were priests and Augustinian monks. They wished not to break with Rome but to reform it of its too worldly and sophisticated and unholy ways. Such hope was short lived and by the 1530s, Protestantism adopted its own, simpler, form of worship (Bratt, 1964).

5.   I wish to emphasize again Wertheim's (1995) point of how making the church schools and universities accessible to men only disenfranchised women. From the twelfth through the nineteenth centuries (when universities did become co-ed and women's colleges did develop), the big broad intellectual movements that have defined Western intellectual thought and culture–the Renaissance, humanism, the scientific revolution and its practical applications–were carried on almost exclusively in relation to these schools and universities. For these seven to eight centuries women were excluded from participating actively in these movements or as in the salons of Paris had to approach these movements in an extracurricular manner. In 1732, Laura Bassi became "the world's first woman professor," at the University of Bologna but could lecture only when the (male) faculty decided she could, namely at "special public occasions...[when she was] put on display to attract fame and attention" (p. 138). Mary Somerville in the early 1800s translated Laplace's monumental book on celestial mechanics into English with copious notes and mathematical derivatives. The book became and stayed for a century the standard text for advanced physics students at the University of Cambridge. Yet she, herself, was "not allowed admission to its hallowed halls" (p. 166). The story of Marie Curie is well known. The world's first twice-honored Nobel recipient, she became, in 1906 (two centuries after Laura Bassi and almost one after Mary Somerville), the University of Paris' first female professor but in spite of these honors was never accepted into the French Academy of Sciences (p. 173). One cannot say the list is endless–it is really quite short.

6. Shortly after Luther's day, the Jesuits began (in the mid-1500s) their series of colleges and since "no uniform system existed" (Fitzpatrick, 1933, p. 28) they began their *ratio studiorum* (rules of study [and administration]). The first fully formed expression of these "rules" appeared in 1599, but the Jesuits had been working on them since 1584 and drew them from Jesuit teaching experiences since the mid-1500s. Hamilton (n.p.) believes that much of the "didacticism conventionally associated with Jesuit practice may have come later through...post-Comenian interpretations" (p. 24).

7. Much of my history of education (with particular reference to the origin of the concepts curriculum and schooling) in sixteenth and seventeenth century Europe is, as the reader has already opined, indebted to the published and unpublished writings of David Hamilton of the University of Liverpool, England.

8. This (new) method–sequential, ordered, efficient (Ong, 1958, p. 225)–was not without its critics. Francis Bacon, in the Preface to his *Novum Organum* (1620/1899), complained that

> those who have assigned so much to logic [the Ramists]...[have] tended more to confirm errors, than to disclose the truth. Our only remaining hope and salvation is to begin the whole labor of the mind again (p. 312).

However, in this fresh start on the concept of understanding, Bacon asserts that we must not leave the mind to itself but must be "directing it perpetually from the very first, and attaining our end as it were by mechanical aid" (p. 312). Thus, a mechanistic methodology was used not only by the Ramists but even by its critics.

As an interesting aside, it is worth noting that the seriation of food serving–course one, two, three, as in a four or seven course meal–came into being around the mid-1600s. Prior to that food was laid out more in a smorgasbord style. See Peterson, 1994, *passim*, especially part I.

9. Ramus was indeed, to use Hamilton's phrase, "the high priest of [shortcutting] method," or, to use Walter Ong's appropriated phrase, "the greatest master of the short-cut the world has ever known." This "teaching" movement, strong from the 1510s on, shifted the intellectual emphasis in education from the classical ideal of a "perfect" orator, etc.

to the classroom ideal of a methodology based on textbooks, teaching manuals, drills (Hamilton, 1990, p. 23-26; Ong, 1958, p. 3).

10. There were, of course, other methodizers: Charles Hoole and his *A New Discovery of the Old Art of Teaching Schoole* (1660) and the Jesuit Order's school manual, *Ratio Studiorum* (1599) stand out in this regard. All of these contributed to the substitution of didactics (rhetorical declamations on teaching and learning) for pedagogics (advice on introducing children to the adult world).

11. Hamilton (1992) strongly makes the point that the work of the methodists (Comenius and his contemporaries) was not merely an extension, even a ramification, of past patterns; rather, they created new educational patterns (maybe even a paradigm) utilizing two new ideas: curriculum and didactics. Now, three hundred years later these patterns are "being challenged by a new set of assumptions that prefigure another educational order" (p. 157). Like Hamilton, I see this new order emerging from complexity theory. The latter part of this paper will introduce complexity theory and muse on the educational (curriculum and instruction) possibilities inherent in this new order.

12. In his *A Reformation of Schooles* (1642, pp. 71 ff.), Comenius talks of

> The Temple of Christian Pansophie to be erected and framed according to the rules, and lawes of Almighty God the supreme Architect, [wherein] by a moft exact forme of Method [and under a] Christian Catholique Church...mans mind turning to every side, may with pleasing contemplation, looke upon every thing in the world, visible and invisable, temporall and eternall, so farre as they are revealed (pp. 71-72).

13. A fine example detailing this ongoing connection can be found in Bjørg Gundem (1992), "Notes on the Development of Nordic Didactics," and in her 1995 Oslo conference on curriculum and didactics.

14. A good development of this both/and rather than either/or theme in Dewey's writing can be found in Chapter Four of Jeanne Robertson's doctoral dissertation: "Reconstructing Educational Experience: A Postmodern Perspective" (1996).

15. Michel Serres (1995) makes an insightful comment about *between* when he says it is an "unexplored space," "an interdisciplinary ground," occupied by conjunctions (p. 70). His comment here comes from a section on method, one in which he looks at method from a mathematical-chaos point of view–i.e., one in which method is nonlinear.

16. There are those who will say I have read too much into one quotation–"basic control resides in the nature of the situations." But no one would argue that Dewey is advocating enforced control and to emphasize individualness exclusively or strongly in Dewey (as some do) is to miss his whole search for an alternative method of development–"an alternative...[that] is not just a middle course or compromise between the two procedures...[but] is something radically different from either" (1934/1964, p. 8). I am arguing that Dewey believed this something radically different to lie in the inter/ transactional nature of situations themselves. This frame Dewey proposes (of "basic control residing in the nature of the situations themselves") is quite akin to Jean Piaget's evolutionary and developmental "tertium quid," to C.H. Waddington's "genetic landscape," and to Humberto Maturana and Francisco Varela's "autopoietic system," and, of course, to Alfred North Whitehead's famous dictum: "It lies in the nature of things that the many enter into complex unity" (see, Doll, 1993, pp. 81-85; Whitehead,1929/1978, p. 21), all of which are, I believe, forerunners to the concept of self-organization.

17. For one view of, and an introduction to, the debate surrounding the randomness of evolution, see Doll, 1993, Chapter Three.

18. More detailed comments about these authors and their views can be found in Doll, 1993, Chapters Three and Four, especially.

19. I also wish to give recognition to Nicolis and Prigogine (1989), Bechtel and Richardson (1993), Cowan, Pines, and Meltzer (1994), and Cohen and Stewart (1994).

20. This issue of the relationship between the abstractness of mathematics and the realness of nature is a key (and controversial) point in Kauffman's cosmology. Fibonacci numbers are those ordered in the pattern of 1,1,2,3,5,8,13,21,34 etc.–always the two previous summing the third. Obviously, this is a mathematical abstraction, one of

thousands, if not of millions. What is interesting about this sequence is how often it is replicated in nature–in the swirls on pine cones, in the branching of trees, in the petals of sunflowers. The phenomenon is well known enough to warrant a name–phyllotaxis (Kauffman, 1995, pp. 151, 185). Indeed, this phenomenon could be looked upon as merely accidental. But for Kauffman and others it is more; it signifies a fundamental tenet (law, if one likes) of the nature of development. The patterns of this development shows up in both Boolean networks and in life itself–at the genetic level and at the cultural level. The patterns of this *emergent* development while not yet well known are, Kauffman believes, natural, not mysterious. They interweave "self-organization, selection, chance, and design" (pp. 185-186). Studying this inter-weaving is Kauffman's project; mine is to look at its curriculum implications.

21. I am also reminded here of Gregory Bateson's (1987) comment that there is "a certain sacredness to the organization of the biological world" (p. 8).

22. Mapping this Boolean network pattern onto genetics is, I believe, complicated enough to not include here. Those wishing to study such are referred to Kauffman's Chapter Five, "The Mystery of Ontogeny," in his *At Home in the Universe* (1995). The simplicity of it all is why Kauffman repeatedly uses the phrase "we the expected; not we the accidental."

23. I am indebted to Jeanne Robertson (1996) for introducing me to the phrase and illuminating the thinking allied with both/and.

24. Too often the "active involvement" present in our modernist classrooms is a *false* active involvement–it is all rigged and too tightly controlled; the flexibility needed is not present. Regretfully, the "discovery method" of a few years back was plagued with this disease.

References
Apple, M. (1975). The hidden curriculum and the nature of conflict. In W. Pinar (Ed.),*Curriculum Theorizing* (pp. 95-119). Berkeley, CA: McCutchan.

Apple, M. (1990). *Ideology and curriculum* (2nd. ed.). New York: Routledge & Kegan Paul.

Apple, M. (1993). *Official knowledge.* New York: Routledge.

Bacon, Francis (1899). *Advancement of learning and novum organum* (rev. ed.). New York: The Colonial Press. (Original work published 1620)

Bateson, G. (1987). Men are grass. In W. I. Thompson (Ed.), *Gaia.* Great Barrington, MA: Lindisfarne Press.

Bechtel, W. & Richardson, R. (1993). *Discovering complexity.* Princeton: Princeton University Press.

Bobbitt, J. F. (1918). *The curriculum.* Boston: Houghton Mifflin.

Bowles, S. and Gintis, H. (1976). *Schooling in capitalist America.* New York: Basic Books.

Bratt, J. H. (1964). *Rise and development of Calvinism.* Grand Rapids, MI: William B. Eerdmans Publishing.

Burtt, E. A. (1967). *The metaphysical foundations of modern science.* London: Routledge & Kegan Paul. (Original work published 1932)

Callahan, R. E. (1962). *Education and the cult of efficiency.* Chicago: University of Chicago Press.

Calvin, J. (1958). *Commentaries.* (Joseph Haroutunian, Trans.). Philadelphia: Westminister Press. (Original works published 1540-1565)

Calvin, J. (1973). *Institutes of the Christian religion* (F.L. Battles, Trans.). Grand Rapids, MI: William B. Eerdmans Publishing. (Original work published 1536)

Cohen, J. and Stewart, I. (1994). *The collapse of chaos.* New York: Viking.

Comenius, J. A. (1896). *The great didactic* (M.W. Keating, Trans.). London: Adam & Charles Black. (Original work published 1657).

Comenius, J. A. (1969). *A reformation of schooles.* Menston, England: The Scholar Press Limited.

Comenius, J. A. (1967). *John Amos Comenius on education* (Classics in Education No. 33). New York: Teachers College Press.

Copernicus, N. (1976). *De revolutionibus* (On the revolutions of the heavenly spheres) (A. M. Duncan, Trans.). New York: Barnes and Noble. (Original work published 1543)

Cowan, G., Pines, D. & Meltzer, D. (1994). *Complexity.* Reading, MA: Addison-Wesley.

Cubberley, E. P. (1916). *Public school administration.* Boston: Houghton Mifflin.

Derrida, J. (1994). *Specters of Marx.* (Peggy Kamuf, Trans.). New York: Routledge.

Descartes, R. (1950). *Discourse on method.* (L. J. Lafleur, Trans.). New York: Liberal Arts Press. (Original work published 1637).

Dewey, J. (1960). *The quest for certainty.* New York: G. P. Putnam. (Original work published 1929).

Dewey, J. (1963). *Experience and education.* New York: Collier Books. (Original work published 1938)

Dewey, J. (1964). The need for a philosophy of education. In R. Archambault (Ed.), *John Dewey on education* (pp. 3-14). New York: Random House. (Original work published 1934).

Dewey, J. (1966). *Democracy and education.* New York: Free Press. (Original work published 1916).

Dewey, J. (1971). *How we think.* Chicago: Henry Regnery. (Original work published 1933 and 1911).

Dewey, J. (1972). The reflex arc concept in psychology. In J. Boydston (Ed.), *John Dewey the early works,* Vol. 5, 1895-98 (pp. 96-109). Carbondale: Southern Illinois University Press. (Original work published in 1896).

Doll, W. E. Jr. (1993). *A post-modern perspective on curriculum.* New York: Teachers College Press.

Doll, W. E. Jr. (n.p.) Ghosts and the curriculum.

Donne, J. (1968). An anatomie of the world. In H. J. C. Grierson (Ed.), *The poems of John Donne* (vol. 1). Oxford: Clarendon Press. (Original work published 1633).

Dreeben, R. (1968). *On what is learned in school.* Reading, MA: Addison-Wesley.

Educational Researcher, (1994, November). 23 (7), 4 - 24.

Fitzpatrick, E. A. (1933). *St. Ignatius and the ratio studiorum.* New York: McGraw-Hill Book Company.

Freeman, W. (1991). The physiology of perception. *Scientific American,* 264, 78-85.

Giroux, H. (1983). *Theory and resistance in education.* South Hadley, MA: Bergin & Garvey.

Goodlad, J. and Klein, F. (1974). *Looking behind the classroom door.* Worthington, OH: Charles A. Jones.

Goodman, P. (1964). *Compulsory mis-education.* New York: Horizon Press.

Grafton, A. and Jardine, D. (1986). *From humanism to the humanities.* London: Duckworth.

Greer, C. (1972). *The great school legend.* New York: Basic Books.

Gundem, B. (1992). Notes on the development of Nordic didactics. *Journal of Curriculum Studies*, 24, 61-70.

Hamilton, D. (1989). *Towards a theory of schooling.* London: Falmer.

Hamilton, D. (1990). *Curriculum history.* Geelong, Victoria: Deakin University Press.

Hamilton, D. (1992). Comenius and the new world order, *Comenius,* 46, 157-171.

Hamilton, D. (n.p.). Notes from nowhere.

Illich, I. (1971). *Deschooling society.* New York: Harper and Row.

Jackson, P. (1968). *Life in classrooms.* New York: Holt, Rinehart and Winston.

Journal for Research in Mathematics Education. (1990). Monograph no. 4: Constructivist views on the teaching and learning of mathematics. Washington, D. C: National Council of Teachers of Mathematics.

Kauffman, S. (1993). *The origins of order.* New York: Oxford University Press.

Kauffman, S. (1995). *At home in the universe.* New York: Oxford University Press.

Kliebard, H. (1986). *The struggle for the American curriculum, 1893-1958.* Boston: Routledge and Kegan Paul.

Kliebard, H. (1992). *Forging the American curriculum.* New York: Routledge.

Lather, P. (1991). *Getting smart.* London: Routledge.

Lewin, R. (1992). *Complexity.* New York: Macmillan.

Maturana, H. and Varela, F. (1980). *Autopoiesis and cognition.* Boston: D. Reidel Publishing.

McClintock, R. (1972). Towards a place for study in a world of instruction, *Teachers College Record,* 73, 161-205.

McLaren, P. (1989). *Life in schools.* New York: Longman.

McNeil, L. (1986). *Contradiction of control.* New York: Routledge and Kegan Paul.

Monod, J. (1971). *Chance and necessity.* New York: Alfred Knopf.

Nicolis, G. and Prigogine, I. (1989). *Exploring complexity.* New York: Freeman and Co.

Ong, W. J. (1958). *Ramus, method and the decay of dialogue.* Cambridge, MA: Harvard University Press.

Oxford English Dictionary (1989). Vol. xiii (see p. 271).

Peterson, T. S. (1994). *Acquired taste.* Ithaca: Cornell University Press.

Pinar, W. (Ed.). (1975). *Curriculum theorizing: The reconceptualists* Berkeley, CA: McCutcheon.

Pinar, W., Reynolds, W., Slattery, P., and Taubman, P. (1995). *Understanding curriculum*. New York: Peter Lang.

Rice, J. M. (1969). *Public school systems of the United States.* New York: Arno Press. (Original work published 1893).

Robertson, J. (1996). *Reconstructing educational experience: A postmodern perspective*. Doctoral Dissertation, Louisiana State University.

Serres, M. (1995). *Conversation on science, culture, and time.* (R. Lapidus, Trans.). Ann Arbor: University of Michigan Press.

Schwiebert, E. G. (1950). *Luther and his times.* St. Louis: Concordia Publishing.

St. Julien, J. (1994). *Cognition and learning: The implications of a situated connectionist perspective for theory and practice in education.* Doctoral Dissertation, Louisiana State University.

Taylor, F. W. (1947). *Scientific management.* New York: Harper and Brothers. (Original work published 1911).

Toulmin, S. (1990). *Cosmopolis.* New York: Free Press.

Triche, S. and St. Julien, J. (1996). Reconceptualizing educational psychology. In *Philosophy of Education Yearbook, 1995* (pp. 483-495). Urbana, IL: Philosophy of Education Society.

Tyler, R. (1950). *Basic principles of curriculum and instruction.* Chicago: University of Chicago Press.

Waldrop, M. M. (1992). *Complexity.* New York: Simon and Schuster.

Wertheim, M. (1995). *Pythagoras' trousers.* New York: Random House.

Whitehead, A. N. (1978). *Process and reality.* (Corrected ed.) (D. Griffin and D. Sherburne, Eds.). (Original work published 1929).

Chapter Fifteen

Curriculum as Affichiste: Popular Culture and Identity

Alan A. Block

Lately, I have been thinking of the Brothers Grimm, who tell us that when Hansel and Gretel set out in the woods on that frightening and foreboding first night, Hansel took the precaution to drop shiny white pebbles along their path to mark the way home, as his father had taught him. And when Hansel and Gretel were, as they had expected, abandoned by their yet-loving father, the children were able–to their father's apparent surprise and delight–to follow the pebble-marked path and arrive back in their home by morning. I keep meditating upon those pebbles dropped by Hansel and Gretel. And of finding one's way home. And of education. And of the myriad ways that we have devised to keep students and teachers on track, in place, observed by the ceaseless trail of writing we have mandated and which defines their and our position. Indeed, I am cognizant of many such mechanisms by which both students and teachers are produced and controlled, indeed, produced by that control, but I would like to explore curriculum–and the possibility of its liberation–in this light for a brief time. For curriculum–a prescribed body of knowledge and methods by which it might be communicated–represents the uninterrupted stream of writing which connects the center with the periphery, which serves as the pebbles by which the path is marked that the teachers and students might always find their way home, even though the father has long since absented himself from that path, ensconced himself at home, and abandoned education for the thrill of exercising control by allowing the teacher and student to assume it. It is no wonder that the father is delighted to see his children, Hansel and Gretel, once again. No children: no control.

Indeed, wasn't it he who taught them about the pebbles in the first place? However, as Henry David Thoreau, a thoroughly disorienting teacher who knew a great deal about paths, tells us, "What does education do? It makes a straight-cut ditch of a free, meandering brook" (Thoreau, 1962, 83). Education, he knew, has nothing to do with marked paths and coming home. Rather, education has more to do with meandering: with getting lost. He declares: "If you are ready to leave father and mother, and brother and sister, and wife and child and friends, and never see them again–if you have paid your debts, and made your will, and settled all your affairs, and are a free man, then you are ready for a walk" (Thoreau, 1980, 94). But increasingly, in the modern era, with talks of national curriculums and national certifications, and with the ferocious battles being fought over the canon and multiculturalism, education has become the functioning of the panopticon, by which the invisible center exercises power by replacing "autocratic power...[with] the more gratifying compulsion of the subject's self-identity" (Eagleton, 1990, 23). In this exercise, control is maintained by the nature of the path and the impossibility–indeed, unthinkability–of deviation from it. When we walk in education today, it is with heavy baggage that we are laden and by which we are easily held down in place and in absolute view.

In *Discipline and Punishment*, Foucault notes how the governors of plague-ridden Paris in order to deal with the pestilence are able to maintain control over the city by a system of surveillance "based on a system of permanent registration" (Foucault, 1979, 96). This panopticonal mechanism, of which Bentham's model of the prison, the Panopticon, is the architectural representation, arranges everything so that the "surveillance is permanent in its effects, even if it is discontinuous in its action." The panopticonal apparatus is "a machine for creating and sustaining a power relation independent of the person who exercises it; the effect of which is that the inmates are caught up in a power situation of which they themselves are the bearers" (201). Confined to their homes for their own personal and social good, the populace is readily observable.

> This enclosed, segmented space observed at every point, in which the individuals are inserted in a fixed place, in which the slightest movements are supervised, in which all events are recorded, in which an uninterrupted work of writing links the center and periphery, in which power is exercised without division,

according to a continuous hierarchical figure, in which each individual is constantly located, examined and distributed among the living beings, the sick and the dead–all this constitutes a compact model of the disciplinary mechanism. The plague is met by order... (Foucault, 1979, 197).

What is created is a perfectly controlled and controlling hierarchy participated in willingly by the subjected as the very means of their existence, as a process establishing individuality. "The liberated subject is the one who has appropriated the law as the very principle of its own autonomy, broken the forbidding tablets of stone on which that law was originally inscribed in order to rewrite it on the heart of flesh. To consent to the law is thus to consent to one's own inward being" (Eagleton, 1990, 19). This panopticonal mechanism organized by a system of endless writing

lays down for each individual his place, his body, his disease and his death, his well-being by means of an omnipresent and omniscient power that subdivides itself in a regular, uninterrupted way even to the ultimate determination of the individual, of what characterizes him, of what belongs to him.... [T]he panoptic mechanism arranges spatial unities that make it possible to see constantly and recognize instantly (Foucault, 1979, 202-3).

The panopticon

reverses the principle of the dungeon; or rather, of its three functions–to enclose, to deprive of light and to hide–it preserves only the first and eliminates the other two. Full lighting and the eye of a supervisor capture better than darkness, which ultimately protects. Visibility is a trap (Foucault, 1979, 200).

The school and the curriculum is such a structure: it promotes incarceration by visibility. In the school we are defined by what we know, which is always linked to written reports delimiting that knowledge, and increasingly, what we know is written by others. We are always to be found by our position on the well-traveled, well-lit and heavily-marked path which is the curriculum. We are defined–we define ourselves–by that position.

He who is subjected to a field of visibility, and who knows it, assumes responsibility for the constraints of power; he makes

them play spontaneously upon himself; he inscribes in himself
the power relation which he simultaneously plays both roles; he
becomes the principle of his own subjection (Foucault, 1979,
202-3).

The unending stream of writing ensures our visibility and our
maintenance on the prescribed path.

But I believe that education is, or at least ought to be, not a
discipline, not a matter of being found or finding self along a set path,
nor of moving progressively along a path defined by others and by
which we can define ourselves by our place along it; education might be
understood as the opportunity of getting lost. And what do I mean by
getting lost? First, it is to abandon the notion of home so that we may
know our home everywhere. Home functions as the controlling center
from which emanate prescribed paths. Home is the place of originary
interpellations, a term I understand to mean to question and therefore to
call into being. I believe with Althusser that "[Even] before its birth,
the child is therefore always-already a subject, appointed as a subject in
and by the specific familial ideological configuration in which it is
'expected' once it has been conceived" (Althusser, 1971, 176). So, too,
in school: even before arrival, students and teachers are all objects of
interpellations–products of the uninterrupted stream of writing which
attributes to them a subjectivity which must then be maintained by that
tie to home. We are discovered by our place along the prescribed path,
and we are welcomed when we can make our way back to home because
we are who we are thought to be and have always been. "Home," says
Warren, in Frost's canonical poem "Death of the Hired Man," "is the
place where when you have to go there, they have to take you in"
(Frost, 1967, 11, 81). Home is the ultimate refuge to which return is
always possible. Except that in Bob Dylan's noncanonical cautionary
tale, "The Ballad of Frankie Lee and Judas Priest," Frankie Lee finds
himself not safe but trapped and threatened within the haven of Judas
Priest's house. Enticed there by Judas Priest with the promise of
warmth and safety, Frankie Lee discovers that he had "soon lost all
control/Over everything that he had made/While the mission bells did
toll" (Dylan, 1966b). Frankie Lee, "stuck inside of Mobile with the
Memphis blues again" (Dylan, 1966a), has forfeited his own life for the
anticipated safety of Judas Priest's home. And "the moral of this story,"
the narrator suggests, is "don't go mistaking Paradise/For that home
across the road" (Dylan, 1966b). Home operates as the determining

center, functions as the defining mechanism, and promises endless return and permanent refuge. And home holds us to the conventional paths by an uninterrupted stream of writing, the many white pebbles we have been taught to drop, the practice and activity of the panopticonal mechanism by which we then are constrained to define ourselves. It is the curriculum along which we move in diachronous regularity. For me, as an educator, that path to home is explicitly marked by the papers by which we are written and by the written papers we are constrained to read: the traditional canonical corpus known as curriculum. It is horrifyingly epitomized most recently in the production of E.D. Hirsch's Cultural Literacy projects organizing what every first and second grader must know. Nor is this to say that all move easily along this path: the path defines the individual, and it is a rare student who can abjure the path and achieve educational success. "The category of the subject is only constitutive of all ideology insofar as all ideology has the function (which defines it) of constituting concrete individuals as subjects" (Althusser, 1971, 171).

But to renounce home–the curriculum–that original centering device, we are then free to become our own centers. "All things are up and down, east and west, to me," Thoreau (1962, 39) declares. "In me is the forum out of which go the Appian and Sacred ways, and a thousand beside, to the ends of the world" (Thoreau, 1962, p. 39). Having recognized home within, there is no longer need for return, no center about which to revolve, no suns to hold us in our orbital place, no way to be but productively lost and decentered. "Having abandoned the reality of the center," Roland Barthes tells us, "the center [becomes] no longer anything but a frivolous idea, subsisting there not in order to broadcast power, but to give to [the city's]...urban movement the support for its empty central, obliging the traffic in a perpetual departure from the normal path" (in Block, 1989, 260). It is, of course, in these perpetual departures which deny home that lostness may be experienced and learning may begin, and it is what the schools might promote by themselves abandoning curricula already in place. "When you got nothing you got nothing to lose," Dylan cries. "You're invisible, you got no secrets to conceal. How does it feel," he asks, "to be on your own/Like a complete unknown/Like a rolling stone?" (Dylan, 1965b). Here, I think, is an appropriate model of the teacher and learner, and of course, of curriculum: its invisibility broadcasts not absence, secrecy and/or reclusiveness masking paranoia, but freedom and possibility; its lostness, when accepted, does not offer to lead the way, but announces rather the knowledge proclaimed by the Grateful Dead: "*If* I knew the way, I would take you home"(Garcia and Hunter, 1971, emphasis added).

Secondly, to get lost is even to abandon the notion of the path. That path, created by the exercise of power which defines it and the traveler who treads upon it, determines direction, supervises the view, and is responsible for controlling thought and action. Thoreau notes how quickly the single path he had worn to the pond for his morning ablutions supervised and determined his way, and how he then knew how that he would have to leave Walden, for "I had other lives to live." I think that as teachers, we must accept Dylan's charge, and offer it challengingly and triumphantly to students, to

> Leave your stepping stones behind, something calls for you.
> Forget the dead you've left, they will not follow you.
> Strike another match, go start anew
> And its all over now, Baby Blue (Dylan, 1965a).

Those stepping stones, the canonical curriculum, are not unlike the pebbles dropped by Hansel, and like those pebbles, only lead home. The educator must accept herself as itinerant, and teach others the freedom of intellectual vagabondage ("To live outside the law you must be honest," cries the narrator looking for Sweet Marie [Dylan, 1965c]) at home nowhere yet everywhere, neither determined nor produced by any path. Thoreau marvels "How many things concur to keep a man at home, to prevent his yielding to his inclination to wander. Man does not travel as easily as the birds migrate. He is not everywhere at home, like flies" (Thoreau, 1962, 245). Paths are the lines holding print to the page denying flight. They are the traditional modes of curriculum and the traditional materials required by it.

At present, education requires that we must learn to write–which I have, and will continue to argue, is to learn to read as well–even as we must teach people to read and write themselves and not to read only what is already written about us by others (see Block, 1989, 1995). To read and write with power is to know that the sign expresses, and that that expression contains everything which has made possible the sign's appearance at this particular time and in this particular place, including what now may be called "me," which too, as a sign, expresses and contains everything which has made possible its appearance. The identity of the sign is thus, established in its relations.

Looked at another way, the conditions of a thing's appearance are equivalent to the thing's identity. Writing and reading are activities which express, and therefore, are relationally, contain everything including the social practices and institutions of the society which make this particular work possible. Writing always denies home and paths because to write is to understand that meaning is situationally dependent, which is to say, that meaning's identity is a product of writing's consumption, even as writing's consumption is a product of its production. Or, as Italo Calvino notes,

> Only the ability to be read by a given individual proves that what is written shares in the power of writing, a power based on something that goes beyond the individual. The universe will express itself as long as somebody will be able to say, 'I read, therefore it writes' (Calvino, 1983, p. 176).

In other words, the meaning of signs–the identity of signs–is a function of relations which are experienced differently as a product of particular historical, sociopolitical, and personal milieus. Writing disavows homes and paths when it recognizes and celebrates the complexities of history as they appear in the sign. Bakhtin says that

> meaning is realized only in the process of active, responsive understanding. Meaning does not reside in the word or in the soul of the speaker or in the soul of the listener. Meaning is the effect of interaction between speaker and listener produced via the material of a particular sound complex (in Volosinov, 1986, p. 102).

In that interaction, both speaker and listener produce identity, which may be known historically, understood relationally and therefore, always already imbued with power. To write is to have existence; not to write–to merely read what is already written, to follow to home the stones already dropped along the path–is alienation, to be separated from one's own center for the comfort of another's assignment of that center. Karl Marx asks,

> What constitutes the alienation of labor? First, that the work is external to the worker, that it is not part of his nature; and that consequently, he does not fulfill himself in his work but denies himself, has a feeling of misery rather than well-being, does not develop freely his mental and physical energies but is physically

exhausted and mentally debased (Marx, 1966, p. 98)

The curriculum, the uninterrupted stream of writing by which teachers and students are held to the path, anchored to home and produced as individuals to serve as their own jailers, demands an attentiveness to reading at the risk of annihilation–and a denial of writing. "Only while we are in action is the circulation perfect. The writing which consists with habitual sitting is mechanical, wooden, dull to read" (Thoreau, 1962, p. 245). Writing originates from the experience of that lostness which renounces all roads to home, indeed, all roads altogether until they have been made strange. Thoreau tells us:

> not till we are completely lost or turned around–for a man needs only to be turned around once with his eyes shut in this world to be lost,–do we appreciate the vastness and strangeness of nature. Every man has once more to learn the points of the compass as often as he awakes, whither from sleep or from any abstraction. In fact, not till we are lost do we begin to realize where we are, and the infinite extent of our relations (Thoreau, 1962, p. 544).

What we must learn, and subsequently offer, then, is the development not of subjectivity but of identity.

Indeed, I return here to the orthodox Marxist belief that the notion of the subject is an entirely bourgeois concept resulting from capitalist ideology. This ideology posits the production of the individual from the notion of private property, from the result of alienated labor producing products which belong not to the worker but to another. "Private property is thus derived from the analysis of the concept of *alienated labor,* that is, alienated man, alienated labor, alienated life and estranged man" (Marx, 1966, 106). And since Marx postulates man and nature relationally, and since alienated labor separates man from nature and alienated man from his own active function, from himself and from his species, alienated labor–which produces private property–makes species life into individual life and creates the individual, the subject. I would prefer to replace the notion of subjectivity with the idea of identity. "Identity for Marx," Bertell Ollman remarks, "is the relation between entities whose role as necessary elements in one another is appreciated for what it is" (Ollman, 1988, 68). To work with Marx's formulation, our effect as teachers on students is not to be viewed causally, but rather, must be understood as an expression of us, the means by which we manifest what we are, and in this, to recognize the student's part of us. This must be appreciated as an historically conditioned phenomenon. Similarly, we must teach students that everything with which they have relations is an expression of them, and is, too, historically situated. Their identity is determined by the totality of their relations. "My own existence," Marx (1966, 130) notes, "is a social activity." Students ought to recognize their identity as a social activity, and must recognize that their identity is made possible by the relations there established. Hence, we must offer them the opportunity to recognize the nature of their internal relations: to teach them by reading and writing about writing and reading. I think that we must see curriculum as the bringing to consciousness of the notion of reading and writing–the always already nature of these processes, the notion of popular culture.

Curriculum as traditionally conceived, and as practiced in the vast majority of schools, is organized about the rationality of order, of linearity, and of diachrony. It is the path we follow to the goal of knowledge. It is the clearly marked passage on which we are always visible. It has been amply argued how the curriculum serves to reproduce the dominant culture, to exclude the cultures of subordinate groups, and to reproduce the power structure. But it has also been shown how this view oversimplifies the actual behaviors of school populations, denying the possibility of agency. It has been amply argued how resistance, which we may define as oppositional behavior which contains emancipatory interests (Giroux, 1983, 110), also oversimplifies the behavior of school populations who engage in resistance by misrepresenting actual human motives which are often contradictory (Roman and Christian-Smith, 1987). Both theories assume a knowledge which they may not have. Reproduction theories assume lack of agency; resistance theories assume consistency of it. And both theories assume that what is offered in and as curriculum is exactly what is received. Both theories fix the populace in ways no less disciplining than the panopticon. If we are to understand life in schools we must look to another model.

Marx has taught us that consumption completes production. The act of consumption actually creates the product, for there would be no sense in production unless consumption was presumed. Thus, if we are to understand education and the curriculum we must look at the process of consumption and not the product to be consumed or the product which results. If we are to understand curriculum, we must study not the knowledge that is transmitted, but what is done with the materials which are said to contain it if and when they are consumed. Knowledge is seen here as process and not as a product, as an activity of knowledge production entered into by the act of consumption. Now, popular culture is the practice of consumption, the art of making do, and is the model we might use to understand curriculum. As John Fiske (1989, 47) makes clear, everyday life is "constituted by the practices of popular culture, and is characterized by the creativity of the weak in using the resources provided by a disempowering system while refusing finally to submit to that power." And this is because popular culture is the practice of meaning making by those who simply are not, or are in active opposition to, the dominant culture which defines its own practices as Culture proper. Of course, dominant cultures prescribe limits to the uses one might put to commodities but can never determine those limits and must maintain flexible boundaries. Consider the market in and price of preripped jeans to understand the dynamic relation between the dominant and subordinate cultures. In any case, however, popular culture exists in the area of meaning production: it is what is made out of what is given. In popular culture, production is completed by consumption.

In this process of consumption is the experience of discovery in the sense of lostness. It is the realization of our own process of knowledge production situated in our several contexts in the world. Each of us consumes in our own particularistic way based on the many and often contradictory arenas in which we act. We produce out of the materials we have at hand. "Men make their own history, but they do not make it just as they please; they do not make it under circumstances chosen by themselves, but under circumstances directly encountered, given and transmitted from the past" (Marx, 1988, 15). And in the school, curriculum is one of the products consumed; indeed, considering curriculum as everything which happens in the school, then it is also everything that is consumed within the school. What we make of what we are given: the definition of popular culture as process (see Fiske, 1989), carries us away from the path and into the creation of our own identities. The examination of those identities ought to be the matter of education. This would be, however, an education *as* popular culture rather than an education *using* popular culture as materials.

Unlike the notion of the subject, or the individual, or the more recent postmodern conjugation, subject-position, the notion of identity accounts for the effects of both ideological interpellation and resistance without accepting the powerless individual wholly subdued by the strategic position of the dominant powers. Indeed, resistance itself is a relational concept, is a product of conflicting knowledges, and is an expression of power. Resistance which takes place within the classroom is always already an expression of power, and is expressed relationally. As Foucault has taught us, power, as do all relations, produces. Pedagogical practice ought then to focus on the nature and sources of this power as it is exercised by the strategic position of *both* students and others, how identity comes to be established in those relations, and therefore revealing the opportunity to change relations, reinscribe power relations, and to alter identity. This pedagogy ought to reveal to students how they already use their knowledge in schools, rather than to instruct them how to follow those paths of knowledge already laid down, ought to teach how to question and not teach how not to answer, how to search for their own answers and not to respond to the question of others. Students must learn to interrogate the sign and discover its expression. Premised on the philosophy of internal relations, which states that the "conditions of a factor's existence are taken to be part of what it is, and is indicated by the fact that it is just this and nothing else" (Ollman, 1988, 27), identity is recognized here as the totality of relations in which a thing engages. Or, as Dietzgen says, "The existence of anything is manifested through qualities which are its relation to other things.... Anything that is torn out of its contextual relations ceases to exist" (in Ollman, 1988, 37). To question–to write –is to interrogate the relations which exist and the identity which is a product of those relations. This knowledge focuses power students already exercise not in oppositional behavior, but in more positive self-directed forms. As teachers, we must educate that though interpellation has already established relations from which identity derives–the functioning of the panopticon–a change in any one factor alters the relations, alters the thing, alters identity. Therefore, to teach identity in relations is to offer strategies for change–which are paths of least resistance.

These paths are ones of least resistance because they already exist. In fact, they are not truly paths at all, but actual lived moments in decentered contexts both produced by and producing meaning. These paths which are not paths, though they are real occupied locuses, cannot be pioneered, illuminated, or populated with pilgrims seeking the way, but must be acknowledged and interrogated as the daily practices, always contradictory and complex, neither linear nor always forward-moving, not without evidences of curtailment, reversal, and even disappearances, by which identity is produced. This production–of identity–ought to be the focus of curriculum, for it is in the production that self-directed change is made possible. Curriculum must reveal the power that always already exists in students and reveal how that power operates.

I believe education ought to be an experience of dislocation in which the sense of lostness is given impetus and validation, and in which in that sense of lostness identity can be achieved. As theorized in the contemporary field, curriculum is the organization of materials for the production of the unified self, which I would suggest does not exist. Lostness, which is to be understood here as neither alienated nor alienation, is the experience of decenteredness and the perpetual realization of identity in relations. Education must acknowledge first the power that always already exists in students and teachers who are its inhabitants, must define that power, and in elucidating its existence, make possible changes in relations, and as a result of this transformation, changes in identity. In this sense, curriculum becomes transformative, and like grace, reflective of internal change. Curriculum in this view is, in the words of the popular iconic hymn, *Amazing Grace*, an engagement with the experience of lostness that the opportunity of being found may occur.

We must begin to practice education which informs us not what we must know and how it can be known, but how what we know has always already been learned. Furthermore, education must be understood as the process by which we produce knowledge from the materials which we are given. The curriculum must return knowledge to its center, within the decentered identity. Education must reveal the process of production in the exercise of consumption.

Now, I would argue that one important development of modern art provides us with a model of this process in, say, the collages of Picasso, Braque, and Miro, the work of the surrealists and the dadaists, the affichistes, the collages of Robert Rauschenberg and Richard Hamilton, and the graffiti artists of the 1980s. These artists, drawing on and from the materials of their daily world, and working with them idiosyncratically, produced in the process a new relationship between art and the world, a new way of being in the world. In their production, they had given up the notion of path and home and experienced lostness. As Braque said of his relationship with Picasso, "The things that Picasso and I said to one another during those years will never be said again, and even if they were, no one would understand them any more. It was like being roped together on a mountain" (in Berger, 1985, 159). This work, begun as a private conversation between Picasso and

Braque "painting still lifes and figure pictures that used newspapers and books as accessories," worked with the idea of

> gluing found paper elements into their works...rerouting the printed ephemera of the cafe table and the city streets into the studio and onto the easel–incorporating, among other things, news headlines, movie bills, cigarette wrappers, package labels, and ads for razors, furs, lingerie, lamps and liqueurs (Varnedoe and Gopnik, 1990, p. 23).

Unlike cubism, which "imagined the world transformed, but not the process of transformation" (Berger, 1985, 171), or like the dadaist who believed that

> art and life was the extreme of individualism...[who] denied that there was any psychic basis common to all humanity...not even a sure means of communication between one man and another... [that] nothing is real or true except the individual pursuing his individual whims, the artist riding his hobbyhorse, his *dada* (Cowley, 1969),

this process of art addressed the world with its own materials but in ways and forms which derived from the individual artist's experience. In other words, contemporary art entered into a relationship with society at large and used public material in the construction of private languages. Those private languages not only were of the world, but were often a critique of it. These works which were derived from the materials of the daily world could be

> authentic new work of great difficulty and contrariness, [could be] powerful new styles of mass persuasion, or [could be] disorienting languages of critique and protest, or trivial manners of decoration. And all of these [could] coexist without contradiction, within the same epoch, the same city, or even the same life, in the compass of a day or an hour (Varnedoe and Gopnik, 1990, p. 63).

This work was the process of knowledge production in the act of consumption of what was available in the everyday world. For example, the particular art of Kurt Schwitters, assembling the printed matter of the world in *papier colles,* whose individual artform was called *Merz,* originally just a clipping from *Commerce,* a work of his youth, was a way of living within but against the grain of the provincial burgher society of Hannover. What Schwitters and others like him attempted was to "make new art forms from the remains of a former culture" (63). In other words, Schwitters attempted to "tear fold by fold and scrap by scrap, the words of a private, intimate dialogue from the mundane registers of the public world" (Varnedoe and Gopnik, 1990, 63). Schwitters work was assembled out of the detritus and leavings of the streets, which he would then shape onto canvas. Employing the materials and/or crap of daily life, Schwitters produced art in his particular use of it.

This is the stuff of popular culture. The affichiste artists of the 1940s and 1950s conjured up the look of daily life and the streets by using mass-produced ephemera in altered ways. Raymond Hains produced *Gypsy Woman* from pieces of posters torn off the walls, as did Jacques de la Villegle in *Sevres-Montparnasse Intersection, July 1961*. Art becomes production by consumption. In Penelope Spheeris' film *Suburbia*, the extended family of outcast teenagers who have taken up residence in an abandoned house in the midst of suburbia, carry strips of lawn sod from the local nursery into the shopping mall, install the grass on the hard concrete in front of the home appliance store, and watch the TVs all alight in the window in what must be seen both a parody of the typical American evening experience and as a touching image of the work of popular culture. This process of making do ought to be the stuff of curriculum. It is the stuff from which art and life are made.

Hence we discover in the affichistes a model of curriculum. These artists acted as collectors or commentators rather than as individual generators of meaning. They recognized that meaning was derived from engagement with the world, from the individual manipulation of the very materials which that world provided, and that art ought to be expressive of that relation to the world.

> The model of linguistic activity within which graffiti was seen as operating had shifted from one emphasizing inner creativity to one emphasizing social interaction and the manipulation of culturally determined conventions. These artists wanted to disrupt established language, rather than revert...to preverbal handwriting (Varnedoe and Gopnik, 1990, p. 91).

In the process, the artists disrupted the order and symmetry of conventional ways of knowing and being, and created a private path available only in a consumption not of their work but of an awareness and exercise of the process in which they themselves engaged and which the work itself displayed. This yet-noncanonical art which developed during the twentieth century offers us a model of curriculum as it produces knowledge in the active consumption of the everyday materials the world makes available. It is an art which is at once personal and social, whose value exists in its originality and not in its reproducibility. Indeed, the reproduction of the work only succeeds in changing the work in a manner which mirrors the process of the original production itself. Art here promotes its own self-destruction as knowledge and offers its process of consumption as a model of knowledge production. It denies the refuge of home, denies the path already defined and marked, and broadcasts lostness as discovery. As should be curriculum, it is a work which instructs in its process, indeed, by its process. As Vardenoe and Gopnik (1990) state about this work:

> it can continue to bring us glad tidings by taking us on extraordinary journeys to familiar places, but only on its own eccentric terms. The deal is that you have to go without a map, and you can only get there on foot (p. 412).

This is what I have argued about curriculum.

Eugene Debs Hartke, Jr. in Kurt Vonnegut's *Hocus-Pocus* (1990), works as a professor at Tarkington College, an institution of higher learning serving learning-disabled children whose parents are also exceedingly rich. But Tarkington College was originally established as a free institute by Elias Tarkington, a brilliant inventor who wanted everyone living within the vicinity of the institution to have access to education. Tarkington's passion was perpetual motion machines, which he built endlessly from pieces of precious metals. But as nothing continues to function ceaselessly as it originally was planned, and even as his idea for an institute of higher learning changed, becoming a place colonized by, in the words of Dr. Helen Dole, an applicant of African American descent, European planters, so too were his machines failures. None of his machines–even his educational institution–ever worked as he desired, and during some research, Hartke discovers that even the workmen who worked on those machines knew all the time that they would never function. Yet, still discovering beauty in these machines, Hartke considers whether beauty is a product not of the commodity itself but of the conditions in which that commodity was produced. Contemplating this, Hartke says, "How is this for a definition of high art: 'Making the most of the raw materials of futility'" (14). I have argued that the work of curriculum is a similar process, and that similarly, it may be the work of high art.

References

Althusser, L. (1971). *Lenin and philosophy* (B. Brewster, Trans.). New York: Monthly Review Press.

Berger, J. (1985). *The sense of sight.* New York: Pantheon Books.

Block, A. (1989). The answer is blowing in the wind: A deconstructive reading of the school text. *Journal of Curriculum Theorizing*, 8(4), 23-52.

Block, A. (1995). *Occupied reading.* New York: Garland Publishing.

Calvino, Italo (1983). *If on a winter's night a traveler.* [Trans. W. Weaver.] NY: Harcourt Brace Jovanovich.

Cowley, M. (1969). *Exile's return.* New York: The Viking Press.

Dylan, B. (1965a). It's all over now, baby blue. On *Bringing it all back home.* New York: Columbia Records.

Dylan, B. (1965b). Like a Rolling Stone. On *Highway 61 revisited.* NY: Columbia Records.

Dylan, B. (1966a). Stuck inside of Mobile with the Memphis blues again. On *Blond on blond.* New York: Columbia Records.

Dylan, B. (1966b). The ballad of Frankie Lee and Judas Priest. On *John Wesley Harding.* New York: Columbia Records.

Dylan, B. (1966c). Absolutely Sweet Marie. From *Blond on blond.* New York: Columbia Records.

Eagleton, T. (1990). *Ideology of the aesthetic.* Cambridge, England: Basil Blackwell.

Fiske, J. (1989). *Understanding popular culture.* Winchester, MA: Unwin Hyman.

Foucault, M. (1979). *Discipline and punishment* (A. Sheridan, Trans.). New York: Vintage Books.

Frost, R. (1967). Death of the hired man. In G. Sanders, J. Nelson, and M. Rosenthal (Eds.), *Chief modern poets of England and America.* New York: The Macmillan Company.

Garcia, J., and Hunter, R. (1971). Ripple. On *American beauty.* New York: Ice Nine Publishing.

Giroux, H. (1983). *Theory and resistance in education; A pedagogy for the opposition.* New York: Bergin and Garvey.

Marx, K. (1966). The economic and philosophical manuscripts. In E. Fromm, *Marx's concept of man* (T. Bottomore, Trans.). New York: Ungar Publishing.

Marx, K. (1988). *The eighteenth brumaire of Louis Bonaparte.* New York: International Publishers.

Ollman, B. (1988). *Alienation.* Cambridge: Cambridge University Press.

Padgham, R. (1988). Contemporary curriculum theory and twentieth century art. In W. Pinar (Ed.), *Contemporary curriculum discourses.* Scottsdale, AZ: Gorsuch Scarisbrick Publishers.

Roman, L., and Christian-Smith, L. (1987). *Becoming feminine: The politics of popular culture.* London: The Falmer Press.

Thoreau, H. D. (1980). *The natural essays.* Salt Lake City, UT: Peregrine Smith.

Thoreau, H. D. (1962). *The journals of Henry David Thoreau* (B. Torrey, and F. Terry, Eds.). New York: Dover Publications.

Varnedoe, K. and Gopnik, A. (1990). *High and low.* New York: Museum of Modern Art.

Volosinov, V. (1986). *Marxism and the philosophy of language.* [L. Matejka, and I. Titunki, Trans.]. Cambridge, MA: Harvard University Press.

Vonnegut Jr., K. (1990). *Hocus-Pocus.* New York: Berkley Books.

Chapter Sixteen

Models of Excellence:
Independent African-Centered Schools

Shariba Rivers and Kofi Lomotey

Introduction

The United States has a history of "bad blood" with its citizens of African descent. Nowhere is this more obvious than in the area of education. African American students have been ridiculed and put under the strictest kind of scrutiny with regard to expected intellectual capacity. Theories of intellectual and cultural inferiority have been posited to explain the low academic achievement of African American students in the public school system (Irvine, 1990). African American students suffer from "low self-esteem" and other psychological problems because they have been at the mercy of an educational system that has systematically excluded and negated their history. Parents and educators have been looking for new ways to improve the education of African American children. They have tried seeking local control of the public schools within their neighborhoods and have asked for the inclusion of culturally relevant curricula for their children (Boateng, 1990). Their requests went unanswered. In response to the public school system's silence, the African American community set out to educate its own children through a network of independent, African-centered preschools, elementary schools, and high schools.

Independent African-centered institutions are not new in this country. Many of them have been in existence for over twenty years. However, their history is even older. The struggle to educate African American children in the U.S. has been a long and tedious one. It began long before the current discussions on multiculturalism and pluralism; it began before the "ethnic studies" movement of the 1960s. Recently, though, there has been discussion about the potential benefits for African American students of African-centered curricula.

In this chapter, we explore the history, structure, successes, and challenges of the independent African-centered school movement. We also discuss the national organization which links these institutions and conclude with a brief analysis of these independent African-centered institutions.

History

Quality education has always been a priority for African American people (Woodson 1933/69) but the disenfranchisement of African American children in public schools in the United States has been persistent, pervasive, and disproportionate (Lomotey, 1990). The United States, steeped in its ideas of superiority and relative aloofness, held the belief that African American students could not sit in a class with white students because African American children were viewed as socially, culturally, economically, and intellectually inferior. In the South, segregation was mandated by law. In the North, although not written in the law books, segregated schools were maintained by the funds provided by the cities (Banks, 1995). Because of this, the obligation of educating African American children became the responsibility of the African American community.

Since the 1700s, African Americans have established their own schools (Independent Black Institutions, or IBIs) designed to meet the particular needs of their children (Ratteray and Shujaa, 1987). African American communities pooled their resources, set up schools, and hired teachers. It was realized, however, that the quality of education at African American schools was not of the same quality as the education at white schools. The method of receiving the education itself may not have been inferior, but the textbooks, the furnishings, and the buildings were all old, dilapidated second-hand items. The information the students received was out of date. The African American community rallied for equality for their students; they wanted the same types of facilities, textbooks and resources that the white students had. However, "this fight was never a battle to sit next to white children in a classroom. It was and still is a struggle for an equal and level playing field in all areas of human endeavor" (Madhubuti, 1994, p. 2).

Later, it became apparent that not only were the resources unequally distributed, but the textbooks and the history that were being used did not include African Americans, with the exception of the slight and distorted treatment of the subject of the enslavement of Africans. In the late 1920s, Carter G. Woodson became one of the leaders of the movement to teach true African American history to all students throughout the country. Woodson warned the nation of the consequences of teaching an inaccurate and incomplete history in his book *The Mis-education of the Negro* (1933/69). He also warned of the false sense of superiority and other harmful attitudes that would be created and maintained if the curriculum and teaching methods were not changed. Many writers and philosophers of the day discussed the need for ethnic studies and inclusion in the curriculum.

As African American communities began to demand inclusion and truthful representation, individual court cases throughout the country were being tried concerning the legality of maintaining separate facilities for African American children. It was not until the U.S. Supreme Court case of *Brown v. Board of Education of Topeka* (1954) that the nation was ordered to discontinue its practice of school desegregation. The court's decision rendered desegregation unlawful.

In the 1960s we witnessed a strong resurgence of movement toward the inclusion of African American history and contributions in textbooks and courses. Educators began to see the effects of the educational system on the children within the system. Woodson's prediction was indeed manifesting itself in many ways. White teachers resented having to teach African American children and began to automatically assign labels to these children–special education, slow learners, culturally deprived (Lomotey and Fossey, in press). Studies were devoted to explaining the cultural and psychological deficits that African American children had. In the end, African American children were described as having low self-esteem and their behavior was labeled as pathological. African American students began to lag behind their white counterparts in academics as well as social mobility (Stanfield, in press). The need to act became imminent. Many people began to recognize the importance of focusing on the African American child, African American history, and African American education. Consequently, the idea of African Americans providing education for African American children resurfaced, and in the late 1960s Independent Black Institutions began to appear. Since then, IBIs have become an integral part of educating the African American youth of this country.

Structure

Although IBIs may vary with regard to teaching methodology and curriculum content, there are certain elements that most of these institutions have in common. They include: 1) the sincere belief that all children can and will learn, and 2) the belief that cultural knowledge is important. The belief that all children can learn permeates the IBI as educators strive to enable every student to achieve at his or her maximum potential at all times. IBI educators emphasize high achievement and academic content beyond the traditional "basics." In addition, IBI educators emphasize manual work and stress the importance of being able to perform both manual and mental work. Self expression is encouraged and students are constantly challenged to think analytically, critically, and independently. They are also charged with working creatively and productively for their personal survival as well as for the survival of the African community/nation.

James Banks (1993) observes that the most productive environment for learning is one where curriculum is consistent with the student's culture and experiences. In addition, "research has clearly shown that it is not merely shared ethnicity but shared cultural and social norms that affect the educational success of ethnic minority students" (Lomotey, 1994, p. 239). Because of this, children in IBIs are given the opportunity to "see themselves in the curriculum" whenever possible. Students are surrounded by images of themselves through pictures on the walls and in textbooks, on field trips, in museums, and through interacting with members of the community. These positive reinforcers motivate students to perform at their best level and they help affirm the student's sense of self-worth.   The curriculum at IBIs is holistic. It involves physical, intellectual, psychological, moral, spiritual, and cultural development. It emphasizes the importance of community and helps to instill in the students a sense of commitment to the continual improvement of the surrounding community and of the African nation as a whole. Teachers use individualized instruction, group sessions, cooperative learning, and other teaching methods as they integrate academic subjects with social and cultural practices. All materials used in IBIs are closely monitored to minimize, if not completely neutralize, the effects of non-African centered teaching aids on students, their perceptions and ideas.

The Nguzo Saba (Kiswahili for "The Seven Principles of Blackness") is used as the value system for most IBIs. In the 1960s, the Nguzo Saba was introduced by Maulana Karenga (1981) in a doctrine called Kawaida. The seven principles are Umoja (Unity), Kujichagulia (Self-determination), Ujima (Collective work and responsibility),

Ujamaa (Cooperative economics), Nia (Purpose), Kuumba (Creativity) and Imani (Faith). These principles are incorporated daily into the curriculum and teaching methods used by the teachers within the IBIs. The Nguzo Saba provide the moral foundation upon which the IBI stands.

A sense of family is also a very important aspect of IBIs. Teachers are enjoined to treat their students as if they were their own children. Students, in turn, are encouraged to love and respect their teachers as they love and respect their parents. IBIs aim to foster these relationships with sincerity and commitment. Parents are encouraged to, and do, participate in IBIs on all levels because it is understood that parents have a right and a responsibility to be involved in the education of their children (Ratteray and Shujaa, 1987). Parents serve as teachers, aides, administrative assistants, and field trip chaperons. They are also very involved in developing the curriculum as they are considered members of the educational team.

Successes and Challenges of the Independent
African-centered School Movement
The majority of IBIs presently in existence began operating within the past twenty years in response to African American parents' community control concerns and their (unsuccessful) efforts to have some say in their children's education in the public schools (Lomotey, 1992). IBIs have continued to grow over the years in response to the African American community's outcry for a curriculum and teaching methods that are culturally relevant to African American children. IBIs have been able to successfully address the problems and issues that have been associated with African American students' low achievement rates. The African-centered approach in IBIs stresses genuine love, concern and respect between students, teacher, and parents (Asante, 1980) and has helped to improve students' self-esteem. Students are performing better academically and their attitudes toward school have changed dramatically. Overall, IBIs have been more successful than their public school counterparts with regard to standardized achievement test scores, attitude, self-esteem, and fostering relationships between school personnel, students, and families (Lomotey and Brookins, 1988).

Although IBIs come under strict scrutiny and criticism, they continue to be an important aspect of educating African American students. Critics have argued that the African-centered approach is nothing but the reverse of the current curriculum being used in public schools today. Their argument is that the proponents of African-centered education are pushing African-centered curriculum as the one best, and only, curriculum that should be used. Critics argue further that if it is not right for the current curriculum to be imposed on others as the one best way, then it should not be right for the African-centered curriculum to be imposed on others. However, King (1995) asserts

> Euro-American cultural knowledge that is represented and valorized in school curricula is culture-centered with respect to its referent... because it serves to *legitimate* the dominant White middle-class normative cultural model.... In contrast, an African-centered worldview refers to the culture-specific social thought or perspective of African-descent people (not in terms of biology but of social and historical experience). In contrast to Eurocentric thought, this worldview does not rationalize or justify a universal or normative cultural model of being and way of knowing the world (p. 270).

An African-centered curriculum does not exclude or negate other peoples and their histories/contributions. It is a holistic approach to education that embraces the African American child.

National Organization

Today, there are a number of IBIs across the country, many of which are part of the Council of Independent Black Institutions (CIBI). CIBI was founded in 1972, in part, "to facilitate the development of Afrikan-centered educational institutions" (CIBI standards of evaluating). Every other year CIBI holds a conference that the members of the IBIs attend to welcome new members, share ideas, concerns and progress reports from the different IBIs within the Council. These conferences are held in even years on the second weekend in November in a different region of the country each time.

CIBI defines Afrikan-centered education as the means by which Afrikan culture–including the knowledge, attitudes, values, and skills needed to maintain and perpetuate it through the nationbuilding process–is developed and advanced through practice. The aim of Afrikan-centered education, therefore, is to build commitment and competency within present and future generations to support the struggle for liberation and nationhood. Nationbuilding is the conscious and focused application of black people's collective resources, energies, and knowledge to the task of liberating and developing the psychic and physical space that we identify as ours. It encompasses both the reconstruction of Afrikan culture and the development of a progressive and sovereign state structure consistent with that culture.

The Council of Independent Black Institutions has worked to provide standards of measure for IBIs and to help these institutions establish an African-centered curriculum. It serves to evaluate schools and offers recommendations for the schools to help bring them into line with nationbuilding and African-centered education. In addition, it emphasizes the importance of African spirituality, self-reliance, familial relations, history, traditions, rituals, and the "discovery of historical truths" (Council of Independent Black Institutions, 1995). The Council provides guidance and support to the IBIs and, in the process, has formed a large network of schools as well as a large family community.

CIBI's evaluation process embodies the commitment to African-centered education and nationbuilding. The standards put forth by CIBI link the institution-building process with nationbuilding. In this context the schools that are built are not themselves ends, but means toward building and maintaining educational institutions that will transmit the cultural knowledge of African people over generations. This aspect of the missions distinguishes CIBI's approach to African-centered education from those that do not connect the aims of education with sovereignty for African people.

The ten categories below represent the essential components of the independent African-centered educational institution. CIBI has developed evaluation criteria for each category that provide CIBI with a means of certifying that its members meet national standards for excellence in African-centered education (Council of Independent Black Institutions, 1995).

Category 1. Cultural and Ideological Context–The way in which the institution expresses and documents its philosophy, mission, and goals as well as its cultural and ideological reference points.

Category 2. Curriculum–The organization of knowledge in ways that guide both the pedagogy and the allocation of instructional time and space. It is the total learning experience to which participants are exposed. It exists in both explicit (written) and implicit (understood/perceived) forms and is reflective of the institutional culture, philosophy, mission, and goals. Explicitly, it is a systematic and comprehensive listing of what is taught. Implicitly, the perception of its content reflects the orientation and centeredness of both the teacher and learner.

Category 3. Institutional Health–The institutional climate and culture; evidence of shared understandings of and commitment to central mission; harmony among interpersonal relationships; capacity for development and continuation beyond the present generation; commitment to learning about the quality of overall performance; and balance and complementarity among roles within the institution.

Category 4. Staff–All persons who implement the curriculum and/or associated support activities and are accountable to the governing structure of the institution. It includes the personnel–paid and volunteer –who participate in providing for the maintenance and growth of the institution, including but not limited to teaching, administration, office, custodial, and transportation roles.

Category 5. Finance System–The methods and means of acquiring and/or maintaining the human and material resources required to maintain and develop the institution. It encompasses the acquisition, management, and investment of the institution's fiscal resources as well as the planning, procedures, and policymaking related to these processes. It is a system for collecting, disbursing, and prioritizing the use of funds.

Category 6. Governance–The structure and the processes by which staff, parents, and board members assign and accept responsibility for institutional operations and its overall management including policies, procedures, and decision making.

Category 7. Services and Community Programs–Benefits that the institution makes available to its internal and surrounding community. It incorporates the process of assessing needs upon which these activities are based.

Category 8. Parent Involvement–The extent to which parents support and participate in the planning, governing, administration, learning, and teaching within the institution.

Category 9. Record keeping–The documentation and organization of institutional data, including but not limited to the areas of financial assets and liabilities, curriculum resources and materials, history, evaluation of students' and staff members' yearly progress and performance, and alumni.

Category 10. Physical environment–The aesthetics, condition, maintenance, planning, and development of the space occupied by the institution.

We add that while these categories and criteria were developed for use in CIBI institutions, they can be useful to individuals working to save the minds of African people in other settings.

Conclusion

IBIs provide inspiration for parents and teachers in the public school because they 1) demonstrate that African Americans can effectively educate their own children, 2) illustrate African American institutional development and financial independence, and 3) provide the training ground for tomorrow's African American leadership. There are many successful IBIs across the country. A great number of these IBIs are members of CIBI, still others are part of the public school model. Whatever the case, IBIs have proven to be successful models for educating African American youth.

IBIs ensure that increased emphasis is placed on the contributions of people of African descent in the curriculum. African-centered cultural content is infused into the curriculum and a conscious effort is made to use only those resources that include truthful and fair representation of African American people. By using these types of materials, IBIs provide an opportunity for their students to accept and acknowledge their own dignity and worth as well as that of others. These resources also help to affirm the differences that children bring to school and to teach students to celebrate and cherish their unique qualities. Finally, curriculum that reflects the faces of the children in the school sends a message to these African American children that they are valued members of the society.

IBIs are even more significant in that, unlike the current public school system, their educators and leaders are African Americans. Part of enabling students to see themselves in the curriculum is allowing them to observe at work those educators and other professionals who share their cultural background. Children are affected in a positive manner because they can envision themselves as leaders and educators and successful entrepreneur. IBIs have been successful primarily because they have incorporated an African-centered curriculum. The remainder of their success lies in their commitment to the children. The public school system would do well by taking these schools as a model to restructure its curriculum to be more inclusive, truthful, and representative of its student body.

References

Asante, M. K. (1980). Afrocentricity: The theory of social change. Buffalo, NY: Amulefi.

Banks, J. A. (1993). Approaches to multicultural curriculum reform. In J. A. Banks and C. A. M. Banks (Eds.), *Multicultural education:*

Issues and perspectives. Needham Heights: Allyn and Bacon.

Banks, J. A. (1995). Multicultural education: Historical development, dimensions, and practice. In J. A. Banks and C. A. Banks (Eds.), *Handbook of Research on Multicultural Education.* New York: Macmillan.

Boateng, F. (1990). Combating deculturalization of the African-American child in the public school system: A multicultural Approach. In K. Lomotey (Ed.), *Going to school: The African-American experience.* Albany: State University of New York Press.

Council of Independent Black Institutions (1995, Spring-Summer). *Fundisha,–Teach!* Buffalo, NY: CIBI.

Irvine, J. J. (1990). *Black students and school failure: Policies, practices, and prescriptions.* Westport, CT: Greenwood Press, Inc.

Karenga, M. (1980). *Kawaida theory: An introductory outline.* Inglewood, CA: Kawaida Publications.

King, J. E. (1995). Culture-centered knowledge: Black studies, curriculum transformation, and social action. In J. A. Banks and C. A. M. Banks (Eds.), *Handbook of research on Multicultural education.* NY: Macmillan Publishing.

Lomotey, K. (1990). Introduction. In K. Lomotey (Ed.), *Going to school: The African-American experience* (pp. 1-9). Albany, NY: State University of New York Press.

Lomotey, K. (1992). Independent black Institutions: African-centered education models. *Journal of Negro Education,* 61 (4), 455-462.

Lomotey, K. (1994). African-American principals: Bureaucrat/ Administrators and ethno-humanists. In M. J. Shujaa (Ed.), *Too much schooling, too little education: A paradox of black life in white societies.* Trenton: Africa World Press, Inc.

Lomotey, K. and Brookins, C. (1988). The independent black institutions: A cultural perspective. In D. T. Slaughter and D. J. Johnson, *Visible now: Blacks in private schools.* Westport, CT: Greenwood Press.

Lomotey, K. and Fossey, R. (In press). School desegregation: Why it hasn't worked and what could work. In K. Lomotey and C. Teddlie. (Eds.), *Forty years after the Brown decision: Implications, perspectives, and future directions.* NY: AMS Press.

Madhubuti, H. (1994). Cultural work: Planting new trees with new seeds. In M. J. Shujaa (Ed.), *Too much schooling, too little education: A paradox of black life in white societies.* Trenton: Africa World Press, Inc.

Ratteray, J. and M. J. Shujaa. (1987). *Dare to choose: Parental choice at independent neighborhood schools.* Washington, DC: Institute for Independent Education.

Shujaa, M. J. and Ratteray, J. D. (1988). Expanding "schools of choice" for African-Americans: Independent neighborhood schools in New Jersey. In New Jersey Public Policy Research Institute, *Blacks in New Jersey, 1987 report: Crisis in urban education* (pp. 39-50). Absecon, NJ: New Jersey Public Policy Research Institute.

Stanfield, J. H. III. (In press). The reproduction of white domination in urban desegregation schools: The post 1970s. In K. Lomotey and C. Teddlie (Eds.), *Forty years after the Brown decision: Implications, perspectives, and future directions.* New York: AMS Press

Weusi, K. J. (1973). *A message from a Black teacher.* New York: East Publications.

Woodson, C. G. (1969). *The mis-education of the Negro.* Washington, DC: Associated Publishers. (Original work published 1933).

Chapter Seventeen

Revolution and Reality: An Interview with Peter McLaren

Carmel Borg, Peter Mayo, Ronald Sultana

You are on record as having argued that the most important ethical question you would ask is not "who are you?", a question we would have been tempted to ask, but "where are you?" How would you answer the latter question?

McLaren: The significant distinction between the questions "where are you?" and "who are you?" was brought to my attention by a contemporary Irish philosopher, Richard Kearney. Both of us are obviously quite influenced by philosophers Emmanuel Levinas and Paul Ricoeur, as some of my commentators and critics have pointed out. I use this distinction a lot in my speeches and I take it right out of some of Kearney's writings on the ethical imagination. The question "where are you" demands an ethical decision: "here I stand." I am here and I am here for you. In other words, the "other" demands of us an ethical response–unalienable right to be engaged as a human being. The phrase "who are you" takes in epistemological and ontological concerns. They are important but before you ask somebody who they are I think you need to establish the possibility of solidarity with them first. As others have pointed out correctly, this characteristic of my work has been influenced by liberation theology. Which disturbs some of my critics who have noticed numerous references to Santeria and Umbanda in my recent work–but that's another story for another interview. Let me say that a praxis of solidarity entails, in Kearney's view, the correlative priority of praxis over theory, ethics as having primacy over epistemology and ontology. I'm always reminded of this when I visit South Central or East Los Angeles, or the ghettos of Mexico or the favelas of Brazil. This summer a group of graduate students brought me to Brazil to teach a course and they actually arranged a lecture tour for me in Florianopolis, Porte Alegre and Sao Paulo. I remember visiting a favela, called Chico Mendez, in Florianopolis with a radical Catholic priest. Father Vilson did not ask people for their identity papers before he gave them assistance. They could be drug dealers, prostitutes, or people dying in their shacks of AIDS. He was committed to all of them. People knew he was there for them–they knew where he stood. I noticed in meeting again with Freire–this time in Sao Paulo–that he reflects where he stands in even the subtleties of his thinking about ordinary events. But let me emphasize that ethical responses are in no way indiscriminate. Our unconditional stance is with the powerless, the dispossessed, the disenfranchised, the immiserated, the wretched of the earth. Those who suffer and who long for comfort. We cannot avoid as educators, as agents for liberation, standing before the concrete other who is in need of our help. When I say, "here I stand" I am implicating, as Kearney notes, a "we" in the "I" and a "there" in the "here." "I stand" takes priority over "I think." The "other" is always a precondition for "I stand" whereas "I think" betrays no responsibility to the other. Kearney points out that the "I" in "I stand" has no significance outside of the call "where are you?" We need to develop an ethical imagination in which others take priority over ourselves. I like to think that in my work I stand on the side of the suffering, the lonely, the desperate, the victims of the global capitalist marketplace. The anguished victims who call out to us–from the classroom corridors, from community "half-way" houses, from the streets of our cities. They even call out to us from the boardrooms of corporations, from the marketing agencies, from the business and church hierarchies, if we would only listen to their cries. We need to know where we stand when they call upon us for assistance. They, in turn, need to know where we stand. I've been greatly influenced by the lives of Che Guevara and Paulo Freire, as you might gather. Both have spoken of the impossibility of revolution consciousness or practice without a love for the people. But a praxis built upon love distilled only into empathy is ultimately too thick for the transformation I am talking about. Empathy is not enough unless it is accompanied by a political agenda to critically intervene in relations of exploitation and domination.

What are some of your key concerns as a citizen, educator, and cultural theorist?

McLaren: My concerns shift in time, space, geopolitically and otherwise, but I shall venture to state, broadly speaking, that my key concerns stem from a struggle to understand the mystery of existence in its historical, material, ethical, and spiritual dimensions and not only to put these dimensions under erasure in some sort of deconstructive enterprise but rather resymbolize, reframe, recode, and reshape such existence in a real material way in the service of liberation and the elimination of needless suffering. I want to hold democracy accountable and responsible for its shortcomings and challenge it to live up to its ideals. I want to contest the anarcho-fascist politics of splayed postmodern will so that we can live in a society that can respect the challenge of Teresa Ebert's refrain: "From each according to her ability, to each according to her need." Freedom from necessity is the key here. My goal as a citizen and educator and cultural theorist is to make the world less exploitative, less cruel, less inhumane than if I had never been born. My goal is to struggle against economic marginalization and abandonment of hope, against ethnoracial power wielded unjustly by whites or any other group, against the unequal proletarianization of the worker and against labor imperialism. And if that gives me the label of a "dangerous man" then so be it. Economics is more than what Bataille refers to as the expenditure of desire. It is about material relations of exploitation and domination. Too often I see criticalists trying to romanticize critical pedagogy or exoticize the precious singularity of the "other"–of that unknowable alterity that escapes representation–and they forget about the politics of collective struggle. They avoid looking at society as a totality for fear that they are entering the realm of universal master narrative as Asians, as Maltese, as Americans, etc. But equally important is the way we interpret those experiences in light of how such experiences have been shaped by the system of social production that produces what we take to be "common sense." I think it was Toni Morrison who said "language is not a substitute for experiences but arches to the place where meaning lies." That statement is the key to the title of one of my speeches, "Building an Arch of Social Dreaming." Some critics have found my metaphor "arch" to be rather confusing but it makes sense to me in light of Morrison's insight about the relationship among language, experience, and meaning. Joan Scott expresses a similar insight to that of Morrison: "Experience is a

subject's history. Language is the site of history's enactment." Liz
Bondi also speaks to this issue which I raise again and again in my
work when she says: "the flaw [within hyphenated feminisms] was to
remain too close to liberal humanism by assuming that knowledge
flowed directly from experience and that experience ensured the
authenticity of knowledge." Of course, experience is important and
needs to be affirmed. To deny experience is to deny voice. And to be
without voice is to be powerless, without agency. Experience may be
relevant and valid but that doesn't mean that it is the arch of
foundational truth. Critical social theory and experience must be
dialectically re-initiating or recursively linked–that's the issue I've been
trying to emphasize. You don't necessarily learn from experiences. You
only learn from experiences that you learn from, as Myles Horton once
put it. Experiences always exhaust the capacity of language and
language always exhausts the capacity of experience. The experiences of
the subaltern should not be essentialized but understood dialectically in
relation to theory. The point is to read the perspectives of the nameless
subaltern along those of the ethnocentrism of the discourse of bourgeois
humanism in order to articulate a counterstance that goes beyond the
philosophical and political norms of the dominant culture. The racism
of Proposition 187 (a California law voted in recently that denies
medical care and education to illegal immigrants) is founded upon a
modernist, bourgeois ethics of law (these are illegal aliens!), but this
must be set against an ethics of liberation articulated from the
perspective of the oppressed and the victims of this Draconian measure
(we are human beings; we are here; we need your help; our children are
sick and wanting). Such a perspective reveals that law to be compli-
citous with racism and the exploitation of the unfree labor of the
migrants. You asked me about my pivotal concerns. One is to try to
fathom the intricacies of subjectivity and historical agency: How can
human beings reconcile their lives in a system that fetishizes their
dreams, commodities their wills, and puts a price tag on their souls?
I've always been amazed–whether it's been my years in Toronto, in
Cincinnati, or in Los Angeles–at why more people don't run through
the streets howling with rage, in the throes and thrall of madness? How
can we live with so little outrage against the evil of global capitalism?
How can we willingly adapt–and sometimes gleefully–ourselves, and
our families, and our children to a system that exploits people on the
basis of their social class, their race, their gender, religion, sexuality?
My work has tried to fathom how the process of motivated amnesia

works on a national scale, through local circuits of subject formation tied together by national myths, so that people refuse to confront their complicity in relations of domination and exploitation. Recently my work has focused on the topic of critical multiculturalism, a topic which is featured throughout my new book, *Critical Pedagogy and Predatory Culture.* Here I try to distinguish different species of multiculturalism: conservative, liberal, left-liberal, and critical. My work in Mexico and also my interest in border culture has led me to formulate a new conception of identity that I call order identity. I've used Gloria Anzaldua's concept of *mestizaje* identity, and recently Margaret Montoya introduced me to Francoise Lionnet's concept of *metissage,* which refers to a type of creolization of subjectivity, a combination of the dominant language with outlaw languages of subaltern groups. Here we are encouraged as teachers and students to redefine and re-invent the language of identity, the language of theory, and the language of research from the perspective of the oppressed. This idea is tied into the concept of how whiteness colonizes the definition of the normal at the level of everyday life and the idea that whiteness serves as a principle of pure exchangeability that tries to become the universalism that white people purport to represent.

Who do you draw your inspiration from as you confront the world, that is to imagine a world that could or should be? On which bases do you construct your "arch of social dreaming?"

McLaren: Nietzsche once wrote: "What does not kill gives me strength." This to me serves as a fitting testament to those revolutionary workers whom I admire, especially those who struggle with young people for a better future. I need to draw inspiration from history, even though history is created retroactively in the context of the present. Last month I went on a march of about 100,000 people in East L.A. We were marching to protest Proposition 187, which subsequently passed and will force teachers into the role of informers of the Immigration and Naturalization Service. If teachers do not report suspected illegal immigrants (those who have brown skin!) they could be fined or lose their jobs. If this proposition becomes law, illegal immigrants will not be allowed to attend school and will not receive medical benefits except in the case of emergencies. I hope that this mean-spirited and Draconian proposition will be declared unconstitutional. I am ashamed to be living in a state that overwhelmingly supported this measure. It doesn't take much of an imagination to think back to an earlier time when people were scapegoated and citizens had to report them to the authorities under threat of serious penalty. So in the face of such challenges, I draw inspiration and inner strength from many individuals: Amilcar Cabral, Memmi Subcommandante Marcos of the Zapatista Army, Trotsky, Fanon, Malcolm X, Althusser, Foucault, and even from some of the ideas of bourgeois thinkers like Jacques Lacan.

I continue to draw inspiration from the works of Tina Modotti, Frida Kahlo, Diego Rivera, the life and works of Paulo Rivera, the Situationists, the life and works of Paulo Freire, Che Guevara, Myles Horton, and El Salvador's Archbishop Romero. The writings of bell hooks and Cornel West figure prominently in my work. I could fill up the page with the names of people that I admire. I find some strong thinking in the work of Maxine Greene, for instance. I draw a great deal of inspiration from numerous individuals. My work in Mexico and Brazil has had a strong effect on my work, obviously, but my visits to Cuba, to Argentina, to Poland, and to Malaysia have also had a powerful impact, both spiritually and politically. My references to Santeria and to Umbanda have not gone unnoticed by readers. Not many people know this, but when I was a young man, I seriously contemplated going into the priesthood or entering a life of spiritual contemplation. Having abandoned this idea, I was drawn, much later, to liberation theology and I felt that, if necessary, priests and ordinary citizens should take up arms to defend oppressed groups. My intellectual life was at that time rich but undisciplined. It wasn't until I started working as a public school teacher that I began the journey into pedagogy that has taken me to the present. It has been a journey towards revolutionary consciousness, and it is a journey that is always and perhaps inevitably a series of beginnings. Modotti's photo entitled "Misery"–her famous depiction of two peasant women passed out in front of a pulqueria–represents for me a metaphor of the material consequences of capitalism. Capitalism is like a leaking nuclear power plant wrapped in a velvet ribbon. I am not against a market economy, but I am against a capitalist economy. The nature of investment should not be at the mercy of supply and demand, for instance. The workers need a more active role in controlling investment decisions. You could say that my arch of social dreaming is built upon the strength and power of the imagination and the courage to face the real. To face the real is to recognize that our actions are the consciousness of our dreams into consciousness. In our unconscious we are capable of the most brutal and horrific acts of violence. Unless we recognize this–unless we recognize the other side of our otherness–we cannot not be other than we are. And who we are now is what we see. We need to build our arch of social dreaming in the liminal, subjective mode of being. We need to transcend who we are so that we can become otherwise and discover where we have always been. I am not trying to be cryptic but I can only answer such a question in the form of positing paradoxes. More concretely, the arch of social dreaming that I continue to dream helps to politicize youth against the seductively violent thrall of capital, to menace passive consciousness like a surly stranger.

In her book, *The Struggle for Pedagogies*, Jennifer Gore remarks that there are few references in your writing, post-*Life in Schools*, to your own teaching or to testing our-your theories of critical pedagogy. Can you comment on this remark? We are particularly interested in learning how your movement from the Jane-Finch corridor to the predominantly white/middle/upper-class Miami University of Ohio has influenced your works.

McLaren: I have met several times Gore and like her personally yet I remain perplexed by her book. I consider feminist theory to be among the most sophisticated critical theoretical work currently being done and the most urgent. I was looking forward to Gore's book, even though I was a little apprehensive, since I had already encountered some difficulties with one of her previously published articles. I readily admit the aporetic status of critical pedagogy, and I also will admit to my gaps, inconsistencies, and confusions, and this certainly includes my own work. It's true that my work–anybody's work–is always incomplete and I have often modified my ideas in reaction to good, sound critique, regardless of who is making it. I have learned much from feminist theorists and writers such as bell hooks, Chandra Mohanty, Rey Chow and others. For instance, hooks' new book, *Teaching to Transgress* is a powerful collection of writings. In comparison, I was very disappointed by Gore's work. Back to your question: I don't know if Gore has actually read much of my post-*Life in Schools* work at all since, if I recall correctly, there aren't many works of mine actually referenced. What works is she talking about? If she had actually read my other books and articles–and there is no indication that she has gone beyond cursory examination of *Life in Schools*—she surely would have found some insights in other works such as *Schooling as a Ritual Performance*—considered by many critics to be my best work prior to *Critical Pedagogy and Predatory Culture*—to contradict some of her criticisms. Is there a motivated amnesia here? I can't really say. It is curious that Gore left out any references to my writings with Canadian feminist critic Rhonda Hammer. But I'm still happy her book is out there because it may provoke some good, productive debate and I hope, perhaps, generate in the long run some alliance-building. Now to the point of your question about empiricism. I went to Miami University, having been denied a full-time contract at Brock University in Canada due to some controversy over my politics. Frankly, it was the only job I could get and I was delighted at the opportunity to work with Giroux. The student body was indeed white and upper middle class and affluent. In fact, it seems to me that if you can reach the hearts and minds of people that have a good chance of occupying positions of power in the social order, then you are doing something worthwhile to contest the reproduction of hegemonic relations of domination and exploitation. I am now at UCLA working with Chicano, Asian, and African American students, but many of my students are still white and upper middle class. I prefer this kind of diversity to that of Miami, obviously, given my ties to Latin America and my revolutionary politics. But I don't regret working with white students nor the work I did at Miami. Don't forget that many of the teachers in my classes worked not only with affluent students but with Appalachian students in rural areas or black students in the inner city of Cincinnati, and they deserve a critical pedagogy, too. And what kind of empirical test does Gore want? Since there is no direct methodology to my work, since it cannot be reduced to a formula, it's hard to measure it empirically. The best empirical test would be perhaps to visit my former students and find out what they are doing in their classrooms. Are the students developing a sensitivity to social issues? Are they exploring the relationship between capital and labor? Are they trying to interpret their experiences and identifications in the cultures that surround them? And are they transforming their experiences? How are they accomplishing these tasks and in what directions? Are they developing a social ethics? A cultural ethics? Is the world less oppressive and less exploitative than if they had not been born? I believe my students are doing some wonderful things. I think it's important to remember, too, that I didn't work only with bourgeois white students at Miami. I also had students from other countries and states in the U.S. who came to work with me and Henry–students from Chicago, California, Argentina, Brazil, and Ireland–and they have all returned to their home states or countries, ready to take on the struggle against exploitation and social injustice and to prepare their own students to do so. I'm proud of the work I did at Miami of Ohio. And I'm proud of the work many of my former students are doing in critical/feminist pedagogy.

The Reagan-Bush years have witnessed an intensification of the New Right onslaught on public education, with the emphasis being placed on new vocationalism, learning the "great books," the market ideology in education, the assertion of a dominant white culture at the expense of subordinated subaltern cultures, etc. We know that people like Michael Apple, Henry Giroux, Stanley Aronowitz, Maxine Greene, Ira Shor, Kathleen Weiler, Joe Kincheloe, and yourself have been in the forefront of the struggle for greater democratic spaces in education. Considering that some of the most important policy making in the United States occurs at the state rather than the federal level, is the Clinton government likely to accomplish anything significant in the way of fostering greater democratization in American education?

McLaren: We are now witnessing the end of democracy as we once knew it and are entering the era of teledemocracy within technocapitalism. Clinton was crushed politically in the elections in November 1994, and the Republicans control a lot. I am amazed at the absolute stupidity of voting. The Republicans have somehow convinced the American public that nationalized health care is the government–Big Brother–legislating health care. So what is the alternative: Health care remains so privatized that nobody can afford it? Republican governments always have more bureaucracy but they manage to camouflage this from the American people. It's democracy through image production, through spin doctors. Issues don't make much of a difference. It's now a democracy through the organization of affect, of emotional economies. The Right does this better than anybody. Clinton will now become more centerist and move towards the right of the Democratic Party. One good thing–he did speak out against Proposition 187 but it didn't make a difference. I hope we can withhold federal funds

from California if the law takes effect. I don't expect Clinton to move
much on education; he's about where Bush was with his Education
2000 plan, except Clinton is more committed to Head Start programs
and federal funding initiatives. After the 1994 Republican win, former
Republican Congressman Bob Doran predicted: "Back to God, family
and country." The Republican vision is that of the carceral society:
more prisons for black males, and more orphanages for children of the
destitute. Some school boards run by the Christian right are eliminating
breakfast programs for starving children on the grounds that eating at
school is anti-family. I think a few ideas of Iris Marion Young can be
helpful here. I agree with Young when she argues that we need to move
away from interest-based and deliberative democracy– discursive
democracy in other words. We need to move towards a communicative
democracy. Proposition 187. Deliberative democracy is a bit better
because it is directed towards agreement by force of better argument. Of
course, we now have a video democracy and argumentation can't match
images on the television screen of rioting blacks in South Central L.A.
Communicative democracy is developed by Young to be based within a
communicative ethics that includes standpoints of the concrete and
generalized other. This is situated in the transformation of people's
preferences and an openness to persuasion. Just as norms are not
transcendentally grounded but are arrived at freely and by maximizing
democracy, according to Young, social understanding occurs from a
multiplicity of social locations, where the politics of greed and self-
interest gives way to a politics of social justice. Majoritarian
democratic procedures often perpetuate social injustice towards minority
groups. This is because social and economic disadvantages prevent
many minority groups from available political resources. Cultural
imperialism has enabled Euro-American values to become the accepted
social norms. Take Proposition 187 as one example. We must analyze
this proposition as it has been developed as a viable social alternative in
this particular conjecture, at this moment in the social formation. We
need to understand this in terms of the way majoritarian democracy
occludes the structure of racism within it. Balibar calls this an age of
"crisis racism" and it is marked by the denial of class solidarities and the
fact that class divisions no longer determine different attitudes towards
the other. Social pathology is condensed into a single cause–
immigrants! What often appears as a democratic consensus–as in
Proposition 187 winning in a landslide vote–really amounts to a form
of exploitation–it's really an empty, artificial consensus brought about

by procedural democracy. We need to start our struggle for equality from the position of social justice in a context of qualitative fairness. The majority of Californians voted for Proposition 187, but it is not a qualitatively fair proposition. It will go down in infamy. It is shameful and inhuman. As Balibar notes, racism is the absence of thought, an oligophreny in the extreme–and that reflection upon it is not enough; rather, it requires a change in the modality of thinking.

Your work is often regarded as being couched in the language of post-colonialism. What would you regard as the basic tenets of a post-colonial education?

McLaren: It's quite true that both of our work is characterized in this way. Speaking about my own work on post-colonial education, I would say that for me the crucial issue is what Negri refers to as the imperialistic process of capital, the ways capital can circulate on a global basis, and the opening up not only of ways of exploitation but also ways of contesting such exploitation. This involves the struggle for spaces of hegemonic rupture out of which new democratizing possibilities may be won. It involves a challenge to Eurocentric, totalizing, and essentialistic notions of identity and the official knowledges of colonialism. I try to locate schooling within the formation of Western forms of metropolitan power and representation. Post-colonial pedagogy, at least as I am attempting to formulate it, sets out to challenge global transnational capitalism and the forms of cultural pluralism that have resulted–forms which I argue really serve to camouflage what I call the neo-colonial cultures of whiteness. Basically it's pedagogy of anti-imperialism. It's really operative in my work at this stage, more heuristically than substantively. It ties into my work on multiculturalism. Schooling tries to commodify black rage, Latino militancy, Asian resistance, and to hellify their world by constantly cannibalizing representations of them and providing prison as the most realistic educational alternative for them. Courses begin at Chino, Folsom, Tehachapi.

In what ways is the ideology of colonialism being repro- duced in the U.S. educational system, and why is it important for educators to unveil the foregoing ideology?

McLaren: Labor power as the source of value in our society has nearly been masked completely. It has been veiled by the multivalent power of the image to reorganize desire into hegemonic blocs, ways that are tied to ideologies and discourses of representation carried over from colonial times. Euro-American concepts of agency, value, self-worth, and citizenship are often not very hospitable to other cultural articulations of identity and subjectivity. The autonomous, stable, ideal self of modernity is profoundly Eurocentric in its attempt to speak from a particular standpoint and for all of humanity. This creates the pre-condition for both the affirmation of the subject of history and its eventual demise as it is put under erasure by the counterstance of cultural workers in the margins and periphery of the dominant culture. Ethics and democracy have become sundered from each other. The commodity form is now internal to the meaning of democracy and democratic citizenship, mediated through the vestiges of colonial sensibility and racial typology. Subjectivities have been created in forms serviceable to the slave-form of capital. Subjectivity has actually become capitalized just as our idea of nature is now seen as the incarnation of capitalism. Human nature is now capitalist. Its power is imprinted on the body, regulates the investment of affect, organizes intricate and often contradictory economies of desire, and creates value from market functions and state powers. It wears a crooked top hat: with iron fists inside velvet gloves, it grasps the throats of its dark-skinned victims, attempting to suffocate the last breath of hope–it has the blood of the workers dripping from its fangs. Labor and the division of labor have not disappeared. The class struggle, as Etienne Balibar and others have noted, is a determining structure affecting all social practices; the antagonistic forms of class struggle may appear in different forms but they have not disappeared.

Given the so-called post-Fordist milieu, in which most educators in the U.S. are operating, how is it possible to build a movement of critical subjectivities that is loud enough to bring about substantial transformation?

What is the ground zero of subjectivity but the movement in which absence is transformed into presence? The internal divisions of fractured, decentered subjectivity have been reunited by the call to nationhood, by myths racialized and incanted in the campaign slogans of the New Right. Racism has become respectable again, as a new book on the genetic inferiority of African Americans in terms of intelligence gets great airplay in the media. Illegal immigrants are to be turned out of schools and medical clinics. Counties in California are planning to evict the homeless. Even attempts to transgressively challenge the confines of control one is trying to resist. Management and labor depend upon one another. Resistance rarely evades the larger circuit, the larger circuit of production and consumption. At the most, we have school reform measures that simply transfer domination from one site to another. The problem has been the centrisms–Anglocentrism, Euro-American centrism, and the discourses and practices of whiteness. But the counter-movements? Take the case of Chicano centrism or Afrocentrism. There is a major problem here. I think that bell hooks and Paul Gilroy have made some good criticisms in their claims that many articulations of Afrocentrism are distinctly European, such as the mythic construction of Africa with Isis and Osiris as superheroes. Some forms of Afrocentrism are grounded, for instance, in nineteenth-century Eurocentric forms of nostalgia–hooks also notes that this is similar to Rousseau's notion of the masculinized public sphere with the household transformed into an opaque space for culture to reproduce itself. Neo-black nationalist views on Afrocentrism, according to hooks, often deny that gender is problematic, creating a fiction of our social reality that avoids recognizing that black women and children will constitute 75% of the black poor in the near future. But the most dangerous centrism right now is white, Euro-American centrism which has colonized most of the other centrisms. The cultures and logics of whiteness shape the very contours of what counts as normative in the United States. Actually, I'm against all and any centrisms. I believe we need to think of difference differently–not in essentialist ways, but discursively and materially. Whiteness tends to define all other groups as it claims to be both everything and nothing–a principle of pure exchangeability. Whiteness should not be the regulating principle of everybody's identity. It needs to be unmasked as linked to forms of ethnicity. White people tend to believe they have transcended the lowliness of ethnicity. Everybody else is ethnic/cultural. They are beyond ethnicity as pure reason, pure rational consciousness. I believe that racialized categories and categories of gender are not linked to the tropic slippage or immanent laws of signification that we hear so much about from the trendy, bourgeois poststructuralists but, rather, are linked to the division of the labor and the regime of the commodity. We can't locate difference outside of the social relations of production which produce exclusion and exploitation. We need to locate difference in a historically materialist way–within a material system of exploitation.

In your work, as well as that of other writers committed to the area of critical pedagogy, we notice an emphasis on multiple forms of oppression. This strikes us as being the trend in a lot of left-wing literature on education coming out of North America. We consider this to be commendable and necessary in the interest of a radical and truly emancipatory democracy. It prevents us from being trapped within an essentialist, reductionist vision of oppression. Yet, judging from the literature emerging from North America, don't you think that we've reached a situation where class analysis is increasingly being placed on the back burner? Furthermore, isn't there a need for coalition building among the various movements and groups struggling to confront different forms of oppression, and what role should intellectuals like yourself play in this process?

McLaren: Yes, in a new global order where societies are being subsumed by capital, and where the state has expropriated all forms of production, the analysis of class is on the back burner among educational theorists, as some of my previous remarks have strongly indicated. Class antagonisms thrive, although their forms and contexts differ within practices of flexible specialization than they do in contexts of Fordism or peripheral Fordism or Taylorism. But class antagonisms also need to be seen in terms of the way they intersect with practices involving racism, sexism, homophobia, xenophobia. Today's political climate favors neoliberal ideology. Private power is now being glorified over government power. Society is to be organized pursuant to the powers of special interests. Responsibility must, neo-liberals argue, rest in private hands and stay out of the hands of the government. Cultural homogeneity is valued above all else. In such a context, it is difficult to organize coalitions–more difficult than with Fordist workers, for instance. The antagonisms among the state, the economy, and the worker, have a different aspect to them in the current context of deregulation and other current realities. Yet, in an important way, the xenophobia reflected in Proposition 187 has sparked resistance across the country, and not only in California. Recently, I spoke at Harvard, and on my way back from my lecture, my spirit began to swell as I witnessed hundreds of students in Cambridge demonstrating against Proposition 187. Did you know that here, in California, more students are leaving schools to march and demonstrate than during the Vietnam War? I think that the anti-immigration discourses that are developing at this particular historical juncture will provide the basis for a new social movement, primarily by Latinos. Many teachers have [joined] or will join them. I am one of them. We can only truly build the necessary revolutionary coalitions needed to challenge the power of capital by our continuous experience of resistance and struggle in organizing counter-vailing powers both strategically and, more importantly, tactically, so that proletarian power can consolidate itself. We need to seize on the constitutiveness of the agent and the possibilities in the building community. New alliances must be made, must be grasped in new and innovative ways. And here I follow Gramsci, Negri, and Foucault in stressing the relation between power and knowledge and how knowledge as an ethical practice can play a central role in the struggle for liberation. The role of the intellectual is important and I applaud much of what Gramsci has said about the role of the "organic intellectual" and Foucault has said about the "specific intellectual." I am also concerned with what I call the "border intellectual." The border intellectual refers to new forms of the social production of subjectivity brought about by determinate antagonisms that can be traced genealogically through the development of modern capitalism. Following Negri, we have entered a new crisis in which deregulation, unemployment, forms of social control through technological means, and global competition have led to the terroristic transformation of subjectivity. Most postmodernists have simply celebrated heterogeneity in such a context and have not, according to Negri, fully explored the possibilities of the constitution of the revolutionary subject form confronting the proliferation of new antagonism brought about by the new crisis of postmodernism. The border intellectual is attentive to such a crisis and the role information and communication plays in the hegemonic production of subjectivity and in terms of controlling the means of production by controlling the way subjects are produced through antagonisms with respect to the formation of common sense. The involves the educator as border intellectual effectively promoting new forms of agency through the transgression of linguistic, cultural, economic, global, and local boundaries–the periphrastic values of the cultural dominant–from the radical perspective and vantage point of a plural self, a non-unitary self, a *mestiza* self, and interspecies self that Gloria Anzaldua writes about. It is obvious how much Anzaldua writes about. It is obvious how much Anzaldua figures in my work by taking a look at my writings on border identity over the last several years. Subjectivity is produced materially and collectively, and that is something I have taken from Negri's work.

Peter, you will recall that, at a 1992 meeting in San Francisco, one or two people from the audience raised the issue of the "difficult," often incomprehensible language in which the work of some writers, in the area of critical pedagogy, is couched. We are sure that this accusation is leveled at you and your colleagues time and time again. That day, as well as on other occasions, you quoted a piece of advice given to you by Paulo Freire, namely, that you should always "be simple but never simplistic." To what extent do you follow this advice in your work?

McLaren: I'm not surprised by this question. This question and I have become good friends, and I have reached the point that I am almost disappointed if it is not asked during an interview such as this. I have always tried to prevent my writing from being imperialized. As is often remarked, I occupy a strange site of enunciation in my work. My work is like an urban hallucination. Half the time I don't know what it means until long after I have put my thoughts to paper. I think it's irresponsible of a writer to claim to know what she is saying before others engage the work. I am a restless thinker. Rarely do I allow myself to be stabilized in one disciplinary domain, trope, genre, or style of writing. I write in order to be otherwise. Some people think I'm just trying to be highfalutin or that I am unwittingly imprisoned by the patrician conceits of the bourgeois metropolitan intellectual, and some-times fellow Marxists admonish me or activists decry my academic prose. And then again I have received letters from leftist intellectuals whose work I admire very much–intellectuals and artists who share a similar admiration for my writing. Writing is an avenue of self-examination and a means to articulate necessary counter-pressures; for me it's an attempt to find a discursive terrain–whether this means treating criticism as a literary artifact or cultural object, or both–in which I can reinvent myself in ways that take into account a deeper reading of social life, so that I can be a more critical agent of social change. Some of this has to do with redemption and self-projection, moral rectitude, and the flight of the spirit into different worlds of meaning. It is an attempt to keep social evil at bay. Writing is a social practice, a political practice, a form of cultural criticism. It enables me to reunite the discourse of critique and joy. My own writing helps me to view the world critically from multiple perspectives–from a grounded aesthetics–that seeks emancipatory transformation of both the world and the word. It is a form of individual self-fashioning for communal emancipation. It would not be wrong to say that I am attempting to create and occupy new subject positions that appear closed-off to the majority of educational critics because of the way educational critics choose to represent themselves that trivialize the political realities at stake. Realities that have to do with human suffering, with exploitation and oppression and racism and hatred. We are now glorifying in the media the authors of Proposition 187, and other states now want to get rid of the immigrants. Supporters of this proposition are at this very moment trying to cut off food for illegal pregnant women and school lunches for illegal immigrant students. All under the banner of being American. Being American is a discourse which has nearly completely displaced an ethical discourse, a discourse of compassion. We have capitulated to an occidental separation of democracy and culture, ethics and aesthetics, criticism and utopian dreaming. For the most part, I hate reading the educational literature. It depresses me. Most of it is junk. Not only does it refuse to admit its ideological presuppositions, it cannily installs you in its ensemble of pre-set identities, and situates you within ideas about gender, race, and class that are formulated in advance–ideas that bear more than just the blemish of patriarchy but which are ravaged by the discourses of white supremacist patriarchal capitalism. It's all about pre-programmed historical agency and the reinscription and reinstitution of sovereign subjectivities which I consider to be a zombification process. It puts you into an arena of expression that chokes the spirit. And where do I get this spiritual inspiration? From the spirit of the jubilee. From the will to resist. From examples set by my compañeros and compañeras in struggle. From my trips to East Los Angeles with my Chicano/a brothers and sisters, from the strength of character exhibited by South Central L.A. homeboys and homegirls, the viscera of the struggles of the Chicanas in the sweatshops–the constueras–who struggle on behalf of the International Ladies' Garment Workers Union, from my work in Mexico, Brazil, Argentina. And visits to places in Europe and Southeast Asia where the revolution is far from dead. From memories of

Toronto. The most inspirational moment in the last few years was
receiving a photograph of a subcommandante sent to me by some
members of the Zapatista army in Chiapas. In all of this I ask myself:
What are the possibilities? What kind of politics is necessary? What
kind of revolutionary struggle? Now when I am working with teachers
in, say, Mexicali, Mexico, or in Los Angeles, I try not to sound like
Derrida. I need to recognize my audience. If I do use some academic
terminology, I try to translate this terminology, I try to translate this
terminology respecting the contextual specificity in which the teachers
find themselves in their classrooms and communities. *Life in Schools*
is a textbook, and that was not a book I really wanted to write, but it
was, I feel, an important political project. I didn't want to summarize
theoretical positions but, rather, advance them and push them further.
But I felt that there was a political necessity for a textbook in critical
pedagogy. And so I tried to be as creative as possible with that book
and because it is a very pedagogical book it sells–surprisingly–more
than many of my other books put together. I am trying to avoid the
traps of white man's journalism, which informs most educational
writing, and I do believe that the assault on experimental academic
prose really is the same kind of assault that we see on the black or
Chicano vernacular. It's an assault on difference. On the other hand,
there is a lot of very bad writing going on in the academy.

**How can theory help cultural workers in their struggle
for justice, given, as Roger Simon remarks, the fear that
they are often believed to harbor with respect to such
theory? We would also argue that certain cultural and
community workers often seem suspicious of academics
and theorists in our field. "Get real" is the exhortation
normally heard.**

McLaren: That's an important question. I think a lot of the criticism
is populist elitism–people feel that closeness to the oppressed is the
key and that academics read in isolation from the real world too much.
Theorizing doesn't guarantee one's politics but neither does brushing
shoulders with the oppressed. You need to be careful of your audience
and your constituencies. You need to translate when you have to in
order to be understood. Theories–reason and rationalities–undergird
everything we do–they shape the contours of our social and institutional
life. They inform our personal and political lives. Theories are agents,

they are constitutive of tradition and prevailing forms of common sense. They organize peoples to and in the world. They formulate our public and private "gaze." But they can also serve as subversive transformative and counter-hegemonic agents in the struggle against domination and exploitation. The key is to make the theories real–to ground them in the contextual specificity of real life and human suffering as well as happiness–to anchor them affectively in people's dreams and agonies, visions and mundane routines. We need to take theories out of the monoculturalism of academic life, out of the monovalent center of the academic mainstream, in order to get democracy off the ground in the streets and in the classrooms. Theories need to help in the mobilization of material resources and not just describe social life in endless forms of deconstructive textual analyses.

You have been criticized for speaking with a voice of authority. What is your reaction to such criticism in view of your pedagogical politics and your location as white, male, middle class, Anglo North American?

McLaren: Let me try to answer that by saying that the voice of authority is something that has been given to me, not something I have sought. This voice has been constructed historically through my writings and international work and, even if I denounce the authority of such a voice, it only paradoxically reinforces its authority. So if I am stuck with being a voice of authority or exhibiting an authoritative style in my work then I will try to make the most of it strategically. And how is this possible at a time when the white North American man is held in such suspicion? Let me first say that I am uncomfortable in the role of the authority. Not because I am white or male and feel guilt about it, or because it carries such a tremendous responsibility, but because it suggests in this climate of expediency in thinking and especially in political thinking, that I–or anyone–can provide expedient solutions to pressing social and educational problems. Many people who have read my work but do not know my ethnicity often assume I am Latino or African American. I've been at more than one conference when somebody has remarked: "You're white!" So there is something going on here that transcends my location as a white male scholar-activist. The only serious criticisms I've had have been from bourgeois white feminists, some of whom consider me apparently to be a "macho Marxist." I still have that working-class sentiment to my work, that of a fighter. I was working class until my father landed a managerial job when I was young–and that turns some people off, I guess. It's in my tone. I sometimes use the "royal we" and have tried to temper that somewhat where I feel it's not helpful to my arguments or to the agency I am trying to develop. But as long as I can remember, I have always been involved with different disadvantaged ethnic groups. I would argue that I am more than my whiteness, more than my maleness, more than my Canadian-ness or my adopted American-ness, or my ancestral Scottishness. The key, I feel, is to remember the privilege that being a white male affords you and to use such privilege to fight against exploitation and economies of power and privilege. I know what being patronizing is all about, what patriarchy is all about. It's not so much who you are but where you stand and for whom. People who know me well know I don't equivocate on this.

In *Schooling as a Ritual Performance* you distinguish between "street corner knowledge" and "knowledge acquired in classroom settings." How can schools accommodate "street corner culture" without simply co-opting it?

McLaren: It is impossible not to co-opt cultural knowledge in some sense. Those who co-opt such knowledge are not unaffected by it. Knowledge always turns into something else. Street corner knowledge is important because it is felt knowledge and occurs in the asignifying dimensions of experience–that is, it occurs on the affective plane and often is supplementary to academic knowledge. In other words, it occurs in the gap between ideology and the body. It is visceral: it is laced with emotional investment–with what Larry Grossberg calls "affective investment." But it is problematic because of the suffusion of capital into mundane and quotidian social relations. This has caused a generalized commodification of desire; desire has been transformed into the performativity of the purchase, of the acquisition of the image. In their attempts to escape the subject positions of adulthood, they try to find a space of their own which, unbeknownst to many, has already been written for them as well in the spectacle of youth anger and alienation. Informed by the necrophiliatic drive of predatory culture rather than the plural versality of being, youth today occupy identities that are crusted over by empty images, like stench-ridden landfill sites. What holds many students together is their collective inability to feel outside of texts of identity that have been already written for them.

They are literally decomposing and want to aestheticize their emptying out of anything meaningful–anything that can be felt. Students need spaces where they can talk about and come to critically interrogate the constant fracturing of their agency, so that they can somehow put life into motion. Teachers absolutely cannot reduce their identities to some unholy criteriology or typology. They need to understand how student identity is constructed at the site of the popular and the national popular. They need to acquire a theoretical language that can help students understand how their desire has been manufactured along with their consensual attitude towards their empty futures. Students need courses in media literacy, in critical social theory, so that they can ask the following: What is it about the way the world has made me that enables me to resist myself and the world?

In countries like the U.S. and Canada, which are characterized by a strong racial mix and which provide the conditions for the emergence of anti-racist education, one is often confronted with the term "multiculturalism." From the experience which two of us had with the Maltese community in Toronto, we have realized that multiculturalism is nothing but a means of keeping the Maltese community entrenched within its own traditional cultural boundaries, boundaries that breed ghettoization and which foster an inorganic sense of the community's traditional cultures. This inorganic sense of Maltese cultures is what feeds into the present hegemony in which a dominant group (Anglo-Canadians) is presented as the visible norm presupposed by the existence of the "insular" other. Is this experience unique to the Maltese community? If not, isn't all the talk that we hear concerning "multicultural education" problematic?

McLaren: That's an important and urgent question. No, it's not unique to the Maltese community. Multiculturalism is a word rightly viewed with suspicion by non-dominant groups. It's become a codeword for absorption and/or containment. Whiteness is the privileging norm, the invisible norm that is able to hide right out in the openness of everyday life. It not only hides in the light–it is the light. Whiteness, as I have said, is equated with rationality while non-whiteness is considered irrational, and the less white you are (the darker you are) the more irrational and more ethnic you are considered to be. White cultures are able to maintain their invisibility and also control of economic, social, and cultural relations. Whiteness is not just about skin color but is entwined in systems of intelligibility enmeshed in colonialism, imperialism, Eurocentrism. I know some African Americans and Latinos who are white, who have accepted the terms of enfranchisement, which means to become culturally stripped and deracinated. Whiteness is an invention–a socially constructed way of looking at others, at oneself from a position of structural privilege and cultural privilege; it is, in short, an inscription into ideological relations that are imbricated in economies of power and privilege also linked to class, race, and gender relations. The issue is not for people of color to simply reverse relations of power so that they assume the same proprietary position as whites, but to create new positions of intensity, new forms of ethnicity, new democratic social realizations and zones of sociality. The notion of pluralism is really an empty notion because pluralism is often just an adding-on of different cultures into a mosaic in which whiteness is the architect. Right now I'm looking at a way outside of identity politics to foster a program of revolutionary struggle. I believe that we need to respect difference but that we also have to understand how differences are deployed by systems of social production within global capitalist relations. How is the difference the product and outcome of material and historical practices–that's the issue that we, as educators, need to explore. As revolutionary cultural workers, we need to become driven by a visceral movement of the spirit, by a ethico-political consciousness, by a commitment to fight against exploitation and oppression in all of its contemporary guises. But unless we are guided by a wisdom born through struggle and love, strengthened by hope, all of this is mere foolishness.

Index

Biographical Notes

Al Alcazar directs the Community Action Program at Loyola University and teaches, part-time, in the philosophy and religious studies departments of its city college. He is a doctoral student at Louisiana State University.

Wendy Atwell-Vasey is assistant professor of education at the Institute for Educational Transformation at George Mason University. Her forthcoming book from SUNY Press's series on feminist theory and education is entitled *Nourishing Words: Bridging Private Reading and Public Teaching*.

Alan Block is an associate professor in the Department of Education, School Counseling and School Psychology, University of Wisconsin-Stout. He teaches courses in curriculum theory and practice and in reading and language arts. Block worked for seventeen years in the public schools teaching high school English. He has published three books, *Anonymous Toil* (1992), *Occupied Reading* (1995) and *It's Alright Ma (I'm only bleeding): Education as the Practice of Social Violence against the Child* (1997). He has published extensively in the areas of curriculum and teaching.

Carmel Borg is a lecturer in the Department of Primary Education, Faculty of Education, University of Malta, working in the areas of curriculum studies and pedagogy.

Deborah P. Britzman teaches at York University in Toronto. She is the author of *Practice Makes Practice: A Critical Study of Learning to*

Teach (1991), as well as essays on identity, self-knowledge, multiculturalism, representation, and psychoanalysis.

Mary K. Bryson, plagued with a name reminiscent of cheap cosmetics, has the dubious distinction of the lowest undergraduate GPA and the shortest dissertation of any student ever to obtain a Ph.D. Suzanne de Castell has five long surnames, and a title about which she tells no-one. This invisible privilege is the source of her shameless dilettant-ism. Her Ph.D. thesis was nearly failed by the University of London for being far, far too long.

Gaile S. Cannella is associate professor at Texas A & M University, and a former early childhood/elementary teacher. In addition to early education, her interests include critical pedagogy in teacher education.

William E. Doll, Jr. is a professor of curriculum theory at Louisiana State University. The author of *A Post-Modern Perspective on Curriculum* (1993), he is interested in formulating new curriculum designs and rationales.

Ivor F. Goodson has accepted the chair of education at the University of East Anglia, where he teaches each spring term. In the fall he teaches at the University of Rochester. He has lectured widely in Europe as well as North America. Among his books are *School Subjects and Curriculum Change* (1983, 1993), *International Perspectives in Curriculum History* (1988), *The Making of Curriculum* (1988, 1994), and with Rob Walker, *Re-interpreting Curriculum Research: Images and Arguments* (1989).

Annette Gough is a senior lecturer in the faculty of education, Deakin University, Australia. Her current teaching and research interests are in feminism and poststructuralism in science and environmental education.

Noel Gough is associate professor in the Deakin Center for Education and Change, Deakin University, Victoria, Australia. His teaching and research interests include narrative theory and popular media culture in education, with particular reference to curriculum studies, science and environmental education, and futures in education. He is editor (Australasia) of the *Journal of Curriculum Studies* and an executive editor of the *Australian Educational Researcher.*

Wen-Song Hwu is an assistant professor at Oklahoma State University. His research interests include curriculum theory, poststructuralism/ postmodernism, critical theory and Eastern philosophy (Zen/Taoism). His upcoming book, *Tao/Zen/Curriculum: East Meets West* (1997), will be published by Peter Lang.

Joe L. Kincheloe teaches cultural studies and pedagogy at Pennsylvania State University. He is the author of *Teachers as Researchers: Qualitative Inquiry as a Path to Empowerment* (Falmer, 1991), the co-editor (with Shirley Steinberg) of *Thirteen Questions* (Peter Lang, 1992), the author of *Toward a Critical Politics of Teacher Thinking: Mapping the Postmodern* (Bergin & Garvey, 1993), and *Toil and Trouble* (Peter Lang, 1995). He is a co-editor (with Shirley Steinberg) of *Measured Lies: The Bell Curve Examined*, *Kinderculture: The Corporate Construction of Childhood,* and *Taboo: The Journal of Education and Culture* (Peter Lang).

Kofi Lomotey is chair and associate professor in the Department of Administrative and Foundational Services in the College of Education at Louisiana State University. His research interests include African American principals, independent African-centered schools, issues of race in higher education, and urban education. He is editor of the *Journal of Urban Education* and the national secretary/treasurer of the Council of Independent Black Institutions, an umbrella organization for independent African-centered schools. In addition, he serves on the editorial boards of several journals, including *Educational Administration Quarterly* and the *Journal for a Just and Caring Education.*

Peter Mayo is a lecturer in the Department of Foundations in Education, Faculty of Education, University of Malta, working in the areas of sociology of education and adult education.

Cameron McCarthy teaches curriculum theory and cultural studies at the University of Illinois in Urbana. He is also a research associate in the Institute for Communication Research. He has published widely on the topics of problems with neo-Marxist writings on race and education, institutional support for teaching, and school ritual and adolescent identities in journals such as the *Harvard Educational Review, Oxford Review of Education, Educational Theory, Curriculum Studies, JCT, Contemporary Sociology,* and the *European Journal of Intercultural*

Studies. He is the author of *Race and Curriculum* (1990) and, with Warren Crichlow, the editor of *Race, Identity, and Representation in Education* (1993).

Peter McLaren teaches cultural studies in UCLA's Graduate School of Education. He is the author *School as Ritual Performance* (1986), *Life in Schools* (1989, 1994), and with Peter Leonard, *Paulo Freire: A Critical Encounter* (1993), and *Critical Pedagogy and Predatory Culture* (Routledge, 1995). He is a faculty advisor for the Chicano Studies Research Center and works in the areas of critical multiculturalism, cultural studies, and Marxist social theory.

Petra Munro is assistant professor in the Department of Curriculum and Instruction and Women's and Gender Studies at Louisiana State University. Her research conducting life history narratives of women teachers focuses on feminist, poststructuralist theories of identity, agency and power/knowledge. She is co-author of "Repositioning Feminism and Education: Perspectives on Educating for Social Change." Her articles have appeared in journals such as *Journal of Curriculum Theorizing, Journal of Curriculum and Supervision,* and *Qualitative Inquiry.*

William F. Pinar teaches curriculum theory at Louisiana State University, where he serves as the St. Bernard Parish Alumni Endowed Professor. He has also served as the Frank Talbott Professor at the University of Virginia and the A. Lindsay O'Connor Professor of American Institutions at Colgate University (both visiting appointments); he taught at the University of Rochester (1972-1985). He is the author of *Autobiography, Politics, and Sexuality* (Peter Lang, 1994), and the senior author of *Understanding Curriculum* (Peter Lang, 1995).

Shariba Rivers is a Ph.D. student at Louisiana State University in educational administration with a concentration in higher education. She has written a book chapter, "The Legacy of Brown 40 Years Later" (with Cheryl Brown Henderson) and an essay review, "Reflection on the Handbook on Multicultural Education: A Long Overdue Synthesis" (with Kofi Lomotey).

Paula M. Salvio is an assistant professor in the Department of Education at the University of New Hampshire. She specializes in curriculum theory with a focus on English education, aesthetics, and feminist pedagogy.

Ronald G. Sultana is Dean of the Faculty of Education at the University of Malta. He works in the areas of sociology of education and comparative education and is the founding Editor-in-chief of the *Mediterranean Journal of Educational Studies*.

Dennis J. Sumara and Brent Davis live with their two cats (Sophie and Finnigan) and their dog (Scooter) in York, Ontario. They share research and teaching interests in areas of curriculum theory, teacher education, and enactivist learning theory, and have published a number of papers on these topics. Brent teaches courses in mathematics education, research methods, and curriculum at the University of British Columbia. He has recently published a book with Garland Publishing entitled *Teaching Mathematics: Toward a Sound Alternative*. Dennis teaches courses in English language arts education, curriculum, and qualitative research at Simon Fraser University. He has recently published a book with Peter Lang entitled *Private Readings in Public: Schooling the Literary Imagination*.